Additional Praise for *America on the Edge*:

"Giroux is one of our most passionate and intelligent public intellectuals, commenting on an impressively wide range of social, political and economic developments, always with a concern for the necessary pedagogical role of culture. He has steadfastly defended the possibilities of a more humane world and criticized every institution, every ideology, every assumption, and every group that has stood in the way of or actively opposed the making of such a world. These essays are Giroux at his best, analyzing and criticizing the changing organizations of power in the United States and their effects on the larger world, and calling out to anyone who will listen that that world is possible."

—Lawrence Grossberg, author of *Caught in the Crossfire: Kids, Politics and America's Future*

Praise for *Take Back Higher Education*:

"Reminiscent of C. Wright Mills' *The Sociological Imagination* . . . this updated, necessary call for action for all academicians is refreshing . . ."

—Choice

"Henry and Susan Giroux are performing an immense public service with this book. It is a sweeping critique of how our culture, especially the educational establishment, has failed to prepare us for the crises of our time. And it offers hope for the possibility of resisting that and creating a new culture, inspirational and profoundly democratic."

—Howard Zinn, author of *A People's History of the United States*

"Henry and Susan Giroux's extraordinary book is an electrifying call to educators to renounce political passivity and to assume the role of public intellectuals prepared to take back schools and universities from the predations of a business driven ideology that silences dissent and undermines democracy. A beautifully fashioned work of cultural history, it is also a rich and stimulating brew of elegant analysis and powerful polemic. Teachers from the kindergarten classrooms to the ivory tower will be grateful for the hope and affirmation the Giroux' have given us. All in all, a magnificent achievement."

—Jonathan Kozol

"Here, at last, is a critical study in the social sciences that explores with brilliant iconoclasm the connection between the post-9/11 de-democratization of America, the erosion of its politics and its civil rights, its inexorable drift into rapid conservatism, and recent attacks on the form and substance of higher education. Argued with enormous conviction and considerable insight, *Take Back Higher Education* does for contemporary pedagogy what the likes of John Dewey did for it long ago: insist that the health of our society depends not on consumption or the rampant production of wealth for the rich, but on educating new generations of citizens for open, informed public engagement, for constructive political involvement, for commitment to a social world built on justice and empowerment for all; in short, for all the things currently under threat in the security-obsessed, frightened USA of the early twenty-first century. Here, in other words, is a charter for real freedom through enlightenment, a charter that ought to have been accomplished two hundred or so years ago, but still requires a good fight. Henry and Susan Giroux have undertaken that fight with vigor, energy, and consummate intelligence."

—John Comaroff, University of Chicago

America on the Edge

Henry Giroux on Politics, Culture, and Education

Henry A. Giroux

AMERICA ON THE EDGE
© Henry A. Giroux, 2006.

First published in 2006 by
PALGRAVE MACMILLAN™
175 Fifth Avenue, New York, N.Y. 10010 and
Houndmills, Basingstoke, Hampshire, England RG21 6XS
Companies and representatives throughout the world.

PALGRAVE MACMILLAN is the global academic imprint of the Palgrave Macmillan division of St. Martin's Press, LLC and of Palgrave Macmillan Ltd. Macmillan® is a registered trademark in the United States, United Kingdom and other countries. Palgrave is a registered trademark in the European Union and other countries.

ISBN 1–4039–7160–9

Library of Congress Cataloging-in-Publication Data

Giroux, Henry A.
    America on the edge : Henry Giroux on politics, culture, and education / Henry A. Giroux.
        p. cm
    Includes bibliographical references and index.
    ISBN 1–4039–7160–9 (alk. paper)
    ISBN 1–4039–7159–5 (pbk. : alk. paper)
    1. Critical pedagogy—United States. 2. United States—Politics and government—2001– I. Title

LC196.5.U6G563 2006
370.11′5—dc22   2005056613

A catalogue record for this book is available from the British Library.

Design by Newgen Imaging Systems (P) Ltd., Chennai, India.

First edition: April 2006

10 9 8 7 6 5 4 3 2 1

Printed in the United States of America.

For Susan, again and again

For Brett, Chris, and Jack

For Micaela and Don

For Grizz

CONTENTS

Preface and Acknowledgments   ix

Introduction

1 Henry Giroux on Critical Pedagogy and the
   Responsibilities of the Public Intellectual   3

Part I America Under Siege: Authoritarianism and Democracy

2 The Conservative Assault on America: Cultural Politics,
   Education, and the New Authoritarianism   23

3 Democracy and the Crisis of Public Education: Co-Authored
   with Susan Searls Giroux   43

4 From Auschwitz to Abu Ghraib: Rethinking Representation
   as Public Pedagogy   53

Part II Against Fundamentalism: Resisting Religious
Extremism and Market Orthodoxy

5 Rapture Politics and the Passion of the Religious Right   71

6 Academic Entrepreneurs: The Corporate Takeover of
   Higher Education   89

Part III Media Pedagogy: Rethinking Political
and Cultural Literacy

7 Roll Over George Orwell: Representations of
   Newspeak in Bush's America   101

8 Breaking into the Movies: Film as Cultural Politics   117

9 Nymphet Fantasies: Child Beauty Pageants and the
   Politics of Innocence   129

Part IV   Race, Surveillance, and Social Justice

10   Racial Politics, Individualism, and the Collapse of the Social   151

11   Disposable Youth, Racism, and the Politics of Zero Tolerance   175

Part V   Militarization, Masculinity, and the Spectre of Fascism

12   Waging War On Democracy: The Militarizing of Public Space   191

13   Private Satisfactions and Public Disorder: *Fight Club*,
Patriarchy, and the Politics of Masculine Violence   205

Part VI   Youth, Pedagogy, and the Politics of Hope

14   The Abandoned Generation: The Urban Debate League
and the Politics of Possibility   229

15   Putting Youth Back into Politics: Reclaiming Education and
Hope in Dark Times   237

16   Translating the Future: Speaking to Graduating Youth   253

Index   257

Preface and Acknowledgments

America on the Edge developed out of an attempt to theorize a number of emerging antidemocratic tendencies that bespeak of an accelerating and dangerous movement toward authoritarianism in the United States. At the current historical moment, the United States is in the hands of extremists who are deeply committed to a politics that serves the needs of those groups who advocate empire, corporate power, religious fundamentalism, militarism, and waging an assault against critical thought at all levels of public and higher education as well as the mass media. Fundamentalisms of various stripes now provide the most powerful governing principles in American society, organizing everything from how we view politics to how we dispense contraceptive drugs for women, inserting biblical literalism into the school curriculum and making the market the template for all social relations. Most disturbing, the plagues of terror and violence have now merged within a war on terrorism that has become the rallying cry for the Bush administration's state of permanent war at home and abroad. The war on terrorism is now being used to camouflage tyranny at home and to launch an imperial war in Iraq through a phony appeal to democracy further mystified by a thick fog of lies and fabrication. As Hannah Arendt once said, we are living in dark times.

At the highest levels of government and business, power betrays a contempt for democratic values, identities, and practices. For example, individuals are abducted by the CIA and sent to foreign countries to be tortured, while helpless prisoners are tortured by U.S. soldiers—and all of this is now common knowledge around the world. Civil liberties are being shredded in the name of a war against terrorism that increasingly mimics the same horrifying practices it condemns. Enron, Tyco International, and Worldcom provide a chilling display of corporate greed, arrogance, and dishonesty, and yet the power of multinational corporations and financial capital to shape and influence major policy decisions at all levels of government has increased just as regulatory government agencies are being dismantled or severely weakened. At the same time, corporate power is unanchored from the boundaries of nation-states and floats above the traditional spheres of politics, regulation, and control—wrecking havoc, poverty, and insecurity as a byproduct of negative globalization. At home, Halliburton is the poster child of political cronyism, and Wal-Mart is the current corporate model for how to cheat workers, break unions, and destroy small businesses. The Bush administration's series of tax cuts for the wealthy, coupled with a tax code designed to levy a tax on consumption instead of on income, has bankrupted both the states and federal government. The goal here is to privatize Social Security, public schooling, all aspects of the welfare system, Amtrak, the postal service, and other public agencies. Without adequate revenue to support public provisions and public goods, the state is reduced to its privatizing and security-policing-surveillance-related functions.

All things public and democratic are now viewed either as a site of disorder or as a metaphor for pathology. Schools have become factories of rote learning and test-taking, as they are increasingly subjected to disciplinary practices associated with prisons. For many black and brown youth, schools simply warehouse them before society offers them either a jobless future or a stint with the criminal justice system, or, if they are lucky, they can end up patrolling the streets of Iraq. Army recruiters now troll the corridors of urban high schools in bright yellow hummers hoping to seduce young people into giving their lives over to a war that was legitimated through a series of governmental lies and that continues to kill both Iraqis and American soldiers with impunity. The most corrupt expressions of power are now legitimated in the name of religion, and "shock and awe" has become the advance calling card for bringing democracy to other countries.

Politics has never been so powerfully exercised while governance so dreadfully ignored. Corruption, greed, and fanaticism are on display for all to see, and yet moral outrage has not been matched by collective resistance. Locked in a privatizing language that only recognizes the social when it fortifies the power of the military, police, and others who equate politics with control, the public is left to its own individual fears, insecurities, and resources in order to address the myriad problems that now shape everyday life—the United States has become a country in which the military appears to be the only institution that matters. Abandoned by a state whose social services have been greatly weakened, the promise of a vibrant global democracy and the possibilities for social struggles have greatly diminished. The bodies of poor blacks and whites left unattended for days in the destructive aftermath of Hurricane Katrina symbolize in a shocking and disturbing way how those marginalized by race and class are now considered expendable; those bodies of the poor also make clear the consequence of the frontal assault that has taken place under the Bush administration against those government infrastructures crucial both to the safety of public life and to the maintenance of a substantive democracy.

Collective shame and political incompetence dissipate in the face of short attention spans and public indifference—fuelled by a media system that refuses to hold government and corporate power accountable. Dark times become even darker as not only the *idea*, but the *reality* and *promise* of democracy are under siege—evident in the ongoing attacks against youth, Social Security, environmental protection, social provisions for the poor, pension programs, and in weakened bankruptcy laws, the dismantling of affirmative action, an immoral occupation of Iraq, and the war against women's reproductive rights. The first mark of an authoritarian regime is to make power unaccountable through secrecy, misinformation, or manipulated consent. This book attempts both to make dominant power visible and to move others to make it accountable. Barbarism is the hallmark signature of the authoritarianism now legitimated by the Bush administration. The lines have to be drawn and the dots have to be connected so that the American people will not only wake up to the grave danger facing American democracy, as distinguished public figures such as Al Gore, Robert Kennedy, Jr., and Seymour Hersh have argued recently, but also put into place those public discourses, values, social relations, and modes of resistance that significantly confront the new authoritarianism, while also resurrecting a politics of hope in which a substantive democracy points to a future that refuses to reproduce eras in American history in which barbarism held sway.

Much of this book was written after Susan Searls Giroux and I decided to leave the United States and take new jobs at McMaster University in Canada. Under the threat of a number of antidemocratic tendencies moving at high speed in the United States, we could no longer live under a government attacking every vestige of democracy. Though this move has proven difficult, it has been made a lot easier for me and Susan as a result of several new and old Canadian friends, including Liss Platt, Jasmin Habib, Janice Hladki, Nasrin Rahimieh, David Clark, Tracy Wynne, Roger and Wendy Simon, and too many others to mention. I want to thank my editor, Amanda Johnson, for supporting this book from its inception. My deepest gratitude goes to my graduate research assistant at McMaster University, Grace Pollock, who edited each chapter, read endless drafts, offered constructive suggestions, and helped to greatly improve the overall quality of the book. I also want to thank my administrative assistant, Maya Stamenkovic, for the kindness of her heart, professionalism, and incredible support. Many friends have read parts of this manuscript over the years and deserve my deepest thanks: John Comaroff, Donaldo Macedo, Roger I. Simon, Chris Robbins, Lawrence Grossberg, Stanley Aronowitz, Arif Dirlik, Olivia Ward, Lewis Gordon, Nick Couldry, Carol Becker, David Theo Goldberg, Douglas Kellner, Paul Youngquist, Kostas Myrsiadas, Paul Street, Jonathan Kozol, Peter McLaren, Brian McKenna, Lynn Worsham, Sut Jhally, Ken Saltman, Jackie Edmundson, Norman Denzin, Robin D. G. Kelly, Micaela Amato, Vorris Nunley, Les Young, Don Schule, Imre Szeman, and Dean Birkenkamp. Lastly, I want to thank my partner, Susan Searls Giroux, my muse, comrade, and heartbeat.

Some of the essays that appear in this book have been extensively revised and bear little resemblance to when they were first published. A different version of chapter 2 appeared as "The Conservative Assault on America: Cultural Politics, Education, and the New Authoritarianism" in *Cultural Politics* 1, no. 2 (July 2005): 139–163. An earlier version of "From Auschwitz to Abu Ghraib: Rethinking Representation as Public Pedagogy" appeared in *Comparative Studies of South Asia, Africa and the Middle East* 24, no. 1 (2004), available online at http://cssaame.com. Chapter 6 appeared earlier as "Academic Entrepreneurs: The Corporate Takeover of Higher Education" in *Tikkun* (March/April 2005): 18–22, 28. "Movies and Public Pedagogy: Film as Cultural Politics" first appeared as "Breaking Into the Movies: Pedagogy and the Politics of Film" in *JAC* 21, no. 3 (Summer 2001): 583–598. Versions of chapters 9 and 10 appeared as "Nymphet Fantasies: Child Beauty Pageants and the Politics of Innocence," *Social Text* 16, no. 4 (1998): 31–53; and "Spectacles of Race and Pedagogies of Denial," *Communication Education* 52, no. 3/4 (July/October 2003): 191–211, available online at http://www.tandf.co.uk/journals/titles/03634523.asp. "Disposable Youths, Racism, and the Politics of Zero Tolerance" first appeared as "Mis/Education and Zero Tolerance: Disposable Youth and the Politics of Domestic Militarization," in *Boundary 2* 28, no. 3 (Fall 2001): 61–94, Copyright © 2001, Duke University Press. Used with permission. A version of chapter 13 was published as "Private Satisfactions and Public Disorders: *Fight Club*, Patriarchy, and the Politics of Masculine Violence," in *JAC* 21, no. 1 (Winter 2001): 1–31.

Introduction

1

HENRY GIROUX ON CRITICAL PEDAGOGY AND THE RESPONSIBILITIES OF THE PUBLIC INTELLECTUAL

Interviewed by Marcia Morales, Mike Pozo, and Sina Rahmani
Edited by Grace Pollock

Henry Giroux is a leading figure in the fields of critical pedagogy and cultural studies, and a major advocate for youth, democracy, and education in the United States. In May 2004, Henry Giroux left Penn State University after twelve years as a Distinguished Professor in the College of Education, moving to McMaster University in Hamilton, Ontario where he holds the Global Television Network Chair in English and Communication.

MARCIA MORALES: In your book *The Mouse That Roared*, you discuss the ways in which the Disney industry operates to construct children's perception of the world. What issues made you write this book?

HENRY GIROUX: I first took an interest in Disney when my three children consistently asked to watch Disney's animated videos. I was appalled by many of the racist and sexist representations in the videos and decided that it was necessary to write a book in which I could address Disney as both a corporate power and a powerful educational force that has enormous influence in deciding what information children have access to in a variety of educational sites. Of course, bigger subjects were here: the changing view of childhood in America; the separation of corporate power from corporate culture; the attempts by business conglomerates to commercially carpet bomb kids and lead them to believe that the only obligations of citizenship were market-driven concerns such as buying goods and making money; the changing nature of culture as a powerful form of public pedagogy; the meaning of play; the relationships between corporations and public life, and between commercial spaces and the destruction of public space.

MM: How do you conceptualize your work?

HG: My work has always been concerned with the interlocking relations between material structures of power and the pedagogical force of cultural politics. In part, this has meant trying to understand how pedagogy both within and outside of schools can be used to link not only learning to social change, but also theory to practice, intellectual scholarship to the problems of public life, and education to the promise of a radical and inclusive democracy. My early work focused on theorizing radical notions of schooling and creating a discourse for linking pedagogy to an understanding of both how domination works in its diverse forms and how public pedagogy can be used as a powerful resource for engaging people in robust forms of dialogue and activism. More recently, I have focused on how public pedagogy works in popular culture, especially in shaping youth culture under the reign of neoliberalism.

MM: **What is your opinion about the role of literacy and the conditions for school reform?**
HG: Critical pedagogy argues for the importance of developing multiple literacies. We need to develop social literacies that are functional, cultural, and critical. In this sense, we need literacies that recognize both the importance of cultural differences and the importance of individuals communicating across various social, cultural, and political borders. Educators and others also need literacies that enable people to critically analyze the new electronic technologies that are shaping everyday life through the popular media, video, television, digital imaging, and film. We need to view literacy as part of a broader critical discourse grounded in a politics of representation in which students and others learn how to analyze the cultural and ideological codes in various forms of signification, including print, visual, and oral texts. At the same time, literacy should never be reduced to the learning of particular forms of knowledge and skills. Literacy should be seen not only as a practice of critical comprehension, but also as an act of intervention in the world. If literacy is a condition for human agency, then pedagogy and education cannot be limited to young people, but should be the right of everyone. Adult education must take on as important a role as public education does today for young people. We must educate various age groups in schools and also in a variety of cultural sites. In order to do this we must completely reform existing schools and programs of education. We must get away from training teachers to be simply efficient technicians and practitioners. We need a new vision of what constitutes educational leadership and social agency so that we can educate teachers to think critically, locate themselves in their own histories, and exercise moral and public responsibility in their role as engaged critics and transformative intellectuals.

MM: **What are the main assumptions and educational implications of critical pedagogy?**
HG: Critical pedagogy is a discourse for asserting the primacy of the political and the ethical as a central feature of educational theory and practice. Critical pedagogy makes clear that schools and other educational spheres cannot be viewed merely as instructional sites, but must be seen as places where culture, power, and knowledge come together to produce particular identities, narratives, and social practices. In this case, critical pedagogy illuminates that schooling is not merely about the

production of skills, but about the construction of knowledge and identities that always presuppose a vision of the future. The critical question here is, Whose future, story, and interests does the school represent? Moreover, critical pedagogy grounds itself in a political vision from which to develop an educational project dedicated to revitalizing democratic public life. Critical pedagogy argues that school practices need to be informed by a public philosophy that addresses how to construct ideological and institutional conditions in which the lived experience of empowerment for the vast majority of students becomes the defining feature of schooling. Critical pedagogy points to redefining the role of the school as a democratic public sphere, educating teachers to be publicly engaged intellectuals who address the most pressing problems of their society as part of a wider politics and pedagogy of solidarity and democratic struggle, and rewriting the curriculum in order to address the lived experiences that different students bring to the school, while not being limited to such knowledge. More specifically, critical pedagogy attempts to create new forms of knowledge through its emphasis on breaking down disciplines and creating interdisciplinary knowledge; it raises questions about the relationships between the margins and centers of power in schools and is concerned with providing a way of reading history as part of a larger project of reclaiming power and identity, particularly as these are shaped around the categories of race, gender, class, and ethnicity; and it rejects the distinction between high and popular culture so as to make curriculum knowledge responsive to the everyday knowledge that constitutes people's lived histories differently, while at the same time recognizing that different forms of knowledge entail different kinds of theoretical and critical work. Critical pedagogy is also concerned with the presences and absences that mark knowledge and texts and how one may be as important as the other in both the construction of such texts and how they are read differently by individuals within diverse historical and social formations. Another major task of critical pedagogy is to link the language of critique to the language of possibility and to be keenly aware that critique and hope must inform each other so as to avoid a crippling cynicism or an empty utopianism. Finally, critical pedagogy illuminates the primacy of the ethical in defining the language that teachers and others use to produce particular cultural practices.

MM: What kind of education promotes a critical democracy?
HG: At the institutional level, we need to develop schools that give teachers an opportunity to exercise power over the conditions of their work. That is, they should have both the time and the power to institute structural conditions that allow them to produce curricula, collaborate with parents, conduct research, and work with communities. Moreover, school buildings must be limited in size to permit teachers and others to provide a sense of democratic community for themselves and their students. We are talking not only about the issue of class size, but about how space is institutionally constructed as part of a political project compatible with the formation of lived, democratic communities. Teaching, learning, and the purpose of schooling itself must emerge out of a project of inclusive democracy. But such a project cannot be merely stated; it must also be experienced in the daily relations of schooling by all

of those involved. Secondly, teachers should construct curricula that draw upon the cultural resources that students bring with them to the school. This suggests not only taking the languages, histories, experiences, and voices of the students seriously, but also integrating what is taught in schools with the dynamics of everyday life. This points to developing curricula that incorporate popular culture, teach media literacy, and address the real problems and concerns that students face on a local, societal, and global level. Curricula must be grounded in a recognition that students need to be educated in order to govern and to exercise power over the conditions of their learning as part of a broader effort that allows them to be the subjects, rather than the objects, of history. Most important, schooling should be organized to provide students with the full range of knowledge, skills, values, and competencies they will need to both understand and experience the importance of an ethical discourse that enables them to develop relations among themselves and others that encourage social, cultural, and economic democracy. In this case, students should be given the opportunity to engage projects as part of their school curricula that provide them with experiences that promote social justice, freedom, and equality. Education, in this sense, suggests inserting learning within an ethical discourse that views achievement as a public, rather than merely a private, consideration. In this case, the school can be used as a strategic site for addressing social problems and for helping students understand what it means to exercise rights and responsibilities as critical citizens actively engaged in forms of social learning that expand human capacities for compassion, empathy, and solidarity.

MM: **Considering the symbolic and economic influences of the media and the Internet, what is the role of schools in the larger culture?**

HG: I think schools must rethink what it means to educate young people to live in a world dominated by entirely new modes of information, communication, and cultural production, such as computers, digital technologies, various modes of electronic communication, and so on. This means at the very least pluralizing the notion of literacy so that we can expand its meaning to mastering the languages, knowledge, skills, tools, new technologies, and methods of a range of modes of communication, including, but going beyond, print culture. Most of the pedagogical influences that students experience do not come from the schools but from popular culture, rooted in a largely electronically driven visual culture. The technologies and content of this culture must be available to students in schools not only so they can read these cultures critically, but also so they can become cultural producers within these new communicative domains. For instance, it is not enough to learn how to read television ads, web pages, sitcoms, or radio programs critically; students must also learn how to master the tools necessary to produce their own radio programs, television ads, and shows. We are in the midst of a second media age, one that fuses technology, power, and human relations in new ways. Media no longer merely transmit information; they create, reorder, and refigure it in ways that make obsolete older notions of literacy, agency, technology, and communication. Educators and students alike will have to rethink how the interface of technology, information, and communication demands a new understanding of the central place the latter occupy in the space of everyday life in a global world.

MM: **How does critical pedagogy view collaboration with families and other social agents in schools?**

HG: Schools should be seen as a resource for the larger community. In this sense, teachers and members of the community become coowners of the school and, as such, collectively determine, within the bounds of reason, how the school is organized, and what role the school might play in the affairs of the community and larger society. Collaboration among the schools, teachers, neighborhood agencies, and parents is essential if the school is to be run democratically and if it is to address seriously the basic social, physical, and cultural needs of students. Schools should foster public values and not merely advance excessive individualism, competitiveness, and intellectual consumerism. Moreover, schools should not lose their connection to the neighborhoods they are intended to serve.

MM: **What is the space for teachers between the discourse of critique and the discourse of possibility?**

HG: The discourse of critique is essential for teachers in two fundamental ways. First, they must be able to critically analyze the ideologies, values, and interests that inform their role as teachers and the cultural politics they promote in the classroom. All of their actions presuppose some notion of what it means to be a citizen and a member of a future society. To the degree that schools are actively engaged in the production of discourses that provide others with a sense of identity, community, and possibility, teachers must be responsible and reflective about their actions. Teachers are not technicians. They are agents whose actions have enormous political, pedagogical, and ethical consequences, and they should be able to work under conditions that enable them to share and exercise power, be reflective about the nature of their work, and work in collaboration with their colleagues and the community. Second, teachers must be able to analyze their relationship with the larger society in order to critically apprehend themselves as social agents capable of recognizing how they might be complicitous with forms of oppression and human suffering. But they must also have a language of possibility, one that allows them to think in terms of the "not yet," to speak the unrepresentable, and to imagine future social relations outside of the existing configuration of power. In this sense, they must be able to understand how power can be harnessed and produced through the poetics of imagination; that is, they must be able to distinguish between reality as a fact and imagining alternative realities as a means of making a better existence into a real possibility. Such dreams must not be forged in isolation, but in solidarity with others. Without hope, there is only the politics of cynicism.

MP: **Have you had time since leaving the United States to reflect on your accomplishments in the field of critical pedagogy over the years? In your opinion, where does critical pedagogy stand today in the United States compared to when you first began writing?**

HG: I am not sure how much I have accomplished other than making clear as an educator that one has to continually fight for social justice and that this is as much a pedagogical as a political task. Hopefully, my work has played a small role in shaping some critical discourses on pedagogy, youth, cultural politics, education, and democracy. Certainly, my generation, which includes a number of intellectuals—Roger Simon, Donaldo Macedo, Stanley Aronowitz, Lawrence Grossberg, William Pinar, Chandra Mohanty, Peter McLaren, bell hooks, and too many others to name—has had a positive effect in extending the reach of critical pedagogy. It is very difficult to be in education today and not be at least aware of the field of critical pedagogy.

Within the last two decades, many diverse groups and individuals have drawn upon critical pedagogy's varied resources to challenge traditional forms of teaching and to provide an entirely new range of discourses for engaging how pedagogy works in shaping power, identities, social relations, and inequality in the classroom. Critical pedagogy has also become an invaluable theoretical tool for helping teachers and others to understand how pedagogy operates outside of the schools in the production of knowledge, values, subject positions, and social experiences. Part of the legacy of critical pedagogy is to make clear that pedagogy is a moral and political practice rather than merely a technique or method. Against an instrumentalized notion of pedagogy, I have argued for years that pedagogy is the outcome of particular conflicts and struggles, and cannot be approached as an a priori method or technique. Pedagogy is directive and is, in part, about the struggle over identities, values, and the future. It articulates and shapes the connection between knowledge and morality, how we get to know and what we know, and it alerts us to how power shapes and is reinvented in the interaction among texts, teachers, and students. At its best, it teaches students to think critically about the knowledge they gain, and what it means to recognize antidemocratic forms of power and to fight substantive injustices in a world marked by deep inequalities. Critical pedagogy also works out of a project of democratization; that is, it is normatively driven in its efforts to create the ideological and material conditions that enable students and others to link education to what it means to be responsible to oneself, work with others, and deepen and extend the possibilities of an inclusive and substantive democracy. Critical pedagogy is not a method looking for an audience or context; on the contrary, it is a practice that emerges out of its allegiance to the imperatives of a democracy that, in turn, expresses itself and the problems it faces differently in different contexts.

Critical pedagogy has produced an entire culture of journals, conferences, courses, research agendas, and an alternative set of pedagogical practices. This is not meant to suggest that it has become some type of dominant paradigm among teachers and in the schools, but its presence is being increasingly felt, to the detriment of traditional educators and supporters of dominant modes of education. Critical pedagogy is also at a crucial historical conjuncture, because all vestiges of critical education are under assault in the United States, and critical pedagogy is one of the few theoretical and pedagogical traditions that offers the history, knowledge, skills, and theories to fight this aggressive attack on the nature of critical education, the connection between learning and social responsibility, and schooling and democracy.

MM: Despite your efforts as well as the work of other radical educators, we still struggle against a very positivist view of education. What would be the ways to overcome such a view?

HG: The first challenge is to defend education as a public good rather than treating it as a private endeavor, and this means struggling against a number of right-wing fundamentalist positions. Education has got to be rescued not from the positivists—though they are a danger—but from those market fundamentalists who want to strip education of any democratic values, while turning it into simply another space dominated by private interests and market relations. This diverse group of corporate and market-based ideologues want to either privatize schools or turn them over to corporations as sources of revenue. The basic choice here is either to run schools as an individual good or to turn them into an outpost of Pepsi, McDonald's, or the Chamber of Commerce. Similarly, defending education as a public good means also resisting the attack on public and higher education being waged by Christian extremists, who want to do away with any critical vestige of secular education, as can be seen in their attempts to substitute "creationism" and theories of "intelligent design" for theories of evolution in the schools. This group is particularly dangerous because they deplore critical education, refuse to respect the boundaries between the state and religion, and want to use the schools to implement a right-wing agenda that includes abstinence education, pro-life curricula, retrograde gender policies, and anti-environmental philosophies. A third attack is emerging from those on the ideological Right who view education as dangerous because, at its best, it teaches students how to be critical citizens, hold power accountable, and extend the most basic impulses of a democratic society. We need both a national and international movement of intellectuals, union activists, social movements, workers, and others who can join together to resist the World Bank view of education, fight for education as a public good, ensure access to those who have been removed from a decent and critical education, overcome the assault by the religious Right, and struggle for economic reforms that provide the financial resources for developing infrastructures essential to decent schooling.

The second challenge is to recover the role of teachers as public intellectuals, intellectuals who do not confuse critical education with training, and who are self-conscious politically, not only about the meaning and purpose of education as a social good, but also about their own role as engaged and critical intellectuals who can energize people to think critically and act differently—that is, who can create the crucial conditions for students and others to combine critical consciousness with the demands of responsible agency and citizenship. Educators need to assume the role of leaders in the struggle for social and economic justice. This means making clear that education is at the heart of what it means to create not only autonomous citizens, but also an autonomous society. Educators must connect what they teach and write to the dynamics of public life, especially those problems and issues that emerge out of the contexts in which they address their students, other educators, and the broader public. At one level, this means rejecting those forms of instrumentalism, positivism, commercialism, and privatization that strip education of its power as a force for democratic politics and critical agency. Of course, schools in this instance become only one site in which such educators can work to illuminate the importance of education as a foundation for creating social movements, for translating private issues into public considerations, and for articulating diverse struggles through the broader concern for a radical and inclusive democracy.

Third, we not only need to provide all students with access to a decent quality education; we need to make sure that the material infrastructure and resources are in place to enable such an education to take place. Under the present system of taxation and distributive justice, the rich are rewarded and the poor are punished. Decent schools that take education seriously are almost entirely defined by property taxes. This is not to suggest that there are not decent schools in poor urban and rural areas as much as to suggest there are many more that are a shocking insult to the children and teachers who attend such schools. The United States is not a generous country either in its system of financing schools or in its tax system, both of which favor the rich. Only when excellence and equity are seen as mutually determining are we going to have a decent public school system. And this issue has to be a top priority for any vestige of educational reform.

MM: September 11, 2001, meant, in many ways, that American hegemony was disturbed. How would you describe the international order now, including the war against Iraq?

HG: I think September 11 has revealed not only that a new notion of the social is emerging, one in which terror and fear become the only basis for solidarity, but also the way in which the world is much more connected and fragile. Of course, September 11 has also given rise to new types of political fundamentalism in which the old rules of international diplomacy and deterrence have been discarded for new and dangerous modes of unilateralism. In this instance, I am referring to the dangerous policy of preemptive strikes adopted by the Bush administration; there is also the religious fundamentalism and moralism that drive President Bush's view of exercising power both at home and abroad in an arrogant and unilateral fashion. Bush's religious discourse is grounded in a moral absolutism and Manichean view of the world in which doubt, if not thoughtfulness itself, is viewed as a weakness and intellectual rigidity an asset. There is also the growing influence of an all-embracing neoliberalism that undermines all democratic public spheres, sees the market as a template of all social relations, and completely subordinates social needs to corporate interests. I think we are living in one of the most dangerous of historical moments. The combination of a ruthless neoliberal global order, the militarization of public space, the influence of religious extremists in setting policy at the highest levels of government, and the rise of the carceral state to take care of those populations who are considered disposable, represents a level of barbarism unlike almost anything we have witnessed in the past. This is evident as the gap between the rich and the poor on a global level is increasing with impunity; whole countries such as Argentina are being held hostage by capital; the environment is systematically being plundered by ruling classes; and public spaces everywhere are being either privatized or destroyed. Moreover, women's reproductive rights are under attack; civil liberties are being whittled away; and homophobic laws are being passed that mimic in a frightening way similar events in Nazi Germany soon after Adolph Hitler came to power.

MM: Is class struggle relevant today?

HG: Around the fault lines of power, the issue of class defined in the broadest sense is moe relevant than ever. What is needed are class struggles that are both symbolic and material, but most importantly, class struggles must be international, concerned with the struggle over life itself. One of the greatest challenges facing the Left today is to create not just national organizations, but international organizations that can once again link political power to economic justice. Globalism under neoliberalism demands a new kind of ethical challenge, and a different and broader notion of responsibility, one that is put into place by a global network of interdependency; the Left must recover the old dream of international solidarity to build political organizations that can overcome the power of multinational corporations and a rampant ideology of neoliberalism that supplies a rationale for global plunder. Globalization demands a global politics because the only effective response to this new form of international political and economic terrorism has to be global and must be reconstituted through notions of solidarity, justice, and social responsibility. At the national level, governments must find ways to redefine the state as guarantor of both social provisions and safety nets for its citizens, especially those who are marginalized by virtue of class, race, gender, disability, and age. Capitalism in its neoliberal varieties must be challenged on the ground, so to speak, within the particularities of specific states, contexts, problems, histories, and issues; but, at the same time, it must be challenged through the emergence of states that are willing to create alliances within international organizations and to fight, regulate, and control rule by the market and capital. The social cannot be defined as the totality of individuals; public life cannot collapse into merely private interests. We need an international struggle to reclaim a notion of the democratic social, one that is appropriate to a globalized world. The task for democracy is the creation of an international social movement that would exercise real influence on governments and international organizations to restore a sense of utopian possibilities and democratic hopes. Historically, real change has always come from active struggles, and such struggles are more important now than ever before.

MP: Is there anything telling in the fact that a prominent university in the United States devalues such a strong proponent of critical thinking such as yourself, while a Canadian university embraces it?

HG: The United States has become a country that appears to have lost its willingness to be reflective about both its own role in the world and its actions at home. It is a country whose commanding governmental and economic institutions are caught in the grip of a group of extremists who are well-organized, well-funded, and absolutely zealous about undoing any vestige of democracy and the social contract. As I mentioned earlier, in many ways this is reflected in the rise of market fundamentalism, militarism, and religious extremism, which now dominate the culture and politics. All of these fundamentalisms, but especially neoliberalism, must be understood within the rising tide of authoritarianism on both a national and global level; we must understand how neoliberalism puts into play both a view of agency that is at odds with a notion of the social endemic to democracy and a form of unbridled self-interest that fits well with neofascism. Under the reign of neoliberalism, politics has become increasingly banal; education has been stripped of its critical functions; and conformity is now lauded as a patriotic act. It is very sad that the most powerful and richest country in the world not only has defaulted on its democratic possibilities, but also undermines those possibilities abroad as it extends its market-based fundamentalism and imperial ambitions around the globe. At the same time, the United States is dominated by one of the most extensive and pervasive conservative propaganda machines the world has ever seen. The educational force of the culture is now mobilized through what I call sites of public pedagogy—radio, television, newspapers, Hollywood films, as well as through the new electronic information technologies. These powerful pedagogical sites are almost entirely dominated by corporate, conservative, and right-wing discourses and values. Consequently, the spaces for critical information and resistance are shrinking dangerously in the United States, and the result, if such a trend is not stopped, will be a new form of authoritarianism. Canada, on the other hand, is a much more liberal society with a strong, social democratic tradition. It values democracy, difference, and diversity to a much greater degree than does the United States. While it has its own problems and inequalities (and these are not minor), it still has at the center of its public discourse a social contract that respects public goods, human life, and democratic values. For instance, Canada has just legalized gay marriages, and it may be only one of three governments in the world that has done so. Some people have argued that I have been too Pollyanna-ish about Canada, but what such criticisms miss is that Canada, when compared to the United States, is light years away from the growing authoritarianism emerging on its southern border. Power is being massively configured in the United States toward the creation of an authoritarian state. Fortunately, that is not happening in Canada. The social visions that sustain a democracy still seem viable in Canada, but this does not seem to be the case for the United States.

MP: Randall Robinson wrote in *Quitting America* (2004), "Three out of five Blacks oppose the War in Iraq, while only one out of five whites opposes the War. Blacks, however, are almost nowhere to be found in the ranks of the American anti-war demonstrations. Why the discrepancy? Oh we know. . . . Know that Whites don't give a shit what we think. Never did. Never will."[1] This is a sobering reminder about how the Left, including the antiwar movement, has forgotten "minorities" and their role in politics. I am also reminded of Jorge Mariscal's writings on the number of Latinos signing up for military duty just to be able to afford a college education, not being fully aware of what a life-altering and often deadly decision they were making. Do you think so-called minorities have been made easy prey to jingoisms or have been converted to a cynical view of political and social change because they have been truly left out—uninvolved—even by the progressives?

HG: Racial justice has become an invisible category in America, camouflaged by the politics of color blindness and obliterated by a racist state that would rather incarcerate people of color than give them rights as citizens. I think there are many people on the Left who care about racial justice, but lack either the language or the politics to do something about it. They often don't know how to speak to a younger generation of black and brown youth; they wrap their politics in a discourse of academic jargon that is uncomprehensible; or they fail to recognize race as one of the most powerful determinants in shaping American society. Race seems to get lost in the discourses of globalization, class, and postmodern aesthetics. In many ways, the Left either has failed to tap into the culture of black and brown youth, or mimics the response of the Right in considering blacks a disposable population with little political currency. The plight of poor black and brown youth in the United States is shameful, giving legitimacy to the claim that the United States has become a carceral state for its people of color. Achille Mbembe, the great African writer, in another context, labels the current state of global race relations, a form of necropolitics—everywhere, though in different degrees, people of color have become disposable, removed from the reach of social and economic justice, their fate in the hands of criminals, thugs, corporate thieves, and occupying armies. The American Left's silence to the state of racial war in the post-9/11 era amounts to shameful indifference, which may say more about the failure of the Left, especially those in the academy, and the crisis of democracy than almost any other political issue. Until matters of race and racial justice become central to progressive politics, the struggle over democracy will have little valence for American progressives.

MP: I think many of us wonder just how one avoids falling into the hopelessness and cynicism that so many people feel and yet have no recourse that might guide them in another direction. How can one see beyond what appears to be the recurrence of political abuses of power, the uncritical manner in which most citizens accept the actions of their leaders and country, and the continued injustices with each passing generation?

HG: The problems we face in the United States and in the world today are too urgent to be either giving up on hope or accepting quietism. At the heart of politics and political agency is the necessity to imagine the impossible, to see beyond the given, and to propose concrete alternative visions. I think that without hope, moral outrage, and a culture of questioning and action, progressive politics becomes unthinkable. The French philosopher Alain Badiou is right in insisting that "emancipatory politics always consists in making seem possible precisely that which, from within the situation, is declared to be impossible."[2] At the same time, false hope is of no use whatsoever. Hope must be tempered by the complex reality of the times, and viewed as a project and condition for providing a sense of collective agency, opposition, political imagination, and engaged participation. Without hope, even in the most dire of times, there is no possibility for resistance, dissent, and struggle. Agency is the condition of struggle, and hope is the condition of agency. Hope expands the space of the possible and becomes a way of recognizing and naming the incomplete nature of the present. It also offers a way of overcoming this debilitating pessimism and manufactured cynicism of the times. Far from being a pipe dream, hope is one of the most important resources we have to promote social change; it is the heartbeat of politics itself. Hope coupled with skepticism reclaims the possibility of ethics, knowledge, criticism, social engagement, and democracy.

SR: Can your emphasis on politics be dangerous?

HG: Any issue can succumb to forms of dogmatism. Anybody who considers themselves a critical intellectual has to be constantly aware of the dangers that can be produced in the name of politics. Simply to say that we are political is not an excuse for dogmatism. The real question here is, How do we refashion politics in a way that resuscitates its democratic possibilities while eschewing both the tendency to be dogmatic and complicitous with power and the refusal to take risks?

SR: Was George W. Bush's reelection in 2004 a failure on the part of progressive academics?

HG: It may testify less to our failure than to the strengths of the conservative opposition. Bush won the election precisely because he was successful in making fear and insecurity into the centerpieces of his campaign. By doing so, he did not have to answer for a disastrous economic record, the bankrupt foreign policy he has pursued, especially in Iraq, the growing militarism in the United States, or his insidious attack on civil liberties. Remember, the Bush administration also controls the means of educational production. It controls the universities and, for the most part, those dominant spaces where ideas can be produced, legitimated, and circulated. I think this means that progressive academics have to rethink not simply their own role as public intellectuals, but also what it might mean to develop a language and theory relevant for inventing a politics adequate to the challenges of the twenty-first century. There is a great educational/cultural/political deficit disorder in the United States. Celebrities are valued over intellectuals, consumer goods over ideas, fashion over social justice, and profits over human needs. This deficit was not caused by a lack of education; it is the outcome of a particular form of education that has become endemic to a neoliberal society, and the right wing knows how to use this type of education to its own ideological ends. Central to such an education is the celebration of conformity, the hatred of intellectuals, and the attack on dissent. This form of conservative pedagogy has to be challenged in all of the forms and sites in which it takes place, suggesting that pedagogy has to become central to any viable attempt to reconnect politics to democracy itself. Intellectuals across the globe have got to bring their resources together, develop new alliances, and begin to play a powerful role in shaping the educational force of political culture. We also need to be more concerned with working alongside groups outside the university. We have to rethink the meaning of politics in the twenty-first century because there is no space outside of politics. To assume that somehow politics is absent from what we do may be comforting for some, but, in the end, it is one of the worst illusions.

MP: **The 1998 Higher Education Act was passed as a means to encourage young people to vote by requiring federally funded schools to make an effort to get young people to register to vote. But a September 14, 2004, article in the** *L.A. Times* **reported that a Harvard study by The Institute of Politics and the** *Chronicle of Higher Education* **found, "only 17% of the schools surveyed were in complete compliance by requesting voter forms at least 120 days prior to the registration deadline."[3] The administrators of the study believed that a general sense of apathy, coupled with the belief that registering kids to vote was not a "higher education priority," was the reason why the Higher Education Act had so little support on campuses. Do you think students are affected by apathy? Why don't more young people get involved in politics?**

HG: I think there are a lot of complex factors involved in why young people largely refuse to participate in the political process, especially around voting. In some cases, they are too poor, overburdened with life's hardships, and simply lack the resources to participate in the process. If they are poor, black, or brown, youth often lack decent jobs and live in a world riddled with fear and insecurity. These economic and social burdens generate a loss of agency and strike a deathblow to politics. In some cases, the state has simply disenfranchised large numbers of youth because of their criminal records. Barred from voting, they become depoliticized by law. In other cases, they are disenfranchised through the mechanisms of corrupt political practices and regulations, as happened in Florida and Ohio in the 2000 and 2004 presidential elections. For others, politics has become a transparent fraud, having little or nothing to do with democracy, and they simply refuse to participate in the swindle that now passes for politics. Some kids, however, participate through the cultural sphere by building alternative spheres where they can narrate themselves through their music, poetry, writing, journals, clubs, Internet exchanges, and so on. Others are caught in a consumerist fantasy produced by a society in which politics is largely about making money, getting rich, or simply buying goods. At another level, depoliticization among youth is the legacy of an educational system that is more about standardization and testing than about learning for public life and civic engagement. At the same time, for those young people who have the time and resources, there is a tremendous sense of moral outrage developing from what they see happening to democracy, the poor, other nations, and their own futures.

MP: In an article in *Tikkun Magazine* (2003), you and Susan Searls Giroux wrote, "Cynicism about politics and skepticism about education have become mutually reinforcing tendencies that to be understood must be analyzed in tandem."[4] Is it just the Bush administration that has converted U.S. citizens against education and political involvement, or is it our market-driven values that make it necessary for citizens to remain uninformed, uneducated, uncritical, and obedient to slogans, sound bites, and catchy images, thereby making participation in two of the most important social forums—education and politics—not worth their time?

HG: Of course, neoliberalism thrives on conformity, uninformed citizens, and a privatized view of the world in which education must be disassociated from public participation in shaping democratic life. But we live at a time in which politics and economic fundamentalism have merged at the highest levels of government. Neoliberal ideology now drives public policy, and part of the policy is dedicated to undermining critical education, allowing power to be unaccountable, and sowing the seeds of cynicism and conformity. Consumerism now seems to be the only obligation of citizenship and civic responsibility. Agency in this view is completely depoliticized, and politics is defined through a discourse of cynicism that suggests that there are no collective structures or agents capable of challenging existing relations of power. At the same time, neoliberalism offers no public spaces for developing a democratic discourse of education or for promoting collective social agents committed to the reproduction of democratic values and institutions. Critical education and democratic politics have become disposable, unnecessary, if not threatening, to a society that privileges inequality over justice, profits over social needs, and short-term gains over the future.

SR: You have commented elsewhere that the intellectual atmosphere at Penn State had degraded in recent years. Is that related at all to the current state of affairs of American political culture?

HG: I think that many universities in the United States are being undermined by both their increasing alliance with corporate values and interests, on the one hand, and the equally dangerous attack on academic freedom, on the other hand. We have witnessed four years in the United States marked by a growing culture of fear, insecurity, and repression. This is a culture largely controlled by religious, political, and free-market fundamentalists, and this combination and the power it has exercised on American life have been profoundly dangerous. The current government is involved in a war at home and a war abroad, both of which are mediated by a messianic view of the world that does not leave much room for dissent, social movements that want to make authority accountable, or forms of public and higher education that act as if they are democratic public spheres. And, of course, with Bush's reelection, this will all get worse. The Bush administration views higher education as a left-wing bastion that needs to be dismantled, and we are already witnessing in Bush's second administration a harsh political assault on the universities.

For example, the Republican-led Pennsylvania House recently passed a resolution, HR 177, that authorizes the state legislature to subpoena faculty about their class reading list, teaching approaches, grading methods, and class assignments. The bill is the outcome of an ongoing struggle by conservatives to convince state legislatures, largely dominated by Republicans, that conservative ideas are being eliminated from college classrooms and that conservative and Christian students are being punished for their views. At the same time, the right-wing attacks on critical intellectuals offer the Bush administration the kinds of diversions that sidetrack people from thinking about the Iraq war, the resources that it is draining, the lives being lost, and the suffering that it is producing. We have seen the beginnings of the attack on higher education already with many academics after the events of September 11 being called "unpatriotic" because they undertook a serious examination of American foreign policy, or called "anti-Semitic" because they dared criticize the Israeli government's policies in the Middle East. Senator Rick Santorum from Pennsylvania even tried to pass a law withdrawing federal funds from those public universities that employed professors who criticized Israeli policy in their classes. These are very disturbing trends and do not bode well for what could happen in higher education over the next four years. So, we are seeing a new war, a war at home, and that war will basically be against the universities. We already see the indications of how that war is going to be organized. We see it in the unjust association made between dissent and treason. We see it in the legislation by which Republicans, through an appeal to academic freedom and balance, attempt to place more conservatives on faculties. We see it in the increasing corporatization of the university and the marginalization of those disciplines that don't translate immediately into profits.

Penn State is one of the largest procurers of military contractors. Susan Searls Giroux and I have written a book called *Take Back Higher Education*[5] on the corporatization of higher education. Essentially, the book is an attack on the corporate university, of which Penn State is a model. There was no question in my mind that there would be retribution, though I never anticipated the shape it actually took. What became clear was that Penn State had become inhospitable to dissent that called into question its involvement with corporations and the defense agencies. To be an academic and to constantly find yourself under pressure and isolated by virtue of an atmosphere of anti-intellectualism and conformity was completely unacceptable. It was a pleasure for Susan and me to leave.

MP: You have been one of the strongest voices warning against the corporatization of universities and the subsequent result of schools encouraging faculty, staff, students, and administration to adopt corporate mentalities toward education. Do you think this was the case with your departure from Penn State University after twelve years?

HG: My leaving Penn State certainly had a great deal to do with the increasing dumbing down and corporatization of the College of Education. The current environment of the college lacks vision regarding the democratic possibilities of higher education as well as the leadership ability to think beyond the most instrumentalized understanding of education. The new research agenda is grounded in "scientifically based research," a term that comes right out of the Bush administration, which used it as a euphemism to undercut any kind of research that connected education to a culture of questioning or to the knowledge and skills that expand the horizons of critical citizenship and social agency. Whatever sense of moral responsibility and democratic vision that had existed in the college were either disregarded or simply undermined. Increasingly, the college has been reduced to a normal school, a relatively uncritical and boring replica of the worse caricature of how a college of education might be constructed.

At the same time, the president of the university boasted in a recent publication that he was proud of what he had done for Penn State, which was to improve its bond rating. This is the type of so-called leadership that emerges under the corporatized university. Generally, universities are now hiring deans and presidents who are either narrow specialists with no connection to civic life or business clones, accountants, and bean counters who impose market values and efficiency standards as the driving force of higher education. What I find particularly disturbing is how provincial and uncritical they tend to be—unable to engage broader issues, reflect thoughtfully about the role of education, or exercise the courage to take risks and make a real difference in the moral lives and political sensibilities of their students. Money, profits, and the creation of particular products become the most important factors driving the hiring of faculty, the support of particular disciplines, the elimination of particular areas of study, and the definition of what constitutes educational leadership, if not vision. Susan and I both worked with a dean in the College of Education who was completely lacking in any type of social vision. In many ways, he was emblematic of how technocratic and indifferent the university had become to the great moral, educational, and social role universities might play as democratic public spheres. He was almost entirely unconcerned with issues connecting education to matters of social and racial justice, ethics, and critical education. When addressing moral and political questions about the relationship between education and democracy, he almost appeared mute, reinforcing the narrowing role of higher education as an appendage of corporate values and power. The direction of the college under his watch invited faculty to function less as critical intellectuals than as either technicians, resigned to grant writing and contract labor, or apologists, rewarded to the degree that, as Zygmunt Bauman put it in another context, "they listen, take notes, or obey."

MP: **Is it safe to say that corporate influence on education in the United States is the most pressing issue that parents, students, and even some teachers are not aware of? How would you encourage people to wake up and recognize the dangers of corporate influence in education?**

HG: Not only are they unaware of it, they generally support corporate values and ideologies. Getting a good job, taking courses on the basis of their exchange value on the market, refusing to take courses or major in areas that embody noncommercialized values, are high priorities for many parents, teachers, and students. Career training and workforce development are the top priorities of the corporate university, and many parents, faculty, administrators, and students support this view. This is not to suggest that students should not learn workplace skills; but they need to be educated both as workers and as critical citizens. Democracy cannot function without educated citizens who are capable of being autonomous, making knowledgeable judgments, and bringing what they learn to bear on understanding and shaping civic culture. Evidence of what happens in a democracy when people are uninformed, misinformed, or not critically educated is on full display with the popular support—though dwindling fast—being given to Bush, in spite of the lies, contradictions, and misrepresentations his administration perpetuates. Neoliberalism has a stake in uncritical education because it thrives on ignorance in order to proceed outside of democratic accountability. What has to be recognized is that neoliberalism is a very powerful ideology, and, in the face of a variety of public pedagogies in the media and elsewhere that both legitimate it and take it for granted, it is often difficult for students, parents, and educators to challenge its basic assumptions or to understand the pernicious influence it is having on public and higher education. At a time when politics is being depoliticized, everyday life is being militarized, and authoritarianism is once again on the rise, it is difficult for many people to get access to alternative views capable of challenging the privatized utopia espoused by corporate ideology. Of course, one doesn't want to carry this position too far. Students and others are protesting the corporatization of the university in many forms and through a variety of issues extending from sweatshop labor to the indentured servitude of teaching assistants and part-time faculty.

MM: **How do you see the relationship between media and popular culture?**

HG: The real issue here is: what is the relationship between the media as a popular and powerful educational force and the state of democracy itself? Without a democratic media, it is impossible to maintain a democratic society or to provide the conditions for a critically informed citizenry. The media in most advanced industrial countries are now the most powerful pedagogical force for framing issues, offering the languages to decipher them, and providing the subject positions that enable people to understand their relationship to others and the larger world. As long as a handful of corporations controls the media, it will also control the conditions under which politics is defined, understood, engaged, and carried out. This is not to suggest that people don't resist these messages or these pedagogical practices; but if they don't have access to alternative sources of information and learning, it becomes more difficult to engage the contradictions between democratic values and market fundamentalisms, and between democratic ideals and various racist, class-specific, and age-related forms of discrimination, exclusion, and exploitation.

sr: The stereotype that seems to pervade public life about academics is that they are detached eggheads with no connection to the world outside. What role do you envision yourself as playing for students?

hg: I think professors and academics in general have a number of obligations to students. In the most limited sense, it means teaching students how to conduct research, pursue knowledge on their own, defend their ideas, be reflective about when to reject their own positions, be aware of the consequences of their ideas and actions, and always be willing to listen critically to others. More specifically there is the obligation to bring into play a body of knowledge that helps to expand their sense of social and individual agency. It's an obligation, in a sense, to make students more critically aware of the world in which they find themselves. This suggests educating students to learn how to be able to live in an inclusive and nonrepressive democracy. It means nurturing those capacities that enable them to take risks, to make democratic politics and public commitments central to their lives. For me, that obligation does not simply rest on expanding the boundaries of knowledge for students. It also rests on making students more aware of how knowledge can be used as a social, intellectual, and theoretical resource to make them more responsible as citizens who can actively shape the larger world. It means using knowledge in more than a narrowly instrumental way—such as preparing for a job. It also means critically embracing knowledge as a means of self-development tied to modes of learning and intellectual work that address matters of human freedom, equality, and social justice. Learning in this instance is linked not just to understanding but also to social change, to those modes of moral witnessing necessary to transform the underlying systemic conditions that produce human suffering and exploit the environment. It seems to me that my obligation, in the long run, is to prepare students for a very complex and contradictory world in which it becomes necessary that they learn how to govern and not just participate in the governance schemes of others. At the same time, they will hopefully associate their own sense of self-determination and agency with modes of governance that are democratic, cosmopolitan, and deeply concerned with matters of economic and social justice. I may be terribly wrong on this issue, but I think academics have to ask themselves very crucial questions about their vision of the future; their responsibilities as citizens; the role of the state, government, and what it means; and what the responsibility of the university might be in terms of its liberatory functions.

sr: You bring up the issue of dissent. What do you see as the role of an oppositional academic?

hg: The role of the oppositional academic is essentially to make power accountable, and to do everything one can, both in one's teaching and research, to make sure that the political and moral stakes are made clear to students about what it might mean to contribute unthinkingly to a culture and social order in which human suffering goes unnoticed and actually becomes normalized. So it seems to me that, as an intellectual, you have a responsibility by virtue of your resources, not to mention the division of labor that academics inhabit, to enter into a discourse in which you can make power visible and to employ a language of critique and possibility to enable students to recognize that they can be important political actors in shaping the world that they inherit. Central to any viable education is the need for both teachers and students to be able to translate private issues into public concerns, use theory as a resource and hope as a pedagogical tool in order to look beyond the horizon of the given, and mediate the memory of loss and the experience of injustice as part of a broader attempt to open up new locations of struggle and undermine various forms of injustice and domination. We live in a world in which educators have a responsibility to rethink the space of the social in order to develop a critical language in which notions of the public good and public life become central to overcoming the privatizing and depoliticizing language of the market. Academics need to address the subversive role of the university, its role in preventing institutions from governing without being challenged. Clearly, as public intellectuals, academics can, as Edward Said has suggested, temper any reverence for authority with a sense of critical awareness. Students need to engage new modes of literacy through which to read the world; they need to be both critics and cultural producers; they need to be able to recognize antidemocratic assaults on public life; and they need a language to defend those vital institutions that are central to every aspect of democratic life. They also need to learn to read the world from the perspectives of those victims of "democracy" who have their own lessons to teach about what it means to live in a global society. I think Jacques Derrida was right in arguing that the university should be a place of unconditional resistance, a place in which nothing is beyond question. At one level, this points to the need for academics to beware of the pitfalls of specialization and professionalism, which often substitute a professional vocation for an intellectual vocation. Professionalism has more to do with reverence than critique, careerism than engagement with public life. At the same time, I think that academics need to view pedagogy as much more than a methodology, or an a priori discourse that simply needs to be uncovered or revealed, and to take seriously the presupposition that the task of pedagogy in its most vital sense is about critically engaging how knowledge, values, desire, and social relations are implicated in power, while also recognizing pedagogy as a moral and political practice that is always an outcome of struggles. Pedagogy is not just a struggle over particular forms of knowledge or identities, although this is important; it is also a struggle over how one views the future and what it might mean to prepare students not simply to imagine a different future, but to make a claim on social justice, solidarity, and the promise of an inclusive democracy.

Notes

1. Randall Robinson, *Quitting America: The Departure of a Black Man from his Native Land* (New York: Dutton Books, 2004), 130.
2. Alain Badiou, *Ethics: An Essay on the Understanding of Evil* (London: Verso, 2001), 121.
3. Emma Schwartz, "Colleges Stumble in Aiding Voter Registration," *Los Angeles Times*, September 14, 2004, A16.
4. Henry A. Giroux and Susan Searls Giroux, "Take Back Higher Education: A Task for Intellectuals in a Time of Crisis," *Tikkun Magazine* 18: 6 (November–December 2003), 28–32.
5. Henry A. Giroux and Susan Searls Giroux, *Take Back Higher Education: Race, Youth, and the Crisis of Democracy in the Post–Civil Rights Era* (New York: Palgrave Macmillan, 2004).

Part I
America Under Siege

Authoritarianism and Democracy

2

THE CONSERVATIVE ASSAULT ON AMERICA

CULTURAL POLITICS, EDUCATION, AND
THE NEW AUTHORITARIANISM

We have frequently printed the word Democracy, yet I cannot too often repeat that it is a word the real gist of which still sleeps, quite unawakened, notwithstanding the resonance and the many angry tempests out of which its syllables have come, from pen or tongue. It is a great word, whose history, I suppose, remains unwritten, because that history has yet to be enacted.
—Walt Whitman, *Democratic Vistas*, 1871[1]

If this were a dictatorship, it'd be a heck of a lot easier, just so long as I'm the dictator.
—George W. Bush, 2000[2]

Democracy is a breeze during good times. It's when the storms are raging that citizenship is put to the test. And there's a hell of a wind blowing right now.
—Bob Herbert, 2004[3]

During the late 1980s, it became clear that the United States government and American popular will were shifting to the ideological Right. From the beginning of the 1980s, President Ronald Reagan and his cohorts breathed new life into the authoritarian Right, using the power of their historical bloc to wage an intense battle to weaken labor unions, dismantle the welfare state, eliminate the Department of Education, support right-wing contras in Nicaragua, and increasingly make use of the state to contain and punish marginalized groups rather than invest in eliminating poverty, racism, and other factors promoting human suffering. What few people anticipated at the time was the degree to which democracy would be under siege in the decades that followed. If the 1980s belonged to Reagan and his brand of social conservatism and militarism, the 1990s belonged to Bill Clinton and a more friendly, though no less pernicious, brand of neoliberalism that placed economics above democratic politics and corporate interests above public considerations. As liberalism dropped its concern for social provisions and morphed into the bloodthirsty, Darwinian politics of neoliberalism, democratic values were subordinated to market values, and corporate interests began to shape the government's interests rather than be subject to its regulatory controls.[4] Politics outside the realm of the marketplace appeared inconceivable just as neoliberalism put into place a notion of agency marked by an unbridled form of self-interest and a value system unconcerned with ethical considerations. While Clinton did not follow the imperial ambitions of his predecessor, he waged a low-intensity war at home against the poor by initiating a reactionary welfare reform package that punished people who were poor, single mothers, and minorities of color. He also abetted the conservative initiative, which had made headway in the Congress and courts in the 1980s, to criminalize social problems by disinvesting in social reform and reinvesting in a state that was increasingly more concerned about punishment, containment, and surveillance than addressing the underlying causes of social problems.

With the election of George W. Bush to the presidency in 2000, democracy was drastically weakened as its most basic underlying principles began to unravel. The corporate state unabashedly began to replace the last vestiges of the democratic state as the central principles of a market fundamentalism were applied with a vengeance to every aspect of society.[5] All things social as well as the very concept of the public good were under attack since they detracted from the interests of profit-making and limited the expansion and possibilities of market identities, values, and relations. Consequently, those noncommodified values that are central to a democracy— liberty, justice, and equality—were either ignored or treated as irrelevant by a new type of social and economic order marked by a shift away from the old forces and values of industrial production to a new emphasis on financial capital and the wealth generated by "immaterial" production within the new knowledge-information industries. Citizenship was now largely defined through a limited notion of choice in which buying and selling constituted the meaning and substance of individual and social agency. Within this shift in which the work ethic was replaced by the ethic of consumption, empire-building and unbridled individualism were substituted for civic responsibility as human needs were almost entirely subordinated to the dictates of the market and the growing spectacle of patriotic jingoism.[6] Tax breaks were given to the wealthy as programs that benefited the poor were cut. Military spending increased as programs such as the peace corps were defunded. The shift from acts of civic responsibility to the demands of consumerism and the spectacle of patriotism not only further devalued the rhetoric of democracy; it also equated dissent with treason and imposed democracy abroad with guns, bombs, and invading armies.

Under the onslaught of market forces unleashed globally during this period, the old social contracts between labor and capital and between the middle class and working poor came under increasing attack. At the same time, all levels of government were hollowed out due to the ongoing attempt on the part of neoliberal advocates to battle against any remnants of the welfare state such as its promise of minimum security through collective safety nets that provided basic social services. Labor now became temporary, flexible, and contingent; and the image of labor as long term, secure, and tied to the traditional notion of the work ethic was now viewed more as a burden than an asset. Job security, always fragile at best, came under increasing attack as deregulation, downsizing, outsourcing, and flexibility reduced work everywhere to part-time and minimum-wage jobs, redundancy, and a future without a vestige of security.[7] Flexibility became the new catchword, signaling that in the new global order nothing is fixed, permanent, or secure, and that the very nature of identity and agency must be amenable to short notice, the dictates of a radical uncertainty, and the whims of a market economy that appeared unchecked by the political power of the nation-state. But the loss of faith in the welfare state did more than inject a radical insecurity, fear, and uncertainty into many people's lives, while increasing the hardships and suffering they experienced; it also signaled the emergence of a political revolution in which economic power was increasingly separated from nation-based and local politics, and all of the gains made during the New Deal were now under aggressive attack by an administration that made an unholy alliance among rigid advocates of neoliberal capitalism, empire-seeking neoconservatives, and a powerful group of evangelical Christians.[8]

On the domestic front, the Bush administration waged an aggressive battle for privatization, deregulation, school vouchers, and the destruction of all of those vital public spheres wedded to providing citizens with social supports, democratic values, and noncommodified ways of "organizing and deepening political, economic, and social freedom."[9] The obsession with privatization accompanied by an unadulterated celebration of excessive individualism and individual choice offered a rationale for implementing policies that brutally destroyed all of those social relations at odds with free-market orthodoxies as well as all of those noncommodified public spheres that called into question the limits of commercial culture and the politically impotent forms of democracy and citizenship it legitimated. Any institution that took seriously the democratic imperative to regenerate public life and address major social problems became a target to be commercialized, privatized, or simply eliminated. With public life being drained of any substance, it became more difficult for the public to even imagine expanding democratic possibilities and hopes. The social costs of a number of draconian policies pursued by Bush and his cronies took their toll in the hard currency of human suffering. For example, the number of people living below the poverty line in 2001 was 33 million; "by 2003 there were almost 36 million."[10] Census Bureau figures reveal that the number of those without healthcare insurance rose to 45 million (up 1.4 million) in 2002. "Hardest hit were women, who for the first time since 1999 saw their earnings decline, and children. By the end of 2003, 12.9 million children lived in poverty."[11] In America 17.6 percent of children live in poverty, and the infant mortality rate increased for the first time in decades in 2002. For African Americans, the poverty rate was "nearly twice the national rate, with 24.4 percent of blacks living below the poverty line in 2003."[12] Bush's policies punished poor African Americans, women, and children but rewarded with massive tax cuts the wealthiest 1 percent of Americans who, with average incomes of $1.1 million per year, saw an average tax cut of $78,460 and their share of the total tax burden fall roughly 32 percentage points to 2.1 percent. The tax cuts for the wealthiest 10 percent of Americans totaled $148 billion.[13] Commenting on Bush's tax cuts, Jim Wallis, editor of *Sojourner Magazine*, claims, "The truth is that hungry people will go without food stamps, poor children will go without health care, the elderly will go without medicine, and school children will go without textbooks, so that the taxes of the wealthiest Americans can be further reduced."[14]

While the Bush administration extended tax cuts to the super rich, it scaled back a range of programs—including job training, housing, higher education, Medicaid benefits, and an array of social services that benefit the poor and the disadvantaged.

Under President Bush's proposed budget for 2006, it has been estimated that the Women, Infant, and Children's program, which supplies food and other vital services to pregnant women and youth, will be cut by "$658 million, with the result that some 670,000 women, babies and youngsters under 5 will not be served."[15] Food stamp programs will be slashed as well as after-school programs, crucial education programs, and heating assistance programs for the poor. But while the poor have suffered under the Bush presidency, the economy has prospered for billionaires. As Holly Sklar points out, "The new Forbes list of the 400 richest Americans has 313 billionaires—up 51 billionaires from 262 [in 2003]."[16]

While the state under the Bush administration was hollowed out—abdicating its power to regulate the social sphere, act as the guardian of the public interest, and provide social guarantees for the needs of children, the poor, and the aged—the state was far from rendered inconsequential. What emerged under Bush's first term was not an impotent state, but a garrison state that increasingly protected corporate interests and glorified financial markets while stepping up the level of repression and militarization on the domestic front. Bush's war on terrorism appeared to mimic the very forces it was fighting as it gutted civil liberties and organized civic society around a culture of fear rather than a discourse of shared responsibility and democratic values. Under a flurry of repressive legislation passed after the events of September 11, American citizens were denied any legal rights and could be detained indefinitely by the American government without due access to a lawyer, family, or friends. Needless to say, the Bush administration's contempt for law and due process emboldened those "defenders of democracy" who blithely argued against freedom in the name of providing security against potential acts of terrorism. In the name of providing security, the fear industry with its massive security system is sprouting up everywhere, making it easier for the government to expand its potential for control, surveillance, and just plain spying on people.[17] Seemingly indifferent to the fact that societies that offer to exchange liberty for security often end up "with neither liberty nor security,"[18] the Bush administration used the spectacle of fear and the culture of insecurity to narrow political dialogue, escalate the forces of authoritarianism, and further promote the militarization of everyday life.

The incessant quest for homeland security took place at the same time that political debate collapsed under the weight of Bush's war on terrorism. One consequence that now shapes the present, as William Greider points out, is that "the [endless] quest for homeland security is heading, in ad hoc fashion, toward the quasi militarization of everyday life."[19] Another consequence of America's infatuation with militarization can be seen in its invasion of Iraq wrapped up in the missionary discourse of democracy brought to life in daily bombings and the unreported killing of thousands of Iraqis, a large percentage of whom are children. The hypocrisy of this contradiction is apparent in the dreadful images of American soldiers torturing detainees at Abu Ghraib as well as a number of other prisons in Iraq, which reflect not only the dark side of the debacle in Iraq, but also seem to represent a "photograph that Americans had taken of themselves—a self-portrait that refracts a collective identity whose spokespersons have conflated pre-emptive war and invasion with liberation."[20] Brute force abroad and the equation of dissent with treason at home set in motion—albeit with flags waving and Fox News Channel blasting at full volume—a wave of fear and repression in which civil society was organized essentially for the production of violence and the shutting down of any critical opposition. Under Bush's first term as president, fear and cynicism became the most powerful values shaping public life, and the United States appeared to be "perilously close to becoming an Orwellian dystopia."[21]

As power was more and more concentrated in the hands of corporate elites and the upper class, government was largely removed from the needs of most people, but especially those who were disadvantaged by virtue of their race, class, age, and gender, a message that was brutally obvious in the government's response to the poor black victims of hurricane Katrina. These groups were often seen either as a political liability or as disposable. Modern democracy was increasingly subverted as public life was progressively militarized, undermined through a government-sponsored culture of fear, and financially weakened by an immoral war that drained valuable resources from social services as it also contributed to a $322 billion deficit. In a shameful act of ethical and political indifference to young people, the Bush administration has saddled future generations with a crippling debt and a bleak future.[22] As Hans Johnson points out, "Today the nation's treasury log reads like a giant ransom note to today's children, rife with red ink from the record . . . deficit they will repay. And the roll call of fewer jobs, lower wages and diminished healthcare coverage revives talk of the 'misery index.' "[23]

Many youthful, critical educators in the late 1980s (including myself) viewed democracy, even with its damaged legacy, as a referent for developing political and social practices that would invigorate critical citizenship, expand the possibilities of public life, and energize an educational system that, in order to be realized, needed to recognize the valuable role it played in strengthening and extending the most important principles of a democracy. In the aftermath of the reelection of George W. Bush to the presidency in 2004, democracy is being threatened as at no other time in the recent past, and the United States may be on the verge of surrendering its democratic ideals, practices, and values to an emerging authoritarianism that is casting a heavy shadow across America at the present historical moment.[24]

A number of powerful antidemocratic tendencies now threaten American democracy. The first is a market fundamentalism that not only trivializes democratic values and public concerns, but also enshrines a rabid individualism, an all-embracing quest for profits, and a social Darwinism in which misfortune is seen as a weakness and the Hobbesian rule of a "war of all against all" replaces any vestige of shared responsibilities or compassion for others. Within neoliberal ideology, the market becomes the template for organizing the rest of society. Everybody is now a customer or client, and every relationship is ultimately judged in bottom-line, cost-effective terms. Similarly, as Paul Krugman points out, "The hijacking of public policy by private interests" parallels "the downward spiral in governance."[25] With the rise of market fundamentalism, economics is accorded more respect than politics; the citizen has been reduced to a consumer; and the buying and selling of goods is all that seems to matter. Even children are now targeted as a constituency from which to make money, reduced to commodities, sexualized in endless advertisements, and shamelessly treated as a market for huge profits. Under such circumstances, hope is foreclosed, and it becomes difficult either to imagine a life beyond capitalism or to believe in a politics that takes democracy seriously.

The second fundamentalism can be seen in a religious fervor embraced by Bush and his cohorts that not only serves up creationism instead of science, but substitutes blind faith for critical reason.[26] This is a deeply disturbing trend in which the line between the state and religion is being erased as radical Christian evangelicals embrace and impose a moralism on Americans that is largely racist, bigoted, patriarchal, uncritical, and insensitive to real social problems such as poverty, racism, the crisis in healthcare, and the increasing impoverishment of America's children. Instead of addressing these problems, a flock of dangerous evangelicals who have enormous political clout are waging a campaign to ban same-sex marriages, privatize Social Security, eliminate federal funding for embryonic stem cell research, and overturn Roe v. Wade and other abortion rights cases. Right-wing religious groups such as the Traditional Values Coalition attempt to impose their religious ideology on scientific research by influencing the awarding of individual government research grants, especially those that deal with sexuality, drug abuse, and HIV/AIDS transmission. In the Republican-controlled Congress, the federal government now finances religious projects under the guise of promoting scientific research that has nothing to do with the principles or methods of rigorous scientific work. For instance, the federal government has funded a $2.3 million project to determine whether praying promotes good health.[27] In February 2004, a group of about sixty scientists, including twenty Nobel laureates, issued a public statement accusing the Bush administration of purposefully distorting, suppressing, and abusing scientific analysis from federal agencies to promote ideologically driven policy goals. For example, the scientists charged that scientific studies about global warming were ignored by the Bush administration. Even worse, government reports were censored "to remove views not in tune with Bush's politics."[28] But not only has the Bush administration undermined scientific facts when they clashed with the politics of his evangelical base; it has also punished researchers and organizations at odds with right-wing religious views through a "steady diet of financial audits, criminal investigations, onerous reporting requirements, and, outright defunding."[29]

A new breed of religious zealot is being elected to the highest level of government. Bill Moyers points out that nearly half the members of the U.S. Congress—"231 legislators in all (more since the 2004 election)—are backed by the religious Right, which includes several powerful fundamentalist leaders, and forty-five senators and 186 members of the 108th Congress earned 80 to 100 percent approval ratings from the most influential Christian Right advocacy groups."[30] George W. Bush did more during his first term to advance the agenda of right-wing evangelicals than any other president in recent history, and has continued to do so in his second term.[31] The perils of theocratic rule are evident; Bush has his own "prayer team," fills his speeches with religious references, allocates billions of dollars to faith-based organizations, and once appointed during his first term an attorney general who claimed that "America has no king but Jesus." What is most disturbing is not simply that many of his religious supporters believe that Bush is their leader, but also that he is embraced as a "messenger from God,"[32] whose job it is to implement God's will. For example, Bob Jones III, the president of fundamentalist Bob Jones University, argued in a letter to President Bush: "Christ has allowed you to be his servant" in order to "leave an imprint for righteousness. . . . In your re-election, God has graciously granted

America—though she doesn't deserve it—a reprieve from the agenda of paganism. You have been given a mandate. We the people expect your voice to be like the clear and certain sound of a trumpet. . . . Don't equivocate. Put your agenda on the front burner and let it boil. You owe the liberals nothing. They despise you because they despise your Christ."[33] Jones goes on to claim that since "Christ has allowed [Bush] to be His servant in this nation. . . . you will have opportunity to appoint many conservative judges and exercise forceful leadership with the congress in passing legislation that is defined by biblical norms regarding the family, sexuality, sanctity of life, religious freedom, freedom of speech, and limited government."[34]

Rampant anti-intellectualism coupled with Taliban-like moralism now boldly translates into everyday cultural practices and political policies as right-wing evangelicals live out their messianic view of the world. For instance, more and more conservative pharmacists are refusing to fill prescriptions for religious reasons. Mixing medicine, politics, and religion means that some women are being denied birth control pills, or any other product designed to prevent conception. Evangelicals are waging battles in the schools in order to incorporate "Creationism" and biblical readings of the world alongside scientifically-backed theories of evolution. But Bush's much exalted religious fundamentalism does more than promote a disdain for science and critical thought while reinforcing retrograde forms of homophobia and patriarchy; it also inspires an aggressive militarism, wrapped up in the language of a holy war. *Agence France-Presse* reported that a group of evangelical marines prepared to "battle barbarians" before their assault on Fallujah in Iraq by listening to heavy metal–flavored lyrics in praise of Christ while a "female voice cried out on the loudspeakers 'You are the sovereign, Your name is holy. You are the pure spotless lamb.'" Just before the battle, a chaplain had the soldiers line up in order to dab their heads with oil, while he told them, "God's people would be anointed with oil."[35] It now appears that Bush's war for "democracy" is defined by many of his followers as a "holy war" against infidels. Inspired to cleanse American society, if not the world, of impurities, evangelical Christians are unleashing a wave of criticism and censorship against all but the most sanitized facets of popular culture, including children's shows that either portray lesbian and gay families positively or offer up perceived homoerotic representations such as those attributed to the cartoon character Spongebob SquarePants.[36] One conservative Texas lawmaker has jumped onto the moralism bandwagon by introducing a bill that would put an end to "sexually suggestive" performances by cheerleaders at sports events and other extracurricular competitions. According to A.L. Edwards, a 26-year veteran of the Texas House: "It's just too sexually oriented, you know, the way they're shaking their behinds and going on, breaking it down. And then we say to them, 'don't get involved in sex unless it's marriage or love, it's dangerous out there' and yet the teachers and directors are helping them go through those kind of gyrations."[37]

The third antidemocratic dogma is visible in the relentless attempt on the part of the Bush administration to destroy critical education as a foundation for an engaged citizenry and a vibrant democracy. The attack on critical education is evident not only in the attempts to standardize curricula, privatize public schooling, and use the language of business as a model for running schools, but also in the ongoing effort to hand over those larger educational forces in the culture to a small group of corporate interests. Schooling is reduced to training, rote learning, and, with regard to poor minorities in poverty stricken neighborhoods, becomes a form of warehousing. Teachers are now viewed as either technicians, depoliticized professionals, or, if they belong to a teachers' union, as former Education Secretary Rod Paige believed, members of a "terrorist organization."[38]

At the same time as democracy is removed from the purpose and meaning of schooling, the dominant media are increasingly reduced to propaganda machines, available to the highest corporate bidder. As is commonly known, the major media outlets in the United States are controlled by six companies and the six largest cable companies reach 80 percent of cable television subscribers.[39] Under the Bush administration, deregulation intensifies such concentration and further undermines any possibility of an independent and critical media. For instance, three firms in the largest radio markets now control access to more than half of the listening audience. One of the firms, Clear Channel Communications, owns 1,225 stations in the United States "and reaches . . . more than 70 percent of the American public."[40] Under such circumstances, democracy is hijacked by private interests, and the marketplace of ideas has almost nothing to do with providing citizens with knowledge that is crucial in order to be active participants in shaping and sustaining a vibrant democracy. On the contrary, the media largely serve to target audiences for advertising, to pander to the antiliberal ideologies of the political elite, to function in large part to reinforce the conventional wisdom of corporate interests, and to help produce a populace absorbed in cynical withdrawal and adrift in a sea of celebrity scandal and mindless info-tainment and mili-tainment. Commenting on the supine role of the press and its refusal to make dominant power accountable, Frank Rich, columnist for the *New York Times*, rightly argues, "The Washington press corps' eagerness to facilitate and serve as dress extras in what amounts to an administration promotional video can now be seen as a metaphor for just how much the legitimate press has been co-opted by all manner of fakery in the Bush years."[41]

Politics is now largely a made-for-TV spectacle in which sound bites replace any vestige of intellectual analysis. Increasingly the poverty of political discourse is matched by the irresponsibility of public-relations intellectuals. Under the sway of a market fundamentalism, the dominant media have deteriorated into a combination of commercialism, propaganda, and entertainment.[42] In such circumstances, the media neither operate in the interests of the public good nor provide the pedagogical conditions necessary for producing critical citizens or defending a vibrant democracy. Instead, as McChesney and Nichols point out, concentrated media depoliticize the culture of politics, commercially carpet-bomb citizens, and denigrate public life.[43] Rather than perform an essential public service, they have become the primary tool for promoting a culture of consent and conformity in which citizens are misinformed and public discourse is debased. Media concentration restricts the range of views to which people have access and, in doing so, does a disservice to democracy itself. For example, *NOW with Bill Moyers* did a radio survey in which it was discovered that "the top-rated talk radio stations across the country ran 310 hours of conservative talk each day and only five hours of views that were not right-wing."[44] But the dominant media do more than peddle conservative ideologies and turn citizens into panting consumers; they also cheapen political discourse, if not intelligence itself. How else to explain *Village Voice* columnist Rick Perlstein's revelation that when he asked a number of political movers and shakers from the Democratic Party about how the Bush administration was stealing our democratic birthright, he was told that he was proposing an "elite argument"? Jeff Shesol, a former speechwriter for President Clinton, exemplifies how the discourse about democracy and politics has been cheapened. According to Shesol, any attempt to talk critically about the future of democracy to a larger public is unproductive because it "pitches too high to reach the mass electorate."[45]

If, as Perlstein claims, highly placed Democratic Party operatives believe that arguments that focus on the fragility or highjacking of democracy are now considered too abstract for public consumption, then surely this suggests an educational as well as a moral failing. Hence, it is not too far-fetched to argue that education as schooling or as public pedagogy now generally functions "to limit the instruments for complex and critical reasoning."[46] Under the Bush administration, especially in its move to create a national security state, various pedagogical sites are increasingly being appropriated in an effort to diminish the capacity of the American public to think critically. For example, public schools are being turned "into factories of rote learning and multiple-choice testing" while the media eschew their critical responsibility to hold dominant authority accountable in favor of assuming the role of an entertainment center.[47] As the critical power of education both within and outside of institutional schooling is reduced to the official discourse of compliance, conformity, and reverence, it becomes more difficult for the American public to engage in critical debates, translate private considerations into public concerns, and recognize the distortions and lies that underlie much of current government policies. How else to explain how Bush was reelected in 2004 in the face of flagrant lies about why the United States invaded Iraq, the passing of tax reform policies that rewarded the ultra-rich at the expense of the middle and lower classes, and the pushing of a foreign policy platform that was largely equated with bullying by the rest of the world? What is one to make of Bush's winning popular support for his reelection in light of his record of letting millions of young people slide into poverty and hopelessness, his continued "assault on regulations designed to protect public health and the environment," and his promulgation of a culture of fear that is gutting the most cherished of American civil liberties?[48]

Finally, a fourth antidemocratic dogma that is shaping American life, and one of the most disturbing, is the ongoing militarization of public life. Americans are not only obsessed with military power; "it has become central to our national identity."[49] Andrew J. Bacevich develops this position by arguing that Americans are enthralled by a dangerous form of militarism. He writes:

> To state the matter bluntly, Americans in our own time have fallen prey to militarism, manifesting itself in a romanticized view of soldiers, a tendency to see military power as the truest measure of national greatness, and outsized expectations regarding the efficacy of force. To a degree without precedent in U.S. history, Americans have come to define the nation's strength and well-being in terms of military preparedness, military action, and the fostering of (or nostalgia for) military ideals.[50]

How else to explain the fact that the United States has "725 official military bases outside the country and 969 at home?" Consider that it "spends more on 'defense' than all the rest of the world put together. . . . this country is obsessed with war: rumors of war, images of war, 'preemptive' war, 'preventive' war, 'surgical' war, 'prophylactic' war, 'permanent' war. As President Bush explained at a news conference on April 13, 2004, 'This country must go on the offense and stay on the offense.' "[51] American militarism shapes a foreign policy that ignores multilateral cooperation with other nations; it is based on a policy "that posits military might as a salvific in a world in which he who has the most and biggest weapons is the more moral and masculine, hence worthy of policing others."[52] But as Cornel West also points out, such aggressive militarism is fashioned out of an ideology that not only supports a foreign policy based on "the cowboy mythology of the American frontier fantasy," but also affects domestic policy because it expands "police power, augments the prison-industrial complex, and legitimates unchecked male power (and violence) at home and in the workplace. It views crime as a monstrous enemy to crush (targeting poor people) rather than as an ugly behavior to change (by addressing the conditions that often encourage such behavior)."[53]

As a politics of fear undermines any feasible attempt to reclaim democratic values conducive to producing and legitimating shared civic responsibilities, the ideology of war and the militarization of public life both legitimate the rise of the military-industrial-prison-educational-entertainment complex and put into play forms of masculinity in which aggression, violence, and a hyped-up bravado set the tone for what it means to be a "real" man in America. Within this climate of degraded masculinity, Governor Arnold Schwarzenegger does not appear troubled using the term "girlie men" to disparage his allegedly liberal counterparts in California who called attention to the consequences of Bush's economic doctrine. Nor is the military unsettled about producing video games, such as *America's Army*, which link masculinity to killing and hunting "foreign" enemies, and are distributed primarily as recruiting tools to get young men and women to join in the "adventure" taking place in Iraq and Afghanistan.[54] The influence of militaristic values, social relations, and ideology now permeates American culture. For example, major universities aggressively court the military establishment for Defense Department grants and, in doing so, become less open to either academic subjects or programs that encourage rigorous debate, dialogue, and critical thinking. In fact, as higher education is pressured by both the Bush administration and its jingoistic supporters to serve the needs of the military-industrial complex, universities increasingly deepen their connections to the national security state in ways that are boldly celebrated. For example, Penn State University, the University of Pennsylvania, Carnegie Mellon University, and a number of other universities have recently created the National Security Higher Education Advisory Board charged with creating a link between major research universities and the FBI. The president of Penn State, Graham Spanier, has been appointed head of the board and claims, in a statement pregnant with irony, that the purpose of the board is "to foster outreach and to promote understanding between higher education and the nation's national security, law enforcement and intelligence agencies. . . . It will also assist in the development of research, degree programs, course work, internships, opportunities for graduates and consulting opportunities for faculty related to national security."[55] This reads like a page out of George Orwell's novel, *1984*, and appears to counter every decent and democratic value that defines higher education as a democratic public sphere. Unfortunately, public schools are faring no better. Public schools not only have more military recruiters; they also have more military personnel teaching in the classrooms. In addition, schools now adopt the logic of "tough love" by implementing zero tolerance policies that effectively model urban public schools after prisons, just as students' rights increasingly diminish under the onslaught of a military-style discipline. Students in many schools, especially those in poor urban areas, are routinely searched, frisked, subjected to involuntary drug tests, maced, and carted off to jail. The not-so-hidden curriculum here is that kids can't be trusted; their actions need to be regulated preemptively; and their rights are not worth protecting. But children and schools are not the only victims of a growing militarization of American society. The civil rights of people of color and immigrants, especially Arabs and Muslims, are being violated, often resulting in either imprisonment, or deportment, or government harassment. Similarly, black and brown youth and adults are being incarcerated at record levels as prison construction outstrips the construction of schools, hospitals, and other life-preserving institutions. In California, beginning correctional officers earn more than the average public school teacher. All of this is happening in the name of antiterrorism laws that are increasingly being used by the Bush administration to justify abusive military campaigns abroad and to stifle dissent at home.

Measures to combat terrorism are now used by the government to support an arms budget that is larger than that of all the other major industrialized countries combined. As the state increasingly functions largely in its capacity to expand the forces of domestic militarization, surveillance, and control, it appears that the Bush administration is waging a war against democracy itself. Militarism has become a new public pedagogy, and one of its consequences is a growing authoritarianism that encourages profit-hungry monopolies, the ideology of faith-based certainty, and the undermining of any vestige of critical education, dissent, and dialogue. Education is either severely narrowed and trivialized in the media as a form of entertainment or converted into training and character reform in the schools. Within higher education, democracy appears as an excess, if not a pathology, as right-wing ideologues and corporate wannabe administrators increasingly police what faculty say, teach, and do in their courses on the grounds that their teaching and research is either insufficiently patriotic or politically biased. And it is going to get worse.

If George W. Bush's first term appeared as an aberration due to "an electoral quirk, the fruit of a Florida fiasco, the arcane algebra of the U.S. electoral system, and a split decision of the supreme court,"[56] his reelection in 2004 appears as a dangerous turning point in American history. Not only did he receive slightly more than 50 percent of the popular vote, but he also garnered a mandate for a mode of leadership and set of domestic and foreign policies that bring the United States close to the edge of a totalitarian regime. George W. Bush's reelection is tantamount to a revolution aimed at rolling back most of the democratic gains of the last century. Paul Krugman is right in arguing that "Bush isn't a conservative. He's a radical—the leader of a coalition that deeply dislikes America as it is. Part of that coalition wants to tear down the legacy of Franklin Roosevelt, eviscerating Social Security and, eventually, Medicare. Another part wants to break down the barriers between church and state."[57] Under Bush's first term as president, growing appeals to fear and insecurity coupled with a growing militarism, authoritarianism, and culture of cynicism became the most powerful values and forces shaping public life. Hence, it is not surprising that Karl Rove, Bush's chief strategist, most admires the Gilded Age under the presidency of William McKinley (1896–1901), a period when robber barons and strikebreakers ruled, and the government and economy were controlled by a cabal that was rich, powerful, and ruthless. Given that Bush's second campaign was run by "dividing the country along [the] fault lines of fear, intolerance, ignorance and religious rule,"[58] the future does not look bright for democracy. Critical race theorist David Theo Goldberg got it right in arguing that the message of the 2004 election was:

> don't get ill, lose your job, or retire; don't breathe, swim in the ocean, travel, or think critical thoughts; invest your life-savings in the stock market even though you will likely lose it all; go to community college for two years of technical training rather than to four-year universities where your mind will be turned to liberal mush; support tax cuts for the wealthy, and military service for the poor. If you step out of line, remember the Patriot Act is there to police you at home and a loaded B52 bomber hovers overhead abroad.[59]

In opposition to this deeply reactionary revolution being waged by political extremists, Christian fundamentalists, and free-market evangelicals, cultural workers— including composition theorists, critical educators, artists, and others need to try to connect to the energies of a deep democratic tradition extending from Horace Mann to W. E. B. Du Bois to John Dewey. Such a critical tradition is both moving and theoretically useful because it not only examines the long legacy of the struggle for democracy in the schools, but also argues for struggling over public and higher education as one of the few public spaces left where democracy can actually be taught, experienced, and defended. Educators, students, and others need to make clear that politics as it is being practiced in Washington, D.C. is no longer about democracy, the public good, public participation, or critical citizenship. What needs to be recognized is that under the auspices of a diverse group of extremists, including political, religious, and market fundamentalists, political and educational culture is being transformed by the discourses of privatization, consumerism, and market-based choice, the spectacle of celebrity, and the revived ethics of social Darwinism. Abstracted from the ideal of public commitment, the new authoritarianism represents a political and economic practice and form of militarism that loosen the connections among substantive democracy, critical agency, and critical education.

In response to the rising tide of authoritarianism, educators must make a case for linking learning to social change, pluralizing and critically engaging the diverse sites where public pedagogy takes place, and must make clear that every sphere of social life is open to political contestation and comprises a crucial site of political, social, and cultural struggle in the attempt to forge the knowledge, identifications, affective investments, and social relations that constitute a political subject and social agent capable of energizing and spreading the basis of a global democracy. Educators need to develop a new discourse whose aim is to foster a democratic politics and pedagogy that embody the legacy and principles of social justice, equality, freedom, and rights associated with the democratic concerns of history, space, plurality, power, discourse, identities, morality, and the future.

Under such circumstances, pedagogy must be embraced as a moral and political practice, one that both initiates and is the outgrowth of struggles designed to resist the increasing depoliticization of political culture that is the hallmark of the current Bush revolution. Education is the terrain where consciousness is shaped; needs are constructed; and the capacity for self-reflection and social change is nurtured and produced. Education has assumed an unparalleled significance in shaping the language, values, and ideologies that legitimate the structures and organizations that support the imperatives of global capitalism. Rather than being simply a technique or methodology, education has become a crucial site for the production and struggle over those pedagogical and political conditions that can enable people individually and collectively to intervene into the processes through which the material relations of power shape the meaning and practices of their everyday lives. Within the current historical context, struggles over power take on a symbolic and discursive as well as a material and institutional form. The struggle over education is about more than the struggle over meaning and identity; it is also about how meaning, knowledge, and values are produced, legitimated, and operate within economic and structural relations of power. Education is not at odds with politics; it is an important and crucial element in any definition of the notion of the political and offers not only the theoretical tools for a systemic critique of authoritarianism, but also a language of possibility for creating actual movements for democratic social change. At stake here is combining an interest in symbolic forms and processes conducive to democratization with broader social contexts and the institutional formations of power itself. The key point here is to understand and engage educational and pedagogical practices from the point of view of how they are bound up with larger relations of power. Educators, students, and parents need to be clearer about how power works through and in texts, representations, and discourses while at the same time recognizing that power cannot be limited to the study of representations and discourses. Changing consciousness is not the same as altering the institutional basis of oppression, but at the same time institutional reform cannot take place without a change in consciousness capable of recognizing the very need for such reform and the need to reinvent the conditions and practices that make it possible. In addition, it is crucial to raise questions about the relationship between pedagogy and civic culture, on the one hand, and what it takes for individuals and social groups to believe that they have any responsibility whatsoever to address the realities of class, race, gender, and other specific forms of domination, on the other. For too long, the Left has ignored that the issue of politics as a strategy is inextricably connected to the issue of political education and to what it means to acknowledge that education is always tangled up with power, ideologies, values, and the acquisition of both particular forms of agency and specific visions of the future.

This suggests that educators need to take positions without standing still and make available those ideas, values, and theories that can critically challenge official knowledge, which indiscriminately embraces both religious fundamentalism and neoliberal ideology. Such a challenge requires struggling to keep alive those institutional spaces, forums, and public spheres (such as the media, higher education, public broadcasting) that support and defend critical education; helping students come to terms with their own power as individual and social agents; exercising civic courage; and engaging in community projects and research that are socially responsible, while refusing to surrender knowledge and skills to the highest bidder. In part, this requires pedagogical practices that connect the production of language, culture, and identity to their deployment in larger physical and social spaces. Such a pedagogy is based on the presupposition that it is not enough to teach students to break with accepted ideas. They must also learn to directly confront the threats from those anti-democratic tendencies that seek to turn democracy into a mall, a sectarian church, or a wing of the coming carceral state.

There are those critics who in tough economic times insist that providing students with anything other than work skills threatens their future viability on the job market. In an age when schooling is reduced to training and excessive testing, and public and higher education are leasing themselves out to the highest corporate bidders, it becomes all the more imperative to view schooling as part of a broader democratic project to provide students with the knowledge, skills, and resources they need to view themselves as critical citizens who can actively participate in understanding and shaping the forces that govern their lives. We must be reminded that education is wedded to an inherently utopian project, one that encourages students and others to reconceptualize themselves as critical social agents able to imagine a world beyond the one they know while struggling to enable the forms and institutions central to a healthy democratic culture and social order.

Unlike some theorists who suggest that politics, as a site of contestation, critical exchange, and engagement, either has come to an end or is in a state of terminal arrest, I believe that the current depressing state of politics points to the urgent challenge of reformulating the crisis of democracy as part of the fundamental crises of vision, meaning, education, and political agency. Within the current discourse of neoliberalism, hope is one of the first casualties, since the notions of the social and the public are banished from the discourse of the future. Similarly, hope is completely at odds with the discourse of many religious fundamentalists, since they are more excited about the world ending so they can be lifted out of their earthly experiences and put on the fast track to heaven. Politics devoid of vision either degenerates into cynicism or appropriates a view of power equated with domination. Lost from such accounts is the recognition that democracy has to be struggled over—even in the face of a most appalling crisis of educational opportunity and political agency. There is also too little attention paid to the fact that the struggle over politics and democracy is inextricably linked to creating and sustaining public spheres where individuals can be educated to function as political agents equipped with the skills, capacities, and knowledge they need not only to actually perform as autonomous political agents, but also to believe that such struggles are worth taking up. It also means taking back people's time in an era when the majority must work more than they ever have to make ends meet. The struggle over time is not merely a work issue; it is also about creating the conditions in which time becomes an asset rather than a liability and offers individuals the opportunity to actually be involved in those deliberative processes and actions that give public life substantive meaning. Jo Ellen Green Kaiser is right in arguing that American culture not only lacks the public spaces in which democracy can flourish; it also "lacks the time for democracy to grow and flourish."[60] The growth of cynicism in American society might say less about the reputed apathy of the populace than it says about the bankruptcy of the old political languages and the need for a new language and vision for clarifying intellectual, ethical, and political projects, especially as they work to reframe questions of agency, ethics, and meaning for a substantive democracy.

Yet crafting a new political language requires what I call educated hope. Hope, in this instance, is the precondition for individual and social struggle, involving the ongoing practice of critical education in a wide variety of sites and the renewal of civic courage among citizens who wish to address pressing social problems. In this sense, educated hope is a subversive force. In opposition to those who seek to turn hope into a new slogan or who punish and dismiss efforts to look beyond the horizon of the given, educators need to resurrect a language of resistance and possibility, a language in which hope becomes anticipatory rather than messianic, mobilizing rather than therapeutic. The longing for a more humane society does not collapse into a retreat from the world but emerges out of critical and practical engagements with present behaviors, institutional formations, and everyday practices. Hope in this context does not ignore the worst dimensions of human suffering, exploitation, and social relations; on the contrary, it acknowledges the need for a "capacity to see the worst and offer more than that for our consideration."[61]

Hence, hope is more than a politics; it is also a pedagogical and performative practice that provides the foundation for enabling human beings to learn about their potential as moral and civic agents. Hope is the outcome of those pedagogical practices and struggles that tap into memory and lived experiences while at the same time linking individual responsibility with a progressive sense of social change. As a form of utopian longing, educated hope opens up horizons of comparison by evoking not just different histories, but different futures; at the same time, it substantiates the importance of ambivalence while problematizing certainty or, as Paul Ricoeur has suggested, it becomes "a major resource as the weapon against closure."[62] Educated hope is a subversive force when it pluralizes politics by opening up a space for dissent, makes authority accountable, and becomes an activating presence in promoting social transformation.

The current limits of the utopian imagination, especially in light of the reelection of George W. Bush, are related, in part, to the failure of many educators and others to imagine what pedagogical conditions might be necessary to bring into being forms of political agency that might expand the operations of individual rights, social justice, and democratic freedoms. At the same time, a politics and pedagogy of hope represent neither a blueprint for the future nor a form of social engineering, but a belief, simply, that different futures are possible, holding open matters of contingency, context, and indeterminacy. Any educational project informed by the promise of a critical and inclusive democracy must recognize that the resurrection of a viable notion of political and social agency is dependent upon a culture of questioning. It is only through critical forms of education that human beings can learn about the limits of the present and the conditions necessary for them to "combine a gritty sense of limits with a lofty vision of possibility."[63] Hope as both an ethical referent and a performative practice poses the important challenge of how to reclaim social agency within a broader struggle to deepen the possibilities for social justice and global democracy.

Coupling education and democracy rests on the assumption that pedagogy plays a crucial role in creating the conditions, knowledge, and skills that allow people to embrace hope rather than cynicism; to be responsible to themselves and others rather than surrender their sense of agency to either corporations or authoritarian despots; to take an essential step toward self-representation rather than mimicking the dictates of a consumer culture; to act from a position of critical agency rather than from a position of subservience; and to break through the modes of alienation that tie them to the "common sense" of neoliberalism and the new global order. In this sense, pedagogy becomes less a manifesto proclaiming a fixed politics than a form of mediation, an intervention, that attempts to connect educators and other activists to old and new locations of struggle in an effort to deepen and broaden both the reality and the possibilities of democratic public life. This suggests modes of critical education that try to come to grips with the changing conditions of politics while at the same time offering educators a language of critique and possibility for becoming public intellectuals capable of linking education to critical agency, and schooling itself to broader public considerations and social issues.

All of this may seem hopelessly romantic, operating largely in the realm of fantasy, but it is crucial to realize, as the journalist Bill Moyers has argued in a different context, that education and "democracy are deeply linked in whatever chance we human beings have to redress our grievances, renew our politics, and reclaim our revolutionary ideals. Those are difficult tasks at any time, and they are even more difficult in a cynical age as this, when a deep and pervasive corruption has settled upon the republic."[64] Of course, too much is at stake for educators and others to ignore this battle over making education a central foundation for a substantive democracy. Rather than retreating into either cynicism or despair, educators need to find new ways to use theory as a resource to rethink the meaning of democracy, the role of educators as public intellectuals, and what it might mean in an age of increasing anti-democratic dogmas and unchecked market authoritarianism to reconsider the nature of politics and forms of intervention that can combine education with a new democratic project infused with both a sense of social justice and a strong hostility to the existence of human suffering and exploitation.

Notes

1. Walt Whitman cited in Cornel West, *Democracy Matters* (New York: The Penguin Press, 2004), 1.
2. Cited in "Elizabeth Farnsworth Reports on President-elect George W. Bush's First Day in Washington" (transcript, *OnLine News Hour With Jim Lehrer*, December 18, 2000, http://www.pbs.org/newshour/bb/politics/july-dec00/trans_12–18.htm).
3. Bob Herbert, "O.K., Folks: Back to Work," *New York Times*, November 5, 2004, A31.
4. For an account of neo liberalism, see David Harvey, *A Brief History of Neoliberalism* (New York: Oxford University Press, 2005).
5. For a brilliant analysis of the Bush administration policies after the events of September 11, see Paul Street, *Empire and Inequality: America and the World Since 9/11* (Boulder, CO: Paradigm Press, 2004). See also, Henry A. Giroux, *Against The New Authoritarianism* (Winnipeg, Canada: Arbeitier Ring Publishing, 2005).

6. Zygmunt Bauman, *Work, Consumerism and the New Poor* (Philadelphia: Open University Press, 1998), especially chapter 2, "From the Work Ethic to the Aesthetic of Consumption," 23–41.

7. Zygmunt Bauman, *The Individualized Society* (London: Polity Press, 2001).

8. William Greider, "The Right's Grand Ambition: Rolling Back the 20th Century," *The Nation*, May 12, 2003, 1–12.

9. Roberto Mangabeira Unger and Cornel West, *The Future of American Progressivism* (Boston: Beacon, 1998), 59.

10. Trudy Lieberman, "Let Them Eat Cake," *The Nation*, May 9, 2005, 7.

11. Cece Connolly and Griff Witte, "Poverty Rate Up 3rd Year In a Row," *Washington Post*, August 27, 2004, A01.

12. Andrea Hopkins, "Nearly 36 Million Americans Living in Poverty," *Common Dreams News Center*, August 26, 2004, http://www.commondreams.org/headlines04/0826-24.htm.

13. These figures can be found at Melvin Claxton and Ronald J. Hansen, "Working Poor Suffer Under Bush Tax Cuts," *Detroit News*, September 26, 2004, http://www.detnews.com/2004/specialreport/0409/26/a01-284666.

14. Jim Wallis, "The War on the Poor," *SojoMail*, May 15, 2003, http://www.sojo.net/index.cfm?action=sojomail.display&issue=050703#3.

15. Lieberman, "Let Them Eat Cake," 8.

16. Holly Sklar, "Boob Time for Billionaires," *Znet Commentary*, October 12, 2004, http://www.zmag.org/sustainers/content/2004-10/12sklar.cfm.

17. I take up this issue in Henry A. Giroux, *The Abandoned Generation: Democracy Beyond a Culture of Fear* (New York: Palgrave, 2004). For a history of free speech under attack in the United States, see Geoffrey R. Stone, *Perilous Times: Free Speech in Wartime, from the Sedition Act of 1798 to the War on Terrorism* (New York: W.W. Norton, 2004).

18. Christopher Hitchens, "War of Words," *New York Times Book Review*, November 7, 2004, 8.

19. William Greider, "Under the Banner of the 'War' on Terror," *The Nation*, June 21, 2004, 14.

20. Allen Feldman, "Abu Ghraib: Ceremonies of Nostalgia," *Open Democracy*, October 18, 2004, 2.

21. Hugh Eakin, "Just Like in the Movies," *New York Times Book Review*, November 7, 2004, 9.

22. This figure comes from Paul Krugman, "Un-Spin the Budget," *The New York Times* July 11, 2005, http://www.nytimes.com/2005/07/11/opinion/11krugman.html?ex=1122436800&en=eac0c83bf5aec4e4&ei=5070&hp&oref=login. On the fiscal irresponsibility of the Bush administration and the politics of the debt limit, see Daniel Gross, "Why Democrats Should be Thankful: At Least They Don't Have to Clean Up the Bush Fiscal Catastrophe," *Slate*, November 4, 2004, http://slate.msn.com/id/2109203/#ContinueArticle.

23. Hans Johnson, "Fiction First, Spin Later," *In These Times*, October 11, 2004, 20.

24. I have taken up the growing authoritarianism in American life in Henry A. Giroux, *The Terror of Neoliberalism: Authoritarianism and the Eclipse of Democracy* (Boulder, CO: Paradigm Press, 2004).

25. Paul Krugman, "Looting the Future," *New York Times*, December 5, 2003, A27.

26. What now seems a typical occurrence is the takeover of school boards by right-wing Christian fundamentalists who then impose the teaching of creationism on the schools. See, for example, Associated Press, "Wisconsin School OKs Creationism Teaching," *Common Dreams News Center*, November 6, 2004, http://www.commondreams.org/headlines04/1106-08.htm.

27. Jim Holt, "The Other National Conversation," *New York Times Sunday Magazine*, November 7, 2004, 17.

28. Associated Press, "Scientists Group Says Bush Administration Ignores, Distorts Research," *SunHerald.com*, February 18, 2004, http://www.sunherald.com/mld/sunherald/business/technology/7982691.htm_18feb04.

29. Esther Kaplan, *With God on Their Side* (New York:The New Press, 2004), 63.
30. Bill Moyers, "Welcome to Doomsday," *New York Review of Books*, March 24, 2005, 10.
31. See Ron Suskind, "Without a Doubt," *New York Times Magazine*, October 17, 2004, 44–51, 64, 102.
32. Esther Kaplan, *With God on Their Side: How Christian Fundamentalists Trampled Science, Policy and Democracy in George W. Bush's White House* (New York: The New Press, 2004).
33. Bob Jones III, "Congratulatory Letter to President George W. Bush From Dr. Bob Jones III" (Bob Jones University website, http://www.bju.edu/letter).
34. Ibid.
35. Agence France-Presse News Line, "Holy War: Evangelical Marines Prepare to Battle Barbarians," *Common Dreams News Center*, November 7, 2004, http://www.commondreams.org/headlines04/1107–02.htm.
36. Frank Rich, "The Year of Living Indecently," *New York Times*, February 6, 2005, AR1.
37. April Castro, "Lawmaker Seeks to End Sexy Cheerleading," *ABC News Online*, May 4, 2005, http://abcnews.go.com/US/wireStory?id=592661.
38. John King, "Paige Calls NEA a 'Terrorist Organization,'" *CNN Washington Bureau*, February 23, 2004, http://www.cnn.com/2004/EDUCATION/02/23/paige.terrorist.nea/.
39. See Ben H. Bagdikian, *The New Media Monopoly* (Boston: Beacon, 2004).
40. Jeff Sharlet, "Big World: How Clear Channel Programs America," *Harper's Magazine*, December 2003, 38–39.
41. Frank Rich, "Laura Bush's Mission Accomplished," *New York Times*, May 8, 2005, Section 4, 13.
42. On the relationship between democracy and the media, see Robert W. McChesney, *Rich Media, Poor Democracy: Communication Politics in Dubious Times* (New York: The New Press, 1999).
43. Robert McChesney and John Nichols, *Our Media, Not Theirs: The Democratic Struggle Against Corporate Media* (New York: Seven Stories, 2002), 52–53.
44. PBS, *NOW with Bill Moyers* (transcript, February 13, 2004, http://www.pbs.org/now/transcript/transcript307_full.html).
45. Cited in Rick Perlstein, "The End of Democracy: Losing America's Birthright, the George Bush Way," *Village Voice*, October 19, 2004, http://www.villagevoice.com/print/issues/0442/perlstein.php.
46. Umberto Eco, "Eternal Fascism: Fourteen Ways of Looking at a Blackshirt," *New York Review of Books*, November–December 1995, 15.
47. Katha Pollitt, "Intelligible Design," *The Nation*, October 3, 2005, 10.
48. Paul O'Neill, former treasury secretary who served in the Bush administration for two years, claimed on the television program *60 Minutes* that Bush and his advisors started talking about invading Iraq only ten days after the inauguration, eight months before the tragic events of September 11. See CBS News, "Bush Sought Way to Invade Iraq" (transcript, *60 Minutes*, January 11, 2004, http://www.cbsnews.com/stories/2004/01/09/60minutes/main592330.shtml). For a chronicle of lies coming out of the Bush administration, see David Corn, *The Lies of George Bush* (New York: Crown, 2003). On the environment, see Seth Borenstein, "Environment Worsened Under Bush in Many Key Areas, Data Show," *Common Dreams News Center*, October 13, 2004, http://www.commondreams.org/headlines04/1013–12.htm.
49. Andrew J. Bacevich, *The New American Militarism* (New York: Oxford University Press, 2005), 1.
50. Ibid., 2.
51. Tony Judt, "The New World Order," *The New York Review of Books* LII:12 (July 14, 2005), 16.
52. Cornel West, *Democracy Matters*, 5.
53. Ibid., 6.

54. See Clive Thompson, "The Making of an X Box Warrior," *New York Times Sunday Magazine*, August 22, 2004, 34–37.

55. Penn State News Release, "Penn State's Spanier to Chair National Security Board," September 16, 2005.

56. Jonathan Freedland, "This is No Passing Phase. This is Now an Era," *The Guardian*, November 4, 2004, http://www.guardian.co.uk/print/0,3858,5054801-112564,00.html.

57. Paul Krugman, "No Surrender," *New York Times*, November 5, 2004, A27.

58. Maureen Dowd, "The Red Zone," *New York Times*, November 4, 2004, A27.

59. David Theo Goldberg, "The Sovereign Smirk," *Open Democracy*, November 3, 2004, 3.

60. Jo Ellen Green Kaiser, "A Politics of Time and Space," *Tikkun* 18, no. 6 (2003): 17–18.

61. Thomas L. Dunn, "Political Theory for Losers," in *Vocations of Political Theory*, ed. Jason A. Frank and John Tambornino (Minneapolis: University of Minnesota Press, 2000), 160.

62. Cited in Zygmunt Bauman, *Work, Consumerism and the New Poor* (Philadelphia: Open University Press, 1998), 98.

63. Ron Aronson, "Hope After Hope?" *Social Research* 66, no. 2 (Summer 1999): 489.

64. Bill Moyers, "Keynote Address to the National Conference on Media Reform," *Common Dreams News Center*, November 12, 2003, http://www.commondreams.org/views03/1112-10.htm.

3

DEMOCRACY AND THE CRISIS OF PUBLIC EDUCATION

CO-AUTHORED WITH SUSAN SEARLS GIROUX

The current crisis of public education in the United States provides the basis for offering some speculation and critical questioning of two events in post–Civil Rights America. The *first* has to do with the current state of American political culture: the declining interest in and cynicism about mainstream national politics, their decidedly negative impact on the democratic process, and how such entrenched dispositions might be reversed. Emptied of any substantial content, democracy appears imperiled as individuals are unable to translate their privately suffered misery into broadly shared public concerns and collective action. Civic engagement now appears impotent and public values are rendered invisible in light of the growing power of multinational corporations to shape the content of most mainstream media as they privatize remaining public space. Political exhaustion, the empty ritual of voting, and, impoverished intellectual visions are fed by the increasingly popular assumption that there are no alternatives to the present state of affairs.[1]

For many people today, citizenship is about the act of buying and selling commodities, rather than increasing the scope of their freedoms and rights in order to expand the operations of a substantive democracy. Politics is uncoupled from democratic values, and market values coupled with rising bigotry undercut the possibility for providing a language in which vital social institutions can be defended as a public good. And as social visions of equity recede from public memory, unfettered, brutal self-interests combine with retrograde social policies to make security and safety a top domestic priority. One consequence is that all levels of government unrelated to the military and police are being hollowed out, reducing their role to dismantling the gains of the welfare state as the government increasingly constructs policies that now criminalize social problems and prioritize penal methods over social investments. For instance, homeless people who panhandle in Key West, Florida, can be "sentenced to 60 days in jail and fined $500."[2] Rather than being disciplined by school officials, student behavioral infractions, however minor, are increasingly being handled by the police. In one instance, a five-year-old girl in Florida was handcuffed by police in her elementary school classroom after she tore some papers off a bulletin board.[3] Under such circumstances, the growing lack of justice in American society rises proportionately to the lack of political imagination and collective hope.[4] Similarly, as public spaces are either commercialized or criminalized, notions of the public cease to resonate as a site of democratic possibilities, as a fundamental space for how we reactivate our political sensibilities and conceive of ourselves as critical citizens, engaged public intellectuals, and social agents.

The *second* trend has to do with the nation's increasing skepticism (even overt hostility) toward the educational system at all levels. Distrust of politicians has become something of a national pastime—accentuated increasingly by the public reaction to the war in Iraq and the failure of the Bush administration to adequately respond to the human suffering inflicted by hurricane Katrina in the Gulf Coast—but why the equal disdain toward educators? Equal opportunity to attend quality educational institutions—both public schools and in higher education—had been one of the defining principles of the Civil Rights movement, and it proved to be a site of that era's most potent victories as schools and universities became more accessible to minorities, women, and students with disabilities. But the backlash was immediate, and discontent with programs like affirmative action and busing were quite visible by the mid-70s among white working-class and middle-class voters, who were feeling pinched by recession and ignored by the federal government. Yet they were careful to avoid the overt racism of their predecessors, who had attacked the rights of minority children to attend desegregated schools or to have access to post-secondary education. Public schooling was increasingly defended as an individual rather than a common good. And with the shift away from public considerations to private concerns, privatization and choice became the catch phrases dominating educational reform for the next few decades. The attack on all things public was accompanied by attempts to empty the public treasury, and public education became one of the first targets of neoliberals, neoconservatives, and religious fundamentalists advocating market and individual interests over social needs and democratic values. With the publication of *A Nation at Risk*, the Reagan administration gave the green light to pass spending cuts in education—cuts that have been obligatory for each administration to follow. Reconceived as a "big government monopoly," public schooling was derided as bureaucratic, inefficient, and ineffectual, producing a product (dim-witted students) who were singularly incapable of competing in the global marketplace. In short, schools had committed "an act of unthinking, unilateral educational disarmament," the report accused. A clever strategy to be sure, as it provided a ready scapegoat to legitimate the flight of U.S. manufacturing to markets overseas. Schools were to blame for increased joblessness and insecurity—not the rapacious greed of corporations eager to circumvent U.S. minimum wage laws, federal taxes, and environmental regulations, while breaking the back of unions at home. Similarly, higher education was accused of harboring a hotbed of leftist academics, who promoted culture wars that derided Western civilization, and, in a post-9/11 era, engaged in dissent that was tantamount to treason. Higher education was portrayed as the center of a class and race war in which the dreams of the white working class were under attack because of the ideological residue of professors tainted by the legacy of radical sixties politics. The division and distrust between "elitist liberals" and a white working class were now complete and utterly secure. Employing a mobile army of metaphors drawn from Cold War rhetoric, the Right succeeded in a propaganda campaign to turn the popular tide against public and higher education.

Though there is nothing new in pointing out these two tragic developments—the popular retreat from politics and disdain of education—we are struck by the fact that they are rarely dealt with together, either as mutually reinforcing tendencies or as indispensable conditions of a free and inclusive democratic society. Democratic politics demands the full participation of an educated populace. It demands a public willing to challenge its elected officials and its laws—and change both when necessary. One can't happen without the other, and now it appears both are in jeopardy.

As we've indicated, neither the decline of democracy nor the crisis of education at all levels has gone unnoticed. But curiously, the progressive advocates and activists clustered around either issue have little regard for the other. Astute readers of the national political scene have little interest in (and are often woefully ignorant of) the state of education beyond a heartfelt sound bite or two. And educators seem to have lost the language for linking schooling to democracy, convinced that education is now about job training and competitive market advantage. While both sides hold common concerns and seek deliberative action to redress public opinion, both suffer, however, from the retreat from what were core American values—a concern for notions of publicness, equal access and opportunity, equality, and autonomy. If the liberal Left seems particularly impotent and disheveled and ineffectual at this point in history, conservatives appear to be the masters of persuasion and organization. Working for decades at grassroots organizing, they have taken both pedagogy and politics deadly seriously. Conversely, mainstream democrats make no mention of an educational agenda that differs significantly from the one adopted by the Bush administration; indeed they appear split on the far more general issue of a national platform, the majority wanting to occupy a kinder, gentler republicanism, while a few "radicals" seek to reclaim the liberal traditions of the Democratic Party. Yet we argue that education—both formal and informal, public and higher—should be their first priority.

In an effort to provide a clear example of what we mean, consider the following statistics: soon after the invasion of Iraq in 2003, the *New York Times* released a survey indicating that 42 percent of the American public believed that Saddam Hussein was directly responsible for the September 11, 2001, attacks on the World Trade Center and the Pentagon. CBS also released a news poll indicating that 55 percent of the public believed that Saddam Hussein directly supported the terrorist organization Al Qaeda. A Knight Ridder/Princeton Research poll found that "44% of respondents said they thought 'most' or 'some' of the September 11, 2001, hijackers were Iraqi citizens." A majority of Americans also believed at one point that Saddam Hussein had weapons of mass destruction, that such weapons had been found, that he was about to build a nuclear bomb, and that he would unleash it eventually on an unsuspecting American public. None of these claims had any basis in fact, as no evidence existed to even remotely confirm these assertions. What does this represent, if not a crisis of pedagogy—both formally and informally—in the public sphere?

While popular support for the Bush administration is now at an all time low, these opinions held by a substantial number of Americans did not simply fall from the sky. They were ardently legitimated by President Bush, Vice President Cheney, Colin Powell, and Condoleezza Rice, while being reproduced daily by an uncritical lapdog media. These misrepresentations and strategic distortions circulated in the popular press either with jingoistic enthusiasm, as in the case of the Fox News Channel, or through the dominant media's refusal to challenge such claims—both positions, of course, in opposition to foreign news sources such as the BBC, which repeatedly contested such assertions. Such deceptions are never innocent, and in this case appear to have been shamelessly used by the Bush administration to muster support for both the Iraqi invasion and an ideological agenda "that overwhelmingly favors the president's wealthy supporters and is driving the federal government toward a long-term fiscal catastrophe."[5] The Bush administration's war against Iraq is analogous to the war being waged at home against young people, and both involve duplicity on the part of the government. As Senator Robert Byrd stated in a senate floor speech, President Bush has no trouble asking Congress for $87 billion in supplemental funds to rebuild Iraq but refuses to allocate the $6 billion needed to fund an educational reform program or, for that matter, to supply the resources required to fully support educational programs for our neediest students. As Byrd puts it, "I wonder how the Senators who object to the cost of my amendment . . . to add $6.1 billion for Title 1 education programs to fully fund money Congress authorized for fiscal year 2004 . . . will view the President's request to add $60 billion or $65 billion or $70 billion to the deficit to fund military and reconstruction activities in Iraq. I wonder if they will be comfortable voting to support a massive spending program for Iraq if they cannot bring themselves to support a comparatively meager increase in education funding for American schoolchildren."[6] Of course, those who suffer from budget shortfalls will be not only school children, but also university students who have to grapple with skyrocketing tuition, decreasing student aid, and fewer course offerings, all of which can delay graduation and result in a generally watered-down education.

Our second example is even more tragic, as we attempt to grapple with the meaning and significance of the torture of Iraqi detainees in what had been Saddam Hussein's most infamous prison, Abu Ghraib. The Bush administration has been quick to denounce the sadistic behavior of a few rogue individuals for denigrating America's claim to moral superiority, or what the president called "the true nature and heart of America." But ongoing revelations—including the administration's position that the Geneva Conventions' protocol against the torture of prisoners does not protect "unlawful combatants," more incidents of human rights violations in other prisons in Iraq and Afghanistan, and Seymour Hersh's claim in the *New Yorker* that Defense Secretary Donald Rumsfeld personally approved interrogation practices legitimating physical assault and mental humiliation—suggest that the events at Abu Ghraib were less about what Bush referred to as "failures of character" than about systemic adherence to policies approved at the highest levels of his administration. Perhaps it was the blasé indifference suggested by the weak arguments about "chain of command" and "following orders" that emerged from defendants in the weeks that followed the infamous *60 Minutes II* report—so eerily reminiscent of the justifications given by German soldiers at Nuremberg—that prompted Susan Sontag to write, "Looking at the photographs, you ask yourself, How can someone grin at the suffering and humiliation of another human being?"[7] It is a ponderous question to be sure, one to which we can only respond with more questions. If we are correct to draw a connection among the failures of a radically underfunded and, for many, decrepit public education system, a profit-driven, corporate-funded media, and a misinformed, politically illiterate public, is it also possible to point to yet another form of illiteracy—a moral and ethical illiteracy—as a direct consequence of such grossly inadequate institutions once entrusted to enable democracy? What happens in the absence of critical thought when blind obedience hardens into boredom, reflection gives way to narcissism, passivity finds solace in extreme and often violent spectacles, and humiliation and despair give way to obscene debauchery? Finding no decent answer to such failures of the nation's schools, there is, it seems, a military answer, as Jonathan Kozol once argued, an "all-American and patriotic answer: basic training, absolute obedience to flag and anthem, suspension of emotion in the face of death, a certain hedonistic joy . . . at the prospect of mechanical annihilation."[8] For those who respond to the crisis of the nation's schools with a demand for work skills, for those who see zero tolerance as the answer to any teen infraction, for those who insist that the nation's professoriate "aim low"[9] in their efforts to shape character and fashion critical citizens, we ask, after Kozol, "Is this the kind of literacy we want? Is this the best that Jeffersonian democracy can do?"[10]

While not downplaying the seriousness of government deception, we believe there is another crucial issue that underlines these events in which the most important casualty is not simply the integrity of the Bush administration, but democracy itself. One of the central legacies of modern democracy, with its roots in the Enlightenment classical liberal tradition, and most evident in the twentieth century in the work of W.E.B. Du Bois, Bertrand Russell, Jane Addams, and John Dewey, among others, is the important recognition that a substantive democracy simply cannot exist without educated citizens. Of course, these views were not universally held. For some, the fear of democracy itself translated into an attack on a truly public and accessible education for all citizens. For others, such as Walter Lippman, who wrote extensively on democracy in the 1920s, it meant creating two modes of education: one for the elite who would rule the country and be the true participants in the democratic process; another for the masses whose education would train them to be obedient workers and passive spectators rather than participants in shaping democratic public life. Du Bois recognized that such a bifurcation of educational opportunity was increasingly becoming a matter of common sense, but rejected it outright.[11] Similarly, in opposition to the enemies of democracy and the elitists, progressives like Dewey and Addams believed that education for a democratic citizenry was an essential condition of equality and social justice and had to be provided through public and higher education.

While Dewey, Du Bois, and others were right about linking education and democracy, they had no way, in their time, of recognizing that the media culture would extend, if not supercede, institutionalized education as the most important educational force in developed societies. In fact, education and pedagogy were synonymous with schooling in the public mind. Challenging such a recognition does not invalidate the enormous importance of formal education to democracy, but it does require a recognition of how the work of education takes place in a range of other spheres, or sites of pedagogy, such as news, advertising, television, film, the Internet, video games, and the popular press. It also underscores with renewed urgency the significance of formal spheres of learning that can counteract popular pedagogies (driven largely by commercial interests that more often than not mis-educate the public) and provide citizens with those critical capacities, modes of lit-eracies, knowledge, and skills that enable them to both read the world and participate in shaping and governing it. We are not claiming that public education is a disinter-ested space, but that, in its best moments, it works through altogether different inter-ests than the commercial values promoted by corporations; that is, it self-consciously educates future citizens capable of participating in and reproducing a democratic society. Universities and colleges, in spite of their present embattled status and contradictory roles, remain uniquely placed to prepare students to both understand and influence the larger educational forces that shape their lives. Such institutions, by virtue of their privileged position and dedication to freedom and democracy, also have an obligation to draw upon those traditions and resources capable of providing a liberal and humanistic education to all students in order to prepare them for a world in which information and power have taken on new and powerful dimensions.[12]

Part of such a challenge means that educators need to reassert the important pre-suppositions that public education cannot be separated from the imperatives of an inclusive democracy and that the crisis of public education must be understood as part of the wider crisis of politics, power, and culture. Recognizing the inextricable link between education and politics is central to reclaiming public education as a democratic public sphere. So, too, is the recognition that politics cannot be separated from pedagogy and the sphere of culture. Of course, acknowledging that pedagogy is political because it is always tangled up with power, ideologies, and the acquisition of agency does not mean that it is by default propagandistic, closed, dogmatic, or uncritical of its own authority. Most important, any viable notion of critical peda-gogy must demonstrate that there is a difference between critical pedagogical prac-tices and propagandizing, and between critical teaching and demagoguery. Such a pedagogy should be open and discerning, fused with a spirit of inquiry that fosters, rather than mandates, critical modes of individual and social agency. Pedagogy should provide the theoretical tools and resources necessary for understanding how culture works as an educational force; how public education connects to other sites of pedagogy; and how identity, citizenship, and agency are organized through pedagog-ical relations and practices. Rather than being viewed as a technical method, peda-gogy must be understood as a moral and political practice that always presupposes particular renditions of what constitutes legitimate knowledge, values, citizenship, modes of understanding, and views of the future. Moreover, pedagogy as a critical practice should provide the classroom conditions that enhance the knowledge, skills, and culture of questioning necessary for students to engage in critical dialogue with the past, to question authority and its effects, to struggle with ongoing relations of power, and to prepare themselves for what it means to be critical, active citizens in the interrelated local, national, and global public spheres.

We believe that if public education is to be a crucial sphere for creating citizens equipped to exercise their freedoms and competent to question the basic assumptions that govern democratic political life, then educators and academics will have to assume their responsibility as citizen-scholars by taking critical positions, relating their work to larger social issues, offering students knowledge, debate, and dialogue about pressing social problems, and providing the conditions for students to have hope and believe not only that civic life matters, but that they can make a difference in shaping it so as to expand its democratic possibilities for all groups. Educators now face the daunting challenge of creating new discourses, pedagogical practices, and collective strategies that will offer students and others the hope and tools necessary to revive the culture of politics as an ethical response to the demise of democratic public life.

Another important challenge facing educators is the need to address the ongoing role that racial politics has played in shaping the curriculum as well as more general questions of how race structures access to and opportunity within public education. One approach might center on addressing the series of intellectual shifts governing the transition from classical rhetoric to philology to an aesthetic formalism that redefines culture as nonpolitical, universal, and race-free. Part of what can be illustrated in such an analysis is that the contemporary call for a "return" to a thoroughly deracinated, formal engagement with the disciplines that make up the curricula is impossible because race historically has always been a part of that construction. Equally important is the need to address the rolling back of educational opportunity and access for minority students at all levels of schooling by challenging iniquitous tax funding schemes and engaging debates over "standards," defending education against overt attacks on (and defunding of) "politically correct" curricula and programs. We need to address these events as so many strategies of a post–Civil Rights backlash that not only threaten the civic mission to prepare all citizens for participation in self-government, but also undermine any pretense to "freedom" and "equality"—tenets once central to liberal democratic politics and to shaping an active and critical citizenry.

Another challenge that needs to be addressed in order to reclaim public education is the threat that neoliberalism and corporate values pose to public education and the necessity to once again remind ourselves that democratic rather than commercial values should be the primary concerns of both public education and the university. While public education should equip students to enter the workplace, it should also educate them to contest workplace inequalities, imagine democratically organized forms of work, and identify and challenge those injustices that contradict and undercut the most fundamental principles of freedom, equality, and respect for all people who constitute the global public sphere. Public education is about more than job preparation and critical consciousness raising; it is also about imagining different futures and politics as a form of intervention into public life. In contrast to the cynicism and political withdrawal that media culture fosters, a critical education demands that its citizens be able to translate the interface of private considerations and public issues, be able to recognize those undemocratic forces that deny social, economic, and political justice, and be willing to give some thought to their experiences as a matter of anticipating and struggling for a better world.

If right-wing reforms in public education continue unchallenged, the consequences will reflect Walter Lippman's desire for a bifurcated civic body. In other words, we will have a society in which a highly trained, largely white elite will be allowed to command the techno-information revolution while a low-skilled majority of poor and minority workers will be relegated to filling the McJobs proliferating in the service sector. In contrast to this vision, we strongly believe that education cannot be confused with training, and that if educators and others are to prevent this distinction from becoming blurred, it is crucial to challenge the ongoing corporatization of public schools while upholding the legacy of a social contract in which all youth, guaranteed the necessary protections and opportunities, once again symbolizes the hope for a democratic future. In short, we need a democratic project, and we need to recapture our commitment to future generations by taking seriously the Protestant theologian Deitrich Bonhoeffer's belief that the ultimate test of morality for any democratic society resides in the condition of its children. If public education is to honor this democratic social contract, it will have to not only reestablish its obligation to young people, but reclaim its role as a democratic public sphere.

This means taking an ethical stand about the purpose and meaning of public education and its crucial role in educating students to participate in an inclusive democracy. It also means a call to action for educators, parents, students, and others to reclaim public education as a democratic public sphere, as a place where teaching is not confused with either training or propaganda and as a safe space where reason, understanding, dialogue, and critical engagement are available to all faculty and students. Public education, in this reading, becomes a site of ongoing struggle to preserve and extend the conditions in which autonomy of judgment and freedom of action are informed by the democratic imperatives of equality, liberty, and justice. Public education has always, though within damaged traditions and burdened forms, served as a symbolic and concrete reminder that the struggle for democracy is, in part, an attempt to liberate humanity from blind obedience to authority. Individual and social agency can be realized only insofar as freedom and justice are guaranteed and protected by the public sphere, where the autonomy of individuals only becomes meaningful under those conditions that also provide for an equal degree of autonomy for every member of society. The educational conditions that make democratic identities, values, and politics possible *and* effective have to be fought for more urgently at a time when democratic public spheres, public goods, and public spaces are under attack by market and ideological fundamentalists who believe either that markets can solve social problems and beneficently govern all human affairs, or that dissent is comparable to aiding and abetting terrorists, strategies that share the common denominator of disabling a substantive notion of ethics, politics, and democracy.

Notes

1. For some sources that have addressed this theme, see Jeffrey C. Goldfarb, *The Cynical Society: The Culture of Politics and the Politics of Culture in American Life* (Chicago: University of Chicago Press, 1991); Joseph N. Capella and Kathleen Hall Jamieson, *Spiral of Cynicism: The Press and the Public Good* (New York: Oxford University Press, 1997); Russell Jacoby, *The End of Utopia* (New York: Basic Books, 1999); William Chaloupka, *Everybody Knows: Cynicism in America* (Minneapolis: University of Minnesota Press,

1999); Zygmunt Bauman, *In Search of Politics* (Stanford, CA: Stanford University Press, 1999); Carl Boggs, *The End of Politics: Corporate Power and the Decline of the Public Sphere* (New York: Guilford, 2000); Henry A. Giroux, *Public Spaces, Private Lives: Democracy Beyond 9/11* (Boulder, CO: Rowman and Littlefield, 2003); Theda Skocpol, *Diminished Democracy* (Norman: University of Oklahoma Press, 2003).

2. Paule Tolme, "Criminalizing the Homeless," *In These Times*, April 14, 2003, 7.
3. ABC Action News, "Police Shown on Tape Handcuffing a Misbehaving 5-Year-Old," April 22, 2005. Available online: http://www.tampabaylive.com/stories/2005/04/050422girlarrest.shtml.
4. On this issue, see Roberto Mangabeira Unger and Cornel West, *The Future of American Progressivism* (Boston: Beacon, 1998).
5. Bob Herbert, "The Art of False Impression," *New York Times*, August 11, 2003, A17.
6. Senator Robert Byrd, "From Bad to Worse . . . Billions for War on Iraq, A Fraction for Poor Kids Education" (Senate floor remarks, *Common Dreams News Center*, September 5, 2003, http://www.commondreams.org/views03/0906-09.htm).
7. Susan Sontag, "Regarding the Torture of Others: Notes On What Has Been Done—and Why—to Prisoners by Americans," *New York Times Sunday Magazine*, May 23, 2004, 28.
8. Jonathan Kozol, *Illiterate America* (New York: Anchor Press/Doubleday, 1985), 85.
9. See Stanley Fish, "Aim Low," *The Chronicle of Higher Education*, May 16, 2003, http://chronicle.com/jobs/2003/05/200305/601c.htm.
10. Jonathan Kozol, *Illiterate America*, 86.
11. W.E.B. Du Bois, *Against Racism: Unpublished Essays, Papers, Addresses, 1887–1961*, ed. Herbert Aptheker (Amherst: University of Massachusetts Press, 1985).
12. This issue is taken up by Stanley Aronowitz, *The Knowledge Factory* (Boston: Beacon, 2000).

4

FROM AUSCHWITZ TO ABU GHRAIB

RETHINKING REPRESENTATION
AS PUBLIC PEDAGOGY

Visual representations of the war have played a prominent role in shaping public perceptions of the United States's invasion and occupation of Iraq. The initial, much celebrated image widely used to represent the war in Iraq was the toppling of the statue of Saddam Hussein in Baghdad soon after the invasion. The second image, also one of high drama and spectacle, portrayed President Bush in full flight gear after landing on the deck of the USS *Abraham Lincoln*. The scripted photo-op included a banner behind the president proclaiming "Mission Accomplished." The mainstream media gladly seized upon the first image since it reinforced the presuppositions that the invasion was a justified response to the hyped-up threat of Saddam's regime and that his fall was the outcome of an extension of American democracy and an affirmation of America's role as a beneficent empire animated by "the use of military power to shape the world according to American interests and values."[1] The second image fed into the scripted representations of Bush as a "tough," even virile, leader who had taken on the garb of a Hollywood warrior determined to protect the United States from terrorists and to bring the war in Iraq to a quick and successful conclusion.[2] The narrow ideological field that framed these images in the American media proved impervious to dissenting views, exhibiting a disregard for accurate or critical reporting as well as indifference to fulfilling the media's traditional role as a fourth estate, as guardians of democracy and defenders of the public interest. Slavishly reporting the war as if they were on the Pentagon payroll, the dominant media rarely called into question the Bush administration's reasons for going to war or its profound implications for domestic and foreign policy, let alone the impact the war was to have on the Iraqi people.

In the spring of 2004, a new set of images challenged the mythic representations of the U.S. invasion: hundreds of gruesome photographs and videos documenting the torture, sexual humiliation, and abuse of Iraqi prisoners by American soldiers at Abu Ghraib. They were first broadcast on the television series *60 Minutes II*, and later leaked to the press, becoming something of a nightly feature in the weeks and months that ensued. Abu Ghraib prison was one of the most notorious sites used by the

deposed Hussein regime to inflict unspeakable horrors on those Iraqis considered disposable for various political reasons, its use by Americans now ironically reinforcing
the growing perception in the Arab world that one tyrant had simply replaced
another. In sharp contrast to the all-too-familiar and officially sanctioned images of
good-hearted and stalwart American soldiers patrolling dangerous Iraqi neighborhoods, caring for wounded soldiers, or passing out candy to young Iraqi children, the
newly discovered photos depicted Iraqi detainees being humiliated and assaulted.[3]
The success of the American invasion was soon recast by a number of sadistic images,
including now infamous photos depicting the insipid, grinning faces of Specialist
Charles A. Graner and Pfc. Lynndie R. England flashing a thumbs-up behind a
pyramid of seven naked detainees; a kneeling inmate posing as if he is performing
oral sex on another hooded male detainee; a terrified male Iraqi inmate trying to ward
off an attack dog being handled by American soldiers; and a U.S. soldier grinning
next to the body of a dead inmate packed in ice. One of the most haunting images
depicted a hooded man standing on a box, with his arms outstretched in Christ-like
fashion, electric wires attached to his hands and penis, and another revealed a smiling
England holding a leash attached to a naked Iraqi man lying on the floor of the
prison.[4] The sheer horror of these images has led some commentators to invoke com-
parisons with the photographs of lynched black men and women in the American
South and the treatment of Jews in Nazi death camps. Susan Sontag, however, points
out a difference between images of atrocities from World War II, which rarely show
Nazi executioners with their victims, and the photos from Abu Ghraib, in which
American soldiers are not only present, but appear gleeful as they orchestrate and
observe the suffering of the prisoners.[5] Like Oscar Wilde's infamous picture of
Dorian Gray, the portrait of American patriotism was irrevocably transformed into
the opposite of the ideal image it sought to present to the world. The fight for Iraqi
hearts and minds was now irreparably damaged as the war on terror appeared to produce only more terror, mimicking the very crimes it claimed to have eliminated.

Sontag has argued that photographs lay down the "tracks for how important conflicts are judged and remembered."[6] But at the same time, she insists that photographs are never transparent, never autonomously existing outside of the "taint of
artistry or ideology."[7] The primary meaning of photographic images resides neither
in the unique vision of their producer nor in the reality they attempt to capture.
Rather, representations privilege those who have some control over self-representation,
and they are largely framed within dominant modes of intelligibility. Lacking any
guaranteed meaning, the photographs of Abu Ghraib prison abuse exist within a
complex of shifting mediations that are material, historical, social, ideological, and
psychological in nature.[8] This is not to suggest that the photographs do not record
reality, as much as to insist that how we render that reality meaningful can only be
understood as part of a broader engagement with questions of ethics, ideology, and
politics and their intersection with various dynamics of power. Reading the Abu
Ghraib photographs and rendering them intelligible is then both a form of cultural
production and a form of public pedagogy.[9]

The pictures of torture at Abu Ghraib prison circulate as a form of public pedagogy not only because they register the traces of racial and cultural mythologies such
as American triumphalism over evil, over terrorists, and the West over East—which

must be critically mediated and engaged—but also because they function to align power and meaning in particular ways that inform how one's response to these images should be organized and represented. As these photographs circulate through various sites including television, newspapers, the Internet, and alternative media, they initiate different forms of address, mobilize different cultural meanings, and offer different sites of learning. The meanings that frame the images from Abu Ghraib prison are "contingent upon the pedagogical sites in which they are considered"[10] that, in turn, limit or rule out certain questions, historical inquiries, and explanations. Often framed within dominant forms of circulation and signification that are marked by disturbing attempts at evading misogynist and racist implications, such images frequently work to legitimate existing power relations and particular types of recognition and meaning (in this instance, soldiers following orders or fraternity pranksters). News programs, such as the Fox Television News, systematically occluded any criticism of the images of abuse at Abu Ghraib that would call into question the American presence in Iraq. If such issues were raised, they were dismissed as unpatriotic. While the media played a vital role informing the American public about the abuse and torture that took place at Abu Ghraib, they have "largely neglected the question of high-level accountability for those acts" and ignored the fact that no "senior officials in the US military or the Bush Administration have yet been held accountable."[11] A similar evasiveness was evident in those politicians who believed that the photographs from Abu Ghraib, not the conditions that produced them, were the real problem, or in the endless commentaries that bemoaned the presence of a few "bad apples" in the military in spite of the evidence of ongoing abuse and torture supplied by recent investigations.

What is often ignored in the debates about Abu Ghraib—its causes and forms of necessary response—are questions that foreground the kinds of education (not ignorance) that enable one to participate in acts of torture, killing, and sexual humiliation as against the kinds of education that prevent such inhumanity or enable one to bear moral witness when degrading acts of abuse occur. Such questions would clearly focus, at the very least, on what pedagogical conditions must be in place to enable people to view the images of abuse at Abu Ghraib not as part of a voyeuristic, even pornographic reception, but through a variety of discourses that enable them to ask critical and probing questions that get at the heart of how people learn to participate in sadistic acts of abuse, sexual abasement, and torture; how they internalize racist assumptions that make it easier to dehumanize people different from themselves; how they accept commands that violate basic human rights; how they become indifferent to the suffering and hardships of others; and how they can view dissent as basically unpatriotic. What pedagogical practices might enable the public to decipher the codes and structures that give photographs their meaning while also connecting the productive operations of photography (as evidence, for example) with broader discourses of justice? In other words, how might the images from Abu Ghraib prison be understood as part of a wider debate about dominant information networks that condone torture and play a powerful role in organizing society around shared fears rather than shared responsibilities? How do we understand the Abu Ghraib images and the pedagogical conditions that produced them without engaging the discourses of security and privatization, particularly the contracting of military labor, the intersection of militarism and the crisis of masculinity, and the war on terrorism and the racism that makes it so despicable? How might one explain the ongoing evaporation of political dissent and opposing viewpoints in the United States that followed the events at Abu Ghraib without engaging the pedagogical campaign of fear-mongering, adorned with the appropriate patriotic rhetoric, waged by the Bush administration? How does the growing political authoritarianism and religious extremism in the United States help to explain "the Bush administration's enthusiasm for torture as the most striking aspect of its war against terrorism?"[12] Photographs demand more than a response to the specificity of an image; they also raise crucial questions about the sites of pedagogy and the technologies that produce, distribute, and frame images in particular ways. At stake here is the role that pedagogy plays as part of a broader discourse of articulation in the context of contemporary representations and politics. What do these pedagogical operations mean in terms of how they resonate with established relations of power, insuring that some meanings have a force that overrides other meanings and putting into play identities and modes of agency that enable established relations of power to be reproduced rather than resisted and challenged? Put differently, how do photographic images translate into ideological practices that define the nature of contemporary politics?

I have suggested that there is a link between how we understand images and the kinds of pedagogical practices that inform our capacity to translate them, because I am concerned with what the events of Abu Ghraib prison might suggest about education as both the subject and object of a democratic society, and how we might engage it differently. What types of critical inquiry would enable citizens to reject the government's argument that Abu Ghraib represents the idiosyncratic behavior of a few "bad apples," and instead raise questions about the nature of American foreign policy and the new American militarism under the influence of radical neoconservatives? That is, people need to recognize and respond to how the "Abu Ghraib debacle showed American soldiers not as liberators but as tormentors, not as professionals but as sadists getting cheap thrills."[13] What kind of education connects pedagogy in its widest articulations to the formation of a critical citizenry capable of challenging the ongoing quasi-militarization of everyday life, the growing assault on secular democracy, the collapse of politics into a permanent war against terrorism, and a growing culture of fear increasingly used by political extremists to sanction the unchecked exercise of presidential power? What kinds of educational practices can provide the conditions for a culture of questioning and engaged civic action? What might it mean to rethink the educational foundation of politics so as to reclaim not only the crucial traditions of dialogue and dissent, but also critical modes of agency and those public spaces that enable collectively engaged struggle? How might education be understood both as a task of translation and as a foundation for enabling civic engagement? How might education be used to question the official arguments legitimating the war on terrorism or to rouse citizens to challenge the social, political, and cultural conditions that led to the horrible events of Abu Ghraib? Just as crucially, we must ponder the limits of education. Is there a point where extreme conditions short-circuit our moral instincts and ability to think and act rationally? If this is the case, what responsibility do we have to challenge the irresponsible violence-as-first-resort ethos of the Bush administration?

Such questions extend beyond the events of Abu Ghraib; but, at the same time, Abu Ghraib provides an opportunity to connect the sadistic treatment of Iraqi prisoners to the tasks of analyzing pedagogy as a political and ethical practice and of reconsidering the sites in which it takes place. I want to emphasize that there is more at stake here than the political responsibilities of criticism; there is also the question, as my friend John Comaroff points out, of what it means to theorize the politics of the twenty-first century as one of the most challenging issues now facing the academy.[14]

In order to confront the pedagogical and political challenges arising from the reality of Abu Ghraib, I want to revisit a classic essay by Theodor Adorno, "Education After Auschwitz," in which he tries to grapple with the relationship between education and morality in light of the horrors of Auschwitz. While I am certainly not equating the genocidal acts that took place at Auschwitz to the abuses at Abu Ghraib, a completely untenable analogy, I do believe that Adorno's essay offers some important theoretical insights about how to imagine the larger meaning and purpose of education as a form of public pedagogy in light of the Abu Ghraib prison scandal. Adorno's essay raises fundamental questions about how acts of inhumanity are inextricably connected to the pedagogical practices that shape the conditions that bring them into being. Adorno insists that crimes against humanity cannot be reduced to the behavior of a few individuals, but often speak in profound ways to the role of the state in propagating such abuses, to the mechanisms employed in the realm of culture that attempt to silence the public in the face of horrible acts, and to the pedagogical challenge that would name such acts as a moral crime against humankind and translate that moral authority into effective pedagogical and political practices throughout society so that such events never happen again. Adorno's plea for education as a moral and political force against human injustice is just as relevant today as it was following the revelations about Auschwitz after World War II. As Roger Smith points out, while genocidal acts claimed the lives of over sixty million people in the twentieth century, sixteen million of them took place since 1945.[15] The political and economic forces fueling such crimes against humanity—whether they are unlawful wars, systemic torture, practiced indifference to chronic starvation and disease, or genocidal acts—are always mediated by educational forces, just as the resistance to such acts cannot take place without a degree of knowledge and self-reflection about how to name these acts and transform moral outrage into concrete attempts to prevent such human violations from unfolding in the first place.

Adorno's essay, first published in 1967, asserted that the demands and questions raised by Auschwitz had so barely penetrated the consciousness of people's minds that the conditions that made it possible continued, as he put it, "largely unchanged."[16] Mindful that the societal pressures that produced the Holocaust had far from receded in postwar Germany and that, under such circumstances, this act of barbarism could easily be repeated in the future, Adorno argued that "the mechanisms that render people capable of such deeds"[17] must be made visible. For Adorno, the need to come to grips with the challenges arising from the reality of Auschwitz was both a political question and a crucial educational consideration. Realizing that education in Germany before and after Auschwitz was separated by an unbridgeable chasm, Adorno contended that education had to be addressed as both an emancipatory promise and a democratic project in order to reveal the conditions that laid the psychological and ideological groundwork for the genocide witnessed at Auschwitz and also to defeat the "potential for its recurrence."[18] Adorno explained how the moral and political imperative of education could be meaningfully realized: "All political instruction finally should be centered upon the idea that Auschwitz should never happen again. This would be possible only when it devotes itself openly, without fear of offending any authorities, to this most important of problems. To do this education must transform itself into sociology, that is, it must teach about the societal play of forces that operates beneath the surface of political forms."[19]

Implicit in Adorno's argument is the recognition that education as a critical practice could provide the means for disconnecting commonsense learning from the narrow framing mechanisms and codes produced and circulated through the mass media, from the regressive tendencies associated with hypermasculinity, from the rituals of everyday violence, from the inability to identify with others, and from the pervasive ideologies of state repression and illusions of empire. Adorno's response to retrograde ideologies and practices was to emphasize the role of autonomous individuals and the force of self-determination, which he saw as the outcome of a moral and political project that rescued education from the narrow language of skills, unproblematized authority, and the seduction of common sense. Self-reflection, the ability to call things into question, and the willingness to resist material and symbolic forces of domination were central to an education that refused to repeat the horrors of the past and engaged the possibilities of the future. Adorno urged educators to teach students how to be critical, to learn how to resist those ideologies, needs, social relations, and discourses that could lead back to a politics in which authority was simply obeyed and the totally administered society reproduced itself through a mixture of state force and orchestrated consensus. Freedom in this instance meant being able to think critically and act courageously, even when confronted with the limits of one's knowledge. Without such thinking, critical debate and dialogue could degenerate into slogans, and politics, disassociated from the search for justice, would become either a power grab or simply banal.

Adorno realized that education played a crucial role in promoting consensus and in creating the psychological, intellectual, and social conditions that made the Holocaust possible, yet he refused to dismiss education as an institution and set of social practices exclusively associated with domination. He argued that those theorists who viewed education simply as a tool for social reproduction had succumbed to the premier supposition of any oppressive hegemonic ideology: nothing can change. Against this disastrous determinism and complicitous cynicism, Adorno argued that the political and critical force of pedagogy could intervene and challenge what he called "reified consciousness." As he put it, "Above all this is a consciousness blinded to all historical past, all insight into one's own conditionedness, and posits as absolute what exists contingently. If this coercive mechanism were once ruptured, then, I think, something would indeed be gained."[20]

Recognizing how crucial education is in shaping everyday life and the conditions that make critique both possible and necessary, Adorno insisted that the desire for freedom and liberation was a function of pedagogy and could not be assumed a priori. At its best, education would take on a liberating and empowering function, refusing to substitute critical learning for mind-deadening training.[21] Such an education would create the pedagogical conditions in which individuals would function as autonomous subjects, capable of refusing to participate in unspeakable injustices, while actively working to eliminate the conditions that make such injustices possible. Human autonomy through self-reflection and social critique becomes, for Adorno, the basis for developing forms of critical agency as a means of resisting and overcoming both fascist ideology and identification with what he called the "fascist collective." According to Adorno, fascism as a form of barbarism defied all educational attempts at self-formation, engaged critique, and transformative engagement. He wrote: "The only true force against the principle of Auschwitz would be human autonomy . . . that is, the force of reflection and of self-determination, the will to refuse participation."[22] While there is a deep-seated tension between Adorno's belief in the increasing power of the totally administered society, on one hand, and his call for modes of education that produce critical, engaged, and autonomous subjects, on the other, he still believed that, without critical education, it would be impossible to think about politics and agency, especially in light of the new technologies and material processes of social integration. Similarly, Adorno did not believe that education as an act of self-reflection alone would produce the necessary changes that could defeat the institutional forces and relations of power that exist beyond institutionalized education and other powerful sites of pedagogy in the larger culture, though he rightly acknowledged that changing such a powerful complex of economic and social forces begins with the educational task of recognizing that such changes are necessary and can actually be carried out through individual and collective forms of resistance. What Adorno brilliantly understood—though in a somewhat limited way given his tendency, in the end, toward pessimism—was the necessity to link politics to matters of individual and social agency.[23] Engaging this relationship involves theorizing what it means to make the political more pedagogical; that is, trying to understand how the very processes of learning provide the educational foundation for constituting both the realm of the social and the political mechanisms through which identities—individual and collective—are shaped, desires are mobilized, and experiences take on form and meaning.

Adorno was acutely aware that education takes place both in schools and in larger public spheres, especially in the realm of media. Democratic debate and the conditions for autonomy grounded in a critical notion of individual and social agency could be realized only if the schools addressed their essential role in fostering democracy. Hence, Adorno argued that the critical education of teachers was essential in preventing the dominant power from eliminating reflective thought and engaged social action. Such an insight appears particularly important at a time when public and higher education are being privatized, commercialized, and test-driven, or, when they serve underprivileged students of color, turned into disciplinary apparatuses that resemble prisons.[24]

Drawing upon Freudian psychology, Adorno was also concerned with addressing those sedimented needs and desires that allow teachers to blindly identify with repressive collectives and unreflectingly mimic their values while venting acts of hate and aggression.[25] If *unlearning* as a pedagogical practice means resisting those social deformations that shape everyday needs and desires, then critical learning means making visible those social practices and ideological and material mechanisms that represent the opposite of self-formation and autonomous thinking, with the aim of resisting such forces and preventing them from exercising power and influence.

Adorno also realized that the media as a force for learning constituted a mode of public pedagogy that had to be criticized for discouraging critical reflection and reclaimed as a crucial force in providing the "intellectual, cultural, and social climate in which a recurrence [such as Auschwitz] would no longer be possible, a climate, therefore, in which the motives that led to the horror would become relatively conscious."[26] Adorno rightly understood and critically engaged the media as a mode of public pedagogy, arguing that it contributed greatly to particular forms of barbarism, and that educators and others must "consider the impact of modern mass media on a state of consciousness."[27] If we are to take Adorno seriously, the role of the media in inspiring fear and hatred of Muslims and Arabs and suppressing dissent regarding the U.S. invasion and occupation of Iraq, as well as the media's determining influence in legitimating a number of myths and lies by the Bush administration, must be addressed as part of the larger set of concerns which led to the horror of Abu Ghraib. Until recently, the media have consistently refused, for example, to comment critically on the ways in which the United States, in its flaunting of the Geneva Accords regarding torture, was breaking international law, favoring instead the discourse of national security provided by the Bush administration. The media's attention has focused mainly on putting into place forms of jingoism, patriotic correctness, and narrow-minded chauvinism, and in celebrating a form of militarization that renders dissent as treason, while the tortures at Abu Ghraib remain largely outside of the discourses of ethics, compassion, human rights, and social justice.

Adorno also insisted that the global evolution of the media and of new technologies that shrank distances yet eroded face-to-face contact (and hence enhanced the ability to disregard the consequences of one's actions) created a climate in which rituals of violence had become so entrenched in the culture that "aggression, brutality, and sadism" had become a normalized part of everyday life. The result was a twisted and pathological relationship with the body that not only tended toward violence, but also promoted what Adorno called the "ideology of hardness."

This ideology of hardness, with its hyped-up masculinity and indifference toward pain inflicted on the self and others, aligns itself, as Adorno put it, all too easily with sadism, and can still be found in the currently fashionable rituals of popular culture, especially reality television programs like *Survivor*, *The Apprentice*, and *Fear Factor*, and in the new vogue of extreme sports. All of these programs condense pain, humiliation, and abuse into digestible spectacles of violence,[28] just as they serve up an endless celebration of retrograde competitiveness and the compulsion to "go it alone," while representing hardness and power over others as central features of masculinity. In such contexts, lies, manipulation, and violence are transformed into nothing more than a sport that lets people connect with each other at some primal level in which the pleasures of the body, pain, and competitive advantage are maximized while violence comes dangerously close to acquiring a glamorous and fascist edge.

The celebration of both violence and hardness (witness the fanfare over Donald Trump's tag-line "You're fired!") can also be seen in those ongoing representations and images that accompany the simultaneous erosion of security (healthcare, work, education) and the militarization of everyday life. The United States has more police, prisons, spies, weapons, and soldiers than at any other time in its history—this coupled with a growing "army" of the unemployed and incarcerated. Yet the military is enormously popular as its underlying values, social relations, and patriotic hyper-masculine aesthetic spread out into other aspects of American culture. The military-industrial complex now joins hands with the entertainment industry in producing everything from children's toys to video games that both construct a particular form of masculinity and serve as an enticement for recruitment. In fact, over ten million people have downloaded *America's Army*, a video game the Army uses as a recruitment tool.[29] Such representations of masculinity and aggression mimic fascism's militariza-tion of the public sphere, through which violence becomes the ultimate language, referent, and currency, making it less difficult to understand how, as Susan Sontag suggested in another context, politics "dissolves . . . into pathology."[30]

The ideology of hardness in its present form, however, also speaks to a disconti-nuity with the era in which the crimes of Auschwitz were committed. As Zygmunt Bauman has pointed out to me in a private correspondence, Auschwitz was a closely guarded secret of which even the Nazis were ashamed. Such a secret could not be defended in light of bourgeois morality (although such denial helped to make Auschwitz possible); by contrast, in the current moral climate of downsizing, pun-ishment, and violence, the infliction of humiliation and pain on those considered weak or less clever is not only celebrated, but also served up as a daily ritual of cul-tural life. Such practices, especially through the proliferation of "reality TV," have become so familiar that the challenge for any kind of critical education is to recognize that the conduct of those involved in the abuse at Abu Ghraib was neither shocking nor unique.[31]

The ideologies of hardness, toughness, and hypermasculinity are constantly being disseminated through a militarized culture that uses forms and sites of public peda-gogy to instill the values and aesthetics of militarization. Such militarized pedagogies play a powerful role in producing identities and modes of agency completely at odds with those elements of autonomy, critical reflection, and social justice that Adorno privileged in his essay. Following Adorno, it is easy to see how the ideology of hard-ness, when combined with neoliberal values that aggressively promote a world based on fear and the narrow pursuit of individual interests, profoundly influences individ-uals who seem increasingly numb to those values and principles that hail us as moral witnesses and call for us to do something about human suffering. Adorno suggested that this indifference toward the pain of others was one of the root causes of Auschwitz.

Adorno's prescient analysis of the role of education after Auschwitz is particularly important in examining those values, ideologies, and pedagogical forces at work in American culture that together suggest that Abu Ghraib, far from being an aberra-tion, was actually an outgrowth of those dehumanizing and demonizing ideologies and social relations characteristic of militarization, expanding market fundamental-ism, systemic racism, and chauvinistic nationalism. While these are not the only forces that contributed to the violations that took place at Abu Ghraib, they do point to how particular manifestations of hypermasculinity, violence, and jingoistic patri-otism are elaborated through forms of public pedagogy that produce identities, social relations, and values conducive to both the ambitions of empire and the cruel, inhuman, and degrading treatment of those who are its victims. What ultimately drives the ideological vision behind these practices, what provides a stimulus for abuse and sanctioned brutality, is the presupposition that a particular society is above the law, either indebted only to God, as John Ashcroft has insisted, or fully justified in its scornful treatment of those individuals and cultures who do not deserve to be accorded human rights because they are labeled part of an evil empire or dismissed as terrorists.[32] The educational force of these ideological practices allows state power to be held unaccountable while legitimizing an "indifference to the concerns and the suffering of people in places remote from our [own] sites of self-interest."[33]

Adorno believed that the authoritarian tendencies in capitalism created individuals who made a cult out of efficiency, suffered from emotional callousness, and had a tendency to treat other human beings as things, ultimate expressions of reification under capitalism. Adorno's insights regarding the educational force of late capitalism to construct individuals who were incapable of empathizing with the plight of others were particularly prescient in forecasting the connections among the subjective mechanisms that produce political indifference and racialized intolerance, the all-encompassing market fundamentalism of neoliberal ideology, escalating authoritarianism, and a virulent nationalism that feeds on the pieties of theocratic pretentiousness.

Under the current reign of free-market fundamentalism in the United States, capital and wealth have largely been distributed upwards while civic virtue has been undermined. Financial investments, market identities, and commercial values take precedence over human needs, public responsibilities, and democratic relations. With its debased belief that profit-making is the essence of democracy, and its definition of citizenship characterized by an energized plunge into consumerism, market fundamentalism eliminates government regulation of big business, celebrates a ruthless competitive individualism, and places the commanding institutions of society in the hands of powerful corporate interests, the privileged, and unrepentant religious bigots. Under such circumstances, individuals are viewed as privatized consumers rather than public citizens. As the Bush administration systemically attacks the New Deal and rolls American society back to the Victorian capitalism of the robber barons, social welfare is viewed as a drain on corporate profits that should be eliminated. Market fundamentalism destroys democratic potential by commercializing public spheres and rendering politics corrupt and cynical.[34]

The impoverishment of public life is increasingly matched by the impoverishment of thought itself, particularly as the media substitute patriotic cheerleading for real journalism.[35] The cloak of patriotism is now cast over retrograde social policies and a coercive unilateralism in which military force has replaced democratic idealism, and war has become the organizing principle of society—a source of pride rather than a source of alarm. In the face of massive corruption, the erosion of civil liberties, and a spreading culture of fear, the defining feature of a domestic politics that celebrates conformity and collective impotence seems to be its insignificance.[36] For many, the collapse of democratic life and politics is paid for in the hard currency of isolation, poverty, inadequate healthcare, impoverished schools, and the loss of decent employment.[37] Within this regime of symbolic and material capital, the other—figured as a social drain on the accumulation of wealth—is feared, exploited, reified, or considered disposable; rarely is the relationship between the self and the other mediated by compassion and empathy.[38]

Adorno's critique of nationalism appears as useful today as it did when it appeared in the late 1960s. He believed that those forces pushing an aggressive nationalism harbored a distinct rage against divergent groups who stood at odds with such imperial ambitions. Intolerance and militarism, according to Adorno, fueled a nationalism that became "pernicious because in the age of international communication and supranational blocks it cannot completely believe in itself anymore and has to exaggerate boundlessly in order to convince itself and others that it is still substantial. . . . [Moreover] movements of national renewal in an age when nationalism is outdated, seem to be especially susceptible to sadistic practices."[39] Surely, such a diagnosis would fit the imperial ambitions of Richard Cheney, Richard Perle, Donald Rumsfeld, Paul Wolfowitz, and other neoconservatives whose dreams of empire are entirely at odds with both a desire to preserve human dignity and a respect for international law. Convinced that the United States should not only maintain political and military dominance in the post–Cold War world, but should also prevent any nation or alliance from challenging its superiority, nationalists across the ideological spectrum advocate a discourse of exceptionalism that calls for a dangerous unity at home and reckless imperial ambitions abroad. Belief in empire has come to mean that the Bush administration would now rather shape than react to world events and, through preemptive acts, use "its overwhelming military and economic might to create conditions conducive to American values and interests."[40] Commenting on America's role in the world under the Bush administration, *Boston Globe* writer, James Carroll, captures something of the "primitive tribalism" that now shapes American policy at home and abroad. He writes:

> Centered on coercive unilateralism, the new doctrine assumes that the United States not only stands apart from other countries but stands above them. The primitive tribalism of boys at football games—"We're number one!"—has been transformed into an axiom of U.S. strategic theory. Military force has replaced democratic idealism as the main source of national influence. Formerly conceived of as essentially defensive, American armed services are now unapologetically on the offense. Aggression is prevention.[41]

American unilateralism buttressed by the dangerous doctrine of preemption has replaced multilateral diplomacy; religious fundamentalism has found its counterpart in the ideological messianism of neoconservative designs on the rest of the globe; and a reactionary moralism that divides the world into good and evil has replaced the possibility of dialogue and debate. Within such a climate, authority demands blind submission at the same time as it rewards authoritarian behavior reproduced "in its own image" so as to make power and domination appear beyond the pale of criticism or change, providing the political and educational conditions for eliminating self-reflection and compassion even in the face of the most sadistic practices and imperial ambitions.

American support for the invasion of Iraq and the "outsourcing of torture"[42] are now defended at least in principle in the name of righteous causes, even by liberals such as Niall Ferguson and Michael Ignatieff, who, like their neoconservative counterparts, revel in the illusion that American power can be used as a force for progress.[43] According to Ignatieff, the war against Iraq, shipping people off to foreign countries to be tortured, and the dismantling of civil liberties by the American government are all justified because the United States's policy of imposing democracy through force is part of its divine mission to save the world from tyranny. As Mariano Aguirre points out, Ignatieff and his ilk have become apologists for the neoconservative crusade. Hence, they are indifferent to the endless violations of democracy perpetrated both at home and abroad by the United States. The intensity of their righteous joy over the benefits of exporting American democracy abroad is matched by their unwillingness to be equally concerned about the rise of the Christian Right, the large-scale racist incarceration of people of color in the United States, and the vast inequalities of wealth and power that turn democracy into a game controlled mostly by the rich; nor do they protest over the "use of doctors at Guantanamo to ensure that prisoners will not die under torture by U.S. forces."[44]

The discourse of empire must be deconstructed and replaced in our schools and other sites of pedagogy with new global models of democracy, models grounded in an ethics and morality in which the relationship between the self and the other extends beyond the chauvinism of national boundaries and embraces a new and critical understanding of the interdependency of the world and its implications for citizenship in global democracy. Memory must serve as a bulwark against the discourse of empire, which is often built on the erasure of historical struggles and conflicts. Memory in this instance is more than counterknowledge; it is a form of resistance, a resource through which to wage pedagogical and political struggles to recover those narratives, traditions, and values that remind students and others of the graphic nature of suffering that unfolded in the aftermath of America's claims for a permanent war on terrorism. Teach-ins, reading groups, public debates, and film screenings should take place in a variety of sites and spaces for dialogue and learning, and they should focus not simply on the imperial ambitions of the United States, but also on the dehumanizing practices informed by a political culture in which human life that does not align itself with official power and corporate ideology is deemed disposable.

The pedagogical implications of Adorno's analysis of the relationship between authoritarianism and capitalism suggest that any viable educational project would have to recognize how market fundamentalism has not only damaged democratic institutions, but also compromised the ability of people to identify with democratic social formations and to invest in crucial public goods, let alone reinvigorate the concept of compassion as an antidote to a commodity-driven view of human relationships. Adorno understood that critical knowledge alone could not adequately address the deformations of mind and character put into place by the conscious and unconscious mechanisms of capitalism. Instead, he argued that critical knowledge had to be produced and democratic social experiences realized through shared values and practices that created inclusive and compassionate communities, which would, in turn, safeguard the autonomous subject through the creation of emancipatory needs. Knowledge, in other words, would become a force for autonomy and self-determination within the space of public engagement, and its significance would be based less on a self-proclaimed activism than on its ability to make critical and thoughtful connections "beyond theory, within the space of politics itself."[45] Students would learn the skills and knowledge to narrate their own futures, resist the fragmentation and seductions of market ideologies, and create shared pedagogical sites that extend the range of democratic politics. Ideas would gain relevance in terms of whether and how they enable students to participate in the worldly sphere of self-criticism and the publicness of everyday life. If Adorno is correct, and I think he is, his call to refashion education in order to prevent inhuman acts has to take as one of its founding tasks today the necessity to understand how free-market ideology, privatization, outsourcing, and the relentless drive for commodified public space radically diminish those political and pedagogical sites crucial for sustaining democratic identities, values, and practices and defending the public spheres vital to a democracy.

Adorno believed that education as a democratic force could play a central role in constructing political and moral agents and in altering the rising tide of authoritarianism on a national and global level. His call to rethink the importance of critical education as a central element of any viable notion of politics offers an opportunity, especially for educators and other cultural workers, to learn from the horrors of Abu Ghraib, and to rethink the value of public pedagogy—produced in a range of sites and public spheres—as constituting cultural practices and the future of public institutions and of global democracy itself. In addition, Adorno brilliantly understood that it was not enough to turn the tools of social critique simply upon the government or other apparatuses of domination. Critique also had to come to grips with the affective investments that tied individuals, including critics, to ideologies and practices of domination. Analyses of the deep structures of domination might help to provide a more powerful critique and healthy suspicion of various appeals to community, the public, and even to the democratic principles of freedom and justice; for, while it is imperative to reclaim the discourses of community, the commons, and the public good as part of a broader discourse of democracy, such terms need to be embraced critically in light of the ways in which they have often served as instruments of dominant power. For Adorno, ongoing critical reflection provided the basis for individuals to become autonomous by revealing the human origins of institutions and, as such, the recognition that society could be open to critique and change. As a condition of politics and collective struggle, agency requires being able to engage democratic values, principles, and practices as a force for resistance and hope in order to challenge unquestioned modes of authority while also enabling individuals to connect such principles and values to "the world in which they [live] as citizens."[46] The capacity for self-knowledge, self-critique, and autonomy becomes more powerful when it is nourished within pedagogical spaces and sites that refuse to be parochial, that embrace difference over bigotry, global democracy over chauvinism, peace over militarism, and secularism over religious fundamentalism. Education after Abu Ghraib must imagine a future in which learning is inextricably connected to social change, to the obligations of civic justice, and to a notion of democracy in which peace, equality, compassion, and freedom are not limited to the nation-state, but are extended to the entire international community. Hopefully, a generation is emerging that will fight for those forms of critical education through which it will be possible to imagine a future that never repeats the horrors of Abu Ghraib, a future in which justice, equality, freedom, respect, and compassion become the guiding principles of a global democracy, and peace is championed as its fundamental precondition.

Notes

1. Ronald Steel, "Fight Fire With Fire," *New York Times Book Review*, July 25, 2004, 12–13.

2. For an interesting comment on how the Bush media team attempted to enhance presidential persona through the iconography of conservative, hyped-up, macho-phallic masculinity, see Richard Goldstein, "Bush's Basket," *Village Voice*, May 21–27, 2003, http://www.villagevoice.com/issues/0321/goldstein.php.

3. A number of sources were instrumental in both exposing the torture at Abu Ghraib and amassing extensive evidence regarding how widespread it was in a number of U.S. military bases. Copies of several reports on the Abu Ghraib prison scandal can be found at Jackie Northam, "One Year Later," *Documenting Abu Ghraib*, April 23, 2005. Available online: http://www.npr.org/templates/story/story.php?storyId=4617138. See also Seymour M. Hersh, *Chain of Command: The Road from 9/11 to Abu Ghraib* (New York: Harper Perennial, 2005); Mark Danner, *Torture and Truth* (New York: New York Review of Books, 2004); Steven Strasser, ed., *The Abu Ghraib Investigations* (New York: Public Affairs, 2004); Karen J. Greenberg and Joshua L. Dratel, *The Torture Papers: The Road to Abu Ghraib* (New York: Cambridge University Press, 2005). For a more extensive commentary on the political context of Abu Ghraib in light of the growing authoritarianism in the United States, see Henry A. Giroux, *The New Authoritarianism* (Winnipeg: Arbeiter Ring Publishing, 2005).

4. Since the release of the initial photos, a new round of fresh photographs and film footage of torture from Abu Ghraib and other prisons in Iraq "include details of the rape and . . . abuse of some of the Iraqi women and the hundred or so children—some as young as 10 years old." One account provided by U.S. Army Sergeant Samuel Provance, who was stationed in the Abu Ghraib prison, recalls "how interrogators soaked a 16-year-old, covered him in mud, and then used his suffering to break the youth's father, also a prisoner, during interrogation." See Ray McGovern, "Not Scared Yet? Try Connecting These Dots," *Common Dreams News Center*, August 11, 2004, http://www.commondreams.org/views04/0809–11.htm. Another account, which appeared in the *Washington Post*, quoted an Army investigation that recorded the use in Abu Ghraib prison of unmuzzled military police dogs as a sadistic game designed to "make juveniles—as young as 15 years old—urinate on themselves as part of a competition." See Josh White and Thomas E. Ricks, "Iraqi Teens Abused at Abu Ghraib, Report Finds," *Washington Post*, August 24, 2004, A01. In July of 2005, lawyers for the Defense Department refused an order by a federal judge to release a computer disk containing eighty-seven photographs and four videos of the abuse and torture that took place at Abu Ghraib. See Kate Zernike, "Government Defies an Order to Release Iraq Abuse Photos," *The New York Times*, July 23, 2005. Available online: http://www.nytimes.com/2005/07/23/politics/23abuse.html?adxnnl=1&adxnnlx=1122488872-OgWWSHOocMYkPc54QclW4Q&pagewanted=print.

5. Susan Sontag, "Regarding the Torture of Others: Notes On What Has Been Done—and Why—to Prisoners by Americans," *New York Times Sunday Magazine*, May 23, 2004, 28.

6. Ibid., 25.

7. Susan Sontag, *Regarding the Pain of Others* (New York: Farrar, Straus and Giroux, 2003), 26.

8. For an excellent discussion of this issue, see John Louis Lucaites and James P. McDaniel, "Telescopic Mourning/Warring in the Global Village: Decomposing (Japanese) Authority Figures," *Communication and Critical/Cultural Studies* 1, no.1 (March 2004): 1–28.

9. This issue is taken up brilliantly in Abigail Solomon-Godeau, *Photography At the Dock* (Minneapolis, MN: University of Minnesota Press, 1994).

10. Jeffrey R. DiLeo, Walter Jacobs, and Amy Lee, "The Sites of Pedagogy," *Symploke* 10, no. 1 & 2: 9.

11. Elizabeth Holtzman, "Torture and Accountability," *The Nation*, July 18, 2005. Available online: www.thenation.com/doc.mhtml?i=20050718&s=holtzman. While 240 soldiers have been punished for prison abuses in Iraq, they all have occupied low-rank positions.

12. William Pfaff, "Torture Reconsidered: Shock, Awe and the Human Body," *International Herald Tribune*, December 22, 2004, http://www.iht.com/articles/2004/12/21/news/edpfaff.html.

13. Andrew Bacevich cited in Chalmers Johnson, "Wake UP! Washington's Alarming Foreign Policy," *In These Times*, April 18, 2005, 22.

14. Personal email correspondence with John Comaroff (April 19, 2003).

15. Roger W. Smith, "American Self-Interest and the Response to Genocide," *Chronicle of Higher Education* 50, no. 47 (July 30, 2004): B6.

16. Theodor Adorno, "Education after Auschwitz," *Critical Models: Interventions and Catchwords* (New York: Columbia University Press, 1998), 191. Adorno's essay was first presented as a radio lecture on April 18, 1966, under the title "Padagogik nack Auschwitz." The first German publication came out in 1967.

17. Ibid., 192.

18. Ibid., 191.

19. Ibid., 203.

20. Ibid., 200.

21. See, for instance, Theodor W. Adorno, "Philosophy and Teachers," in *Critical Models*, 19–36.

22. Peter Uwe Hohendahl, *Prismatic Thought: Theodor Adorno* (Lincoln: University of Nebraska Press, 1995), 58.

23. Some might argue that I am putting forward a view of Adorno that is a bit too optimistic. But I think that Adorno's political pessimism, given his own experience of fascism, which under the circumstances seems entirely justified to me, should not be confused with his pedagogical optimism, which provides some insight into why he could write the Auschwitz essay in the first place. Even Adorno's ambivalence about what education could actually accomplish does not amount to an unadulterated pessimism as much as a caution about recognizing the limits of education as an emancipatory politics. Adorno wanted to make sure that individuals recognized those larger structures of power outside of traditional appeals to education while clinging to critical thought as the precondition, but not absolute condition, of individual and social agency. I want to thank Larry Grossberg for this distinction. I also want to thank Roger Simon and Imre Szeman for their insightful comments on Adorno's politics and pessimism.

24. On the relationship between prisons and schools, see Henry A. Giroux, *The Terror of Neoliberalism: The New Authoritarianism and the Eclipse of Democracy* (Denver, CO: Paradigm Press, 2004).

25. Adorno, "Education after Auschwitz," 192.

26. Ibid., 194.

27. Ibid., 196.

28. George Smith refers to one program in which a woman was tied up in a clear box while some eager males "dumped a few hundred tarantulas onto her. . . . you can hear the screaming and crying from her and witnesses. Some guy is vomiting. This is critical, because emptying the contents of the stomach is great TV. Everyone else is laughing and smirking, just like our good old boys and girls at Abu Ghraib." George Smith, "That's Entrail-Tainment!" *Village Voice*, August 3, 2004, http://www.villagevoice.com/issues/0431/essay.php.

29. Clive Thompson, "The Making of an X Box Warrior," *New York Times Magazine*, August 22, 2004, 34–37.

30. Cited in Carol Becker, "The Art of Testimony," *Sculpture* 16, no. 3 (March 1997): 28.

31. This paragraphs draws almost directly from personal correspondence with Zygmunt Bauman (August 31, 2004).

32. This issue is taken up with great insight and compassion in Robert Jay Lifton, *Super Power Syndrome: America's Apocalyptic Confrontation with the World* (New York: Thunder Mouth Press, 2003).

33. Akeel Bilgrami, "Forward," in Edward Said, *Humanism and Democratic Criticism* (New York: Columbia, 2004), x.

34. I take up this issue in great detail in Henry A. Giroux, *Public Spaces, Private Lives: Democracy Beyond 9/11* (Lanham, MD: Rowman and Littlefield, 2003).

35. One of the best books examining this issue is Robert W. McChesney, *Rich Media, Poor Democracy* (New York: The New Press, 1999).

36. Zygmunt Bauman, *In Search of Politics* (Stanford, CA: Stanford University Press, 1999).

37. See Kevin Phillips, *Wealth and Democracy* (New York: Broadway, 2003).

38. Constructions of the impoverished other have a long history in American society, including more recent manifestations that extend from the internment of Japanese Americans during World War II to the increasing incarceration of young black and brown men in 2004. Of course, they cannot be explained entirely within the discourse of capitalist relations. The fatal combination of chauvinism, militarism, and racism has produced an extensive history of photographic images in which depraved representations such as blacks hanging from trees or skulls of "Japanese soldiers jammed onto a tank exhaust pipe as a trophy" depict a xenophobia far removed from the dictates of objectified consumerism. See Lucaites and McDaniel, 4. See also Zygmunt Bauman, *Wasted Lives* (Cambridge, UK: Polity, 2004).

39. Adorno, "Education after Auschwitz," 203.

40. Janadas Devan, "The Rise of the Neo Conservatives," *Straits Times*, March 30, 2004, http://www.straitstimes.asia1.com.sg/columnist/0,1886,145–180171-,00.html.

41. James Carroll, *Crusade: Chronicles of an Unjust War* (New York: Owl Books, 2004), 185.

42. The outsourcing of torture refers to the U.S. program known as "extraordinary rendition," defined as the policy of seizing individuals and taking them to authoritarian regimes where they can be tortured outside any semblance of the law. The tragic and outrageous effects of this program have been revealed by Maher Arar, a Canadian citizen who was born in Syria but lived in Canada since he was a teenager. He was seized by the U.S. government on September 26, 2002, and eventually interned and tortured in Amman, Jordan. See Bob Herbert, "Torture, American Style," *New York Times*, February 11, 2005, A23. For an extensive and damning analysis of the U.S. outsourcing of torture, see Jane Mayer, "Outsourcing Torture: The Battle Over 'Extraordinary Rendition,' " *The New Yorker*, February 14 & 21, 2005, 106–123.

43. See, for instance, Niall Ferguson, *Colossus: The Price of America's Empire* (New York: Penguin, 2004) and Michael Ignatieff, *The Lesser Evil: Political Ethics in an Age of Terror* (Princeton, NJ: Princeton University Press, 2004).

44. Mariano Aguirre, "Exporting Democracy, Revising Torture: The Complex Missions of Michael Ignatieff," *Open Democracy*, July 15, 2005. Available online: http://www.opendemocracy.net/democracy-americanpower/jefferson_2679.jsp.

45. Nick Couldry, "In the Place of a Common Culture, What?" *The Review of Education, Pedagogy, and Cultural Studies* 26, no. 1 (January–March 2004): 15.

46. Said, *Humanism and Democratic Criticism*, 6.

PART II
AGAINST FUNDAMENTALISM

RESISTING RELIGIOUS EXTREMISM
AND MARKET ORTHODOXY

5

Rapture Politics and the Passion of the Religious Right

Unique among the nations, America recognized the source of our character as being godly and eternal, not being civic and temporal. And because we have understood that our source is eternal, America has been different. We have no king but Jesus.

—John Ashcroft[1]

With the reelection of George W. Bush, religious fundamentalism seems to be in overdrive in its effort to define politics through a reductive and somewhat fanatical moralism. This kind of religious zealotry has a long tradition in American history, extending from the arrival of Puritanism in the seventeenth century to the current spread of Pentecostalism. This often-ignored history, imbued with theocratic certainty and absolute moralism, has been quite powerful in providing religious justification to the likes of the Ku Klux Klan, the parlance of the robber barons, the patriarchal discourse of "family values," the National Association of Evangelicals' declaration of war on "the bias of aggressive secularism," and the right-wing Christian attack against a judiciary that is allegedly waging an assault on people of faith.

Evidence of an American theocracy is reflected by a host of powerful politicians, judges, and religious leaders, including Supreme Court Justice Anton Scalia, whose pronouncements against the separation of church and state are well known; former attorney general, John Ashcroft, who held regular prayer meetings in his Washington office and covered up the marble breasts of the statue of Justice; and Senator Rick Santorum, a right-wing Catholic, who in his new book, *It Takes a Family*, compares abortion to slavery, rails against two-income families, and states his preference for religious over public schools.[2] There is also George W. Bush's decision to kick off his first presidential campaign by speaking at Bob Jones University and his appointment soon afterward of Ralph Reed, former head of the Christian Coalition, as one of his top advisers. Reed, a long-time crusader against divorce, single-parent families, and abortion, has argued that the religious conservative movement helped to elect Bush, views him as its leader, and that the movement is no longer on the outskirts of power. Referring to the newfound role of the Christian Right, he claimed, "You're no longer throwing rocks at the building; you're in the building."[3] Religious fundamentalism in its most recent incarnation extends far beyond the parameters of extremist sects or the isolated comments of radical Christian politicians, evangelical leaders, and pundits; it is now operative in the highest reaches of government and is far "more radical and far-reaching than in the past."[4] Bill Moyers rightfully insists that in the United States a coupling of ideology and theology increasingly "makes it impossible for a democracy to fashion real-world solutions to otherwise intractable challenges."[5]

The historical lesson here is that absolute moralism when mixed with politics not only produces zealots who believe they have a monopoly on the truth and a biblical mandate for refusing to engage ambiguities; it also fuels an intolerance toward others who do not follow the scripted, righteous path of officially sanctioned beliefs and behavior. For example, Christian cadets at the American Air Force Academy, with the support of faculty and the chaplain's staff, have been putting pressure on "peers who believe differently, or who do not believe. Jewish cadets, in particular, have been targeted, charged with the murder of Christ."[6] This particular scandal illustrates how widespread the culture of intolerance has become in a country in which religious zeal is coupled with moral absolutism and ideological certitude. Another example of religious intolerance and religious zeal can be found in James Dobson, the founder and chairman of Focus on the Family and one of the most right-wing evangelicals in America. Dobson is heard on radio broadcasts "in ninety-nine countries and his estimated listening audience is more than 200 million worldwide."[7] Chris Hedges accurately summarizes Dobson's brand of politics, fear, hatred, and sectarianism:

> He likens the proponents of gay marriage to the Nazis, has backed political candidates who called for the execution of abortion providers, defines embryonic stem-cell research as "state-funded cannibalism," and urges Christian parents to pull their children out of public-school systems. He has issued warnings to the Bush Administration that his extremist agenda must begin to be implemented in Washington and by the federal courts if the Republican party wants his continued support. Dobson apparently believes that he is a man without sin.[8]

The use of fear and intimidation by the Bush administration panders to the religious Right just as it transforms dissent into a threat and wields power in a manner consistent with "not only the character of the deity portrayed in the Old Testament but also with the modus operandi of the Corleone and Gambino crime families."[9] "Family values" is now joined with an emotionally charged rhetorical appeal to "faith" as the new code words for cultural conservatism. As Lewis Lapham notes, "merchants of salvation" such as Jerry Falwell, Sun Myung Moon, and James Dobson united in endorsing Christian evangelist Pat Robertson's claim that feminists "leave their husbands, kill their children, practice witchcraft, destroy capitalism, and become lesbians."[10] Giddy with power and a newfound legitimacy in American politics, these moral apparatchiks now believe that Satan's influence shapes everything from the liberal media to "how Barbra Streisand was taught how to sing."[11] This is a form of "Rapture politics" in which the Bible is read as literally true; dissent is a mark of the anti-Christ; and all "sinners will be condemned to eternal hellfire."[12]

As right-wing religion conjoins with conservative political ideology and corporate power, it not only legitimates intolerance and antidemocratic forms of religious correctness; it also lays the groundwork for a growing authoritarianism that easily derides appeals to reason, dissent, dialogue, and secular humanism. How else to explain the growing number of Christian conservative educators who want to impose the teaching of creationism in the schools, ban sex education from the curricula, and subordinate scientific facts to religious dogma? What is one to make of the passing of laws in Texas and other states banning gay and lesbian couples from adopting children, or the not-so-subtle message of Christian triumphalism that now celebrates the embrace of faith and politics by fundamentalist religious groups that receive political and financial support from the Bush administration? Or the uncritical media coverage given to religious fanatics such as televangelist Pat Robertson, who recently claimed that he would be "wary of appointing Muslims to top positions in the U.S. government, including judgeships"?[13] Or, even worse, former House Majority Leader Tom DeLay's thinly veiled threat against federal judges who declined to reopen the Terry Schiavo case, warning them that "the time will come for the men responsible for this to answer for their behavior"?[14] This is far from an innocent comment coming from one of the most powerful politicians in the government, especially in light of the recent violence committed against a number of judges throughout the United States, for example, the killing in Chicago of the husband and mother of Federal Judge Joan Lefkow. Moreover, the recklessness of this threat is mediated by an ideological jihad evident in DeLay's view of the courts as "the left's last legislative body."[15] DeLay also claimed, "Our entire system is built on the Judeo-Christian ethic, but it fell apart when we started denying God. If you stand up today and acknowledge God, they will try to destroy you. . . . My mission is to bring us back to the Constitution and to Absolute Truth that has been manipulated and destroyed by a liberal world view."[16] John Ashcroft added another layer to this type of religious fervor when he told a crowd at the National Religious Broadcasters Convention in Nashville, Tennessee, in February 2002, that the freedoms that Americans enjoy appear to have little to do with the men who wrote the U.S. Constitution, since such freedoms are made in heaven. Ashcroft stated, "We are a nation called to defend freedom—a freedom that is not the grant of any government or document but is our endowment from God."[17] DeLay, Ashcroft, and other hard-wired Christian evangelicals, along with George W. Bush, believe that they are doing "God's will," and, at the same time, believe they are doing us all a favor as a result of their divinely inspired political interventions in shaping public life. What is implied for democracy when morality is equated with religious doctrine in political life, and religious belief becomes the litmus test for one's political views and actions both in and out of public office?

The emergence of a government-sanctioned religious fundamentalism has its counterpart in a political authoritarianism and market fundamentalism that undermine not only the democratic tenets of social justice and equality, but also the most basic tenets of religious faith. In other words, this type of religious fundamentalism, supported largely by politicians and evangelical missionaries who run to the prayer groups and Bible study cells sprouting up all over the Bush White House, has little to do with genuine religion or spirituality. Joseph Hough, the head of the Union Theological Seminary, speaks for many Americans and religious leaders when he claims that what passes for Christianity in the Bush administration is simply a form of political machination, masquerading as religion when it is actually a grab for power.[18] Fundamentalist politicians who believe that biblical creationism rather than evolution should be taught in schools, or that the United States, as Wills notes, "must extend God's will of liberty for other countries, by force if necessary," do not represent the compassionate traditions in Islam, Christianity, or Judaism, which should serve as important counterpoints to the reactionary evangelicalism now setting policy in the White House.[19]

Education appears to be the next target of right-wing Christian extremists. Amply funded and ideologically determined, right-wing religious groups are spreading out across college campuses in the United States. For example, the Campus Crusade For Christ has raised "more from private donors than the Boy Scouts of America, the Public Broadcasting Service and Easter Seals" and is targeting students at all levels of higher education, especially the Ivy Leagues.[20] The group's aims are to recruit Christian missionaries among college students and to promote Bible study groups in order to help students fight off the temptations of sex and the satanic influence of gays, feminists, and any other group that supports the rampant "secular humanism" on college campuses that allegedly threatens the moral, social, and religious fabric of America. Instead of reading philosophy, history, literature, science, and political science, the true believers now urge students to immerse themselves in a biblical worldview by organizing prayer groups and reading books such as the fiction series *Left Behind*, which argues that "Christians should be willing to fight humanists with 'blood, sweat, and tears to defeat this very real enemy.' "[21] Rod Paige, the secretary of education, made it clear how he feels about the separation of church and state when he told a Baptist publication that he believed that all schools should teach Christian values. When asked to resign by a number of critics, Paige refused and his office declined to clarify, let alone repudiate, his suggestion that either schools should teach Christian values or parents should remove their kids from publicly funded schools and enroll them in private institutions. To the criticisms, his office simply replied: "The quotes are the quotes."[22]

With George W. Bush's mandate to govern for four more years, religious correctness appears to be exercising a powerful influence on American society. The morality police seem to be everywhere, denouncing everything from Janet Jackson's out-of-wardrobe display to the wanton satanic influence of the television show *Desperate Housewives*. But the morality police do more than censor and impose their theocratic moralism on everyone else's behavior; they also elect politicians, and this does not augur well for the future of democracy in the United States. The rise of the religious zealot as politician is readily apparent not only in high-profile religious hucksters such as John Ashcroft, Senator Rick Santorum, and the current "chosen" occupant of the White House, but also in the emergence of a new group of faith-bearing politicians being elected to the highest level of government—readily supported by a media largely controlled by conservative corporate interests and a growing evangelical base of Christian fundamentalists. Conservative Christian moralism now travels straight to the highest levels of power, as can be seen in the recent election of a new crop of "opportunistic ayatollahs on the right" to the U.S. Senate.[23] For instance, the newly elected senator from Oklahoma, Tom Coburn, has not only publicly argued for the death penalty for doctors who perform abortions, but also insisted that lesbianism is so rampant in the schools in Oklahoma that school officials only let one girl at a time go to the bathroom. Jim DeMint, the new senator from South Carolina, stated that he would not want to see "a single woman who was pregnant and living with her boyfriend" teaching in the public schools.[24] He has also argued that he wants to ban gays from teaching in public schools. John Thune, the newly elected senator from South Dakota, supports a constitutional amendment banning flag burning, not to mention making permanent Bush's tax cuts for the rich.

Since George W. Bush's reelection, the rhetoric of the religious Right has grown both more brazen and politically aggressive. Appearing on the NBC News program *Meet the Press*, Jerry Falwell, founder of the Moral Majority, stated, "my prayer, my hope, [is] that he will appoint men or women to the court who will overturn Roe v. Wade."[25] This is the same "man of God" who claimed that the tragic events of 9/11 had been caused by "the pagans, and the abortionists, and the feminists, and the gays and lesbians, the ACLU, People for the American Way—all of them who have tried to secularize America."[26] Many right-wing Christian movements and politicians are planning strategies designed "to strip the federal judges of their right to hear cases involving the separation of church and state."[27] For instance, Republican Rep. John Hostettler of Indiana plans to introduce a bill in Congress "that would deny federal courts the right to hear cases challenging the Defense of Marriage Act, which bans same-sex marriage."[28] According to Hostettler, "When the courts make unconstitutional decisions, we should not enforce them. Federal courts have no army or navy. . . . The court can opine, decide, talk about, sing, whatever it wants to do. We're not saying they can't do that. At the end of the day, we're saying the court can't enforce its opinions."[29] Recent attempts by the dominant wing of the Republican Party to rail against so-called activist judges who allegedly commit judicial overreach against people of faith were also evident in an event called "Justice Sunday: Stopping the Filibuster Against People of Faith," organized by Christian conservatives on April 24, 2005, from Highview Baptist Church near Louisville, Kentucky, and simultaneously broadcast to as many as sixty-one million households all over the United States via cable and satellite. One of the rally's organizers, Tony Perkins of the Washington, D.C.–based Family Research Council, argued that activist judges and courts pose "a greater threat to representative government than terrorists groups."[30] One of the scheduled speakers at the rally was Senate Majority Leader Senator Bill Frist, who supports imposing right-wing political dominance over the federal judiciary. On August 14, 2005, Justice Sunday II took place reaching an estimated seventy nine million households in fifty states and featured house majority leader Tom Delay as one of its speakers.

Needless to say, with the retirement of Sandra Day O'Connor from the Supreme Court and the death of Chief Justice Rehnquist, evangelical Christians were aggressively mobilizing in their efforts to pressure President Bush to appoint right-wing justices in order to implement their conservative moral agenda, including banning same-sex marriages and abortion rights. Right-wing conservatives have been waiting for this opportunity for over a decade, and Falwell, on July 1, 2005, bluntly expressed how important the fight over judicial appointments is for evangelical Christians with the comment: "This is do or die." He also indicated a few weeks later, according to the *New York Times*, that "Someone from the White House called me . . . asking for any input I might have." The bitter Senate battle in 2005 over lower-level judicial nominees indicates how tenaciously religious conservatives are willing to fight to ensure that Bush elects a conservative judge. Bush's nominee, John Roberts, Jr., is described as a "solidly conservative" appeals-court judge who as a lawyer cowrote a brief calling on the Supreme Court to overturn the 1973 *Roe v. Wade* ruling that legalized abortion in the United States. At age fifty, Roberts will serve for years on the Supreme Court now that his nomination was confirmed. Many religious extremists, such as Dobson, view such an appointment not only as ground zero for every other issue on the conservative agenda, but also as political payback for allegedly delivering the 2004 election to Bush. There is every reason to believe that the Falwells and Dobsons of the world will continue to get their way with Bush and, if that happens, their brand of religious zealotry will be influencing judicial policy long after such fanatics have passed from the American religious and political landscape.

Such opportunism reflects more than a call by Christian social conservatives and "power puritans," as Maureen Dowd calls them, to appoint conservative judges, prevent homosexuals from securing jobs as teachers, dismantle the power of the federal judiciary, and approve legislation that would stop stem cell research and eliminate the reproductive rights of women; it is also an example of the "bloodthirsty feelings of revenge" that now motivate many of Bush's religious boosters.[31] For millions of evangelical Christians, fear, hatred, and bigotry reminiscent of the vengeful God of the Old Testament is now a defining feature of politics and is on full display in a belief that combines a terrible punishment for God's enemies with a delirious wish for the final showdown in the valley of Armageddon, when "true believers will be transported to heaven where, seated at the right hand of God, they will watch their political and religious opponents writhe in the misery of plagues—boils, sores, locusts, and frogs—during the several years of tribulation that follow."[32] The diminishing separation of politics and religion and the rise of Rapture politics are apparent in the growth of conservative religious organizations, such as the National Association of Evangelicals, whose membership is over thirty million strong, which together total "one fourth of the nation's voters." As Lewis Lapham points out, the recent twelve-page manifesto, "An Evangelical Call to Civic Responsibility," represents not merely a merging of politics and theocratic values, but a "bullying threat backed with the currencies of jihadist fervor and invincible ignorance" in which "the latter-day bringers of joy and righteousness from the suburbs of Los Angeles and the mountains of Colorado believe themselves obliged to cleanse the world of its impurities—to render justice, reward merit, [and] mete out punishments" to those unworldly inhabitants of the planet who do not pledge "allegiance to the King of Kings."[33] Within this discourse and its appeal to fear and moral absolutes, hatred, bigotry, character assassination, and racism have become the norm for the translation of religion into political discourse. The problem, of course, lies not merely with the madness or simply antidemocratic nature of such beliefs, but with the fact that the religious organizations that embody such views exercise a far-reaching and powerful influence over politics in the United States.

The dogmatic allegiance, if not call for vengeance, that drives many of Bush's Christian fundamentalist supporters is readily apparent every day on many of the 1,600 Christian radio and television broadcasts, which reach as many as 140 million listeners and viewers. The message that unites these broadcasts is that America is destined to become a Christian nation, and for that to happen Christian fundamentalists of various doctrinal stripes will have to unite to overthrow and take control of secular society. Chris Hedges, who has studied the religious Right, paints a very disturbing picture of some of the ideological elements that hold together a curious mix of fundamentalists who are part of a large movement known as Dominionism, which is unified by a strong desire for political power, change, and control. He is worth quoting at length:

> Dominionists preach that Jesus has called them to build the kingdom of God in the here and now, whereas previously it was thought that we would have to wait for it. America becomes in this militant biblicism, an agent of God, and all political and intellectual opponents of America's Christian leaders are viewed, quite simply, as agents of Satan. Under Christian dominion, America will no longer be a sinful and fallen nation but one in which the Ten Commandments form the basis of our legal system, Creationism and "Christian values" form the basis of our educational system, and the media and the government proclaim the Good News to one and all. Aside from its proselytizing mandate, the federal government will be reduced to the protection of property rights and "homeland" security. Some dominionists would further require all citizens to pay "tithes" to church organizations empowered by the government to run our social-welfare agencies, and a number of influential figures advocate the death penalty for a host of "moral crimes," including apostasy, blasphemy, sodomy, and witchcraft. The only legitimate voices in this state will be Christian. All others will be silenced.[34]

The religious arrogance and blind obedience that fuel this quest for political power are also clear in the words of Bush supporter Hardy Billington, who states, "To me, I just believe God controls everything, and God uses the president to keep evil down, to see the darkness and protect this nation. Other people will not protect us. God gives people choices to make. God gave us this president to be the man to protect the nation at this time."[35] Bush seems to harbor the same arrogant illusion, and out of that illusion has emerged a government that pushes aside self-criticism, uncertainty, and doubt in favor of a faith-based certainty and moral righteousness bereft of critical reflection. In fact, fear, slander, and God were the cornerstones of the Bush 2004 presidential campaign. First, Cheney argued that if John Kerry was elected, it would mean the country would be subjected to terrorists attacks, which amounted to "Vote Bush or Die." Second, the Swift Boat campaign successfully led the American people to believe that Kerry was a coward, rather than a war hero, in spite of the five medals he won in Vietnam. And, finally, God became the ultimate referent to mobilize millions of additional votes from Christian fundamentalists. Matthew Rothschild, editor of *The Progressive*, points out that the Republicans sent out pieces of literature in Arkansas and West Virginia, "claiming the Democrats were going to take everyone's Bibles away. . . . On the front of one such envelope, sent from the Republican National Committee, was a picture of a Bible with the word 'BANNED' slapped across it. 'This will be Arkansas . . . if you don't vote,' it said."[36] It appears that the high-pitched righteousness proclaimed by Bush's evangelical army of supporters took a vacation in order to play dirty politics during the Bush versus Kerry campaign.

The fundamentalist tendencies of President Bush are now commonplace and can be seen in his official recognition of "Jesus Day" when he was governor of Texas, his ongoing faith-based initiatives, his endless use of religious references and imagery in his speeches, and his public support for teaching intelligent design in the public schools. Believing he is on a direct mission from God, Bush openly celebrates the virtues of evangelical Christian morality and expresses his fervent belief in Christianity in both his rhetoric and policy choices. For example, while running as a presidential candidate in 2000, Bush proclaimed that his favorite philosopher was Jesus Christ. Further, in a speech in which he outlined the dangers posed by Iraq, he stated, "We do not claim to know all the ways of Providence, yet we can trust in them, placing our confidence in the loving God behind all of life, and all of history. May He guide us now."[37] In *The Faith of George W. Bush*, Stephen Mansfield claims that Bush told James Robinson, a Texas preacher: "I feel like God wants me to run for president. I can't explain it, but I sense my country is going to need me. . . . I know it won't be easy on me or my family, but God wants me to do it."[38] Bush also told Bob Woodward, as cited in *Plan of Attack*, that he "was consulting a higher father" rather than his own foreign policy experts or Colin Powell, the secretary of defense, in determining whether he could trust Vladimir Putin, president of the Russian Federation.[39] Surrounded by born-again missionaries and guided by God, rather than the most basic tenets of American democracy, Bush has relentlessly developed policies based less on social needs than on a highly personal and narrowly moral sense of divine purpose. Melding fundamentalist ideology and political power, Bush gives voice to a form of religious correctness that mocks the country's secular roots, history, and values, particularly, as Susan Jacoby points out, those embedded in the "Constitution which omits any mention of God and instead assigns supreme power to 'We the People.' "[40] From shocking and incredulous statements made by Bush, such as "We need common-sense judges who understand our rights were derived from God. And those are the kind of judges I intend to put on the bench,"[41] to his use of religious rhetoric to defend Middle Eastern policy—particularly in support of Israel[42]—as well as to generate what Jim Wallis has called "the language of righteous empire,"[43] it is clear that Bush has ushered in a politics of "true believers" and evildoers that not only blurs the line between religion and state, but is dangerously authoritarian.

Bush's religious fundamentalism is never far removed from the dictates of money and power, and it includes the distribution of billions of dollars to fund religious institutions, activities, and symbols. As Hendrik Hertzberg points out:

> The money is both withheld and disbursed: withheld from international family-planning efforts, from domestic contraceptive education, and from scientific research deemed inconsistent with religious fundamentalism; disbursed to "abstinence-based" sex-education programs, to church-run "marriage initiatives," and, via vouchers, to drug-treatment and other social-service programs based on religion.[44]

Using the privilege of executive action, President Bush has aggressively attempted to empower faith-based social service groups—whose express purpose is often less to address social issues than to convert and proselytize in the name of Christianity—by making more federal funds available than any other president to Christian religious groups that provide a range of social services. He has also eased the rules "for overtly religious institutions to access $20-billion in federal social service grants and another $8-billion in Housing and Urban Development money. Tax dollars can now be used to construct and renovate houses of worship as long as the funds are not used to build the principal room used for prayer, such as the sanctuary or chapel."[45] He has provided over $60 billion in federal funds for faith-based initiatives organized by religious charitable groups.[46] Not all religious groups, however, receive equal funding. The lion's share of federal monies goes to Christian organizations, thus undermining, via state sanction of some religions over others, the very idea of religious freedom. In addition, he has promised that such agencies can get government funds "without being forced to change their character or compromise their mission."[47] This means that such organizations and groups can now get federal money even though they discriminate on religious grounds in their hiring practices. The two programs that Bush showcased during his January 2003 State of the Union speech both "use religious conversion as treatment."[48] Bush has also created an office in the White House entirely dedicated to providing assistance to faith-based organizations applying for federal funding. Moreover, Bush is using school voucher programs to enable private schools to receive public money, and he is refusing to fund schools that "interfere with or fail to accommodate 'prayer for Bible study' by teachers or students."[49]

The Bush administration has also refused to sign a United Nations declaration on children's rights unless it eliminates sexual health services such as providing teenage sex education in which contraception or reproductive rights are discussed. On the domestic front, Bush has passed legislation halting "late term" abortions, tried to pass legislation stopping the distribution of the morning-after pill, and eliminated financial support for international charities that provide advice on abortion. David Hager, appointed by Bush to the FDA's Advisory Committee for Reproductive Health Drugs, "refuses to prescribe contraceptives to unmarried women (and believes the Bible is an antidote for premenstrual syndrome)."[50] These measures undertaken by the Bush administration not only call into question the traditional separation between church and state; they also undercut public services and provide a veneer of government legitimacy to religious-based organizations that prioritize religious conversion over modern scientific techniques. As Winnifred Sullivan, a senior lecturer at the University of Chicago Divinity School, puts it, the conservative evangelical proponents of the faith-based initiatives "want government funds to go to the kinds of churches that regard conversion as part of your rehabilitation. It's a critique of secular professional social service standards."[51]

Ron Suskind has argued that the one key feature of Bush's faith-based presidency is that it scorns "open dialogue, based on facts, [which] is not seen as something of inherent value."[52] Jim Wallis, a progressive evangelical pastor who was called upon by Bush to bring together a range of clergy to talk about faith and poverty, discovered rather quickly that the president was not open to inconvenient facts or ideas at odds with what he often refers to as "his instincts." Wallis claims that as he worked over time with Bush in the White House, he began to see the man who "would emerge over the next year—a messianic American Calvinist. He doesn't want to hear from anyone who doubts him."[53] Bush became widely recognized as a president who exhibited a dislike, if not disdain, for contemplation, examining the facts, or dealing with friendly queries about the reasons for his decisions.

The government has become a handmaiden to religious extremists, or what commentator Andrew Sullivan calls a conservatism of faith. Unlike a conservativism of doubt, this movement wants to use politics and government power to impose a

morality in which ideology trumps doubt and ignores evidence, while theology substitutes faith and unquestioning belief for science and skepticism. The political outcome is a series of policies that are as authoritarian and antidemocratic as they are
ideologically rigid and politically reactionary. Sullivan provides a succinct outline of
such policies. He writes:

> The state, therefore, has a duty to protect, at a minimum, all human life, meaning it
> must regulate abortion and end-of-life decisions. The conservatism of faith sees nothing
> wrong with channelling $2 billion of public money to religious charities, as the Bush
> administration boasts; or with spending government money to promote sexual absti-
> nence as a moral good; or with telling parents in government literature that a gay child
> may need therapy. Science must be hedged by faith, as the teaching of evolution is ques-
> tioned and pharmacists are allowed to refuse prescriptions for contraception on reli-
> gious grounds. And public education must have a moral component. As President Bush
> said in his first State of the Union, "Values are important, so we have tripled funding for
> character education to teach our children not only reading and writing, but right from
> wrong." The "we" referred to here is the federal government. The alternative, in the eyes
> of faith-conservatives, would be to allow those with a different morality to promote a
> rival agenda. Since neutrality is impossible, conservative truths trump secular values.[54]

Bush's religious fervor appears more indebted to the God of the Old Testament,
the God who believes in an eye-for-an-eye, a God of vengeance and retribution.
Hence Bush appears indifferent to the seeming contradiction between his claim to
religious piety and his willingness as the governor of Texas to execute "more prisoners
(152) than any governor in modern U.S. history."[55] Nor does he see the contradiction between what it means to uphold the word of God and impose democracy on
the largely Muslim population of Iraq through the rule of force and the barrel of a
gun. And yet, while Bush and his religious cohorts claim they are working to exercise
great acts of charity, it appears that the poor are being punished and the only charity
available is a handout for the rich. For instance, as funds were being distributed for
faith-based initiatives, Congress not only passed legislation that eliminated a child tax
credit that would have benefited about two million children; it also agreed to a $350
billion tax cut for the rich while slashing domestic spending for programs that support the poor, the elderly, and children. Combining fundamentalist notions of religion and the market, Bush has implemented draconian social policies that reproduce
stark class and racial divisions, promote ecological disasters, and legitimate the most
anti-intellectual and callous forms of behavior. Katha Pollitt is right in arguing that
the botched government response to Hurricane Katrina made clear that "Bush's ownership society turns out to be the on-your-ownership society. The rising tide that was
supposed to lift all boats is actually a flood that only those who already have a boat
can escape."[56]

Behind the rhetoric of religious commitment are the realities of permanent war,
the further immiseration of the poor, and the ongoing attacks on the notion of the
secular state. There is also the force of intolerance and bigotry, which demonizes,
scapegoats, and scrutinizes immigrants, African Americans, and others marked by
differences in class, race, gender, and nationality. The refusal to recognize the multiplicity of religious, political, linguistic, and cultural beliefs and practices acts to
suppress those vast and diverse elements that constitute the democratic global sphere

at its best. Hints of this bigotry are not only visible in the culture of fear and religious fundamentalism that shape the world of Bush and Ashcroft, but also in those followers who serve them with unquestioning loyalty. This became visible when the national press revealed that a high-ranking Defense Department official called the war on terrorism a Christian battle against Satan.[57] Lt. General William Boykin, in his capacity as deputy under secretary of Defense for Intelligence, while standing in front of pictures of Osama bin Laden, Saddam Hussein, and Kim Jong-Il, asked the parishioners of the First Baptist Church of Broken Arrow, Oklahoma, the following question: "Why do they hate us? . . . The answer to that is because we are a Christian nation. We are hated because we are a nation of believers." He continued, "Our spiritual enemy will only be defeated if we come against them in the name of Jesus." For Boykin, the war being fought in Iraq, Afghanistan, and maybe eventually at home against non-believers, is a holy war. Boykin appears deadly serious when claiming that other countries "have lost their morals, lost their values. But America is still a Christian nation."[58] This is not the ranting of a religious fanatic; it is symptomatic of a deeper strain of intolerance and authoritarianism that is emerging in this country.

What progressives and others need to acknowledge and make visible is that the Bush administration's attempt to undo the separation between church and state is driven by a form of fundamentalism that discredits democratic values, public goods, the social state, and critical citizenship. Similarly, Bush's never-ending efforts aimed at undermining church and state distinctions spawn an irrationality evident in the innumerable contradictions arising from the administration's professed religious commitment and its profound intolerance of difference, from its rhetoric of "compassionate conservativism" and its relentless grab for economic and political power—an irrationality that is the hallmark of both the old European fascism and the new authoritarianism that is now casting a long shadow on American life. Religious fundamentalism poses a direct challenge to the secular traditions that inform the most basic foundations of American democracy, and it is the roots and heritage of this tradition that must become an object of historical recovery and pedagogical engagement.

The turn to religion as a central element of politics suggests some important and related considerations that need to be addressed by those of us who believe in a democracy that maintains the legitimate separation of church and state as fundamental to religious freedom and the flourishing of diverse public spheres. There is a growing need to address the search for community through social formations, values, and movements that bring people together through the discourse of public morality, civic engagement, and the ethical imperatives of democracy. This is not just a matter of discovering America's secular roots, but also of creating a cultural politics in which the language of community, shared values, solidarity, and the common good plays an important pedagogical and political role in the struggle for an inclusive and substantive democratic society. This means developing a language of critique in which the rabid individualism and atomism of neoliberal market ideology can be unmasked for their antidemocratic and utterly privatizing tendencies. It means rooting out all those fundamentalisms so prevalent in American society, including those market, political, religious, and militaristic fundamentalisms that now exercise such a powerful influence over all aspects of American culture.

At the same time, it is crucial to understand that religion cannot simply be dismissed as antidemocratic or evil. Not only can religion provide a sense of hope and community; it can also be a force for addressing the needs of the poor, sick, and disadvantaged. Defending the separation between church and state is not about denying the validity of religious beliefs; it is about protecting the recognition that religion is much too powerful a force in shaping everyday life to be handed over to bigots and aggressive fundamentalists. As the welfare state declines, many right-leaning Christian churches offer not only eternal salvation, but also material assistance in the form of daycare, low-priced dinners for poor families, psychological help for the abused, and a ministry for inner-city, at-risk youth. As social services are privatized, the churches are one of the few public spheres left where people can form a semblance of community, find soup kitchens, and become part of a support group.[59] Religion—even fundamentalism—performs a certain kind of work that taps into very real individual and collective needs. Right-wing, faith-based groups provide people not only with a sense of identity in a time of crisis; they also offer a sense of public efficacy. That is, they furnish the promise of social agency through which individuals can exercise solidarity and develop a sense of meaning and action in their lives, though right-wing religious groups often provide only what Ernst Bloch once called the "swindle of fulfillment" by promising moral values while still supporting the party that produced the horror of Abu Ghraib.[60]

In a world in which the social state has abandoned its comprehensive welfare-bearing role, a global social order has emerged that lacks both a sense of moral purpose and a meaningful sense of the future. The future has now become the enemy of possibility as short-term gains become the only viable language of the market, demanding both an embrace of a present that endlessly repeats itself and a refusal to address the political and social responsibilities owed to future generations. Collective security from poverty, illness, old age, unemployment, and the loss of the most basic social provisions such as healthcare and a decent education have been replaced by market forces that view misfortune with disdain and treat welfare institutions as a poisonous reminder of Marxist orthodoxy. Deregulation, fragmentation, privatization, rabid individualism, uncertainty, and outsourcing are now the order of the day, and one consequence is a world that increasingly appears inhospitable, insecure, and unnerving.[61] Abandonment, exclusion, and disposability are the only categories left to mark the space of the social, citizenship, and the idea of humanity itself. As long as politics is divorced from addressing what it means to provide a sense of meaning, purpose, and dignity to people's lives, religious fundamentalists will step in and take up this task. As long as neoliberal capitalism rules the global social order and the future no longer provides a referent for addressing matters of social justice inspired by a discourse of hope, fundamentalisms of all stripes will flourish in the United States and elsewhere around the globe.

If democratic politics, religious tolerance, and secular humanism are worth investing in, defending, and fighting for, cultural studies theorists, educators, and other progressives need more than a language of critique; they also need a language of possibility. Such a discourse should both challenge the antidemocratic values claimed by the Right and offer up a notion of moral values in which "care and responsibility, fairness and equality, freedom and courage, fulfilment in life, opportunity and

community, cooperation and trust, honesty and openness" are wedded to the principles of justice, equality, and freedom.[62] Barbara Ehrenreich is right on target in arguing that progressives need to

> articulate poverty and war as the urgent moral issues they are. Jesus is on our side here,
> and secular liberals should not be afraid to invoke him. Policies of pre-emptive war and
> the upward redistribution of wealth are inversions of the Judeo-Christian ethic. . . . At
> the very least, we need a firm commitment to public forms of childcare, healthcare,
> housing and education—for people of all faiths and no faith at all. . . . Progressives
> should perhaps rethink their own disdain for service-based outreach programs. Once it
> was the Left that provided "alternative services" in the form of free clinics, women's
> health centers, food co-ops and inner-city multi-service storefronts. Enterprises like
> these are not substitutes for an adequate public welfare state, but they can become the
> springboards from which to demand one.[63]

In addition to revitalizing democratic communities, identity must be experienced
beyond the atomizing call of market forces. For identity to become meaningful in a
democratic society, it must be nourished through a connection to others, a respect for
social justice, and a recognition of the need to work with others in order to experience both a sense of collective joy and a measure of social responsibility. Hence, there
is a need for educators, artists, parents, activists, and others not only to defend existing democratic public spheres, but also to develop alternative ones where the language and practice of democratic community, public values, civic engagement, and
social justice can be taught, learned, and experienced. Educators and cultural studies
theorists must fight against the manufactured cynicism based on the culture of fear
and insecurity that is so rampant in the United States. This means resurrecting hope
both as a condition for individual and social agency and as a basis for opposing an
immobilizing politics of fatalism. Education must be seen as a moral and political
practice that, as Paulo Freire points out, calls us to venture beyond ourselves and create the possibilities for social transformation.[64] Our capacity for agency is based on
the ability to invest in the future, ask disturbing questions, make authority accountable, and recognize that hope is an essential component of politics.

The directive nature of pedagogy operates through a radical notion of hope in
which it is assumed that students can learn how to be critical as well as socially
responsible; that is, they can learn to both read the word critically and act on the
world in order to deepen the possibilities for social, racial, economic, and cultural justice. A pedagogy without hope is an educational practice that forecloses on any
chance of challenging those forms of cynicism and despair that cripple our willingness to act as engaged citizens in a world in which democracy becomes more than a
promise. Right now, the dominant visions available to us demand our loyalty as passive citizens and eager consumers. And, for those millions of Christians who believe
in the Rapture, the apocalypse is welcomed as the decisive moment when they alone
will be transported to heaven. In this discourse of exclusion, politics is constructed on
a denial both of a worldly future and of a responsibility toward society as a whole, and
campaigns against the very possibility of hope. Educated hope, by contrast, unsettles
the present and opens up horizons of comparison; it provides what Zygmunt
Bauman calls an "activating presence" that offers the possibility of a vision that

"brings us back in touch with our deep democratic energies and sense of possibility."[65] In this case, hope is articulated as both a project and a pedagogical condition for providing a sense of opposition and engaged struggle. As a project, Andrew Benjamin insists, hope must be viewed as "a structural condition of the present rather than as the promise of a future, the continual promise of a future that will always have to have been better."[66] As part of a pedagogical struggle, hope is not viewed merely as an individual proclivity, but as part of a broader politics that acknowledges those social, economic, spiritual, and cultural conditions in the present that make certain kinds of agency and democratic politics possible. At its best, hope pluralizes politics and dissent while enticing us to be attentive to those democratic public spheres in which a language of critique, possibility, and vision can be nurtured by evoking not just different histories but different futures.

Different futures, if they are to be imagined, need public spaces where the language of critique and hope can become a reality. All too often, progressives pay very little attention to the fact that the struggle over politics and democracy is inextricably linked to the need to create, sustain, and defend those vital public spheres where individuals can be engaged as political agents equipped with the skills, capacities, and knowledge they need not only to actually perform as autonomous political agents, but also to believe that such notions of agency are worth taking up. What is becoming increasingly clear is that public and higher education may be two of the few sites left in which public values can be learned and experienced, and both should be defended vigorously by broadening the terms of learning to define a new democratic mission for educational institutions. Public and higher education, when approached as democratic public spheres, not only offer a space where dialogue and the expansion of the intellect can be encouraged, but also prepare students to be critical agents capable of intervening in the world in order to make good on the promise of a substantive and inclusive democracy. At the same time, democracy needs to be supported and nourished across a wide range of overlapping sites, from film and television to the Internet and talk radio, which engage in diverse forms of public pedagogy—that is, widely organized practices in which the production of a society's ideas, values, and knowledge is a central feature and outcome. Cultural politics is alive and well in the United States; unfortunately, it is a politics controlled by the Right and largely ignored by progressives of various ideological stripes. While it may be true, as the *New York Times* columnist Frank Rich points out, that the morality police actually have much less support among the American populace than Bush supporters and the dominant media would have us believe, the problem that Rich seems to overlook is that this minority now exercises an enormous influence in shaping legislation and political policy and that is where the danger lies—not in their numbers, but in their influence.[67]

The merging of religion and dominant politics echoes the claim made by Nobel Prize winner Wole Soyinka that religion has become the central problem of the twenty-first century. According to Soyinka, "It is not so much religion itself but what religion has turned into, the use to which religion is being put, which is a highly political, sectarian one. In other words, religion is being taken over by the fundamentalist extremists—and that's the problem."[68] Religious fundamentalism is only one type of authoritarianism emerging in the United States. Authoritarianism takes many forms and its most recent expression in faith-based politics appears to be gaining ground through the relentless force of a "moral values" crusade at home and abroad. Not only are the most basic principles of reason and freedom being undermined, but the very idea of democracy is under assault. The war against tolerance, secular humanism, and democratic values is being fought intensively on the cultural front, in the media, schools, newspapers, churches, and other sites of public pedagogy. What is at stake here is the challenge of rethinking the very meaning of politics and democracy for the twenty-first century. This is a challenge that cannot be left to those in the "My God's Better Than Yours" crowd, who disavow democratic values for a politics of "Horns and Halos."

Notes

1. Ashcroft cited in John Perr, "The American Taliban," *Perspectives*, April 19, 2005, http://www.perrspectives.com/features/Taliban.htm.
2. Rick Santorum, *It Takes a Family: Conservativism and the Common Good* (Wilmington, DE: Intercollegiate Studies Institute, 2005). This has to be one of dumbest books ever written. It is filled with right-wing clichés about the need for women to stay home, the corrupting influence of gays, the sanctity of marriage, and the evil nature of television shows like *Sex in the City* and *Friends*. Even the cover, which has an image that looks as if it were modeled after the Nativity, is just over the top.
3. Reed cited in Dana Milbank, "Religious Right Finds Its Center in Oval Office," *Washington Post*, December 23, 2001, A02.
4. Andrew Sullivan, "Crisis of Faith: How Fundamentalism is Splitting the GOP," *New Republic Online*, May 25, 2005, http://www.tnr.com/docprint.mhtml?i=20050502&s=sullivan050205.
5. Bill Moyers, "Welcome to Doomsday," *New York Review of Books*, March 24, 2005, 8.
6. James Carroll, "Climate Change," *Boston Globe*, May 17, 2005, http://www.boston.com/news/globe/editorial_opinion/oped/articles/2005/05/17/climate_change?mode=PF.
7. Chris Hedges, "Feeling the Hate with the National Religious Broadcasters," *Harper's Magazine*, May 2005, 60.
8. Ibid.
9. Lewis Lapham, "The Wrath of the Lamb," *Harper's Magazine*, May 2005, 8.
10. Lewis Lapham, "Tentacles of Rage—The Republican Propaganda Mill—A Brief History," *Harper's Magazine*, September 2004, 37.
11. Ibid., 39.
12. Moyers, "Welcome to Doomsday," 8.
13. Tam Hamburger, "Robertson Says Giuliani Would be 'Good President,'" *Los Angeles Times*, May 2, 2005, http://www.latimes.com/news/nationworld/nation/la-na-robertson2may02,1,3131285,print.story?ctrack=2&cset=true.
14. Fox News, "DeLay Rips Justice Kennedy," *FOXNews.com*, April 20, 2005, http://www.foxnews.com/printer_friendly_story/0,3566,154009,00.html.
15. Ibid.
16. Cited in Stephen Pizzo, "Tom Delay in his Own Words," *Alternet*, May 16, 2002, http://www.alternet.org/story/13152.
17. Ashcroft, "Remarks to National Religious Broadcasters Convention," *Department of State*, February 19, 2002, http://usembassy-australia.state.gov/hyper/2002/0219/epf204.htm.
18. Hough cited in *NOW With Bill Moyers* (transcript, "Bill Moyers Interviews Union Theological Seminary's Joseph Hough," October 24, 2003).
19. Garry Wills, "With God on His Side," *New York Times Sunday Magazine*, March 30, 2003, 26.

20. Laurie Goodstein and David Kirkpatrick, "On a Christian Mission to the Top," *New York Times*, May 22, 2005, 22.

21. John Giuffo, "Debunked'd: The CFI's Campus Crusade for Common Sense," *Education Supplement 2005*, January 11, 2005, 2.

22. Paige cited in A. Cooperman, "Paige's Remarks on Religion in Schools Decried," *Washington Post*, April 9, 2003, A06.

23. The phrase "opportunistic ayatollahs on the right" comes from Frank Rich, "The Great Indecency Hoax," *New York Times*, November 28, 2004, Section 2, 1.

24. Maureen Dowd, "The Red Zone," *The New York Times*, November 4, 2004, A27.

25. NBC News, *Meet the Press* (transcript, November 28, 2004, http://www.msnbc.msn.com/id/6601018).

26. A transcript of Falwell's comments from Pat Robertson's *700 Club* telecast on September 13, 2001, can be found on "Jerry Falwell and Pat Robertson say Immorality and Anti-Christian Groups Should Share in the Blame for the Terrorist Attacks on America—Truth!" *TruthOrFiction.com*, http://www.truthorfiction.com/rumors/f/falwell-robertson-wtc.htm.

27. George McEvoy, "Courts First to Go in Right-Wing Revolution," *Palm Beach Post*, November 27, 2004, http://www.palmbeachpost.com/opinion/content/opinion/epaper/2004/11/27/m11a_mcevoy_1127.html.

28. Ibid.

29. Cited in ibid.

30. Frank Rich, "A High-Tech Lynching in Prime Time," *New York Times*, April 24, 2005, WK13.

31. Both the quote and the comments are from Maureen Dowd, "Slapping the Other Cheek," *New York Times*, November 14, 2004, Section 4, 11.

32. Moyers, "Welcome to Doomsday," 8.

33. Lapham, "The Wrath of the Lamb," 7.

34. Hedges, "Feeling the Hate," 58.

35. Cited in Ron Suskind, "Without a Doubt," *New York Times Magazine*, October 17, 2004, 102.

36. Matthew Rothschild, "Fear, Smear, and God," *The Progressive*, November 2004, 4.

37. Bush cited in J. Lawrence, "Bush's Agenda Walks the Church-State Line," *USA Today*, January 29, 2003, http://usatoday.com/news/washington/2003-01-29-bush-religion_x.htm.

38. Bush cited in S. H. Schanberg, "The Widening Crusade," *Village Voice*, October 15–21, 2003, http://www.villagevoice.com.issues/0342/schanberg.phb. See also Stephen Mansfield, *The Faith of George W. Bush* (New York: Tarcher/Penguin, 2003).

39. Bush cited in N. Gibbs, "The Faith Factor," *Time Magazine*, June 21, 2004, 30. See also Bob Woodward, *Plan of Attack* (New York: Simon & Schuster, 2004).

40. Susan Jacoby, "In Praise of Secularism," *The Nation*, April 19, 2004, 14.

41. Cited in A. Stanley, "Understanding the President and his God," *New York Times*, April 29, 2004, B1.

42. See G. Monbiot, "Their Beliefs Are Bonkers, But They Are at the Heart of Power," *The Guardian/UK*, April 20, 2004, http://www.guardian.co.uk/comment/story/0,3604,1195568,00.html (accessed May 20, 2004); and R. Perlstein, "The Jesus Landing Pad," *Village Voice*, May 18, 2004, http://www.villagevoice.com/print/issues/0420/perlstein.phb.

43. Cited in ibid.

44. Hendrik Hertzberg, "New Time Religion," *The New Yorker*, June 7, 2004, 34.

45. R. Blumner, "The Politics of Conversion," *St. Peterburg Times*, September 28, 2003, 7D.

46. P. Harris, "Bush Says God Chose Him to Lead His Nation," *The Guardian*, November 2, 2003, http://observer.guardian.co.uk/international/story/0,6903,1075950,00.html.

47. J. L. Conn, "Faith-based Fiat," *Americans United for the Separation of Church and State*, January 2002, http://www.au.org/churchstate/cs01031.htm.

48. Blumner, "The Politics of Conversion," 7D.
49. J. Turley, "Raze the Church/State Wall? Heaven Help Us!" *Los Angeles Times*, February 24, 2003, B11.
50. H. Wokusch, "Make War Not Love: Abstinence, Aggression, and the Bush White House," *Common Dreams News Center*, October 23, 2003, http://www.commondreams.org/views03/1026–01.htm.
51. Sullivan cited in Blumner, "The Politics of Conversion," 7D.
52. Suskind, "Without a Doubt," 47.
53. Ibid., 50.
54. Sullivan, "Crisis of Faith," Ibid.
55. G. Carter, "The President? Go Figure," *Vanity Fair*, December 2003, 70.
56. Katha Pollitt, "Intelligible Design," *The Nation*, October 3, 2005, p. 10.
57. B. Erbe, "Who Turned This Idiot Loose?" *Scrips News Service*, http://www.commondreams.org/views03/1021–08/htm (accessed May 24, 2004).
58. Boykin cited in W. M. Arkin, "The Pentagon Unleashes a Holy Warrior," *Los Angeles Times*, October 16, 2003, B17.
59. All of these examples are taken from Barbara Ehrenreich, "The Faith Factor," *The Nation*, November 29, 2004, 6.
60. Cited in Anson Rabinach, "Unclaimed Heritage: Ernst Bloch's *Heritage of Our Times* and the Theory of Fascism," *New German Critique* (Spring 1977): 8.
61. These ideas are drawn from Zygmunt Bauman, *Identity* (London: Polity, 2004), especially 85–87.
62. George Lakoff, "Our Moral Values," *The Nation*, December 6, 2004, 6.
63. Ehrenreich, "The Faith Factor," 7.
64. Paulo Freire, *Pedagogy of Freedom* (Lanham, MD: Rowman and Littlefield, 1999).
65. Peter Beilharz, *Zygmunt Bauman: Dialectic of Modernity* (London: Sage, 2000), 59; Cornel West, "Finding Hope in Dark Times," *Tikkun* 19, no. 4 (2004): 18.
66. Andrew Benjamin, *Present Hope: Philosophy, Architecture, Judaism* (New York: Routledge, 1997), 1.
67. Rich, "The Great Indecency Hoax," AR1, AR17.
68. Soyinka cited in Felicia R. Lee, "Basking in the Glow of Literary Lights," *New York Times*, April 30, 2005, B11. See also Wole Soyinka, "Faiths that Preach Tolerance," *The Guardian*, May 4, 2004, http://www.guardian.co.uk/Archive/Article/0,4273,4406539,00.html.

6

ACADEMIC ENTREPRENEURS

THE CORPORATE TAKEOVER OF
HIGHER EDUCATION

Under a Bush administration that seems increasingly intent on corporatizing the public sphere and shifting wealth from the working poor and middle class to the rich, too little attention has been given to the condition of the American university and its professors. Usually considered an elite class due to their educational status and the practice of tenure, professors and their work within universities have largely been ignored throughout the course of American history. However, given the university's key role in public life as the protector and promoter of democratic values, it is worthwhile to take a look at how public policy is changing the conduct of American higher education.

In a country in which corporations such as Halliburton and Bechtel rapaciously profit from the war in Iraq and government agencies such as the Food and Drug Administration and Homeland Security appear concerned more with the financial well-being of the pharmaceutical and defense industries than with the health of the general public, the Bush administration extends massive tax cuts to the rich amid increasing poverty, hunger, and job losses. Unfortunately, the university offers no escape and little resistance. Instead, the humanistic knowledge and values of the university are being excised as higher education becomes increasingly corporatized. Such corporatization affects not only the culture of the campus, but also the very content delivered by the university, as academic labor is increasingly based on corporate needs, rather than on either the demands of research for the public good or education designed to improve public life. In the corporate university, academics are now expected to be "academic entrepreneurs," valuable only for the money and prestige they bring, and not for the education they can offer. Sacrificed in this transformation is any notion of higher education as a crucial public sphere in which are formed critical citizens and democratic agents capable of addressing the antidemocratic forces in the United States and abroad.

The University as Brand-Name Corporation

Anyone who spends any time on a college campus in the United States these days cannot miss how higher education is changing. Strapped for money and increasingly defined through the language of corporate culture, many universities seem less interested in higher learning than in becoming licensed storefronts for brand-name corporations—selling off space, buildings, and endowed chairs to rich corporate donors. University bookstores are now managed by corporate conglomerates such as Barnes & Noble, while companies such as Sodexho-Marriott (also a large investor in the U.S. private prison industry) run a large percentage of college dining halls, and McDonald's and Starbucks occupy prominent locations on the student commons. Student IDs are now adorned with MasterCard and Visa logos, providing students who may have few assets with an instant line of credit and the identity of a full-time consumer.

In addition, housing, alumni relations, healthcare, and a vast array of other services are now being leased out to private interests for operation and management. One consequence is that spaces once marked as public and noncommodified—places for quiet study or student gatherings—now have the appearance of a shopping mall. Commercial logos, billboards, and advertisements plaster the walls of student centers, dining halls, cafeterias, and bookstores. Everywhere students turn outside of the university classroom, they are confronted with vendors and commercial sponsors who are hawking credit cards, athletic goods, soft drinks, and other commodities that one associates with the local shopping center. Universities and colleges compound this marriage of commercial and educational values by signing exclusive contracts with Pepsi, Nike, Starbucks, and other contractors, further blurring the distinction between student and consumer. The message to students is clear: customer satisfaction is offered as a surrogate for learning and "to be a citizen is to be a consumer, and nothing more. Freedom means freedom to purchase."[1]

Why should we care? Colleges and universities do not simply produce knowledge for students; they also play an influential role in shaping their identities, values, and sense of what it means to become citizens of the world. If colleges and universities are to define themselves as centers of teaching and learning vital to the democratic life of the nation and globe, they must acknowledge the real danger of becoming mere adjuncts to big business, the Department of Defense, or corporate entities in themselves.

And the danger is real. Commercial deals are no longer just a way for universities to make money. Corporate branding drives the administrative structure of the university. College presidents are now called CEOs and are known less for their intellectual leadership than for their role as fundraisers and their ability to bridge the world of academe and business. Venture capitalists now scour colleges and universities in search of big profits to be made through licensing agreements, the control of intellectual property rights, and investing in university spinoff companies. Deans are often hired from the ranks of the business community and evaluated on the basis of their ability to attract external funding and impose business models of leadership and accountability. The dean at my former university completely collapsed the distinction between scholarship and grant-getting by handing out distinguished professorships to academics who secured large grants and did very little in the way of either making important theoretical contributions or publishing widely recognized scholarly work. What is missing from the space of the corporate university is any perspective suggesting that, at the very least, university administrators, academics, students, and others need to exercise political, civic, and ethical courage in order to refuse the commercial rewards that would reduce them to becoming simply another brand name, corporate logo, or adjunct to corporate interests.

Public Policy and Corporate Education

The Bush administration willingly supports the corporatization of higher education, both through overt statements and by reinforcing the conditions that make such corporatization possible. Reductions in grants for students, pressure on students to use their education as job training, and the replacement of government grants with corporate funding all are speeding the process. As the Bush administration cuts student aid, plunders public services, and pushes states to the brink of financial disaster, higher education increasingly becomes a privilege rather than a right. As the *Chronicle of Higher Education* recently reported, young people from poor and disadvantaged families face even more difficult hurdles in trying to attain a college education because the Bush administration has decided to cut Pell Grants, the nation's largest federal student aid program. In addition, because Congress changed the federal needs-analysis formula, more than 90,000 disadvantaged students have been disqualified in 2005 from receiving not only Pell Grants, but also state financial aid. As a result, universities cannot balance their budget through tuition increases or federal grants. Instead, they turn to corporate money and self-branding to balance their budgets. Students become "customers," both of the university's own brand and of corporations who sell to them directly through university deals.

Although higher education has never been free of the market, there is a new intimacy between higher education and corporate culture, characterized by what Larry Hanley has called a "new, quickened symbiosis."[2] The result is "not a fundamental or abrupt change perhaps, but still an unmistakable radical reduction of [higher education's] public and critical role."[3] What was once the hidden curriculum of many universities—the subordination of higher education to capital—has now become an open and much celebrated policy of both public and private higher education. As the line between for-profit and not-for-profit institutions of higher education collapses, the tensions between democratic values and market interests blur, and the distinction between education and job training collapses.

An even closer symbiosis of corporate and university culture takes place among faculty who traditionally have sought outside support for research. As government grant money dries up, such researchers increasingly must turn for support to corporate funders. At the same time, as universities increasingly begin to pattern themselves after multinational businesses, they are more willing to allow corporations that sponsor research to influence the outcome or place questionable restrictions on what can be published. The *New England Journal of Medicine* reported that "medical schools that conduct research sponsored by drug companies routinely disregard guidelines intended to ensure that the studies are unbiased and that the results are shared with the public."[4] Hence, it is not surprising to find, as the journal stated, that "studies reported by the tobacco industry reported pro-industry results [and that] studies on pharmaceuticals were affected by their source of funds as well."[5] In some instances, corporations place pressure on universities to suppress the publication of those studies whose data questions the effectiveness of the wares, threatening not only academic integrity, but also public health and safety. For example, Canada's largest pharmaceutical company, Apotex, attempted to suppress the findings of a University of Toronto researcher, Dr. Nancy Olivieri, when she argued that the "drug the company was manufacturing was ineffective, and could even be toxic."[6] The University of Toronto not only refused to provide support for Dr. Olivieri; it also suspended her from her administrative role as program director and warned her and her staff not to talk publicly about the case. It was later disclosed that "the university and Apotex had been for some years in discussions about a multimillion-dollar gift to the university and its teaching hospitals."[7]

The Academic Entrepreneur

As corporate culture and values shape university life, academic labor is increasingly being transformed in the image of the new multinational conglomerate workforce. While corporate values such as efficiency and downsizing in higher education appear to have caught the public's imagination at the moment, this belies the fact that such "reorganization" has been going on for some time. The modern university was once governed by faculty, with the faculty senate naming the university president. That era of faculty control is long gone, with presidents being named by boards of trustees and governing through hand-picked (and well-paid) bureaucrats rather than through faculty committees. John Silber, the former president of Boston University, best exemplifies this trend. Faculty power had rested in the fact that most faculty were full-time, and a large percentage of them had tenure, so they could confront administration without fear of losing their jobs. One of the first steps taken by the newly corporatized university in the 1980s was to limit faculty power by hiring fewer full-time faculty, promoting fewer faculty to tenure, and instituting "post-tenure" reviews that threatened to take tenure away.

The American Council of Education reported in 2002, "The number of part-time faculty members increased by 79 percent from 1981 to 1999, to more than 400,000 out of a total of one million instructors over all," and the "biggest growth spurt occurred between 1987 and 1993, when 82 percent of the 120,000 new faculty members hired during that period were for part-time positions."[8] In fact, more professors are working part-time and at two-year community colleges now than at any other time in recent history. The American Association of University Professors reported in 2004 that "44.5 percent of all faculty are part-time, and non-tenure-track positions of all types account for more than 60 percent of all faculty appointments in American higher education."[9] Creating a permanent underclass of part-time professional workers in higher education is not only demoralizing and exploitative for many faculty who have such jobs; it also de-skills both part- and full-time faculty by increasing the amount of work they have to do. With less time to prepare, larger class loads, almost no time for research, and excessive grading demands, many adjuncts run the risk of becoming ineffective.

As power shifts away from the faculty to the administrative sectors of the university, adjunct faculty increase in number while effectively being removed from the faculty governance process. In short, the hiring of part-time faculty to minimize costs simultaneously maximizes managerial control over faculty and the educational process itself. As their ranks are depleted, full-time faculty live under the constant threat of either being given heavier workloads or having their tenure contracts weakened or eliminated through "post-tenure reviews." These structural and ideological factors send a chilling effect through higher education faculty and undermine the collective power that faculty need to challenge the increasing corporate-based, top-down administrative structures that are becoming commonplace in many colleges and universities. The ease with which tenured faculty can now be replaced has been demonstrated in recent years by major universities such as Penn State, which fired lesbian, feminist drama professor Nona Gerad for writing derogatory e-mails in which she complained about the lack of resources for her program, criticizing the performance of some of her colleagues, and for staging a play that a right-wing donor found offensive because of its partial nudity and sexually explicit language![10] Such academic downsizing has been legitimized through a cult of professionalism that bears little resemblance to its once-stated emphasis on quality teaching, creative research, and public service. Professionalism now positions and rewards educators as narrow specialists, unencumbered by matters of ethics, power, and ideology. No longer concerned with important social issues, democratic values, or the crucial task of educating students about important historical, cultural, social, and theoretical traditions, corporate-inspired notions of professionalism now shift the emphasis from the quality of academic work to a crude emphasis on quantity; from creativity and critical dialogue in the classroom to standardization and rote learning; from supporting full-time tenured positions to constructing an increasing army of contract workers; and from emphasizing rigorous scholarship and engagement with public issues to pushing for grant writing and external funding.

University presidents, such as Lee C. Bollinger of Columbia University, now view academics as professionals who should ignore a partisan mentality, which Bollinger equates with indoctrination.[11] He urges academics not to speak to pressing social issues in their work or in the classroom, but to address only the meaning of an issue or idea without considering the historical and material contexts in which it has arisen and through which it continues to impact people's lives. The appeal here is to method, nonpartisanship, and elevated qualities of the mind such as tolerance and the originality of ideas. But there is also a deeply elitist anti-utopianism at work in such appeals. For instance, Bollinger is quite clear that he believes institutions of higher education should remove themselves from the public realm and not take political positions, just as academics should not confuse the distinct roles of "scholar professional and that of the citizen" for fear of turning "the campus into a political convention."[12] Both the space and the idea of citizenship become dangerous in this discourse just as politics itself is stripped of its pedagogical possibilities and relegated to the dustbin of propaganda. What is ironic is that Bollinger says nothing about how higher education is already political by virtue of the network of political, economic, cultural, and ideological forces and values that bear down on and connect it to the larger society. As a site of power, higher education institutions always harbor, though differentially depending upon the institution, links with the defense establishment, corporate interests, religious groups, trustees who are far from ideologically innocent, and an endless slew of politicians. Moreover, they reproduce, mediate, and sometime challenge those values and ideologies, which, in all of their complexity, maintain the deeply embedded registers of class, racial, and gender inequality that characterize the larger society. Bollinger makes a plea for professionalism but it is really an apology for a system of higher education that is inextricably tied to militarism, corporate power, religious fundamentalism, and a range of other antidemocratic tendencies. Moreover, against such forces, higher education appears mute, if not irresponsible, in asserting its obligation as a democratic public sphere. Bollinger's insistence for a scholarly ethos is really a call for academics to ignore the larger world, to desist from linking learning to social change, and to turn a blind eye to what it might mean to educate students to make authority and power accountable while simultaneously expanding the space and idea of engaged citizenship, social justice, and a substantive democracy.

A stern critic of what he called the cult of professionalism, the late Edward Said condemned its sham quietism, obsession with specialized languages, cult of elitism, expertise rooted in all the obvious gendered, racial, and class-specific hierarchies, and bogus claims to objectivism. Said was especially critical of those intellectuals such as Bollinger and Stanley Fish who slipped into a kind of professional somnambulism in which matters of theory had less to do with a conscious challenge to politics, power, and injustice than with either a deadening scholasticism, unworldly academicism, or a kind of arcane cleverness—a sort of narcotic performance in fashionable irony—that neither threatened anyone nor opposed anything. He was extremely disheartened by the rise of the cult of professionalism in higher education, and he viewed such a turn as an unacceptable retreat from two of the primary obligations of intellectual work: to expand the horizons of knowledge and critical understanding, and also to address serious social issues in order to lessen the hatred and violence that often mark human social relations.

But the cult of professionalism did more than resurrect a trendy retreat into the realms of arcane discourse and weightless theory; it also inspired fear and insecurity in academics terrified about obtaining tenure, maintaining it, or, for that matter, simply securing a part-time position. Pressured by the harsh lessons of financial deprivation, overburdened by workloads, and having lost power to shape the governance process, many faculty now live under the constant threat of being downsized, punished, or fired, and are less concerned about the realm of high theory than about following the new rules of corporate-based professionalism in order to simply survive in the new corporatized academy.

A Strategy to Retake the University

As full-time academic labor is outsourced to temporary or contract labor, the intellectual culture of the university declines as overworked graduate students and part-time faculty assume the role of undergraduate teaching. Undergraduate teaching in many universities is now largely being done by graduate students and contingent faculty who have no role in the university governance process, are detached from the intellectual life of the university, rarely have time to engage in sustained scholarship, and appear largely as interchangeable instructors acting more like temporary visitors than faculty whose commitment is secured by full-time positions. Power now resides in the hands of a new cadre of corporate-oriented trustees and administrators who actually define themselves largely as academic entrepreneurs and CEOs than as educational leaders. As the power of higher education is reduced in its ability to make corporate power accountable, it becomes more difficult for faculty, students, and administrators to challenge the logic of the bottom line and to address pressing social and ethical issues. This suggests a perilous turn in American society, one that threatens our understanding of democracy as fundamental to our basic rights and freedoms as well as the ways in which we can rethink and reappropriate the meaning, purpose, and future of higher education. Situated within a broader context of issues concerned with social responsibility, politics, and the dignity of human life, higher education should be engaged as a public sphere that offers students the opportunity to involve themselves in the deepest problems of society, to acquire the knowledge, skills, and ethical vocabulary necessary for modes of critical dialogue and forms of broadened civic participation. This suggests developing educational conditions for students to come to terms with their own sense of power and public voice as individual and social agents by enabling them to examine and frame critically what they learn in the classroom as part of a broader understanding of what it means to live in a global democracy. At the very least, students need to learn how to take responsibility for their own ideas, take intellectual risks, develop a sense of respect for others different than themselves, and learn how to think critically in order to shape the conditions that influence how they function in a wider democratic culture.

But more is needed than defending higher education as a vital sphere in which to develop and nourish the proper balance between democratic values and market fundamentalism, between identities founded on democratic principles and identities steeped in forms of competitive, self-interested individualism that celebrate their own material and ideological advantages. Given the current assault on critical educators in light of the tragic events of September 11 and the conservative backlash against higher education being waged by the Bush administration, it is politically crucial that educators at all levels of involvement in the academy be defended as public intellectuals who provide an indispensable service to the nation. Such an appeal cannot be made in the name of professionalism, but in terms of the civic duty such intellectuals provide. Noam Chomsky has rightly argued that "the social and intellectual role of the university should be subversive in a healthy society . . . [and that] individuals and society at large benefit to the extent that these liberatory ideals extend throughout the educational system—in fact, far beyond."[13] The late Edward Said took a similar position and argued in *The Nation* that academics should engage in ongoing forms of permanent critique of all abuses of power and authority, "to enter into sustained and vigorous exchange with the outside world," as part of a larger project of helping "to create the social conditions for the collective production of realist utopias."[14]

Following Chomsky and Said, I believe that intellectuals who inhabit American universities should represent the conscience of this society because they not only shape the conditions under which future generations learn about themselves and their relations to others and the outside world, but also because they engage pedagogical practices that are, by their very nature, moral and political, rather than simply technical. And at its best, such pedagogy bears witness to the ethical and political dilemmas that animate the broader social landscape. Such pedagogical approaches are important because they provide spaces that are both comforting and unsettling, spaces that both disturb and enlighten. Pedagogy in this instance not only works to help students think critically about the issues affecting their lives and the world at large, but potentially energizes them to seize such moments as possibilities for acting on the world, engaging it as a matter of politics, power, and social justice. The appeal here is not merely ethical; it is also an appeal that addresses the materiality of resources, access, and politics, while viewing power as generative and crucial to any viable notion of individual and social agency.

Organizing against the corporate takeover of higher education also suggests fighting to protect the jobs of full-time faculty, turning adjunct jobs into full-time positions, expanding benefits to part-time workers, and putting power into the hands of faculty and students. Protecting the jobs of full-time faculty means ensuring that they have the right to academic freedom, are paid a decent wage, and play an important role in governing the university. A weak faculty translates into a faculty without rights or power, one that is governed by fear rather than shared responsibilities and is also susceptible to labor-bashing tactics such as increased workloads, contract labor, and the suppression of dissent. Adjunct or part-time labor must be given the opportunity to break the cycle of exploitative labor and within a short period of time be considered for full-time positions with full benefits and the power to influence governance policies. Within the universities and colleges today, power is top-heavy, largely controlled by trustees and administrators and removed from those groups who actually do the work of the university, which include the faculty, staff, and students. Moreover such struggles must consider addressing the exploitative conditions under which many graduate students work, constituting a de facto army of service workers who are underpaid, overworked, and shorn of any real power or benefits.

The challenge for faculty in higher education is both structural and ideological. On the structural side, faculty, students, and staff need to organize labor movements and unions to challenge the corporatization of the university. Universities have ample resources that can be mobilized to oppress faculty, exploit staff, and deny the rights of students to a decent education. To fight against such power demands a labor and student movement capable of exercising enormous power collectively in both influencing and shaping academic policies. Such movements must connect to local communities, reach out to national and international organizations, and develop multiple strategies in taking back the universities from the corporations while simultaneously dismantling the ideological and institutional framing mechanisms of a rabid capitalism. I want to stress here the need for multiple interventions extending from anti-sweatshop movements to taking control of academic departments to organizing larger faculty structures and organizations. At best, faculty and students must unionize whenever they can in order to speak with a voice of collective opposition.

Ideologically, faculty must find ways to contribute their knowledge and skills to understanding how corporate values, identities, and practices create the conditions for devaluing critical learning and undermining viable forms of political agency.

Academics, as Imre Szeman puts it, need to figure out how corporate power, culture, and values "constitute a problem of and for pedagogy."[15] Academics need to be attentive to the oppositional pedagogies put into place by various student movements in order to judge their "significance . . . for the shape and function of the university curricula today" as well as their rhetorical and material impact on public spheres.[16] Within the last few years, protests on and off campuses have picked up and spawned a number of student protest groups, including the United Students Against Sweatshops, with chapters in over two hundred schools, the nationwide 180/Movement for Democracy and Education, and a multitude of groups protesting the policies of the World Trade Organization and the International Monetary Fund. The challenge here is for faculty to learn as much as possible from these student movements about what it means to deepen and expand the struggle for establishing pedagogical approaches and labor movements that can be used, on one hand, to mediate the fundamental tension between the public values of higher education and the commercial values of corporate culture and to fight against the more crucial assaults waged against the welfare state and other public goods, on the other. If the forces of corporate culture are to be challenged, educators must consider enlisting the help of diverse communities, interests, foundations, social movements, and other forces to make certain that public institutions of higher learning are adequately funded so that they will not have to rely on corporate sponsorship and advertising revenues.

The language of the emerging corporate university radically alters the vocabulary available for appraising the meaning of citizenship, agency, civic virtue, and democracy itself. Within this discourse, everything is for sale, and what is not has no value as a public good or practice. It is in the spirit of such a critique and act of resistance against neoliberalism that educators need to break with what Pierre Bourdieu has described as a "new faith in the historical inevitability professed by the theorists of liberalism" and "invent new forms of collective political work" capable of confronting the march of corporate power and capitalism in its global forms.[17] This will not be an easy task, but it is a necessary one if democracy is to be won back from the reign of financial markets and the Darwinian values of an unbridled neoliberalism. Academics can contribute to such a struggle by, among other things, defending higher education for the contribution it makes to the quality of public life, using organized resistance to realize the full potential higher education can exercise pedagogically in asserting the primacy of democratic values over commercial interests, and struggling collectively through a powerful union movement to preserve the institutional and ideological conditions necessary to provide both faculty and students with the capacities they need for civic courage and engaged critical citizenship.

Notes

1. Jennifer L. Croissant, "Can This Campus be Bought?" *Academe*, September–October 2001, http://www.aaup.org/publications/Academe/2001/01SO/so01cro.htm.
2. Larry Hanley, "Conference Roundtable," *Found Object* 10 (Spring 2001): 103.
3. Masao Miyoshi, " 'Globalization,' Culture, and the University," in *The Cultures of Globalization*, ed. Fredric Jameson and Masao Miyoshi (Durham, NC: Duke University Press, 1998), 263.

4. Cited in Katherine S. Mangan, "Medical Schools Routinely Ignore Guidelines on Company-Sponsored Research, Study Finds," *Chronicle of Higher Education*, Daily News Online, October 25, 2002, http://chronicle.com/daily/2002/10/200210250ln.htm.

5. Cited in Lila Guterman, "Conflict of Interest is Widespread in Biomedical Research, Study Finds," *Chronicle of Higher Education*, Daily News Online, January 22, 2003, http://chronicle.com/daily/2003/01/2003012202n.htm.

6. Cited in Mangan, "Medical Schools."

7. Derek Bok, *Universities in the Marketplace* (Princeton, NJ: Princeton University Press, 2003), 75.

8. Sharon Walsh, "Study Finds Significant Increase in Number of Part-Time and Non-Tenure-Track Professors," *Chronicle of Higher Education*, Daily News Online, October 29, 2002, http://chronicle.com/daily/2002/10/2002102904n.htm. The full text of the American Council of Education study can be found on the council's web site.

9. American Association of University Professors, "Contingent Faculty Appointments," *AAUP Bulletin*, September 29, 2004, http://www.aaup.org/Issues/part-time/.

10. Paula Reed Ward, "PSU Fires Tenured Theater Professor," *Post-Gazette.Com*, March 2, 2004, http://www.post-gazette.com/[g/04062/279825.

11. Lee C. Bollinger, "The Value and Responsibilities of Academic Freedom," *Chronicle of Higher Education*, April 8, 2005, B20.

12. Ibid.

13. Noam Chomsky, "Paths Taken, Tasks Ahead," *Profession* (2000): 35.

14. Edward W. Said, "The Public Role of Writers and Intellectuals," *The Nation*, October 1, 2001, 4.

15. Imre Szeman, "Introduction: Learning to Learn from Seattle," in Special Double Issue: Learning From Seattle, ed. Imre Szeman, *The Review of Education, Pedagogy, and Cultural Studies* 24, no. 1 & 2 (January–June 2002): 4.

16. Ibid., 5.

17. Pierre Bourdieu, *Acts of Resistance* (New York: New Press, 1999), 26.

PART III
MEDIA PEDAGOGY

RETHINKING POLITICAL AND CULTURAL LITERACY

7

ROLL OVER GEORGE ORWELL

REPRESENTATIONS OF NEWSPEAK
IN BUSH'S AMERICA

The worst betrayal of intelligence is finding justification for the world as it is.
—Jean Guehenno, French philosopher (1890–1978)

In times of universal deceit, telling the truth becomes a revolutionary act.
—George Orwell (1903–1950)

One of the more significant characteristics of an authoritarian society is its willingness to distort the truth while simultaneously suppressing dissent. For instance, Umberto Eco argues that one element of authoritarianism is the rise of an Orwellian version of newspeak, or what he labels as the language of "eternal fascism," whose purpose is to produce "an impoverished vocabulary, and an elementary syntax [whose consequence is] to limit the instruments for complex and critical reasoning."[1]

Dwight Macdonald, writing in the aftermath of World War II and the horrors of the Nazi Holocaust, situates the rise of authoritarianism in a broader context. He argues that as more and more people are excluded from the experience of political agency and exhibit "less and less control over the 'policies' of their governments," ethics is reduced to the status of mere platitudes, and politics becomes banal.[2] According to Macdonald, as the state becomes more tightly controlled, organized, and rationalized, it empties politics and morality of any substance and relevance, thus making it difficult for people either to care about the obligations of critical citizenship or to participate in the broader landscape of politics and power. Under such circumstances, language becomes the mechanism of choice for promoting political powerlessness in that it is used by the state to misrepresent the truth and is also trivialized—experienced as a collection of mere platitudes reinforcing moral indifference and political impotence. In the current political landscape, the truth is not merely misrepresented, it is overtly mocked. For example, Bush administration officials seem to delight in consistently repeating claims that have already been discredited in the public arena, demonstrating a barely disguised contempt for the public and for democratic principles.

Under the Bush administration, especially since the horrible events of September 11, we have witnessed an extension of the concept of war not only to include traditional, strategic, defense-oriented objectives, but also to discipline civil society, reproduce all aspects of public life in the image of official power, and establish the ideology of militarism as the very foundation for effective governance. Accompanying this increasing form of discursive and material repression is an attempt to refashion the tools of language, sound, and image in an effort to diminish the capacity of the American public to weigh evidence critically, exercise thoughtful discrimination, and make informed judgments. As the critical power of language is reduced in official discourse to the simulacra of communication, it becomes more difficult for the American public to engage in critical debates, translate private considerations into public concerns, and recognize the distortions and omissions that underlie much of the current government policies. What happens to critical language under the emergence of official newspeak can be seen in the various ways in which the Bush administration and its official supporters both misrepresent by misnaming government policies and simply engage in deceit to cover up their own regressive politics and policies.[3]

Many people have pointed to Bush himself as a mangler of the English language, but this charge simply repeats the obvious while privatizing a much more important issue connecting language to power.[4] Bush's discursive ineptness may be fodder for late night comics such as Jon Stewart and Jay Leno, but such analyses miss the more strategic issue of how the Bush administration actually manipulates discourse. For instance, Bush describes himself as a "reformer" while he promotes policies that expand corporate welfare, give tax benefits to the rich, and "erode the financial capacity of the state to undertake any but the most minimal welfare functions."[5] He defines himself as a "compassionate conservative," but he implements policies that result in "billions of dollars in cuts . . . proposed for food stamp and child nutrition programs, and for health care for the poor."[6] Bush's public speeches, often mimicked in the media, are filled with what Renana Brooks has called "empty language," that is, statements that are so abstract as to be relatively meaningless, except to reinforce in simplistic terms an often reactionary ideological position. Brooks cites the example of Bush's comment on the complex relationship between malpractice suits and skyrocketing healthcare, which he reduces to: "No one has ever been healed by a frivolous lawsuit."[7] While Bush's own ideological position becomes clear in this comment, the complexity of the issue is completely trivialized and removed from public discussion. As Bob Herbert reported in *The New York Times*, Bush's language often reveals that he just doesn't "get it," as when he flew to New Orleans five days after Katrina's wrath had done its damage and "Instead of urgently focusing on the people who were stranded, hungry, sick and dying, he engaged in small talk, reminiscing at one point about the days when he use to party in New Orleans, and mentioning that Trent Lott had lost one of his houses but that it would be replaced with a 'fantastic house–and I am looking forward to sitting on the porch.'"[8]

Sometimes the distortions of official language are hard to miss, even among the media guards so quick to invoke patriotic correctness. For instance, critics who argue that public welfare programs such as Social Security—which provide at least some measure of economic security for working-class Americans—"should have priority over tax cuts for the rich" are discredited by the Bush administration with the charge that they are practicing "class warfare."[9] One glaring example happened in an interview between Terry Gross, host of National Public Radio's *Fresh Air*, and Grover Norquist, president of Americans for Tax Reform, also considered to be the chief architect of President Bush's tax plan. The topic for discussion was the estate tax, reviled as the "death tax" by conservative elites to gain popular support for its repeal, though the vast majority of Americans will not be affected by this tax. Gross suggested that since the estate tax only effects a small minority of people who get over $2 million in inheritance, the law eliminating it clearly privileges the rich, not the average American. Norquist responded by arguing that the morality behind her argument was comparable to the same type of morality that resulted in the deaths of millions of Jews during the Holocaust. When Gross challenged this specious analogy, Norquist argued illogically that people (read liberals) who attacked the estate tax could now be placed on the same moral plane as the Nazis who killed over six million Jews and untold others.[10] Under this logic, any critique of a minority group, but especially the rich, can be dismissed as being comparable to the kind of discrimination waged by the perpetrators of one of the worst mass murders in human history. Of course, there is the further implication that liberal critics should also be punished for these views just as the Nazis were punished in Nuremberg for their crimes against humanity. This is not just a matter of using a desperate logic to dismiss counterarguments, or of silencing one's critics through distortion, but actually of demonizing those who hold the "wrong" views. Norquist's position is a contortion that fails to hide the market fundamentalism that often drives this type of language. A similar example can be found in those Bush supporters who claim that any concern over the enormously wide gap between the rich and the poor is just another example of the "politics of envy."[11] Another example can be found in newly appointed federal appeals court justice Janice Rogers Brown's argument that liberalism leads to slavery or, to be more exact, "In the heyday of liberal democracy, all roads lead to slavery."[12]

Official newspeak also trades in the rhetoric of fear in order to manipulate the public into a state of servile political dependency and unquestioning ideological support. Fear and its attendant use of moral panics create not only a rhetorical umbrella to promote other agendas, but also a sense of helplessness and cynicism throughout the body politic. Hence, the Bush administration's increased dependency upon issuing terror and security alerts and its panic-inducing references to 9/11 are almost always framed in Manichean language of absolute good and evil. The administration's newspeak also employs the discourse of evangelicalism, and its attendant suggestion that whatever wisdom Bush has results from his direct communion with God—a position not unlike that of Moses on Mount Sinai, and which, of course, cannot be challenged by mere mortals.[13]

While all governments sometimes resort to misrepresentations and lies, the Bush administration's newspeak makes such action central to its maintenance of political power and its manipulation of the media and the public. Language is used in this context to say one thing, but to actually mean its opposite.[14] This type of discourse mimics George Orwell's dystopian world of *1984*, where the Ministry of Truth actually produces lies and the Ministry of Love is actually used to torture people. Ruth Rosen points out that the Bush administration engages in a kind of newspeak right out of Orwell's novel. For instance, Bush's Healthy Forest Initiative "allows increased logging of protected wilderness. The 'Clear Skies' initiative permits greater industrial air pollution."[15] With respect to the latter, the Bush administration has produced Spanish-language public service commercials hawking "Clear Skies" legislation, ads that claim such legislation promotes "cleaner air," when in fact it has weakened restrictions on corporate polluters and eased regulations on some toxic emissions such as mercury. In fact, J. P. Suarez, the Environmental Protection Agency's chief of enforcement, notified his staff that "the agency would stop pursuing Clean Air Act enforcement cases against coal burning power plants."[16] Eric Pianin reported in the *Washington Post*, "The Bush administration has decided to allow thousands of the nation's dirtiest coal-fired power plants and refineries to upgrade their facilities without installing costly anti-pollution equipment as they now must do."[17] In addition, the Bush administration has weakened federal programs for cleaning up dirty waters and has removed scientific studies offering evidence of global warming from government reports.[18] It gets worse.

In a speech delivered in Tennessee in April 2005, Bush stated, "We didn't create this earth but we have an obligation to protect it!"[19] This is an odd statement coming from a president who supports oil drilling in the wilderness of Alaska and fashions an energy policy developed by multinational corporations. On the matter of foreign policy, Bush's use of the term "democracy" is truly Orwellian. On the one hand, he fashions a unilateral foreign policy that rejects dialogue and collaboration with other major powers while "promoting" democracy in Iraq with bombs, a brutal military occupation, and what *New York Times* writer Bob Herbert calls "an exercise in extreme madness, an absurd venture that would have been rich in comic possibilities except for the fact that many thousands of men, women and children have died, and tens of thousands have been crippled, burned or otherwise maimed."[20] In an exercise of extreme arrogance and hypocrisy, Bush seems undaunted in lecturing President Putin of Russia on the virtues of democracy, all the while currying favor with some of the most virulent authoritarian regimes in the world, including Saudi Arabia, Turkey, and Afghanistan. It is difficult to understand why the media, intellectuals, educators, and other citizens do not robustly challenge and take to the streets in protest when President Bush uses the rhetoric of democracy to defend his foreign and domestic policies. What is one to make of his statement in a speech at National Defense University, "It should be clear that authoritarian rule is not the wave of the future; it is the last gasp of a discredited past"?[21] Surely he cannot be referring to his own record of policies that undermine civil liberties; promote torture and other human rights violations at Abu Ghraib and other prisons in Iraq and Afghanistan; plunder the environment in the interest of corporations; align his government with right-wing religious extremists who are working to eliminate the separation between church and state; and endorse a foreign policy that is utterly militaristic and empire-driven. For all his pretense to moral righteousness, Dick Cheney is like the spouse, who, so full of contempt for his partner, openly flaunts his adultery and mocks the pain it is designed to induce.

Even when it comes to children, Bush is undaunted in his use of deceptive language. In arguing for legislation that would shift financial responsibility to the states for the highly successful Head Start program, which provides over one million poor children with early educational, health, and nutrition services, Bush employed the phrase "opt in" to encourage Congress to pass new legislation reforming Head Start. While "opt in" sounds as if it refers to expanding the program, it actually undermines it because the states that are facing crushing deficits do not have the money to fund the programs. Thus, the legislation would drastically weaken Head Start. Such language calls to mind the Orwellian logic that "war is peace, freedom is slavery, and ignorance is strength." Not surprisingly, the Bush administration more recently announced that it will cut funding for Head Start programs in the 2005 budget.

There is also the now obvious ways in which the Bush administration manipulated intelligence to legitimate a claim for preemptive war with Iraq. The list of misrepresentations and rhetorical contortions includes the following claims: Iraq was building nuclear weapons and engaged in the production of biological and chemical agents, and Saddam Hussein was working with Osama bin Laden and had direct ties to Al Qaeda.[22] Even after the CIA reported that the charge that Saddam Hussein had bought uranium from Niger in pursuit of developing a nuclear weapon was fabricated, Bush included the assertion in his 2003 State of the Union Address.[23] And, of course, Vice President Dick Cheney seemed relentless in repeating these lies in practically every speech and interview, even when they were refuted by the high-ranking intelligence services that cannot any longer credibly support such misrepresentations. In fact, Cheney—like former House Majority Leader Tom DeLay—when confronted with contradictions in his story, simply issues absurd pronouncements and goes his merry way. For instance, when Cheney was caught on videotape and questioned by reporters who claimed that he had fabricated a rationale for the U.S. invasion of Iraq by insisting that an alleged meeting took place between Mohammed Atta and an Iraqi intelligence official, Cheney denied he had ever made the claim even though another videotape existed of him making such an assertion on the television news program *Meet the Press*. As Eric Alterman points out, "It was left to the *Daily Show* to run the two tapes of Cheney together" to expose Cheney's almost allergic reaction to telling the truth. One senses that Cheney's goal is not one of persuasion or winning consent, but of reinforcing the public's sense of cynicism and powerlessness.

Charges of newspeak do not come exclusively from the Left or from cantankerous critics. *New York Times* op-ed writer and liberal economist, Paul Krugman, asserts that "misrepresentation and deception are standard operating procedure for [the Bush] administration, which—to an extent never before seen in U.S. history—systematically and brazenly distorts the facts." And, in referring to Bush's record on the selling of the Iraqi war, he argues that it "is arguably the worst scandal in American political history—worse than Watergate, worse than Iran-contra. Indeed, the idea that we were deceived into war makes many commentators so uncomfortable that they refuse to admit the possibility."[24]

In what has to rank as one of the most egregious distortions (or as maybe a delusional raving, as the *New York Daily News* suggests) that has emerged from the Bush administration, President Bush in an interview with *New Yorker* reporter Ken Auletta, claimed, "No president has ever done more for human rights than I have."[25] Such a statement is extraordinary given that Amnesty International condemned the United States in 2002 for being one of the world leaders in human rights violations. Similarly, several organizations such as Human Rights Watch, U.S. Human Rights

Network, the ACLU, the Center for Constitutional Rights, and Amnesty International have accused the Bush administration itself of engaging in various human rights violations. These include: preventing foreign nationals held as prisoners at Guantanamo Bay from gaining access to U.S. courts; executing juvenile offenders; engaging in racial profiling, detention, inhumane treatment, and deportation of Muslim immigrants after September 11, 2001; refusing to ratify the American Convention on Human Rights, the Kyoto Protocol, the International Covenant on Civil and Political Rights, the International Criminal Court, the Convention on the Rights of the Child, and numerous other international agreements aimed at protecting human rights.

The Bush administration is exceptionally adept at hiding some of its most flagrant violations of human rights by labeling them with names that appear either perfectly legitimate or incomprehensible. For example, a policy that allows people to be kidnapped, put on a plane, and sent to a foreign country to be tortured is denoted as "extraordinary rendition." Of course, in actuality, "extraordinary rendition" is just a euphemism for torture. The pilots and crews who flew the planes to Syria, Egypt, Morocco, and Jordan—all countries which have been identified by the State Department as practicing torture in their prisons—were labeled as " 'The Special Removal Unit.' "[26] Military intelligence officials in agreement with the CIA hid certain detainees at Abu Ghraib from international rights organizations by not assigning them internment numbers and keeping their names off the books. These prisoners were quaintly named "ghost" prisoners. While the language may seem harmless, the act violated international law and ignored the most basic precepts of human rights.[27] Bob Herbert discussing the case of Maher Arar, a Canadian citizen abducted by the U.S. while changing planes in New York and eventually shipped off to Syria where he was tortured for a year and later freed, without any charges lodged against him, raised the question of whether anything, including murder, is permissible in post-9/11 America. He writes:

> Mr. Arar's is the case we know about. How many other individuals have disappeared at the hands of the Bush administration? How many have been sent, like victims of a lynch mob, to overseas torture centers? How many people are being held in the C.I.A.'s highly secret offshore prisons? Who are they and how are they being treated? Have any been wrongly accused? If so, what recourse do they have? President Bush spent much of last week lecturing other nations about freedom, democracy and the rule of law. It was a breathtaking display of chutzpah. He seemed to me like a judge who starves his children and then sits on the bench to hear child abuse cases. In brussels Mr. Bush said he planned to remind Russian President Vladimir Putin that democracies are based on, among other things, "the rule of law and the respect for human rights and human dignity."[28]

Under such circumstances, democracy as both a moral referent and a political ideal appears to have lost any vestige of credibility when it is used by the Bush administration. Rather than viewed as a system of governance, the Bush administration invokes democracy as a ritual incantation to be marshalled as a curative for everything from terrorism to ethnic atrocities. Unfortunately, the hyper-rhetoric of democracy reveals more about its actual absence than its influence in shaping

U.S. domestic and foreign policies. Even in the face of events that reveal the enormous gap between the rhetoric and reality of democracy in the U.S., the Bush administration assumes the moral high ground of democracy while refusing to acknowledge how it is being undermined by their own policies. For instance, *Newsweek* published in its May 9, 2005, issue a short report in its "Periscope" section in which it inaccurately stated that American interrogators had flushed a copy of the Koran, the sacred Muslim text, down a toilet. The story triggered several days of rioting in Afghanistan and other countries, resulting in a number of people being injured and at least fifteen killed. *Newsweek* quickly retracted the story and apologized for publishing an inaccurate report on the defiling of the Koran. The Bush administration used the story not only to amp up its relentless attack on the news media and to accuse its most trusted voices, like Dan Rather, of irresponsibility, but also to suggest that *Newsweek* was solely responsible for the anti-American demonstrations and deaths. Bullying the media has been a favorite pastime of the Bush administration, and it has worked well as part of a larger attempt to "cover up its own fictions and failings in Iraq."[29] What is so amazing about this response is that it completely ignores the history of ongoing violence by American forces against Muslim detainees in Guantanamo Bay in Cuba, Abu Ghraib prison in Iraq, and the Bagram detention center in Afghanistan. The *Newsweek* story simply publicized one incident in a long chain of abuse and violence that has angered Muslims all over the world. While the *Newsweek* story may have been wrong, the practice and pattern of abuse it revealed have been going on for some time. Yet, the Bush administration and the dominant media completely ignored the history of such cruel and inhumane treatment of detainees as a factor in producing the protests and riots against the U.S. government, not only in Afghanistan, but around the world, especially in many Arab countries. In light of the numerous reports by a number of government agencies, the International Committee of the Red Cross, and Amnesty International, which document cases of torture, beatings, and sexual humiliation against Muslim prisoners, it is not difficult to imagine why the anger of many people outside of the U.S. escalated in a violent reaction to the *Newsweek* story about the defiling of the Koran. Moreover, even before the *Newsweek* incident, there were numerous reports of the Koran being defiled by American interrogators, in addition to revelations regarding numerous abuses and Muslim-baiting practices such as "depriving prisoners of published religious items or materials and forcing the removal of beards and clothing" as well as authenticated cases "in which female interrogators 'touched and spoke to detainees in a sexually suggestive manner in order to incur stress based on the detainees' religious beliefs.' "[30] Two weeks after the *Newsweek* imbroglio, the Pentagon released a "report certifying desecrations of the Koran by American guards." The report was released "at 7:15 P.M. on a Friday, to assure it would miss the evening newscasts and be buried in the Memorial Day weekend's little-read papers."[31] The attempt on the part of the Bush administration to claim that *Newsweek* should take the blame for anti-American demonstrations is laughable.[32] In fact, after the original story ran, U.S. forces fired on demonstrators in Afghanistan, killing at least fourteen people and injuring many more. In addition, on May 20, 2005, the *New York Times* ran a front-page story detailing the brutal deaths of two inmates at the Bagram prison. Such stories bespeak an ongoing accumulation of incidents, ranging from the merely inflammatory to the deeply inhumane, any of which might prove to be the breaking point for a wave of protests, riots, and violence against American forces and interests.

The short account in the *New York Times* was based on a report by Army investigators detailing how a twenty-two-year-old taxi driver known as Dilawar was chained by his wrists to the top of his cell for four days, beaten, and injured so badly his legs could no longer bend. He eventually died in his cell while chained to the ceiling. But the Army investigators not only documented the brutal deaths of Mr. Dilawar and another detainee named Habibullah; they also revealed a systemic pattern of abuse by American interrogators that has now become commonplace. In what has become a typical incident of abuse of Muslim detainees, the *Times* included the following example of an interrogation: "In sworn statements to Army investigators, soldiers describe one female interrogator with a taste for humiliation stepping on the neck of one prostate detainee and kicking another in the genitals. They tell of a shackled prisoner being forced to roll back and forth on the floor of a cell, kissing the boots of his interrogators as he went. Yet another prisoner is made to pick plastic bottle caps out of a drum mixed with excrement and water as part of a strategy to soften him up for questioning."[33]

Shortly after the *Newsweek* story broke, Amnesty International issued a report that further undermined Bush's efforts to allegedly spread democracy to the Middle East and other parts of the world. Detailing the U.S. mistreatment of prisoners in the context of the "war on terror," the report, "Guantanamo and Beyond: The Continuing Pursuit of Unchecked Executive Power," compared the U.S. detention centers in Guantanamo Bay, Iraq, Afghanistan, and other secret locations to new forms of Soviet-style "Gulag" labor camps.[34] In top Orwellian fashion, President Bush, Vice President Cheney, Donald Rumsfeld, and other high-level members of the government responded to the report by suggesting that its contents were simply the result of lies being peddled by former detainees. Cheney, appearing on the Larry King television program, attempted to substantiate the government position by claiming, without irony, that the detainees at Guantanamo, for instance, "have been well treated, treated humanely and decently."[35] The official government response to the *Newsweek* incident, coupled with its ongoing policy of abuse, torture, secrecy, and distortion, bankrupts any attempt on the part of Bush and his cohorts to use the rhetoric of democracy to characterize American domestic and foreign policy.

The perceived gap between rhetoric and deeds in the Bush administration not only damages the credibility of the American government throughout the world; it also functions as a space in which all kinds of stealth phenomena can be made visible and addressed as part of a larger politics of lying, corruption, secrecy, and media manipulation. Official newspeak is part of a larger politics to silence critics, control the media, and allow governmental power to operate without any checks and balances. Eric Alterman rightly points, for instance, to the ways in which the current administration is undermining the ability of journalists to hold power accountable. He writes:

> But the White House and its supporters are doing more than just talking trash—when they talk at all. They are taking aggressive action; preventing journalists from doing

their job by withholding routine information; deliberately releasing deceptive information on a regular basis; bribing friendly journalists to report the news in a favourable context; producing their own "news reports" and distributing these free of charge to resource-starved broadcasters; creating and crediting their own political activists as "journalists" working for partisan operations masquerading as news organizations.[36]

Official newspeak not only raises questions regarding the abuse of power; it also leads us to ask what kind of cultural politics is necessary to expose such myths and to defeat what Edward Said has called "the imposed silence and normalized quiet of unseen power."[37] Pointing to these issues is both a political and pedagogical task that demands that intellectuals and others speak out, break through the haze of official discourse and memory, and take seriously a cultural politics that connects critical knowledge and understanding with the possibility of social engagement and transformation. At the very least, this suggests recognizing the many sites of pedagogy (from the Internet to alternative magazines) in which ideological mystifications can be challenged and rearticulated in the interest of transforming the conditions that impose silence and perpetuate human suffering. It means connecting the sites in which we work, whether in higher education, the arts, journalism, the media, or other dominant and alternative public spheres, with those individuals, groups, and issues that make up everyday life. At stake here is the need to reconnect matters of theory and practice, critical understanding and civic engagement, and to do so from the recognition that we need to reach as many people as possible. Evidence of such attempts to make the pedagogical more political can be found in the work of MoveOn.org, which offers a wide array of information for activists.[38] Educator and filmmaker Sut Jhally provides numerous film and video sources about crucial political issues through his organization, The Media Education Foundation.[39] Web sites such as CommonDreams.org make available not only a vast number of critical commentaries by left-wing and progressive critics, but also numerous web sites and homepages for a diverse number of left media sources and organizations.[40] Regardless of the ideological oversights and theoretical sloppiness that mark Michael Moore's work, it should be studied as one model for redefining public pedagogy as a crucial tool for political engagement. Recognizing that progressives and others need to reach out to young people who are under attack by the Bush administration, Adam Fletcher has pioneered The Freechild Project, which connects children, youth, and adults with a wide range of resources on social change.[41] Making the political more pedagogical means that progressives and others need to be attentive to how people connect intellectually and affectively to the language, values, and political issues that shape their lives. This is no small matter because consciousness is the basic condition for agency to develop and for political action to become realizable.

How might matters of resistance and politics be engaged when FBI agents can arrest a 16-year-old girl at a high school in East Harlem, detain her in an immigration detention center in Pennsylvania, and justify such actions with the claim that she poses a threat to the United States as a "would-be suicide bomber?" And there is barely a public outcry. Her teachers describe the young girl as someone whose "biggest worry was whether she'd done her homework or studied for a science test."[42] This script is right out of the movie *Minority Report,* based on the story by Philip K. Dick, in which the Washington, D.C., police initiate a policy of "pre-crime." Using a trio of psychics to identify people who are about to commit a crime, the police arrest such individuals before they complete the deed. Unfortunately, the movie in many ways imitates reality, except that the FBI are now the psychics who use their "uncanny abilities" (that is, racial profiling) to arrest future terrorists, and there is virtually no significant resistance to this incident from the press, media, or academics. This is more than shameful; it is an utter capitulation in the face of an Orwellian rhetoric that only thinly veils an egregious form of authoritarianism and racism. At the same time, such events should also register the potential power of a critical discourse to disrupt authoritarian ideologies and material relations of power. Power has to be made visible, if it is to be held accountable, though, of course, that is not where politics ends. Critical consciousness, autonomy, the ability to make visible power relations and abuses of power, and to become aware of alternative histories and communities of struggle are, after all, not merely the stuff of political awareness, but what makes democratic politics possible in the first place.

In the face of the Bush administration's Orwellian newspeak, it is important to raise serious questions about what happens when critical education is detached from an engaged democratic politics and how public forms of resistance are increasingly replaced by a mood of despair, buttressed by a cynicism manufactured at the highest levels of government and aided and abetted by various apparatuses of cultural production. The widespread use of newspeak by politicians and media pundits alike has dire consequences for a society rooted in new historical conditions in which matters of pedagogy and learning have become central to new and emerging forms of market and religious fundamentalisms. The production of individual identities and social agency is no longer limited to the traditional spheres of learning such as schools; it is now being organized and disseminated across a wide range of educational spheres inhabited by newspapers, talk radio, magazines, films, television, the Internet, and other instruments of public pedagogy that are deployed by cultural apparatuses to reshape the nature of the relationship among power, learning, and agency. The result, on one level, is the widespread use of newspeak, and, on the other, a conception of the political that is stripped of its democratic, transformative possibilities. A misinformed citizenry is increasingly mobilized to support reactionary policies at home and abroad. Language, sound, and images are disseminated across a wide variety of traditional and electronically mediated public spheres to inspire identification with a militaristic way of life, the familiar associations of fraternal bonding, and hypermasculinity; a religious revolution has made patriarchal family structure and sexual purity its battle cry; and everyday existence is now shaped through a media apparatus that promotes a deep fear and suspicion of foreign others.

At the same time, the hollowed-out civic discourse that permeates American society is parallelled by a lack of political imagination among critical intellectuals and social movements. The impoverishment of everyday life is matched by a growing intellectual impoverishment in which politics loses its theoretical and social vibrancy as critique is reduced to arcane vocabularies or simplistic jingles, and academic work is largely removed from the worldly space of social crises and political issues. Where scholarly criticism does appear in the publications of liberals such as Michael Ignatieff, Christopher Hitchins, and Norman Geras, it serves generally as an apology for official power, overlooking official lies and generally defending U.S. actions either in the name of some spurious cost-benefit defense of democracy or by dismissing left critiques of U.S. foreign policy as one-sided, unpatriotic, or overly severe (while ignoring the very real suffering of those enduring the daily attacks, abuses, and disruptions of the American occupation).[43] While left critics are often insightful about U.S. foreign and domestic policies, their work is too often tainted by attempts to reduce all problems in the world and their solutions to the exclusive expression of economic self-interest. Capitalizing on the intellectual impoverishment of public discourse and the ever-growing complicity of liberal intellectuals, the ideologically driven conservative corporate media substitute entertainment or patriotic correctness for any responsible effort to make dominant authority and institutions accountable for their actions. Adding insult to injury, Lynne Cheney, Joseph Lieberman, and other right-wing political operatives and ideological cheerleaders for the Bush administration capitalize on the media-induced culture of fear by arguing that the best way to save American culture is "to remove it from any thought that isn't utterly conformist with the opinion of 'the public at large.' "[44] In the place of public debates across a wider number of pedagogical sites, we now have the spectacle of fully staged and scripted "town hall meetings" and a few talking/shouting heads posing as experts in a limited number of tightly controlled media spheres. As politics is emptied of any substantive meaning, mysticism and religious extremism are on the rise, often filling the void left by the retreating social state.

Despair, insecurity, and uncertainty increasingly translate into cynicism as the capacity to think in terms of the common good or a more general notion of freedom collapses into an utterly privatized politics. In some cases, insightful commentators such as Curtis White come dangerously close to stoking the fires of cynicism by claiming that the American public suffers from what he calls the "New Censorship," which "functions by making everything known and naked to a paralysing degree."[45] In this discourse, consent does not require the duplicity of Orwellian language. On the contrary, allegedly exposed to full view are the truth of corruption, reactionary policies designed to serve the rich, and rigged elections, but nobody challenges these charades. In another words, the basic principle of the "New Censorship" is that the truth, read as "bad news," is transparent and readily recognized by the public. Unlike Jean Baudrillard, who argues in *In the Shadow of Silent Majorities* that rather than being apathetic, the masses simply refuse to play the game, White suggests that the public cannot distinguish between the daily betrayals of the public trust and entertainment.[46] In this instance, White insists that deception is no longer needed by those in power, because the public is both overwhelmed by the lies and seemingly unable to do anything—because so removed from power—about the consequences of such manufactured deception. Of course, White's implication that everything is known by the public needs to be challenged, as does the presupposition that critical knowledge has no relationship with critical action. This is a position that invents its own truth through a discourse of cynicism that attempts to hide its own despair while justifying, in spite of its own intentions, a politics of indifference. Despite White's claims, knowledge is not always shock entertainment and thus consumable as passive information. In the end, White offers up a politics without a pedagogy, a manifesto of cynicism parading as political insight. Matt Miller is more on target with his claim

that "the gap between the cartoon of public life that the press and political establishment often serve up and the pragmatic open-mindedness of most Americans explains
why so many people tune out—and how we might get them to tune back in.
Alienation is the only intelligent response to a political culture that insults our intelligence."[47] Powerlessness in this case has its roots not in paralysis, but in a lack of
knowledge that both challenges official accounts and is capable of persuading an
alienated public. Dwight Macdonald, in a different context, goes further than both
of these positions. He also understands how language is used by those in power to
strip people of their moral imagination and political sensitivity, but rather than
collapse into cynicism or succumb to alienation, Macdonald makes politics more relevant by connecting the language of politics to everyday life so that people do not
merely assume ethical and political positions, but also experience them as central to
their own problems and sense of individual and collective agency. Macdonald insists
on connecting language and ideology to people "on the ground," mediated through
the problems, principles, and structures of feeling that they share. At stake here is the
recognition that knowledge can be made meaningful in order to be made critical and
thus transformative, and the latter is what makes a pedagogical intervention both
political and worthwhile.

The appearance of indifference, even in the face of the truth, is more complicated
and emerges from a plethora of conditions and social formations, as I have repeated
throughout this chapter. For instance, within an increasingly privatized world, the
space of an engaged politics is often eroded as public spheres are commercialized or
privatized; critical vocabularies are replaced by the discourses of religious and market
fundamentalism; and democratic values are replaced by the logic of a rabid individualism and disdain for, if not fear of, public life. Couple this utter privatization of
everyday life with the systemic forces unleashed by neoliberal politics in the production of all manner of giant economic, social, and personal transformations and
accompanied by massive insecurities, uncertainties, dislocations, and the haunting
"spectre of exclusion."[48] What is really being learned by the American public is that
while power is everywhere and can be struggled over, it is, in the final analysis, largely
removed from their lives. But, at the same time, knowledge is not produced in a
totally administered society and, since different publics mediate knowledge out of
different social and historical formations, how knowledge is engaged, understood,
and acted upon suggests widely diverse modes of interpretation.

If intellectuals, activists, citizens, young people, and others are to revive the
possibilities of a democratic politics, they are going to have to locate the energy of
resistance in a revitalized struggle over old and newly fashioned sites of public pedagogy as well as in the material conditions of power that make them possible. This is
not simply a call for linking critical education and pedagogical practices to making
visible the "facts" necessary for exposing, for example, the lies behind Orwellian
newspeak, however important such a task might be. Making the abuse of power and
its consequences visible within the existing discourse of conservative politics is an
important political strategy, but it is not enough. What must be explored in greater
detail is the need to enlarge politics into more than a search for truth or a discourse
of critique. Rendering intelligible the techno-tele-media field of analysis and the
categories it deploys in the interest of dominant power is an important form of

critique; however, it needs to be accompanied by a positive intervention in which alternative public spheres can be constructed out of a sense of hope and a struggle for justice animated by the ideals of democracy and emancipation. Politics must become more attentive to those everyday conditions that have allowed the American public to become complicitous in the barbaric policies of the Bush regime even though the rationales buttressing such policies have often been exposed as willful lies serving the rich and the powerful. The spirit of critique must be supplemented with an affirmative sense of individual and social agency capable of becoming both a witness to injustice and a force for social transformation. Dominant power now operates not only within the naturalized logic of common sense, but also in a multiplicity of sites and systems fused within new connections between technology and culture that occupy ever larger social spheres and spaces. Politics emerges in new forms in the age of virtual reality as global modes of information constitute a new interface between smart machines and humans. Beheadings are taped by radical Muslim insurgents and shown on the Internet in order to force occupying governments to withdraw their troups; students use video cameras to monitor the exploitation of under paid workers by giant corporations such as Nike, and different movements for global justice use computers to communicate with their allies across national boundaries.

At the same time, as Mark Poster brilliantly illustrates, it is critical to acknowledge that while the imbrication of technology and culture is at the heart of "new conditions of social space," agency is not obliterated but offers new possibilities for resistance through a reimagining of both the forms that public spheres might take in the information age and how the very nature of agency and politics might be reconfigured within new forms of participatory electronically mediated discourses, experiences, and social practices.[49] Stanley Aronowitz has further argued that while it is crucial to recognize that a "new conception of the public sphere is necessary," it would be a mistake to suggest that older public spheres, such as neighborhoods, workplaces, clubs, churches, and other embodied sites in which people meet face-to-face, talk, organize, share stories, and work, have either disappeared or have become irrelevant to any notion of radical politics in a post-fordist age.[50] Aronowitz is right when he suggests that any new politics that takes words, images, and sounds seriously must come to grips with the new electronically mediated technologies, but must not do so at the expense of erasing an older politics in which the conditions for agency and struggle were embodied in the particularities and specificities of place, history, bodies, and materiality. The possibilities for understanding how political agency is both interfered with and enabled cannot be limited to analyzing those new public spaces produced at the intersection of new electronic communication systems and emerging cultural landscapes such as the electronic café or interactive blogger communities. There is a broader question at work here in which older notions of politics and the public sphere must be combined with new understandings of how culture and the electronic communication systems have intervened in and refigured the historical dialectics of knowledge and power, teaching and learning, thinking and acting.

In addition, any concern for a democratic politics has to rethink the role of social movements and the task they face in reclaiming the values of the common good, public life, and social justice and the promise of a global democracy. The curse of neoliberal ideology with its incessant war against all things public, social, and democratic has weakened the ability of many people in the U.S. to prevent public issues from being relegated to merely private concerns. Consequently, language has lost its civic functions; citizenship no longer bears the challenge of social responsibilities; and education is largely reduced to a private affair. As discourse is hermetically sealed within an often privatized conception of the world, politics becomes either banal or fascistic, reduced to game shows, empty electoral rituals, military salutes, and dangerous incursions into ever-widening circles of political, racial, and social-cultural exclusion. If democracy in its most substantive and inclusive forms is to become a rallying cry at a moment of incipient authoritarianism, engaged citizens must struggle to overcome the disconnection between discourse and social responsibility, politics and critical education, market interests and democratic values, privately felt pain and joys of lived experience and larger public considerations. This suggests a renewed struggle over the mutually determining forces of cultural politics and material relations of power, a more complex understanding of the centrality of cultural politics to any viable struggle for democratic forms of identity and agency, and a reclaiming of a notion of hope in which the gritty realities of everyday life can be used to mobilize social movements intent on making the promise of global democracy a reality rather than merely a utopian dream.

Notes

1. Umberto Eco, "Eternal Fascism: Fourteen Ways of Looking at a Blackshirt," *New York Review of Books*, November–December 1995, 15.

2. Dwight Macdonald, *The Responsibility of Intellectuals and Other Essays in Political Criticism* (London: Victor Gollancz, 1957), 44–45.

3. The now famous "Downing Street memo" published by the *Times* (London) on May 1, 2005, revealed that the Bush administration decided to overthrow Saddam Hussein in the summer of 2002 and "fixed" the intelligence in order make the case for weapons of mass destruction.

4. Mark Crispin Miller, *The Bush Dyslexicon: Observations on a National Disorder* (New York: W.W. Norton, 2002); Jacob Weisberg, *Still More George W. Bushisms* (New York: Fireside, 2003).

5. Abbott Gleason, "The Hard Road to Fascism," *Boston Review*, Summer 2003, http://www.bostonreview.net/BR28.3/gleason.html.

6. Bob Herbert, "Casualties at Home," *New York Times*, March 27, 2003, A27.

7. Renana Brooks, "The Language of Power, Fear, and Emptiness," *The Nation*, June 24, 2003, http://reclaimdemocracy.org/weekly-2003/bush-language-power- fear.html.

8. Bob Herbert, "A Failure of Leadership," *New York Times*, September 5, 2005. Available online: http://www.nytimes.com/2005/09/05/opinion/05herbert.html?incamp = articles_popular. Maureen Dowd goes even further in highlighting Bush's indifference to the suffering of others; see Maureen Dowd, "United States of Shame," *New York Times*, September 3, 2005. Available online: http://www.nytimes.com/2005/09/03/opinion/03dowd.html?8hpib.

9. Paul Krugman, "Losing Our Country," *New York Times*, June 10, 2005, A23.

10. The relevant excerpt from this interview can be found in "Millions and Millions Lost," Platform Section, *Harper's Magazine*, January 2004, 16.

11. Paul Krugman, "Losing Our Country," *New York Times*, June 10, 2005, A23.

12. Janice Rogers Brown cited in David D. Kirkpatrick, "Seeing Slavery in Liberalism," *New York Times*, June 9, 2005, 1.

13. This insight comes from Juan Stam, "Bush's Religious Language," *The Nation*, December 22, 2003, 27.

14. Bush's use of newspeak is so pronounced that the National Council of Teachers of English awarded him its 2003 Newspeak Award. See: http://www.govst.edu/users/ghrank/Introduction/bush2003.htm.

15. Ruth Rosen, "Bush Newspeak," *San Francisco Chronicle*, July 14, 2003, http://www.commondreams.org/views03/0714-10.htm. In January 2004, former vice president Al Gore, in a major speech on Bush's environmental policies, said, "Indeed, they often use Orwellian language to disguise their true purposes. For example, a policy that opens national forests to destructive logging of old-growth trees is labeled Healthy Forest Initiative. A policy that vastly increases the amount of pollution that can be dumped into the air is called the Clear Skies Initiative." Gore cited in Bob Herbert, "Masters of Deception," *New York Times*, January 16, 2004, A21.

16. Jennifer Lee, "U.S. Proposes Easing Rules on Emissions of Mercury," *New York Times*, December 3, 2003, A20.

17. Eric Pianin, "Clean Air Rules to Be Relaxed," *Washington Post*, August 23, 2003, http://www.washingtonpost.com/ac2/wp-dyn/A34334-2003Aug22?.

18. The *New York Times* reported that the Environmental Protection Agency actually eliminated references to any studies that "concluded that warming is at least partly caused by rising concentrations of smokestack and tail pipe emissions and could threaten health and ecosystems." Cited in Huck Gutman, "On Science, War, and the Prevalence of Lies," *The Statesman*, June 28, 2003, http://www.commondreams.org/views03/0628-04.htm.

19. George W. Bush, "President Bush Delivers Remarks in Tennessee on Earth Day," *GOP.com* (speech, April 22, 2005, http://www.gop.com/News/Read.aspx?ID = 5385).

20. Bob Herbert, "Stranger than Fiction," *New York Times*, May 9, 2005, A19.

21. George W. Bush, "Remarks by the President on the War on Terrorism" (speech, National Defense University, March 8, 2005, http://www.usembassy.it/file2005_03/alia/a5030801.htm).

22. For all of the direct government sources for these lies, see *One Thousand Reasons to Dump George Bush*, especially the section titled "Honesty" (http://thousandreasons.org/the_top_ten.html). See also David Corn, *The Lies of George Bush* (New York: Crown, 2003). For an excellent source for examining the ongoing deceptions practised by the Bush administration, see Douglas Kellner, *From 9/11 to Terror War: The Dangers of the Bush Legacy* (Denver: Rowman and Littlefield, 2003).

23. See Corn, *The Lies*, 228–230.

24. Both quotations can be found in Paul Krugman, "Standard Operating Procedure," *New York Times*, June 3, 2004, A17.

25. See Lloyd Grove, "Lowdown," *New York Daily News*, January 11, 2004, www.unknownnews.net/insanity011404.html; Bush cited in Paul Krugman, "Going for Broke," *New York Times*, January 20, 2004, A21.

26. Jane Mayer, "Outsourcing Torture," *The New Yorker*, February 4, 2004, 106.

27. Josh White, "Army, CIA Agreed on 'Ghost' Prisoners," *Washington Post*, March 11, 2005, A16.

28. Bob Herbert, "It's Called Torture," *The New York Times*, February 28, 2005, A27.

29. Frank Rich, "It's All *Newsweek*'s Fault," *New York Times*, May 22, 2005, WK13.

30. Ibid.

31. Frank Rich, "Don't Follow the Money," *New York Times*, June 12, 2005, 14.

32. What the dominant press ignored almost entirely was that both Gen. Richard Myers, the chairman of the Joint Chiefs of Staff, and Afghanistan's president, Hamid Karzai, publicly stated that the riots responsible for the seventeen deaths were unrelated to the *Newsweek* story.

33. Tim Golden, "In U.S. Report, Brutal Details of 2 Afghan Inmates' Deaths," *New York Times*, May 20, 2005, A12.

34. A copy of the report is available online: http://web.amnesty.org/library/Index/ENGAMR510632005.

35. Cheney cited in CNN.com News, "Cheney Offended by Amnesty Criticism," *CNN.com International Edition*, May 31, 2005, http://www.cnn.com/2005/US/05/30/cheney.amnestyintl/.

36. Eric Alterman, "Bush's War on the Press," *The Nation*, May 9, 2005, 11.

37. Edward Said, *Humanism and Democratic Criticism* (New York: Columbia University Press, 2004), 135.

38. See: http://www.moveon.org/front/.

39. See: http://www.mediaed.org/.

40. See: http://www.commondreams.org/.

41. See: http://www.freechild.org/.

42. Nina Bernstein, "Teachers and Classmates Express Outrage at Arrest of Girl, 16, as a Terrorist Threat," *New York Times*, April 9, 2005, B3.

43. See, for example, Michael Ignatieff, "The Burden," *New York Times Magazine*, January 5, 2003, http://www.mtholyoke.edu/acad/intrel/bush/burden.htm; and Norman Geras, "Reductionism," *Dissent*, Winter 2005, 55–60.

44. Curtis White, "The New Censorship," *Harper's Magazine*, August 2003, 16.

45. Ibid., 17.

46. Jean Baudrillard, *In the Shadow of Silent Majorities* (New York: Semiotexte, 1998).

47. Matt Miller, "Is Persuasion Dead?" *New York Times*, June 4, 2005, A15.

48. Zygmunt Bauman, *Identity: Conversations with Benedetto Vecchi* (London: Polity, 2004), 46.

49. Mark Poster, *The Information Subject* (Amsterdam: Gordon and Breach, 2001).

50. Stanley Aronowitz, "Commentary," in ibid., 176.

8

BREAKING INTO THE MOVIES

FILM AS CULTURAL POLITICS

Without a politically guaranteed public realm, freedom lacks the worldly space to make its appearance.
> —Hannah Arendt, "What is Freedom?" 1961[1]

My memories of Hollywood films cannot be separated from the attractions that such films had for me as a young boy growing up in Smith Hill, a working-class neighborhood of Providence, Rhode Island, in the 1950s. While we had access to the small screen of black and white television, it held none of the mystery, fascination, and pleasure that we found in the five or six grand movie theaters that populated the downtown section of Providence. Every Saturday afternoon, my friends and I would walk several miles to the business district, all the while making plans to get into the theaters without having to pay. None of us could afford to buy a ticket so we had to be inventive about ways to sneak into the theaters without being caught. Sometimes we would simply wait next to the exit doors, and as soon as somebody left the theater we would rush in and bury ourselves in the plush seats, hoping that none of the ushers spotted us. We were not always so lucky. At other times, we would pool our money and have one person buy a ticket, and at the most strategic moment he would open the exit door from the inside and let us in. Generally, we would sit in the balcony so as to avoid being asked for a ticket if the ushers came along and spotted us.

Hollywood film engendered a profound sense of danger and otherness for us. Gaining access to the movies meant we had to engage in illicit behavior, risking criminal charges, or possibly a beating by an irate owner, if caught. But the fear of getting caught was outweighed by the lure of adventure and joy. Once we got inside the movie theater we were transported into an event. We were able to participate in a public act of viewing that was generally restricted for kids in our neighborhood because films were too expensive, and removed from the daily experiences of kids too poor to use public transportation; we were also too restless to sit in a movie theater without talking, laughing, and being allegedly too rough to inhabit a public space meant for family entertainment. Silence in the movie theaters was imposed on us by the fear of being noticed. Yet the thrill of adventure and the expectation of what was about to unfold before us was well worth the self-imposed discipline, the contained silence, and the focus that such viewing demanded. Back on the street, the movies enabled a space of dialogue, criticism, and solidarity for us. Movies were a source of shared joy, entertainment, escape, and, though we were too young to realize it at the time, a source of knowledge. A source of knowledge that, unlike what we were privy to in school, connected pleasure to meaning. Sometimes we saw as many as three double features in one day. When we left the movie theater, the cinematography and narratives that we had viewed filled our conversations and our dreams. We argued, sometimes actually fought, over their meaning and relevance for our lives. Hollywood films took us out of Smith Hill, offered narratives that rubbed against the often rigid identities we inhabited, and offered up objects of desire that both seduced us and left us thinking that the movies were not about reality but fantasy, remote from the burdens and problems that dominated our neighborhoods. Films pointed to a terrain of pseudo-freedom located in an inner world of dreams, reinforced by the privatized experience of pleasure and joy offered through the twin seductions of escape and entertainment.

All of these memories of my early exposure to Hollywood films came rushing back to me during a visit not too long ago to Universal Studios in Los Angeles. While on one of the tours of the studio lots, the guide attempted to capture the meaning of contemporary films by proclaiming, without hesitation, that the great appeal of movies lies in their capacity to "make people laugh, cry, and sit on the edge of their seats." Surely, I believed this as a child, as much as the tourists listening to the guide seemed to believe it almost forty years later. My first reaction was to dismiss the guide's comments as typical of Hollywood's attempt to commodify experience through simplification and reification, relieving pleasure of the burden of thinking, let alone critique, and positioning the public as passive tourists traveling through the Hollywood dream machine. But there was something about the guide's comments that warranted more than a simple dismissal. While the mythic fantasy and lure of entertainment demand a challenge to the utterly privatized realm of mass-mediated common sense, it also requires more than the arrogance of theory, which often refuses to link the pleasure of film-watching with the workings and structures of the public domain. Films do more than entertain; they offer up subject positions, mobilize desires, influence us unconsciously, and help to construct the landscape of American culture. Deeply imbricated within material and symbolic relations of power, movies produce and incorporate ideologies that represent the outcome of struggles marked by the historical realities of power and the deep anxieties of the times; they also deploy power through the important role they play in connecting the production of pleasure and meaning with the mechanisms and practices of powerful teaching machines. Put simply, films both entertain and educate.

In the 1970s, I began to understand, though in a limited way, the constitutive and political nature of films, particularly how power is mobilized through their use of images, sounds, gestures, talk, and spectacles in order to create the possibilities for people to be educated about how to act, speak, think, feel, desire, and behave. Films provided me with a pedagogical tool for offering students alternative views of the world. Of course, films not only challenged print culture as the only viable source of knowledge; they were attractive cultural texts for students because they were not entirely contaminated by the logic of formal schooling. As a young high school teacher, I too was attracted to films as a way of challenging the constraints imposed by the rigidity of the text-based curriculum. In opposition to the heavy reliance on the lock-step, traditional curriculum, I would rent documentaries from a local Quaker group in order to present students with a critical perspective on the Vietnam War, poverty, youth-oriented issues, the Cold War, and a host of other social concerns. Films now became crucial texts for me, useful as a resource to offset dominant textbook ideologies and invaluable as a pedagogical tool to challenge officially sanctioned knowledge and modes of learning.

The choices I made about what films to show were determined by their overtly educational content. At that point in my teaching experience, I had not figured out that all films played a powerful role pedagogically, not only in the schools, but also in the wider culture. Nor did I ever quite figure out how my students felt about these films. Far removed from the glamor of Hollywood, these documentary narratives were often heavy-handed ideologically, displaying little investment in irony, humor, or self-critique. Certainly my own reception of them was marked by ambivalence. The traditional notion that films were forms of entertainment or the more radical argument that dismissed films as one-dimensional commodities seemed crass to me. One option that I pursued in challenging these deeply held assumptions was to engage films performatively as social practices and events mediated within the give-and-take of diverse public spheres and lived experiences. My students and I discussed the films we viewed both in terms of the ideologies they disseminated and how they worked to move mass audiences and break the continuity of common sense. In addition, films became important to me as a way of clarifying my role as a critical teacher and of broadening my understanding of critical pedagogy. But there was a price to pay for such an approach. Films no longer seemed to offer me pleasure in as much as my relationship to them was now largely conceived in narrow, instrumental terms. As a subversive resource to enhance my teaching, I focused on films in ways that seemed to ignore how they functioned as emotionally charged sites, mobilizing a range of desires while invoking the incidental, visceral, and transitory. Films became for me, though unconsciously, formalized objects of detached academic analysis. I attempted to organize films around important pedagogical issues, but in doing so I did not use theory to link films to broader aspects of public life (audiences, publics, and events within the concrete relations of power). I used theory as a way of legitimating film as a social text, rather than as a site where different possibilities of uses and effects intersect. I wanted students to read films critically, but I displayed little concern with going beyond examining how films as relatively isolated texts were implicated in the production of ideologies regarding everything from how to define masculinity and patriotism to forming particular views about race, class, and gender. Missing from my approach then was any sustained attempt to address how both documentary and popular films might be used to prepare students to function as critical agents capable of understanding, engaging, and transforming those discourses and institutional contexts that closed down democratic public life. In addition, by being overly concerned with how films might be used as alternative educational texts, I failed to understand and impart to my students the powerful role that films now played within a visual culture employing new forms of pedagogy, signaling different forms of literacy, and exemplifying a mode of politics in which "culture [becomes] a crucial site and weapon of power in the modern world."[2]

I am not suggesting, in retrospect, that films are overburdened by theoretical discourses per se or that they should be removed from the sphere of engaged textual analysis. But I do want to challenge those versions of textuality and theory that isolate films from the broader social issues and considerations that structure the politics of everyday realities. Drawing upon a distinction made by Lawrence Grossberg, I am more interested in a theorizing politics than in a politics of theory, the former which suggests less an interest in theory as an academic discourse than as a resource understood and strategically deployed in relation to particular projects, contexts, and practices that both make pressing problems visible and offer the tools to expand the promises of a substantive democracy.[3]

At the same time, as film, particularly Hollywood film, becomes more commodified, ubiquitous. and increasingly abstracted from serious forms of critical analysis, it is all the more important to engage the varied film theoretical discourses produced by feminists, mass culture theorists, Marxists, and others. These approaches have performed an important theoretical service in enabling us to understand the aesthetic and political significance of film texts, on the one hand, and the specific industrial and economic formations that shape how they are produced and consumed, on the other.[4] But while academic film studies dramatically offset the commonplace assumption that films are either simply about entertainment or not worthy of serious academic analysis, such discourses have often become so narrow as to find no way to talk about film as a public pedagogy or to fully engage how film relates to public life. These discourses often treat film in a manner that is overly formalistic and pretentiously scientific, trapped in a jargon that freezes the worldly dimensions of film as a public transcript that links meanings to effects, forged amid the interconnecting registers of knowledge, desire, agency, and power. The refusal to fully engage film as a public medium that, as Gore Vidal points out, provides both a source of joy and knowledge, is all the more problematic, especially since film has become so prevalent in popular and global culture as a medium through which people communicate to each other.[5]

The potency and power of the movie industry can be seen in its powerful influence upon the popular imagination and public consciousness. Unlike ordinary consumer items, film produces images, ideas, and ideologies that shape both individual and national identities. The power of its reach and extent of its commodification can be seen as film references are used to sell t-shirts, cups, posters, bumper stickers, and a variety of kitsch. But at the same time, the growing popularity of film as a compelling mode of communication and form of public pedagogy—a visual technology that functions as a powerful teaching machine that intentionally tries to influence the production of meaning, subject positions, identities, and experience—suggests how important it has become as a site of cultural politics. Herman Gray captures this sentiment in arguing that "culture and the struggles over representation that take place there are not just substitutes for some 'real' politics that they inevitably replace or at best delay; they simply represent a different, but no less important site in the contemporary technological and postindustrial society where political struggles take place."[6]

As a form of public pedagogy, film combines entertainment and politics, and as I have attempted to argue, lays claim to public memory, though in contested ways given the existence of distinctly varied social and cultural formations. Yet films are more than "vehicles of public memory," mining the twin operations of desire and nostalgia; they are also sites of educated hopes and hypermediated experiences that connect the personal and the social by bridging the contradictory and overlapping relations between private discourses and public life. While films play an important role in placing particular ideologies and values into public conversation, they also provide a pedagogical space that opens up the "possibility of interpretation as intervention."[7] As public pedagogies, they make clear the need for forms of literacy that address the profoundly political and pedagogical ways in which knowledge is constructed and enters our lives in what Susan Bordo calls "an image saturated culture."[8] For critical educators, this might mean educating students to ethically and practically analyze how films function as social practices that influence their everyday lives and of positioning them within social, cultural, and institutional machineries of power; it also means considering how the historical and contemporary meanings produced by film align, reproduce, and interrupt broader sets of ideas, discourses, and social configurations at work in the larger society.[9]

How we think about film as a public pedagogy and form of cultural politics is all the more crucial to address as traditional, if not oppositional, public spheres such as religious institutions, schools, trade unions, and social clubs become handmaidens to neoliberal social agendas that turn such noncommodified public spheres into commercial spaces.[10] The decline of public life demands that we use film as a way of raising questions about issues that are increasingly silenced by the forces of the market, commercialization, and privatization. As the opportunities for civic education and public engagement begin to disappear, film may provide one of the few mediums left that enables conversations that connect politics, personal experiences, and public life to larger social issues.[11] Not only is film more of a pedagogical form compared to television and popular music, but film carries a kind of pedagogical weight that other mediums lack. Films allow their ideologies to play out pedagogically in a way that a three-minute pop song or a twenty-two-minute sitcom cannot do and, by doing so, offer a deeper pedagogical register for producing particular narratives, subject positions, and ideologies. In addition, young people inhabit a culture in which watching film demands a certain degree of attention, allowing them to enter into its discourse intertextually in a way that they cannot, or often refuse to do, with television programs and other electronic media. As a backdrop for a wide range of social practices, television, video games, and popular music are a kind of distracted media that do not offer the pedagogical possibilities that appear relatively unique to film's mobilization of a shared and public space.

Using films in my classes during the last decade, it became clear to me that film connects to students' experiences in ways that oscillate between its lure as entertainment and its provocation as a cultural practice. On one hand, many students, feeling powerless and insecure in a society marked by a cutthroat economy, increasing privatization, and a breakdown of all notions of public life, find a sense of relief and escape in the spectacle of film. On the other hand, many students see in the public issues addressed by film culture a connection to public life that revitalizes their sense of agency and resonates well with their sense of the importance of the cultural terrain as both an important source of knowledge and critical dialogue. At best, films offer my students an opportunity to connect the theoretical discourses we engage in classes with a range of social issues represented through the lens of Hollywood movies. Reading about youth seems more compelling when accompanied by a viewing of Spike Lee's film, *Sucker-Free City*. Theorizing masculinity in American society becomes more meaningful and concrete when taken up within a film such as *Fight Club*, especially since many students identify with the film and only after seeing and talking about it as part of a critical and shared dialogue do they begin to question critically their own investment in the film. Films no longer merely constitute another method of teaching, a view I held as a high school teacher. They now represent a new form of pedagogical text—one that does not simply reflect culture but actually constructs it—that signals the need for a radically different perspective on literacy and the relationship between film texts and society. The power and pervasiveness of films not only call into question their status as cultural products, but raise serious questions about how their use of spectorial pleasure and symbolic meaning work to put into play people's attitudes and orientation toward social others and the material circumstances of their own lives. The importance of film as a form of public pedagogy also raises questions about the educational force of the larger culture, and the recognition that to make knowledge meaningful in order also to make it critical and transformative, it is necessary to understand, engage, and make accountable those modes of learning that shape students' identities outside of the school. Of course, there is always the risk of using popular cultural forms such as films as a way of policing students' pleasures and, in doing so, undermining the sense of joy and entertainment that films provided. But, as Margaret Miles points out, it would be an ethical and pedagogical mistake to allow students to believe that films are merely about entertainment, or at the same time to suggest that the pleasure of entertainment is identical to the "learned pleasure of analysis."[12] Scrutinizing the pleasure of entertainment in films, James Snead suggests, "It never has been enough to just see a film—and now, more than ever, we need, not just to 'see,' but to 'see through' what we see on the screen."[13] Snead is not denying that students make important affective investments in film, but he wants educators to recognize that such investments often work well to connect people and power through mechanisms of identification and affect that effectively undermine the energies of critical engagement. Snead's comments suggest that students must think seriously about how films not only give meaning to their lives but also mobilize their desires in powerful ways. Seeing through films means, in this sense, developing the critical skills to engage how the ideological and affective work in combination to offer up particular ways of viewing the world that come to matter to individuals and groups. Films assume a major educational role in shaping the lives of many students, and bell hooks is right in claiming that the pedagogical importance of such films, both in terms of what they teach and the role that they can play as objects of pedagogical analysis, cannot be underestimated. hooks's comments about her own use of such films is quite instructive: "It has only been in the last ten years or so that I began to realize that my students learned more about race, sex and class from movies than from all the theoretical literature I was urging them to read. Movies not only provide a narrative for specific discourses of race, sex, and class, they provide a shared experience, a common starting point from which diverse audiences can dialogue about these charged issues."[14]

As a teaching form, film often puts into play issues that enter the realm of public discourse, debate, and policy-making in diverse and sometimes dramatic ways—whether we are talking about films that deal with racism, challenge homophobia, or address the themes of war, violence, masculinity, sexism, and poverty. Uniquely placed between the privatized realm of the home and other public spheres, film provides a distinct space in which a range of contradictory issues and meanings enter public discourse, sometimes in a subversive fashion, by addressing pressing and urgent issues in American society. As a space of translation, they also bridge the gap between private and public discourses, play an important role in putting particular ideologies and values into public conversation, and offer a pedagogical space for addressing how a society views itself and the public world of power, events, politics, and institutions.

Engaging movies as a form of public pedagogy in my recent work, I have not been particularly interested in defending film as an art form.[15] Aside from the residue of nostalgia and elitism that guides this position, it is a view that seems particularly out of date, if not irrelevant, given the important role that popular culture, including film, now plays pedagogically and politically in shaping the identities, values, and broader social practices that characterize an increasingly postmodern, electronic culture. Similarly, I have avoided addressing or taking up films within the disciplinary strictures of contemporary media and film studies that are designed, in part, to legitimate film as a serious academic subject. Thus, I have chosen not to position my particular approach to discussing film in relation to what is admittedly a vast literature of film theory and viewer response theories. Absent from my analysis is a sustained focus on those specialized film theories that engage films as either self-contained texts or largely focus on film through the narrow lens of specific theoretical approaches such as semiotics, Lacanian psychoanalysis, or feminist theories of pleasure. Film and media studies are bound up within a complex philosophical debate surrounding the meaning and importance of film theory. I have pointed to these traditions in my classes but have not addressed them with any depth because of the specialized nature of their focus. At the same time, I often provide students with resources to address such traditions in ways that do justice to the complexity of such work. While this work is enormously important, my aim pedagogically is much more modest. I try to address film more broadly as part of a public discourse, cultural pedagogy, and civic engagement that participates in a kind of ideological framing and works to structure everyday issues around particular assumptions, values, and social relations. I make no claims suggesting that there is a direct correlation between what people see, hear, and read and how they act, between the representations they are exposed to and the actual events that shape their lives. But I do argue that film as a form of civic engagement and public pedagogy creates a climate that helps to shape individual behavior and public attitudes in multiple ways, whether consciously or unconsciously.

The entertainment industry is America's second largest export—behind only military aircraft—and it is estimated that a successful film is seen by ten million people in theaters, and millions more when it is aired on cable, sold on DVDs, and exported to foreign markets.[16] Moreover, the film industry is controlled by a very limited number of corporations that exercise enormous power in all major facets of moviemaking, including production, distribution, and circulation in the United States and abroad.[17] At the same time, the media is not an unchanging, monolithic bastion of corporate culture and ruling-class power; a critical approach to media and film requires an understanding of film as neither monolithic nor its audiences as passive dupes. Films, like other media, work to gain consent and operate within limits set by the contexts in which they are taken up. Moreover, as numerous film scholars have indicated, audiences mediate such films rather than simply inhabit their structures of meaning. My own writing and teaching in which I use film to address a number of important social issues has been directed at educators, students, and others who want to explore film in their classes and other educational sites as part of an interdisciplinary project aimed at linking knowledge to broader social structures, learning to social change, and student experience to the vast array of cultural forms that increasingly shape their identities and values.

Rather than focus on film theory in my classes, I have been more concerned with what it means to situate films within a broader cultural context as well as to take up the political and pedagogical implications of films as teaching machines. Theory in this approach is used as a resource to study the complex and shifting relations between texts, discourses, everyday life, and structures of power. Rather than reduce analysis to an academic exercise rooted in a specific theoretical trajectory, I attempt to analyze films in ways that link texts to contexts, culture to the institutional specificity of power, pedagogy to the politics of representation, affective investments to the construction of particular notions of agency, and learning to public intervention. By taking up films intertextually, I attempt to foreground not just questions of meaning and interpretation, but also questions of politics, power, agency, and social transformation.

The ubiquity and importance of film as a mode of public pedagogy offer educators both an opportunity and a challenge to connect film as a cultural practice to broader public considerations, social relations, and institutional formations, as well as to important social issues. How films derive their meanings and how specific claims are made by different audiences on films must be addressed, not through the narrow lens of film theory or the somewhat limited lens of reception theory, but within an assemblage of other cultural texts, discourses, and institutional formations. Meaning should not be sutured into a text, closed off from the myriad contexts in which it is produced, circulated, and renegotiated. Nor should the priority of signification exist at the expense of engaging material relations of power. On the contrary, films become relevant as public pedagogies to the degree to which they are situated within a broader politics of representation, a politics that suggests that the struggle over meaning is, in part, defined as the struggle over culture, power, and politics. I have purposely avoided in my pedagogical practices focusing exclusively on films either as isolated texts or on what Doug Kellner refers to as narrow and one-sided ethnographic approaches to audience reception of texts.[18] These approaches are important, but they do not necessarily yield a productive way of dealing with films as a form of public pedagogy. Rather, they often fail to address questions of effects because they do not theorize the relationship of meaning to historical and institutional contexts, and, in doing so, largely ignore the material and power-saturated relations that structure daily life, which, in turn, provides the contexts that films both reflect and help to construct. Often missing from such analyses are the ways in which films are located along a circuit of power that connects the political economy and regulation of films with how they function as representational systems implicated in processes of identity formation and consumption.[19] The problem of movies is not that they can be understood in multiple ways, but that some meanings have a force that other meanings do not; that is, some meanings gain a certain legitimacy and become the defining terms of reality because of how well they resonate and align under certain conditions with broader discourses, dominant ideologies, and existing material relations of power. For instance, a brilliant documentary such as *Why We Fight,* which explores and dissects the rise of American militarism and imperialism throughout the world, viewed against the widespread influence of a rampant jingoism in which disagreement with government foreign policy is viewed as un-American has a good chance of being understood by the general public less as an historical analysis of American foreign policy than as an unpatriotic expression of dissent. Similarly, a film such as *Crash* might be viewed less as a commentary on the pervasive nature of systemic racism than as an expression of the diverse forms of prejudice that varied individuals harbor, thus echoing the popular perception that racism is a private issue rather than a public problem.

In my own approach to the pedagogy of cultural politics, I emphasize that I approach films as a serious object of social, political, and cultural analysis; moreover, as part of an attempt to read films politically, I make it clear that I bring a certain set of assumptions, experiences, and ideas to my engagement with films. But at the same time, I try to emphasize that, in doing so, I am not suggesting that my analyses make a claim to either certainty or finality. Not only do I encourage a critique of my own interpretations and analyses of film, but I also urge students to develop their own positions as part of a critique and engagement with varied positions, including my own, that develop amid class dialogue and in conjunction with outside readings and critical reviews. The pedagogical challenge in this instance is to make a convincing case, through the very process of auto critique and student engagement, that my analyses of films are necessarily partial, incomplete, and open to revision and contestation. Rather than closing down student participation, my own interpretations are meant to be strategic and positional, eschewing the notion that any type of closure is endemic to my perspectives on particular films, while at the same time using my own position to encourage students to think more critically about their own interpretations as they enter into dialogue about films. Critical analysis under such circumstances is not replaced or shut down, but expanded, by encouraging students to enter into dialogue with both the films and the interpretations that frame them, thus engaging the meaning, function, and role of film as a pedagogical, moral, and political practice that can only be understood within a range of theoretically constructed practices, relations, and frameworks. Addressing films within a framework that is both defined and problematized, I try to signal to students and others the pedagogical value of their taking a position while not standing still.

Films both shape and bear witness to the ethical and political dilemmas that animate the broader social landscape, and they often raise fundamental questions about how we can think about politics and political agency in light of such a recognition. Critique as both a form of self-analysis and a mode of social criticism is central to any notion of film analysis that takes seriously the project of understanding just how cultural politics matters in the everyday lives of people and what it might mean to make interventions that are both critical and transformative. Films can enable people to think more critically about how art can contribute to constructing public spaces that expand the possibilities for pleasure and political agency, democratic relations, and social justice. At the same time, film as a form of public pedagogy encourages students and others outside of the academy to examine critically not only how Hollywood films—in spite of their unquestioned fetishization of entertainment, spectacle, and glamor—want us to understand (or misunderstand) the wider culture, but also how they influence us to live our lives.

In every class that I teach, I use films that are widely accessible to the public and that deal with complex and provocative subject matter, highlighting a number of important social issues, problems, and values that provoke the public imaginary, and, in many cases, have generated substantial controversy. In addressing film as a form of cultural politics and an important mode of public pedagogy, progressive educators can engage the pedagogical and political practice of film in ways that render due account of the complexities of film culture itself. At the same time, such educators need to challenge a voyeuristic reception of films by offering students the theoretical resources necessary to engage critically how dominant practices of representation work to secure individual desires, organize specific forms of identification, and regulate particular modes of understanding, knowledge, and agency. Taking films seriously as a vehicle of public pedagogy means, in part, examining how their practices and values embody relations of power and ideological assumptions, admittedly in contradictory ways, that both mirror and construct the interests, fears, longings, and anxieties of the periods in which they were produced. Accordingly, this suggests developing pedagogical practices that promote political engagement, challenge conventional ways of thinking about film as simply entertainment, and using film as a cultural text to bridge the gap between the academic discourse of the classroom and those social issues and public concerns that animate the larger society.

As a young boy watching films in Providence, Rhode Island, I believed that movies provided only the diversion of entertainment. I had no idea that they also played an active role in shaping my sense of agency, offering me a moral and political education that largely went unnoticed and uncontested. Films have been a great source of joy throughout my lifetime. Now they not only provide pleasure, but also enable me to think more critically about how power operates within the realm of the cultural, and how social relations and identities are forged. All films disseminate ideologies, beckon in sometimes clear and often contradictory ways toward visions of the future, and encourage and stultify diverse ways of being in the world. But most important, film constitutes a powerful force for shaping public memory, hope, popular consciousness, and social agency, and, as such, invites people into a broader public conversation. As a horizon of "sensory experience and discursive contestation," films engender a public space in which knowledge and pleasure intersect—no small matter as public life becomes increasingly controlled and regulated, if not militarized.[20] It is in this promise of education and sensuality that films become other, gesturing toward public spheres, beyond those spaces offered by the presence of film, in which critical dialogue, pleasure, shared interaction, and public participation flourish. Film, in this instance, registers a public dialogue and set of experiences that offer the opportunity to revitalize those democratic public spheres in which the popular intersects with the pedagogical and the political in ways that suggest film cannot be dismissed simply as a commodity, but instead becomes crucial to expanding democratic relations, ideologies, and identities.

Notes

1. Hannah Arendt, "What is Freedom?" *Between Past and Future: Eight Exercises in Political Thought* (1961; New York: Penguin, 1977), 149.
2. Lawrence Grossberg, *Bringing It All Back Home: Essays on Cultural Studies* (Durham, NC: Duke University Press, 1997), 143.
3. Lawrence Grossberg, "The Cultural Studies' Crossroad Blues," *European Journal of Cultural Studies* 1, no. 1 (1998): 65–82.
4. For a representative example of film studies scholarship, see Toby Miller and Robert Stam, eds., *A Companion to Film Theory* (Malden, MA: Basil: Blackwell, 2003); Joanne Hollows, Peter Hutchings, and Mark Jancovich, eds., *The Film Studies Reader* (New York: Oxford University Press, 2000); Christine Gledhill and Linda Williams, eds., *Reinventing Film Studies* (New York: Oxford University Press, 2000); Richard Dyer, E. Ann Kaplan, Paul Willemen, John Hill, eds. *Film Studies: Critical Approaches* (New York: Oxford University Press, 2000); Gilberto Perez, *The Material Ghost* (Baltimore: Johns Hopkins University Press, 1998); Noell Carroll, *Mystifying Movies* (New York: Columbia University Press, 1988); and Norman K. Denzin, *The Cinematic Society* (Thousand Oaks, CA: Sage, 1995). Though not focused on cinema, Durham and Kellner provide a very useful book in which to understand film within the larger body of theoretical work produced around media and cultural studies; see Meenakshi Gigi Durham and Douglas M. Kellner, eds., *Media and Cultural Studies: Key Works* (Malden, MA: Basil Blackwell, 2001).
5. Gore Vidal, *Screening History* (Cambridge, MA: Harvard University Press, 1992).
6. Herman Gray, *Watching Race: Television and the Struggle for "Blackness"* (Minneapolis: University of Minnesota Press, 1995), 6.
7. Homi Bhabha cited in Gary Olson and Lynn Worsham, "Staging the Politics of Difference: Homi Bhabha's Critical Literacy," *JAC: Journal of Advanced Composition* 18, no. 3 (1999): 29.
8. Susan Bordo, *Twilight Zones: The Hidden Life of Cultural Images from Plato to O.J.* (Stanford: University of California Press, 1997), 2.
9. Gray, *Watching Race*, 132.
10. See Mike Hill and Warren Montag, eds., *Masses, Classes and the Public Sphere* (London: Verso Press, 2000).
11. See Henry A. Giroux, *Public Spaces/Private Lives: Beyond the Culture of Cynicism* (Lanham, MD: Rowman and Littlefield, 2001).
12. Margaret Miles, *Seeing and Believing: Religion and Values in the Movies* (Boston: Beacon Press, 1996), 14.
13. James Snead, *White Screens/Black Images* (New York: Routledge, 1994), 131.
14. bell hooks, *Reel to Real: Race, Sex, and Class in the Movies* (New York: Routledge, 1996), 2.
15. See Henry A. Giroux, *Fugitive Cultures: Race, Violence & Youth* (New York: Routledge: 1996), *Channel Surfing: Racism, the Media, and the Destruction of Today's Youth* (New York: St. Martin's Griffin, 1997), *Stealing Innocence: Corporate Culture's War Against Youth* (New York: Palgrave, 2000).
16. Edward Asner, "Foreword," in *The Political Companion to American Film*, ed. Gary Crowus (Chicago: Lakeview Press, 1994), ix.
17. See Robert W. McChesney, *Rich Media, Poor Democracy: Communication Politics in Dubious Times* (New York: The New Press, 2000).

18. Douglas Kellner, *Media Culture* (New York: Routledge, 1995), 199.

19. I am drawing here from the "circuit of culture" paradigm that has been developed by Stuart Hall and others in the Culture, Media, and Identities series published by Sage. For example, see *Representation: Cultural Representations and Signifying Practices*, ed. Stuart Hall (Thousand Oaks, CA: Sage, 1997).

20. Mariam Bratu Hansen, "*Schindler's List* is Not *Shoah*: The Second Commandment, Popular Modernism, and Public Memory," *Critical Inquiry* 22 (Winter 1996): 312; see Giroux, *Public Spaces/Private Lives*.

9

NYMPHET FANTASIES

CHILD BEAUTY PAGEANTS AND THE POLITICS OF INNOCENCE

Only in a climate of denial could hysteria over satanic rituals at daycare centers coexist with a failure to grasp the full extent of child abuse. (More than 8.5 million women and men are survivors). Only in a culture that represses the evidence of the senses could child pageantry grow into a $5 billion dollar industry without anyone noticing. Only in a nation of promiscuous puritans could it be a good career move to equip a six-year-old with bedroom eyes.
—Richard Goldstein, *Village Voice*

The Disappearing Child and the Politics of Innocence

The notion of the disappearing child and the myth of childhood innocence often mirror and support each other. Within the myth of innocence, children are often portrayed as inhabiting a world that is untainted, magical, and utterly protected from the harshness of adult life. In this scenario, innocence not only erases the complexities of childhood and the range of experiences different children encounter, but it also offers an excuse for adults to evade responsibility for how children are firmly connected to and shaped by the social and cultural institutions run largely by adults. Innocence in this instance makes children invisible except as projections of adult fantasies—fantasies that allow adults to believe that children do not suffer from their greed, recklessness, perversions of will and spirit and that adults are, in the final analysis, unaccountable for their actions.[1]

If innocence provides the moral ethos that distinguishes children from adults, the discourse that deals with the disappearance of childhood in our culture signals that it is being threatened by forces that tend to collapse that distinction. For example, in cultural critic Neil Postman's thoroughly modernist view of the world, the electronic media, especially television, present a threat to the existence of children and the civilized culture bequeathed to the West by the Enlightenment.[2] Not only does the very character of television—its fast-paced format, sound-bite worldview, information overload, and narrative organization—undermine the very possibility for children to engage in critical thinking, but its content works to expel images of the child from its programming by both "adultifying" the child and promoting the rise of the "childfied" adult.[3] But Postman is quick to extend his thesis to other spheres, noting, for example, the disappearance of children's clothing and children's games, the entry of children into professional sports, and the increasing willingness of the criminal justice system to treat children as miniature adults. Postman's lament represents less a concern with preserving childhood innocence than a cry for the passing of a world in which popular culture threatens high culture, and the culture of print loses its hold on a restricted and dominant notion of literacy and citizenship education. The loss of childhood innocence in this scenario marks the passing of a historical and political time in which children could be contained and socialized under the watchful tutelage of such dominant regulatory institutions as the family, school, and church.

Many politicians eager to establish themselves as protectors of childhood innocence also have appropriated the spectre of the child as an endangered species. In their rush to implement new social and economic policies, numerous politicians hold up children as both the inspiration for and prime beneficiaries of their reforms. Lacking opportunities to vote, mobilize, or register their opinions, young children become an easy target and referent in discussions of moral uplift and social legitimation. They also become pawns and victims. Far from benefiting children, many of the programs and government reforms enacted in the late 1990s by Clinton and the Republican-led Congress represent what connection Senator Edward Kennedy (D-MA) has called children "legislative child abuse."[4] Of course, the Bush administration has practically waged a war on all programs designed to benefit young people and children. Protecting the innocence of children appears to have a direct connection with the disappearing child, although not in the sense predicted by the late Neil Postman. The draconian cuts in welfare reform enacted in the 1996 Personal Responsibility and Work Opportunity Reconciliation Act are having a devastating effect on a great number of poor families and their children. While welfare roles have declined since 1996, a report released by the National Conference of State Legislatures indicated that 40 to 60 percent of the poor people who leave welfare obtain employment but often at below-poverty-level wages. Moreover, assistance has been terminated for substantial numbers of children with disabilities. Meanwhile, thousands of families are losing welfare aid because of penalties for noncompliance with new welfare reform rules, and many of those who lose benefits do not find work. Harsh compliance measures, inadequate child care, marginal employment, low wages, and lack of adequate transportation for poor families all combine to make a mockery of welfare reform.[5] In this instance, children are indeed disappearing—right into the hole of poverty, suffering, and despair.[6] In short, the language of innocence suggests a concern for all children but often ignores or disparages the conditions under which many of them are forced to live, especially those who are generally excluded because of race or class from the privileging and protective invocation of innocence.

Politicians have little interest in the welfare of kids who are poor and nonwhite. In view of this fact, innocence emerges less as a term used to highlight the disappearance of kids than as a metaphor for advancing a conservative political agenda based on so-called family values, in which middle-class white children are viewed as more valued and deserving of the material resources and cultural goods of the larger society than are poor and nonwhite children.[7] In this selective appropriation, innocence turns with a vengeance on its humanitarian impulse: the everyday experience of childhood is held hostage to the realities of power and the disingenuous rhetoric of political pragmatism.

As the rhetoric of child welfare heats up in the public consciousness, innocence is increasingly being redeployed by politicians, journalists, and media pundits to rearticulate which specific children are deserving of entitlements and adult protection and what forces pose a threat to them. Imbued with political and ideological values, innocence as used by the popular press is not merely selective about which children are endangered and need to be protected; it also is used to signal who and what constitute a threat to children.

As politicians, the popular press, and the media increasingly use "the child" as a moral yardstick it becomes more difficult for adults to fail to take responsibility for what they do to kids. Consequently, childhood innocence appears both threatened and threatening. According to popular wisdom, the enemies of children are not to be found in the halls of Congress, in the poisonous advertisements that commodify and sexualize young children, or even in the endless media bashing that blames children for all of society's ills.[8] On the contrary, the child molesters, pedophiles, abductors, and others who prey on children in the most obscene ways imaginable are the biggest threat to children. Here the notion of childhood innocence does more than produce the rhetoric of political opportunism; it also provides the basis for moral panic. Both conservatives and liberals have fed off the frenzy of fear associated with a decade of revelations of alleged child abuse. Starting with the 1987 McMartin preschool case, a wave of fear-inspired legislation has swept the nation to protect children from pedophiles, child molesters, predatory priests and teachers, and anyone else who might be labeled as a sexual deviant who poses a threat to the innocence of children.[9] Child abuse in this scenario is reduced to the individual pathology of the molester and pedophile; the fear and anger it arouses are so great that the Supreme Court is willing to suspend certain constitutional liberties in order to keep sexual predators locked up even after they finish serving their sentences.[10]

But the issue of widespread child abuse has done more than inspire a national fear of child molesters. It points beyond the language of individual pathology to the more threatening issue of how society treats its children, exposing the degree to which children have not been provided with the security and resources necessary to insure their safety and well-being. While the most disturbing threat to innocence may be child abuse, this form of abuse cannot be assessed only through the horrible behavior of sexual predators. Such abuse needs to be situated within a broader set of political, economic, and social considerations; such considerations probe deeply into the cultural formations that not only make children visible markers of humanity and public responsibility but also see them as a menacing enemy or as merely a market to be exploited. The social investment in children's innocence may be at the center of political rhetoric in the halls of Congress, but other forces in American society aggressively breed a hatred and disregard for young people, especially those who are excluded because of their class, race, gender, or status as non-U.S. citizens.

Here I argue that the central threat to childhood innocence lies not in the figure of the pedophile or sexual predator but in the diminishing public spheres available for children to experience themselves as critical agents. Children must be able to develop their capacities for individual and social development free from the debilitating burdens of hunger, poor healthcare, and dilapidated schools, while simultaneously being provided with fundamental social services such as state protection from abusive parents. As cities become increasingly ghettoized because of the ravaging effects of deindustrialization, loss of revenue, and white flight, children are left with fewer educational, social, and economic services to fulfill their needs and desires. As public schools are abandoned or surrendered to the dictates of the market, children increasingly find themselves isolated and removed from the discourses of community and compassion. As the state is hollowed out and only its most brutal apparatuses—police, prisons, etc.—remain intact, children have fewer opportunities to protect themselves from an adult world that offers them dwindling resources, dead-end jobs, and diminished hopes for the future.[11] At the same time, children are increasingly subjected to social and economic forces that exploit them through the dynamics of sexualization, commodification, and commercialization.[12]

JonBenet Ramsey, Race, and the Perils of Home

While the concept of innocence may incite adults to publicly proclaim their support for future generations, more often than not it protects adults from the reality of society and the negative influence they have in contributing to the ever-increasing impoverishment of children's lives. Of course, flash points in a society often signal that children are in danger and that certain elements in the culture pose a threat to their innocence. Conservatives, for example, have focused on the dangers presented by rap music, cinematic violence, and drugs to launch an attack on Hollywood films, the fashion world, single teen moms, and what it calls the cultural elite. But rarely do conservative and liberal critics focus on the ongoing threats to children at the center of dominant economic, political, and cultural relations—the dismantling of welfare benefits for poor children, particularly cuts in health insurance, food stamps, and housing allowances; the growing assault on young black males through an ever-expanding criminal justice system, and the increasing demonization of young teens in the media.

Poverty, racism, sexism, and the dismantling of the welfare state do great harm to children, but the press does not report most of the stories exemplifying the effects of these social conditions; if it does, little public discussion or self-examination follows.

One recent exception can be found in the case of JonBenet Ramsey, the six-year-old who was found strangled in her wealthy Boulder, Colorado, home the day after Christmas in 1996. Throughout the first half of 1997, the press fixated on the case. Major media networks, newspapers, and tabloids besieged the public with photographs and television footage of JonBenet, dubbed the slain little beauty queen, posing coquettishly in a tight dress, wearing bright red lipstick, her hair bleached blond. The case revealed once again that the media gravitate toward victims that fit the dominant culture's image of itself. Not only are children who are white, blond, and middle-class invested with more humanity; they become emblematic of a social order that banishes from consciousness any recognition of abused children who "don't fit the image of purity defiled."[13]

Consider the case of a nine-year-old African American child, labeled in the press Girl X. Girl X was raped, beaten, blinded, murdered, and dumped in a stairwell in the rundown Cabrini Green Housing Project in Chicago. The brutal murder aroused a great deal of publicity in Chicago but was virtually ignored by the national media. Race and poverty relegated Girl X to a nonentity. Innocence is applied primarily to children who are white and middle-class, often tucked away in urban townhouses and the safe sanctuaries of segregated suburban America. But there is something equally disturbing about the JonBenet Ramsey case. Innocence also masks the sexualization and commodification of young girls who are taught to identify themselves through the pleasures and desires of the adult gaze. The child becomes the principal incitement of adult desire, but the educational and commercial practices at work remain unexamined because they take place within acceptable cultural forms such as children's beauty pageants. This murder also challenges the assumption that privileged families are immune to accusations of child abuse or neglect. The death of the young beauty queen raises serious questions about the cultural practices and institutions of everyday life that shape children's lives, often in ways that undermine children's chances of entering adulthood free from violence, intimidation, and abuse.

I argue that by critically examining the beauty pageant we can begin to see how the language of innocence obscures from the public's view the appropriation, sexualization, and commercialization of children bodies. In pursuing this argument, I examine how the culture of child beauty pageants functions as a site where young girls learn about pleasure, desire, and the roles they might assume in an adult society. I also examine how such pageants are rationalized; how they are upheld by commercial and ideological structures within the broader society; and how they are reproduced, reinforced, and sustained in related spheres such as advertising and fashion photography—spheres that also play an important role in marketing children as objects of pleasure, desire, and sexuality. Here I attempt to challenge the concept of such rituals as innocent, to reconsider the role they play as part of a broader cultural practice in which children are reified and objectified. This is not meant to suggest that all child beauty pageants constitute a form of child abuse. Pageants vary both in the way they are constructed and in how they interact with local and national audiences. Moreover, their outcomes are variable and contingent. But beauty pageants, as sites of representation, identity formation, consumption, and regulation, have to be understood in terms of how they articulate and resonate with other cultural sites engaged in the production and regulation of youth, the packaging of desire, and the sexualized body.

Beauty Pageants and the Shock of the Real

The Ramsey case challenges and disrupts ideological conventions that typically apply to narratives of childhood innocence. The blitz of media coverage following the brutal murder of six-year-old JonBenet Ramsey gives evidence to that fact. On one level, JonBenet's case attracted national attention because it fed into the frenzy and moral panic Americans are experiencing over the threat of child abuse—fueled by horrific crimes like the kidnap and murder of Polly Klaas in California. Similarly, it resonated with the highly charged public campaigns of various legislators and citizen groups calling for the death penalty for sex offenders such as Jesse Timmendequas, the child molester who killed seven-year-old Megan Kanka. On another level, it opened to public scrutiny another high-profile example of a child succeeding at the make-believe game of becoming an adult. Not unlike Jessica Dubroff, the seven-year-old would-be Amelia Earhart who, while attempting to be the youngest pilot to cross the United States, died in a plane crash, JonBenet Ramsey also projected the uncanny ability to present herself as an adult. But if the boundary between innocence and impurity, child and adult, became blurred in both cases, JonBenet's notoriety as an object of public fascination revealed a dark and seamy element in American culture.

Night after night the major television networks aired videotapes of little JonBenet Ramsey in a tight, off-the-shoulder dress, bright red lipstick, and teased, bleached blond hair pulling a feathered Mardi Gras mask coyly across her eyes as she sashayed down a runway. Playing the role of an alluring sex kitten, JonBenet seemed to belie the assumption that the voyeuristic fascination with the sexualized child was confined to the margins of society, inhabited largely by freaks and psychopaths.

The JonBenet Ramsey case revealed not only how regressive notions of femininity and beauty are redeployed in this conservative era to fashion the fragile identities of young girls but also how easily adults will project their own fantasies onto children, even if it means selling them on the beauty block. The JonBenet case offered the public a spectacle in which it became both a voyeur and a witness to its own refusal to address the broader conditions that contribute to the sexualization and commercialization of kids in the culture at large. The general public has come to recognize that child abuse often takes place at home and that the conventional image of the molester as an outsider is less than credible thanks to the recent attention given to child abuse by celebrities such as Roseanne Barr and Oprah Winfrey. The view of the home as a safe space for children also became questionable, as it became clear that the Ramseys imposed their own strange fantasies on their daughter and in doing so denied her an identity suitable for a six-year-old. Instead, they positioned her within a child beauty pageant culture that stripped her of her innocence by blurring the boundary between child and adult. Not allowed to be a child, JonBenet was given the unfortunate job of projecting herself through a degrading aesthetic that sexualized and commodified her. Collapsing the (hardly clear-cut) boundaries between the protective parental gaze and the more objectifying adult gaze, JonBenet's parents appear to have stripped their daughter of any sense of agency, independence, or autonomy in order to remake her in the image of their own desires and pleasures. Parental "care" in this case appears to have been wielded tyrannically to prevent JonBenet from experiencing childhood pleasures and needs outside the gaze of pleasure-seeking, narcissistic adults.

Images of six-year-olds cosmetically transformed into sultry, Lolita-like waifs are difficult to watch. They strike at the heart of a culture deeply disturbed in its alleged respect for children and decency. Whereas the blame for the often-violent consequences associated with this eroticized costuming is usually placed on young women, it is hard to blame JonBenet Ramsey for this type of objectification. The public's usual attacks on kids, suggesting that they are responsible for society's ills, breaks down in this case as it becomes more difficult for adults to evade responsibility for what they do to children—their own and others.[14] JonBenet's image violently transgresses a sacred responsibility associated with protecting the innocence of children. Writ large across the media coverage of the JonBenet case was the disturbing implication and recognition that childhood innocence is tarnished when children can no longer expect "protection . . . consistency and some sort of dignity" from adults.[15]

The JonBenet Ramsey case prompted an unusual debate in the media and national press. Lacking the theoretical tools or political will to analyze the institutional and ideological forces in the culture that generate such disregard for children, the media focused on what was often termed "the strange subculture of child beauty pageants." More often than not it suggested that the abuse children suffered in such pageants was due to overbearing mothers trying to control their daughters' lives. It seems that if young girls are unavailable for scapegoating, their mothers will suffice. Rarely did the media raise the larger issue of how young girls are being educated to function within such a limited sphere of cultural life or how such a regressive education for young girls is more often the norm rather than the exception.

The traditional moral guardians of children's culture who would censor rap lyrics, remove "dangerous" videos and CDs from public circulation, boycott Disney for pro-gay and lesbian labor practices, and empty school libraries of many classic texts have had little to say about the sexualization of young children in children's beauty pageants, a social form as American as apple pie. Nor are they willing to acknowledge that such pageants must be considered within a broader set of practices which increasingly includes youth sport events that appeal to middle- and upper-class parents who seem willing to sacrifice their children's welfare to the imperatives of success and celebrity. Amid the silence of conservatives and the family values crowd, liberal and progressive reporters have begun to raise some important questions. For example, CBS anchorman Dan Rather criticized the television networks for running the JonBenet tapes, claiming that they amounted to nothing less than kiddy porn. Columnist Frank Rich wrote a courageous piece in the *New York Times* in which he argued that the "strange world of kids' pageantry is not a 'subculture'—it's our culture. But as long as we call it a subculture, it can remain a problem for somebody else."[16] Reporter Richard Goldstein followed up Rich's insights with a three-part series in *The Village Voice* in which he argued that the marketing of the sexual child has a long history in the United States and that the JonBenet case "brings to the surface both our horror at how effectively a child can be constructed as a sexual being and our guilt at the pleasure we take in such a sight."[17] For Goldstein, the JonBenet case challenges the American public to confront the actual nature of child abuse, which is all too often a part of family life and is further legitimated by a culture willing to capitalize on children as the new arena for the production of pleasure and commercial exploitation.

All of these critiques raise valid concerns about the role of child beauty pageants and how they produce particular notions of beauty, pleasure, and femininity that are as culturally gender-specific as they are degrading. Such criticisms also prompt a debate about the nature of adult needs and desires that push kids into pageants, and how such pageants correspond with other social practices that "silently" reproduce roles for children that undermine the notion of child innocence and reinforce particular forms of child abuse. In what follows, I examine these issues in detail by focusing on the scope and popularity of children's beauty pageants, what they attempt to teach young girls, and the broader commercial forces that sustain them. I also locate the phenomenon of child beauty pageants within a broader, related set of cultural practices, especially the world of high-fashion advertising and the rise of the teenage model.

Beauty and the Beast: A Genealogy of Child Beauty Pageants

Frank Rich is on target in arguing that child beauty pageants represent more than a subculture in American society. Ted Cohen, president of World Pageants Inc., which publishes an international directory of pageants, estimates that the pageantry industry represents a billion-dollar-a-year industry, with sponsors such as Procter and Gamble, Black Velvet, and Hawaiian Tropics.[18] An estimated 3,000 pageants a year are held in the United States in which more than 100,000 children under the age of twelve compete.[19] In some cases, girls as young as eight months are entered in pageants. California, Florida, and New York hold the most pageants, and the number of pageants in the United States appears to be growing, despite the fact that many contests, especially at the national level, charge entrants between $250 and $800.[20] Most contestants who enter local pageants are from working-class families driven by mobility fantasies and the lure of a small cash prize. The larger and more expensive pageants appear to be dominated by middle- and upper-class parents like the Ramseys, who have lots of money and resources to spend on costly voice and dance lessons, pageant coaches, expensive costumes, and entry fees.[21]

Pageants are a lucrative business. Promoters market prurient pleasure and rake in big dividends, with some making as much as $100,000 on each event. In addition, child beauty pageants have produced a number of support industries, including costume designers, grooming consultants, interview coaches, photographers, and publishers,[22] not to mention the cosmetics, weight reduction, and other "beauty-aid industries." Trade magazines such as *Pageant Life*, which has a circulation of 60,000, offer their readers images and advertisements celebrating ideals of femininity, glamour, and beauty while marketing young girls in the image of adult drives and desires. In some cases, parents invest big money for makeup artists, hairstylists, and coaches to teach prepubescent kids particular "pro-am modeling styles and tornado spins."[23] A story that appeared in *Life* magazine in 1994 featuring Blaire, an eleven-year-old seasoned beauty pageant performer, documented this trend. Blaire's fortunes at winning got better when her mom and dad hired Tony, a voice coach and makeup artist, who charges $40 an hour, to completely redesign her. When Blaire father was asked why he was so involved with entering Blaire in child beauty pageants, he answered: "I am a plastic surgeon only from the neck up. I enjoy the beauty of the face. No doubt that's why I am so involved with Blaire." The article reports that "Bruce is captivated by his daughter's beauty but prefers it enhanced: He apologizes to strangers when she is not wearing makeup. Some parents have accused Bruce of enhancing Blaire's looks with surgery." Blaire indicates that she loves pageants; they are all she is interested in. The article ends by pointing out that Blaire lacks a child's spontaneity and then conjectures that she "shows so little offstage emotion because she's so busy editing herself with adults."[24]

Blaire's case may appear to some a caricature of pageant life, narrowly depicting parents who push their kids too hard and who impose their own interests and desires on children too young to decide whether they actually want to participate in the pageants. But the popular literature is replete with such stories. Many parents involved in these pageants do not seem concerned about the possible negative consequences of dressing their children in provocative clothing, capping their teeth, putting fake eyelashes on them, and having them perform before audiences in a manner that suggests a sexuality well beyond their years.

The popular literature that supports the child beauty pageant culture fails to acknowledge that "sexualized images of little girls may have dangerous implications in a world where 450,000 American children were reported as victims of sexual abuse in 1993."[25] Trade magazines such as *Pageant Life* and *Babette's Pageant and Talent Gazette* are filled with ads in which toddlers strike suggestive poses. Full-page spreads of contest finalists depict contestants ranging in age from two to twenty-four years. All of the entrants are defined by the same aesthetic: the makeup, pose, smile, and hairstyles of the six-year-olds are no different from those of the young women. Within the beauty pageant aesthetic, the line between children and adults is blurred; all of the images depict the cool estrangement of sexual allure that has become a trademark of the commodities industry. In addition, the magazines are full of ads hawking outfits from companies called, for example, "Hollywood Babe" and "Little Starlet Fashions"—with many ads invoking the warning "Don't Be Left Behind."[26] One even gushes that contestants may enter a particular pageant for the fee of only $1.00 per pound. Success stories for the younger-age set (four- to eight-year-olds) consistently focus on the thrill of competition, on winning titles, and on the successful modeling careers of the pageant winners.

Parents and pageant sponsors often respond to public criticisms by arguing that the press overreacted to JonBenet Ramsey's death by unfairly focusing on beauty pageants as somehow being implicated in her murder. Others legitimate the child beauty pageant culture as a route to get their kids into lucrative careers such as modeling or to win college scholarships, financial awards, and other prizes. The most frequently used rationale for defending pageants is that they build self-esteem in children, "help them to overcome shyness, and [teach them how] to grow up."[27] One pageant director in Murrieta, California, refuted the criticism that pageants are detrimental for young girls, arguing that "many young girls look at pageants as a protracted game of dress up, something most young girls love."[28] Pam Griffin, another pageant proponent, whose daughter trained JonBenet Ramsey, remarked that "more girls are trying pageants after seeing how much fun JonBenet had."[29] Even *Vogue* reporter Ellen Mark concluded that most kids who participate in beauty pageants end up as success stories. The reason for their success, according to Mark, is that "pageants made them feel special . . . Little girls like to look pretty."[30]

This argument, in appropriating the ideology of liberal feminism, emphasizes that girls gain affirming self-direction, autonomy, and a strong competitive spirit through their participation in pageants. But such critiques often fail to recognize that self-esteem is actually being defined within a very narrow standard of autonomy, one that is impervious to how gender is continually made and remade within a politics of appearance that is often reduced to the level of a degrading spectacle. Self-esteem in this context means embracing rather than critically challenging a gender code that rewards little girls for their looks, submissiveness, and sex appeal. Coupled with the ways in which the broader culture, through television, music, magazines, and advertising, consistently bombards young girls with a sexualized ideal of femininity "from which all threatening elements have been purged,"[31] self-esteem often becomes a euphemism for self-hatred, rigid gender roles, and powerlessness.

There is a certain irony in appropriating the language of self-esteem to defend child beauty pageants, especially since the pageants provide young children with standards of beauty that 1 of 40,000 young women will actually meet. Must we ask what is wrong with young girls wanting to become fashion models who increasingly look as if they will never grow up (e.g., Kate Moss), and for whom beauty is not only defined by the male gaze but appears to be one of the few requisites to enter "into the privileged male world."[32] Cultural critic Naomi Wolf is right in arguing that the problem with linking standardized notions of sexualized beauty to self-esteem is that it does not present young girls or adult women with many choices. This is especially true when issues regarding sexual pleasure and self-determination are held hostage to notions of femininity in which it becomes difficult for women to move beyond such infantilized representations in order to express themselves in ways that are empowering.[33] Moreover, on the other side of the cheap glamorization of the waif-child as the fashion icon of beauty is the reality of a patriarchal society in which the nymphet fantasy reveals a "system by which men impose their authority on women and children alike."[34]

In short, rarely do the defenders of child beauty pageants address the consequences of stealing away a child's innocence by portraying her as a sexualized nymphet. Once again, they have little to say about what children are actually learning in pageants, how a child might see herself and mediate her relationship to society when her sense of self-worth is defined largely through a notion of beauty that is one-dimensional and demeaning. Nor do parents and other pageant participators seem to question the wisdom of allowing children to be sponsored by corporations. The message that often informs such relations is that the identities of the young girls who enter the pageants become meaningful only when tied to the logic of the market. What a young girl learns is that "in order to enter [the] contest she must represent someone other than herself."[35]

Unlike contests that took place ten or fifteen years ago, pageants, especially the national ones, now offer bigger prizes and are backed by corporate sponsors. Moreover, as the commercial interests and level of investment have risen, so have their competitive nature, hype, and glitz. V. J. LaCour, publisher of *Pageant Life Magazine* and a firm supporter of child beauty pageants, thinks that many parents have resorted to makeup and other "extreme" measures because "the parents are trying to get a competitive edge."[36] In some cases, parents resort to mentally punitive and physically cruel practices to get their kids to perform "properly." Lois Miller, owner of the Star Talent Management in Allentown, Pennsylvania, reports that she has "seen parents who have pinched their children for messing up their dress or not looking appropriate or not wiggling enough or not throwing kisses."[37] Parents often respond to such criticisms by claiming that their kids are doing exactly what they want to do and that they enjoy being in the pageants. This argument is strained when parents enter children as young as eight months into pageants, or when parents decide, as reported in *Money* magazine, that their four-year-old child needed a talent agent to make the "right connections" outside of the beauty pageants.

Sixty Minutes, the television program highly acclaimed for its investigative reporting, aired a segment on child beauty pageants on May 18, 1997, in the aftermath of the JonBenet Ramsey controversy. The premise of the program, announced by commentator Morley Safer, was to explore whether "child beauty pageants exploit children to satisfy ambitions of parents." To provide a historical perspective on such pageants, *60 Minutes* aired cuts from child beauty pageants that had been seen on the program in 1977 and then presented videotaped shots of JonBenet and other children performing in a recent pageant. The contrast was both obscene and informative. The children in the 1977 pageants wore little-girl dresses and ribbons in their hair; they embodied a childlike innocence as they displayed their little-girl talents—singing, tap, and baton twirling. Not so with the more recent pageant shots. The contestants did not look like little girls but rather like coquettish young women whose talents were reduced to an ability to move suggestively across the stage. Clearly, as Morley Safer indicated, "By today's beauty pageant standards, innocence seems to have vanished." When he asked one of the stage mothers who had appeared in the 1977 program what she thought of today's pageants, she responded that she recently went to a child beauty "walked in the door and walked out. It was disgusting to see the beaded dresses and blown-up hair on kids." The program's take on child beauty pageants was critical, yet it failed to consider the broader social practices, representations, and relations of power that provide the context for such pageants to flourish in the United States. Nor did it analyze the growing popularity of the pageants as part of a growing backlash against feminism reproduced in the media, culture, and fashion industries as well as in a growing number of conservative economic and political establishments.[38] Morely Safer was, however, clear about the assumption that the root of such abuse toward children was to be placed squarely on the shoulders of overly ambitious and exploitative parents.

The feminist backlash has not stopped more informed criticisms from emerging. For example, some child psychologists argue that the intense competition at pageants compounded with the nomadic lifestyle of traveling from one hotel to another when school is not in session make it difficult for young children to make friends, putting them at risk for developing problems in social interactions with other children. Other child specialists argue that it is as developmentally inappropriate to "teach a six-year-old to pose like a twenty-year-old model as it is to allow her to drive [and] drink alcohol."[39] Of course, there is also the stress of competition and the danger of undermining a child's self-confidence, especially when she loses, if the message she receives is that how she looks is the most important aspect of who she is. Psychologist David Elkind argues that parents used to be concerned with the ethical behavior of kids. A decade ago, when kids got home from school, their parents asked them if they were good. Now, because of the new economic realities of downsizing and deindustrialization, parents are fearful that their kids will be losers.[40] Parents, too often, now focus on how well their kids are competing. Journalist Marly Harris writes that the "massive restructuring of the economy creates a winner-take-all society in which parents believe that if kids don't end up as one of the few winners they will join the ranks of the many losers."[41] Thus the question kids get when they come home in the 1990s is no longer "Have you been good?" but "Did you win?" The message here is did you get the highest grades? Harris also believes that the money spent on child pageants by parents, up to $10,000 per child a year in some cases, could be invested in more productive ways, say in savings plans to help them finance the cost of a college education. But the attributes that are accentuated when defining their identities and self-esteem in pageants offer them limited opportunities to develop and express themselves.[42]

In spite of such criticisms, child beauty pageants are enormously popular in the United States, and their popularity is growing. Moreover, they have their defenders.[43] In part, such popularity can be explained, as I mentioned previously, by their potential to make money for promoters, but there is more to the story. Children's beauty contests also represent places where the rituals of small-town America combine with the ideology of mass consumer culture. Pageants with titles such as "Miss Catfish Queen," "Miss Baby Poultry Princess," and "The Snake Charmer Queen Ritual Competition" suggest that such rituals are easily adapted to "local meanings and familiar symbols, values, and aesthetics—those relevant to the producers, performers, and consumers of the contest."[44] Such rituals are easy to put on; are advertised as a legitimate form of family entertainment; resonate powerfully with dominant Western models of femininity, beauty, and culture; and play a crucial role at local and national levels of reproducing particular notions of citizenship and national identity. Child beauty pageants are often embraced as simply good, clean entertainment and defended for their civic value to the community. Moreover, while adult beauty contests, such as the annual Miss America pageant, have been the target of enormous amounts of feminist criticism,[45] few academics and cultural critics have focused on child beauty pageants as a serious object of cultural analysis.[46]

Beyond the Politics of Child Abuse

Any attempt to challenge the sexist practices and abuses at work in children's beauty pageants must begin with the recognition that pageants represent more than trivial entertainment. Educational theorist Valerie Walkerdine argued that forms of popular culture such as the beauty pageant offer a way for working-class girls to escape the limiting discourses and ideologies found in schools and other institutions. Popular culture becomes a realm of fantasy offering the promise of escape, possibility, and personal triumph. Desire in this instance gains expression through an endless parade of highly sexualized images and narratives that not only provide the promise of erotic fantasies that "belong to them" but also constitute for these young girls an important strategy for survival.[47] According to Walkerdine, popular cultural forms such as child beauty pageants occupy a reputable public space in which preadolescent working-class girls are offered forms of identification they can appropriate as survival practices in a society stacked against them. But what Walkerdine ignores is that such fantasies often are founded on forms of identification and hope that offer nothing more than the swindle of fulfillment, providing limited choices and options to young girls. Moreover, while such strategies cannot be dismissed as politically incorrect but must be considered within a broader understanding of how desire is both mediated and acted upon, the social costs for such identifications go far beyond the benefits they provide as a buffer against hard times. In the long run, such investments serve to limit, often exploit, and disrupt working-class lives. At the same time, the emergence of cultural forms such as the child beauty pageant makes clear the degree to which viable public spheres are diminishing for children. As public funding decreases, support services dry up, and extracurricular activities are eliminated from schools because of financial shortages, society contains very few noncommercial public spaces for young people to identify with and experience. As market relations expand their control over public space, corporations increasingly provide the public spheres for children to experience themselves as consuming subjects and commodities with limited opportunities to learn how to develop their full range of intellectual and emotional capacities to be critical citizens.

While many progressives are well aware that the struggle over culture is tantamount to the struggle over meaning and identity, it is also important to recognize that any viable cultural politics also must locate specific cultural texts within wider relations of power that shape everyday life. Understood within a broader set of relations, child beauty pageants become an important object of critical analysis for a number of reasons. First, the conservative and rigid gender roles that are legitimated at many child beauty pageants must be analyzed both in terms of the specific ideologies they construct for children and how these ideologies find expression in other parts of the culture. What I want to suggest is that the values and dominant motifs that shape beauty pageants gain their meaning and appeal precisely because they find expression in related cultural spheres throughout American society. For instance, by examining advertising campaigns such as those produced by Calvin Klein or the increasing use of advertising that depicts the ideal modern American female as young, extremely thin, sexually alluring, and available, it becomes clear that the processes at work in the objectification of young children are not altogether different from the social relations that take place in other sites. All of these sites use the bodies and body parts of young girls to market desire and sell goods. What often makes such connections untenable in the public eye is that beauty pageants appropriate innocence as a trope for doing what is best for children, often in the name of dominant family values. And yet, it is precisely in the name of innocence that practices that might be seen in other contexts as abusive to children are defined within the dominant culture as simply good, clean, family entertainment.

In advertisements for Calvin Klein's Obsession perfume and in his well-known jeans ads, innocence becomes a fractured sign and is used unapologetically to present children as the objects of desire and adults as voyeurs. Innocence in this instance feeds into enticing images of childlike purity as it simultaneously sexualizes and markets such images. Sexualizing children may be the final frontier in the fashion world, exemplified by the rise of models such as Kate Moss who represent the ideal woman as a waif—sticklike, expressionless, blank-eyed, and more recently snorting cocaine.[48] Or the media culture simply makes celebrities out of teenage models such as Ivanka Trump, who in their waning teen years are left wondering if they are too old to have a career in those culture industries that reduce a woman's talents to elusive and shortlived standards of desire, sexuality, and beauty. What connects the beauty pageants to the world of advertising and fashion modeling is that young girls are being taught to become little women, while women are being taught to assume the identities of powerless, childlike waifs. In this instance, Lolita grows up only to retreat into her youth as a model for what it means to be a woman.[49] Here innocence reveals a dark quality; not only are youth being assaulted across a variety of public spaces but their identities, especially those of young women, are being appropriated in different ways in diverse public sites for the high pleasure quotient they evoke in satisfying adult desires and needs.

As an ethical referent, innocence humanizes children and makes a claim on adults to provide them with security and protection. But innocence gains its meaning from a complex set of semiotic, material, and social registers. And what is happening to children in many cultural spheres as seemingly unrelated as child beauty pageants and the world of advertising and fashion modeling suggests how vulnerable children actually are to learning the worst social dimensions of our society: misogyny, sexism, racism, and violence. Innocence needs to be understood as a metaphor that is open to diverse uses and whose effects can be both positive and devastating for children. If innocence is to become a useful category for social analysis, the term must be understood politically and ethically only through the ways in which it is represented and used within everyday life, shaped by language, representations, and the technologies of power. Central to analyzing a politics of innocence is the need to address why, how, and under what conditions the marketing of children's bodies increasingly permeates diverse elements of society. Likewise, educators and others must uncover not only the political and ideological interests and relations of power at work in the construction of innocence but also the actual ways in which cultural practices are deployed to influence how children and adults learn about themselves and their relationships to others.

Innocence becomes both a mystifying ideology and a vehicle for commercial profit. In the first instance, innocence is a highly charged term that points to pedophiles and sexual perverts as the most visible threats to children in our society. Such a restricted notion of innocence fails to understand how child abuse connects to and works its way through the most seemingly benign of cultural spheres such as the beauty pageant. Thus beauty pageants are not only ignored as serious objects of social analysis but are dismissed as simply a subculture. Here innocence protects a particular notion of family values that is class-specific and racially coded. In a society in which working-class youth and youth of color are represented as a threat and menace to public order, innocence becomes an ideological trope defined through its contrast with children who are constructed as "other." Innocence as ideological trope reinforces a politics of innocence that legitimates the cultural capital of children who are largely white, middle-class, and privileged. Moreover, the discourse of innocence provides little understanding of how the conditions under which children learn in specific places resonate and gain legitimacy through their connection to other cultural sites.

In the second instance, innocence falls prey to the logic of the market and the successful teaching operations of consumerism. The myth of innocence is increasingly appropriated through a glitzy aesthetic in which children provide the sexualized bait that creates images and representations that tread close to the border of pornography. In this scenario, children's sense of play and their social development are transformed through marketing strategies and forms of consumer education that define the limits of their imaginations, identities, and sense of possibility while simultaneously providing through the media a "kind of entertainment that subtly influence[s] the way we see [children], ourselves, and our communities."[50]

Concerned educators, parents, and activists must begin to challenge and counter such images, ideologies, and social practices as part of a cultural politics that makes issues of teaching and power central to its project. This means taking seriously how beauty pageants and other popular cultural sites teach children to think of themselves through the representations, values, and languages offered to them.[51] It also means expanding our understanding of how education is played out on the bodies of young children in pageants and how this practice resonates with what children are taught in other cultural spheres. Schools and other educational sites must treat popular culture as a serious area of analysis. This suggests teaching kids and adults how to read popular culture critically. It also means teaching them how to be cultural producers capable of using new technologies to create texts that honor and critically engage their traditions and experiences. In strategic terms, students must be offered texts, resources, and strategies that provide a complex range of subject positions that they can address, inhabit, mediate, and experiment with. Students and adults also should be taught how to organize social movements at the local and national levels to pressure and boycott companies that engage in abusive practices toward children. Underlying this merging of the political and the educational is the overt political goal of "enabling people to act more strategically in ways that may change their context for the better"[52] and the educational goal of finding ways for diverse the better groups of children and adults to work together to transform popular public spheres into sites that address social problems by way of democratic, rather than merely market, considerations.[53]

In short, the socialization of children must be addressed within a larger discussion about citizenship and democracy, one that resists what philosopher Theodor Adorno calls the "obscene merger of aesthetics and reality."[54] What Adorno means here is precisely the refutation of those ideologies and social practices that attempt to subordinate, if not eliminate, forms of identity fundamental to public life, to an economy of bodies and pleasures that is all surface and spectacle. Such a discussion not only calls into question the conditions under which kids learn, what they learn, and how this knowledge shapes their identities and behavior; it also raises questions about the material and institutional relations of power that are fundamental for maintaining the integrity of public life—a condition that is essential for all children to learn in order to be critical participants in the shaping of their lives and the larger social order. Child abuse comes in many forms, and it has become a disturbing feature of American society. The current assault being waged on children through retrograde policy, the dismantling of the welfare state, and the pervasive glut of images that cast them as the principal incitements to adult desire suggest that democracy is in the throes of a major crisis. If democracy is to carry us forward into the next century, surely it will be based on a commitment to improving the lives of children, but not within the degrading logic of a market that treats their bodies as commodities and their futures as trade-offs for capital accumulation. On the contrary, critical educators and other progressives need to create a cultural vision and a set of strategies informed by "the rhetoric of political, civic, and economic citizenship."[55] The challenge to take up that commitment has never been so strained nor so urgent.

Notes

1. Marina Warner, *Six Myths of Our Time* (New York: Vintage, 1995), esp. chap. 30. Of course, the concept of childhood innocence as a historical invention has been pointed out by a number of theorists. See, for example, Philip Aries, *Centuries of Childhood* (Harmondsworth: Penguin, 1979); Lloyd deMause, ed., *The Evolution of Childhood* (New York: Psychohistory Press, 1974).

2. Neil Postman, *The Disappearance of Childhood* (New York:Vintage, 1994).

3. See ibid., esp. chap. 8. The notion that television and popular culture represent the main threat to childhood innocence is central to the conservative call for censorship, limiting sex education in the schools, restricting AIDS education, redefining the home as the most important source of moral education, and the "Gumping" of American history (in which the 1960s often are seen as the source of the country's current social ills). The quintessential expression of this position can be found in the speeches, press releases, and writings of former secretary of education and "drug czar" William Bennett. It also can be found in legislation supported by groups such as the Christian Coalition, especially the Parental Rights and Responsibilities Act of 1995. Examples of the conservative position on child abuse, the loss of innocence, and the "poisonous" effects of popular culture abound in the popular press. See, for example, Jeff Stryker, "The Age of Innocence Isn't What It Once Was," *New York Times*, July 13, 1997, E3.

4. Cited in Peter Edelman, "The Worst Thing Bill Clinton Has Done," *The Atlantic Monthly* 279 (March 1997), 45.

5. All of these figures are taken from two articles on the Children's Defense Fund web site (www.childrensdefense.org/): "The New Welfare Law: One Year Later," October 14, 1997, 1–5, and "CDF, New Studies Look at Status of former Welfare Recipients," May 27, 1998, 1–4. See also Jennifer Wolch, "American's New Urban Policy: Welfare Reform and the Fate of American Cities," *Journal of American Planning Association* 54:N1 (Winter 1998), 8–11.

6. For specific statistics on the state of youth in the United States, see Children's Defense Fund, *The State of America's Children Yearbook 1998* (Boston: Beacon Press, 1998); Ruth Sidel, *Keeping Women and Children Last* (New York: Penguin, 1996).

7. For an analysis of the ideological underpinnings of the right-wing family values crusade, see Judith Stacey, *In the Name of the Family: Rethinking Family Values in the Postmodern Age* (Boston: Beacon Press, 1996).

8. For an analysis of the widespread assault currently being waged against children, see: Henry A. Giroux, *Channel Surfing: Race Talk and the Destruction of Today's Youth* (New York: St. Martin's Press, 1997); Mike A. Males, *The Scapegoat Generation: America's War on Adolescents* (Monroe, Me.: Common Courage Press, 1996); Charles R. Acland, *Youth, Murder, Spectacle: The Cultural Politics of "Youth in Crisis"* (Boulder, CO: Westview Press, 1995); Holly Sklar, "Young and Guilty by Sterotype," *Z Magazine* (July–August 1993): 52–61; Deena Weinstein, "Expendable Youth: The Rise and Fall of Youth Culture," in Jonathan S. Epstein, ed., *Adolescents and Their Music* (New York: Garland, 1994), 67–83; and various articles in *Microphone Fiends*, ed. Andrew Ross and Tricia Rose (New York: Routledge, 1994); Lawrence Grossberg, *We Gotta Get Outta Here* (New York: Routledge, 1992).

9. For a brilliant analysis of how the image of the sexual predator is used to preclude from public discussion the wide range of social factors at work in causing child abuse, see James R. Kincaid, *Child-Loving: The Erotic Child and Victorian Culture* (New York: Routledge, 1992).

10. For an analylsis of the Supreme Court's decision, see Linda Greenhouse, "Likely Repeaters May Stay Confined," *New York Times*, June 24, 1997, A19.

11. The concept of the hollow state comes from Stanley Aronowitz, *The Death and Birth of American Radicalism* (New York: Routledge, 1996).

12. The literature on advertising and the marketing of children's desires is too extensive to cite, but one of the best examples is Stephen Kline, *Out of the Garden: Toys, TV, and Children's Culture in the Age of Marketing* (London: Verso Press, 1993).

13. Richard Goldstein, "The Girl in the Fun Bubble: The Mystery of JonBenet," *Village Voice*, June 10, 1997, 41.

14. For a sustained treatment of the current assault on kids, especially those who are poor, nonwhite, and urban, see Henry A. Giroux, *Fugitive Cultures* (New York: Routledge, 1996). See also Angela McRobbie, *Postmodernism and Popular Culture* (New York: Routledge, 1994).

15. Annie Gottlieb, "First Person Sexual," *The Nation*, June 9, 1997, 26.

16. Frank Rich, "Let Me Entertain you," *New York Times*, January 12, 1997, Section 1, 23.

17. Goldstein, "The Girl in the Fun Bubble," 41.

18. Cited in Karen de Witt, "All Dolled Up," *New York Times*, January 12, 1997, D4.

19. While the statistics on children's beauty pageants vary, a number of sources cite similar figures to the ones I cite here. See, for example, Rich, "Let Me Entertain You"; Ellen Mark, "Pretty Babies," *Vogue*, June 1997, 240; Beverly Stoeltje, "The Snake Charmer Queen Ritual Competition and Signification in American Festival," in Colleen Ballerino, Richard Wild, and Beverly Stoeltje, eds., *Beauty Queens* (New York: Routledge, 1996), 13.

20. Cited in Pat Jordan, "The Curious Childhood of an Eleven-Year-Old," *Life*, April 1994, 38.

21. In the wake of JonBenet's death, a sharp decline in the popularity of child beauty pageants has resulted in a rise in entry fees. Fees that were once $200 are now $500, thus weeding out all but the most wealthy contestants. See Alex Kuczynski, "Tough Times on the Children's Pageant Circuit," *New York Times*, September 13, 1998, Section 9, 1, 8.

22. Mark, "Pretty Babies," 240.

23. Linda Caillouet echoes a point made by many academics and journalists across the country: "Pageants have changed over the past 30 years. Grade-schoolers are wearing makeup, modeling swim wear and sashaying down runways. Today's little girls' parents often invest big money in coaches to teach the children the pro-am modeling style and tornado spins. They pay for makeup artists and hair stylists to accompany the children to pageants. Some of the kids use tanning beds. Seven-year-olds have reportedly worn false teeth, false eyelashes, and colored contact lenses." Cited in Linda Caillouet, "Slaying Has Child Pageants on Defensive," *Arkansas Democrat-Gazette*, April 14, 1997, 1A.

24. Jordan, "Curious Childhood," 62, 68.

25. Michael F. Jacobson and Laurie Ann Mazur, *Marketing Madness* (Boulder, Colo.: Westview, 1995), 79.

26. Cited in ad for "Debbrah's: Nation's Top Pageant Designers," *Pageant Life*, Winter 1996, 26.

27. Elliot Zaren, "Eyebrows Life at Child Strutting in Sexy Dresses, Markup," *Tampa Tribune*, January 14, 1997, 4.

28. Cited in Jodi Duckett, "In the Eyes of the Beholder: Child Beauty Pageants Get Mixed Reviews," *Morning Call*, April 6, 1997, E1.

29. Ibid.

30. Mark, "Pretty Babies," 283.

31. Susan Bordo, *Unbearable Weight: Feminism, Western Culture, and the Body* (Berkeley: University of California Press, 1993), 162.

32. Ibid., 179.

33. Naomi Wolf, *The Beauty Myth* (New York: Anchor Books, 1992).

34. Richard Goldstein, "Nymph Mania: Honoring Innocence in the Breach," *Village Voice*, June 17, 1997, 71. This is not to suggest that women and children do not mediate and resist such domination as much as to make clear the determinate relations of power that lie behind the resurrection of the nymphet in the culture.

35. Stoeltje, "The Snake Charmer," 23.

36. Cited in Caillouet, "Slaying Has Child Pageant on Defensive," 1A.

37. Cited in Duckett, "In the Eyes," E1.

38. See, for example, Susan Faludi, *Backlash: The Undeclared War Against American Women* (New York: Anchor Books, 1991).

39. This paragraph relies heavily on comments by pediatric psychologists cited in Rebecca A. Eder, Ann Digirolamo, and Suzanne Thompson, "Is Winning a Pageant Worth a Lost Childhood?" *St. Louis Post-Dispatch*, February 24, 1997, 7B.

40. David Elkind, "The Family in the Postmodern World," *National Forum* 75, Summer 1995, 24–28.

41. Marly Harris, "Trophy Kids," *Money Magazine*, March 1997, 102.

42. As Annette Corrigan points out, "Young girls should have the freedom to explore the unlimited possibilities of their humanity and to be valued, as men are, for much more than how they look or their capacity to stimulate desire in the opposite sex." Annette Corrigan, "Fashion, Beauty, and Feminism," *Meanjin* 51: 1 (1992), 108.

43. For an academic defense of beauty pageants as simply an acting out of community standards, see Michael T. Marsden, "Two Northwestern Ohio Beauty Pageants: A Study in Middle America's Cultural Rituals," in Ray B. Browne and Michael T. Marsden, eds., *The Cultures of Celebration* (Bowling Green, Ohio: Bowling Green State University Press, 1994), 171–180. Marsden is so intent in seeing pageants as ritualistic performances that he does not notice how ideological his own commentary is when focusing on some of the most sexist aspects of the pageant practices. Hence, for Marsden, bathing suit competitions simply prove that "beauty can be art." For a more complex analysis see Robert H. Lavender, " 'It's Not a Beauty Pageant' Hybrid Ideology in Minnesota Community Queen Pageants," in *Beauty Queens*, 31–46. See also Susan Orlean's insipid defense of child beauty pageants as public rituals that offer mothers pride when their daughters win and provide pageant contestants the comfort of a family "in which everyone knows each other and watches out for each other." Susan Orlean, "Beautiful Girls," *The New Yorker*, August 4, 1997, 29–36.

44. Stoeltje, "The Snake Charmer Queen Ritual Competition," 13.

45. For an important analysis of the different critical approaches to beauty and the politics of appearance that feminists have taken since the appearance of the first Miss America pageant in 1968, see Corrigan, "Fashion, Beauty, and Feminism," 107–22. What is so interesting about this piece is that nothing is said about child beauty pageants. This is especially relevant since many of the conceptual approaches dealing with the politics of appearance simply do not apply to six-year-olds. For instance, the notion that beauty can be appropriated as an act of resistance and turned against the dominant culture seems a bit far-fetched when talking about children who can barely read.

46. One exception can be found in the collection of the essays in Cohen et al., eds, *Beauty Queens*.

47. Valerie Walkerdine, *Daddy's Girl: Young Girls and Popular Culture* (Cambridge, Mass: Harvard University Press, 1997), 166.

48. While I have not developed in this chapter the implications such depictions have for women, many feminists have provided some excellent analysis. See especially Bordo, *Unbearable*. For a shameful defense of thinness as an aesthetic in the fashion industry, see Rebecca Johnson, "The Body," *Vogue*, September 1997, 653–58. Johnson goes a long way to legitimate some of the most misogynist aspects of the beauty industry, but really reaches into the bottom of the barrel in claiming resentment is the primary reason that many women criticize the image of waiflike models permeating the media. Claiming that thinness is only an aesthetic and not a morality, Johnson seems to forget that within the dominant invocation of thinness as a standard of beauty is the suggestion that overweight women are slovenly, older women are ugly, and nonwhite women are not as beautiful as the ever-present blond waifs who populate the media.

49. The classic work on this issue is Mary Pipher, *Reviving Ophelia: Saving the Selves of Adolescent Girls* (New York: Ballantine Books, 1994). See also Nicole Peradotto, "Little

Women: A New Generation of Girls Growing Up Before Their Time," *Buffalo News*, January 26, 1997, 1F.

50. Cohen et al., eds., Introduction to *Beauty Queens*, 10.

51. For a critical analysis of how young girls are represented in popular culture and what is learned by them, see Walkerdine, *Daddy's Girl;* see also McRobbie, *Postmodernism and Popular Culture.*

52. Lawrence Grossberg, "Toward a Genealogy of the State of Cultural Studies," in Cary Nelson and Dilip Parameshwar Gaonkar, eds., *Disciplinarity and Dissent in Cultural Studies* (New York: Routledge, 1996), 143.

53. This suggests that adults not only take responsibility for how children's identities are constructed within oppressive social relations but also that such adults support those youth such as Free Children, a youth group consisting of kids between ten and sixteen years of age who are organizing at the national and international level to "to help children being abused and exploited, but to also empower young people to believe in themselves and to believe that they can play an active role as citizens of this world," Craig Kielburger, "Children Can Be Active Citizens of the World," *Rethinking Schools,* Summer 1997, 19.

54. Adorno cited in Geoffrey Hartman, "Public Memory and Its Discontents," *Raritan* 8:4 (Spring 1994), 27.

55. Stanley Aronowitz, "A Different Perspective on Inequality," in Henry A. Giroux and Patrick Shannon, eds., *Education and Cultural* (New York: Routledge, 1998), 193.

PART IV
RACE, SURVEILLANCE, AND SOCIAL JUSTICE

10

RACIAL POLITICS, INDIVIDUALISM, AND THE COLLAPSE OF THE SOCIAL

Race relations in the United States have changed considerably since W.E.B. Du Bois famously predicted in *The Souls of Black Folks* that "the problem of the 20th century is the problem of the color line."[1] This is not to suggest that race has declined in significance, or that the racial conditions, ideologies, and practices that provided the context for Du Bois's prophecy have been overcome; rather the point is that they have been transformed, mutated, recycled, and have taken on new and, in many instances, more covert modes of expression.[2] Du Bois recognized that the color line was not fixed—its forms of expression changed over time, as a response to different contexts and struggles—and that one of the great challenges facing future generations would be not only to engage the complex structural legacy of race, but also to take note of the plethora of forms in which it was expressed and experienced in everyday life. For Du Bois, race fused power and ideology, and was deeply woven into both the public pedagogy of American culture and its geography, economics, politics, and institutions.

The great challenge Du Bois presents to this generation of students, educators, and citizens is to acknowledge that the future of democracy in the United States is inextricably linked "to the outcomes of racial politics and policies, as they develop both in various national societies and the world at large."[3] In part, this observation implies that how we experience democracy in the future will depend on how we name, think about, experience, and transform the interrelated modalities of race, racism, and social justice. It also suggests that the meaning of race and the challenges of racism change for each generation, and that the new challenges we face demand a new language for understanding how the symbolic power of race as a pedagogical force as well as a structural and materialist practice redefines the relationship between the self and the other, the private and the public. It is the changing political and ped-alogical practices of race relations, in particular, that need to be more fully addressed if racism is not to be reduced to an utterly privatized discourse that erases any trace of racial injustice by denying the very notion of the social and the operations of power through which racial politics are organized and legitimated.

When Du Bois wrote *The Souls of Black Folk*, racism was a visible and endemic part of the American political, cultural, and economic landscape. The racial divide was impossible to ignore, irrespective of one's politics. As we move into the new millennium, the politics of the color line and representations of race have become far more subtle and complicated than they were in the Jim Crow era, when Du Bois made his famous pronouncement. And though far from invisible, the complicated nature of race relations in American society no longer appears to be marked by the spectre of Jim Crow. A majority of Americans now believe that antiblack racism is a thing of the past, since it is assumed that formal institutions of segregation no longer exist. Yet, surveys done by the National Opinion Research Center at the University of Chicago have consistently found "that most Americans still believe blacks are less intelligent than whites, lazier than whites, and more likely than whites to prefer living on welfare over being self-supporting."[4] Contradictions aside, conservatives and liberals alike now view America's racial hierarchy as an unfortunate historical fact that now has no bearing on contemporary society. Pointing to the destruction of the Southern caste system, the problematizing of whiteness as a racial category, the passing of civil rights laws, a number of successful lawsuits alleging racial discrimination against companies such as Texaco and Denny's, and the emergence of people of color into all aspects of public life, the color line now seems in disarray, a remnant of another era that Americans have fortunately moved beyond. Bestselling books such as Dinesh D'Souza's *The End of Racism*, Jim Sleeper's *Liberal Racism*, and Stephan and Abigail Thernstrom's *America in Black and White: One Nation, Indivisible* all proclaim racism as an obsolete ideology and practice.[5] And a large number of white Americans seem to agree. In fact, poll after poll reveals that a majority of white Americans believe that people of color no longer face racial discrimination in American life. For example, a recent Gallup survey on "Black-White Relations" observes that "7 out of 10 whites believe that blacks are treated equally in their communities. . . . Eight in ten whites say blacks receive equal educational opportunities, and 83% say blacks receive equal housing opportunities in their communities. Only a third of whites believe blacks face racial bias from police in their areas."[6] For many conservative and liberal intellectuals, the only remaining remnant of racist categorization and policy in an otherwise color-blind society is affirmative action, which, ironically, is alleged to provide blacks with an unfair advantage in higher education, the labor force, entitlement programs, and "even summer scholarship programs."[7]

The importance of race and the enduring fact of racism are relegated to the dustbin of history at a time in American life when the discourses of race and the spectacle of racial representations saturate the dominant media and public life. The color line is now mined for exotic commodities that can be sold to white youth in the form of rap music, hip-hop clothing, and sports gear. African American celebrities such as Michael Jordan, Etta James, 50 Cent and George Foreman are used to give market legitimacy to everything from gas grills to high-end luxury cars to clothes. Black public intellectuals such as Patricia Williams, Cornel West, Michael Dyson, and Henry Louis Gates, Jr., command the attention of the *New York Times* and other eye-catching media. African Americans now occupy powerful positions on the Supreme Court and in the highest levels of political life. The alleged collapse, if not transformation, of the color line can also be seen in the emergence of the black elite, prominently on display in television sitcoms, fashion magazines, Hollywood movies, and music videos. On the political scene, however, the supposedly race-transcendent public policy is complicated by ongoing public debates over affirmative action, welfare, crime, and the prison-industrial complex, all of which suggests that whereas the color line has been modified and dismantled in certain places, race and racial hierarchies still exercise a profound influence on how most people in the United States experience their daily lives.[8] Popular sentiment aside, race—rather than disappearing—has retained its power as a key signifier in structuring all aspects of American life. As Michael Omi keenly observes: "Despite legal guarantees of formal equality and access, race continues to be a fundamental organizing principle of individual identity and collective action. I would argue that, far from declining in significance (as William Julius Wilson would have us believe), the racial dimensions of politics and culture have proliferated."[9]

Representations of race and difference are everywhere in American society, and yet racism as both a symbol and condition of American life is either ignored or relegated to an utterly privatized discourse, typified in references to individual prejudices or to psychological dispositions such as expressions of "hate." As politics becomes more racialized, the discourse about race becomes more privatized. While the realities of race permeate public life, they are engaged less as discourses and sites where differences are produced within iniquitous relations of power than as either unobjectionable cultural signifiers or desirable commodities. The public morality of the marketplace works its magic in widening the gap between political control and economic power while simultaneously reducing political agency to the act of consuming. One result is a growing cynicism and powerlessness among the general population as the political impotence of public institutions is reinforced through the disparaging of any reference to ethics, equity, justice, or any other normative referent that prioritizes democratic values over market considerations. Similarly, as corporate power undermines all notions of the public good and increasingly privatizes public space, it obliterates those public spheres in which there might emerge criticism that acknowledges the tensions wrought by a pervasive racism that "functions as one of the deep, abiding currents in everyday life, in both the simplest and the most complex interactions of whites and blacks."[10] Indifference and cynicism breed contempt and resentment as racial hierarchies now collapse into power-evasive strategies such as blaming minorities of class and color for not working hard enough, for refusing to exercise individual initiative, or for practicing reverse racism. In short, marketplace ideologies now work to erase the social from the language of public life so as to reduce all racial problems to private issues such as individual character and cultural depravity.

Black public intellectuals such as Shelby Steele and John McWhorter garner national attention persuading the American people that the subject and object of racism have been reversed. For Steele, racism has nothing to do with soaring black unemployment, struggling and segregated schools for black children, a criminal justice system that resembles the old plantation system of the South, or police brutality that takes its toll largely on blacks in urban cities such as Cincinnati and New York. On the contrary, according to Steele, racism has produced white guilt, a burden that white people have to carry as part of the legacy of the Civil Rights movement. To remove this burden from white shoulders, blacks now have to free themselves from their victim status and act responsibly by proving to whites that *their* suffering is unnecessary.[11] They can do so through the spirit of principled entrepreneurialism— allowing themselves to be judged on the basis of hard work, individual effort, a secure family life, decent values, and property ownership.[12] It gets worse. John McWhorter, largely relying on anecdotes from his own limited experience in the academy at UCLA-Berkeley argues that higher education is filled with African American students who are either mediocre or simply lazy, victims of affirmative action programs that coddle them because of their race while allowing them to "dumb down" rather than work as competitively as their white classmates. The lesson here is that the color line now benefits blacks not whites, and, in the end, for McWhorter, diversity rather than bigotry is the enemy of a quality education and functions largely to "condemn black students to mediocrity."[13]

Within this discourse, there is a glimmer of a new kind of racial reference, one that can only imagine public issues as private concerns. This is a racism that refuses to "translate private sufferings into public issues," a racism that works hard to remove issues of power and equity from broader social concerns.[14] Ultimately, it imagines human agency as simply a matter of individualized choices, the only obstacle to effective citizenship and agency being the lack of principled self-help and moral responsibility. Racism, in this view, is only intelligible in the discourse of American individualism. In what follows, I want to examine briefly the changing nature of the new racism by analyzing how some of its central assumptions evade notions of race, racial justice, equity, and democracy altogether. In the process, I analyze some elements of the new racism, particularly the discourse of color-blindness and neoliberal racism. I then address the ways in which the controversial Trent Lott affair demonstrated neoliberal racism as well as the racism of denial. I will conclude by offering some suggestions about how the new racism, particularly its neoliberal version, can be addressed as both a pedagogical and political issue.

Neoliberalism and the Culture of Privatization

The public morality of American life and social policy regarding matters of racial justice are increasingly subject to a politics of denial. Denial in this case is not merely about the failure of public memory or the refusal to know, but an active ongoing attempt on the part of many conservatives, liberals, and politicians to rewrite the discourse of race so as to deny its valence as a force for discrimination and exclusion either by translating it as a threat to American culture or relegating it to the language of the private sphere. The idea of race and the conditions of racism have real political effects, and eliding them only makes those effects harder to recognize. And yet, the urgency to recognize how language is used to name, organize, order, and categorize matters of race not only has academic value, it also provides a location from which to engage difference and the relationship between the self and the other and between the public and private. In addition, the language of race is important because it strongly affects political and policy agendas as well. One only has to think about the effects of Charles Murray's book *Losing Ground* on American welfare policies in the 1980s.[15] But language is more than a mode of communication or a symbolic practice that produces real effects; it is also a site of contestation and struggle. Since the mid-1970s, race relations have undergone a significant shift and acquired a new character as the forces of neoliberalism have begun to shape how Americans understand the notions of agency, identity, freedom, and politics itself.[16]

Part of this shift has to be understood within the emerging forces of transnational capitalism and a global restructuring in which the economy is separated from politics and corporate power is largely removed from the control of nation-states. Within the neoliberal register, globalization "represents the triumph of the economy over politics and culture . . . and the hegemony of capital over all other domains of life."[17] Under neoliberal globalization, capital removes itself from any viable form of state regulation, power is uncoupled from matters of ethics and social responsibility, and market freedoms replace long-standing social contracts that once provided a safety net for the poor, the elderly, workers, and the middle class. The result is that public issues and social concerns increasingly give way to a growing culture of insecurity and fear regarding the most basic issues of individual livelihood, safety, and survival. Increasingly, a concern with either the past or the future is replaced by uncertainty, and traditional human bonds rooted in compassion, justice, and a respect for others are now replaced by a revitalized social Darwinism, played out nightly in the celebration of reality-based television, in which rabid self-interest becomes the organizing principle for a winner-take-all society. As insecurity and fear grip public consciousness, society is no longer identified through its allegiance to democratic values but through a troubling freedom rooted in a disturbing emphasis on individualism and competitiveness as the only normative measures to distinguish between what actions are right or wrong, just or unjust, proper or improper action. Zygmunt Bauman captures this deracinated notion of freedom and the insecurity it promotes in his observation that

> Society no longer guarantees, or even promises, a collective remedy for individual misfortunes. Individuals have been offered (or, rather, have been cast into) freedom of unprecedented proportions—but at the price of similarly unprecedented insecurity. And when there is insecurity, little time is left for caring for values that hover above the level of daily concerns—or, for that matter, for whatever lasts longer than the fleeting moment.[18]

Within this emerging neoliberal ethic, success is attributed to thriftiness and entrepreneurial genius while those who do not succeed are viewed as either failures or utterly expendable. Indeed, neoliberalism's attachment to individualism, markets, and antistatism ranks human needs as less important than property rights and subordinates "the art of politics . . . to the science of economics."[19] Racial justice in the age of market-based freedoms and financially driven values loses its ethical imperative to a neoliberalism that embraces commercial rather than civic values, private rather than public interests, and financial incentives rather than ethical concerns. Neoliberalism negates both racism as an ethical issue and democratic values as a basis for citizen-based action. Of course, neoliberalism takes many forms as it moves across the globe. In the United States, it has achieved a surprising degree of success but is increasingly being resisted by labor unions, students, and environmentalists. Major protests against economic policies promoted by the World Bank, International Monetary Fund, and World Trade Organization have taken place in Seattle, Prague, New York, Montreal, Genoa, and other cities around the world. In the United States, a rising generation of students is protesting trade agreements like GATT and NAFTA as well as sweat-shop labor practices at home and abroad and the corporatization of public and higher education. In Latin America, counties such as Argentina, Venezuela, and Brazil are rejecting the neoliberal model for governing their markets and social order. Unfortunately, antiracist theorists have not said enough about either the link between the new racism and neoliberalism, on the one hand, or the rise of a race-based carceral state, on the other. Neither the rise of the new racism nor any viable politics of an antiracist movement can be understood outside of the power and grip of neoliberalism in the United States. Hence, at the risk of oversimplification and repetition, I want to be a bit more specific about neoliberalism's central assumptions and how it frames some of the more prominent emerging racial discourses and practices.

Neoliberalism and the Politics of the New Racism

Under the reign of neoliberalism in the United States, society is largely defined through the privileging of market relations, deregulation, privatization, and consumerism. Central to neoliberalism is the assumption that profit-making be construed as the essence of democracy and consuming as the most cherished act of public participation. Strictly aligning freedom with a narrow notion of individual interest, neoliberalism works hard to privatize all aspects of the public good and simultaneously narrow the role of the state to both a gatekeeper for capital and a policing force for maintaining social order and racial control. Unrestricted by social legislation or government regulation, market relations as they define the economy are viewed as a paradigm for democracy itself. Central to neoliberal philosophy is the claim that the development of all aspects of society should be left to the wisdom of the market. Similarly, neoliberal warriors argue that democratic values should be subordinated to economic considerations, social issues be translated as private dilemmas, part-time labor replace full-time work, the trade unions be weakened, and everybody be treated as a customer. Within this market-driven perspective, the exchange of capital takes precedence over social justice, the making of socially responsible citizens, and the building of democratic communities. There is no language within neoliberalism for recognizing anti-democratic forms of power, developing nonmarket values, or fighting against substantive injustices in a society founded on deep inequalities, particularly those based on race and class. Hence, it is not surprising that under neoliberalism, language is often stripped of its critical and social possibilities as it becomes increasingly difficult to imagine a social order in which all problems are not personal, in which social issues provide the conditions for understanding private considerations, critical reflection becomes the essence of politics, and matters of equity and justice become crucial to developing a democratic society.

It is under the reign of neoliberalism that the changing vocabulary about race and racial justice has to be understood and engaged. As freedom is increasingly abstracted from the power of individuals and groups to actively participate in shaping society, it is reduced to the right of the individual to be free from social constraints. In this view, freedom is no longer linked to a collective effort on the part of individuals to create a democratic society. Instead, freedom becomes an exercise in self-development rather than social responsibility, reducing politics to the privileging of a market-based notion of agency and choice that appears quite indifferent to how power, equity, and justice offer the enabling conditions for real individual and collective choices to be both made and acted upon. Under such circumstances, neoliberalism undermines those public spaces where noncommercial values and crucial social issues can be discussed, debated, and engaged. As public space is privatized, power is disconnected from social obligations and it becomes more difficult for isolated individuals living in consumption-oriented spaces to construct an ethically engaged and power-sensitive language capable of accommodating the principles of ethics and racial justice as a common good rather than as a private affair. According to Bauman, the elimination of public space and the subordination of democratic values to commercial interests narrows the discursive possibilities for supporting notions of the public good, creates the conditions for "the suspicion against others, the intolerance of difference, the resentment of strangers, and the demands to separate and banish them, as well as the hysterical, paranoiac concern with 'law and order.' "[20] Positioned within the emergence of neoliberalism as the dominant economic and political philosophy of our times, neoracism can be understood as part of a broader attack not only on difference, but on the value of public memory, public goods, and democracy itself.

The new racism represents both a shift in how race is defined and a symptom of the breakdown of a political culture in which individual freedom and solidarity maintain an uneasy equilibrium in the service of racial, social, and economic justice. Individual freedom is now disconnected from any sense of civic responsibility or justice, focusing instead on investor profits, consumer confidence, the downsizing of governments to police precincts, and a deregulated social order in which the winner takes all. Freedom is no longer about either making the powerful responsible for their actions or providing the essential political, economic, and social conditions for everyday people to intervene in and shape their future. Under the reign of neoliberalism, freedom is less about an act of intervention than about the process of individuals withdrawing from the social and enacting a sense of agency as an almost exclusively private endeavor. Freedom now cancels out civic courage and social responsibility while it simultaneously translates public issues and collective problems into tales of failed character, bad luck, or simple indifference. As Amy Elizabeth Ansell points out:

> The disproportionate failure of people of color to achieve social mobility speaks nothing of the justice of present social arrangements, according to the New Right worldview, but rather reflects the lack of merit or ability of people of color themselves. In this way, attention is deflected away from the reality of institutional racism and towards, for example, the "culture of poverty," the "drug culture," or the lack of black self-development.[21]

Appeals to freedom, operating under the sway of market forces, offer no signposts theoretically or politically for engaging racism as an ethical and political issue that undermines the very basis of a substantive democracy. Freedom in this discourse collapses into self-interest and as such is more inclined to organize any sense of community around shared fears, insecurities, and an intolerance of those "others" who are marginalized by class and color. But freedom reduced to the ethos of self-preservation and brutal self-interest makes it difficult for individuals to recognize the forms that

racism often takes when draped in the language of either denial, freedom, or individual rights. In what follows, I want to explore two prominent forms of the new
racism—color-blindness and neoliberal racism—and their connection to the New
Right, corporate power, and neoliberal ideologies.

Unlike the old racism, which defined racial difference in terms of fixed biological
categories organized hierarchically, the new racism operates in various guises proclaiming among other things race-neutrality, asserting culture as a marker of racial
difference, or marking race as a private matter. Unlike the crude racism with its biological referents and pseudoscientific legitimations, buttressing its appeal to white
racial superiority, the new racism cynically recodes itself within the vocabulary of
the civil rights movement, invoking the language of Martin Luther King, Jr., to argue
that individuals should be judged by the "content of their character" and not by the
color of their skin. Ansell, a keen commentator on the new racism, notes both
the recent shifts in racialized discourse away from more rabid and overt forms of racism
and its appropriation particularly by the New Right in the United States and Britain:

> The new racism actively disavows racist intent and is cleansed of extremist intolerance,
> thus reinforcing the New Right's attempt to distance itself from racist organizations
> such as the John Birch Society in the United States and the National Front in Britain.
> It is a form of racism that utilizes themes related to culture and nation as a replacement
> for the now discredited biological referents of the old racism. It is concerned less with
> notions of racial superiority in the narrow sense than with the alleged "threat" people
> of color pose—either because of their mere presence or because of their demand for
> "special privileges"—to economic, socio-political, and cultural vitality of the dominant
> (white) society. It is, in short, a new form of racism that operates with the category of
> "race." It is a new form of exclusionary politics that operates indirectly and in stealth via
> the rhetorical inclusion of people of color and the sanitized nature of its racist appeal.[22]

What is crucial about the new racism is that it demands an updated analysis of how
racist practices work through the changing nature of language and other modes of
representation. One of the most sanitized and yet most pervasive forms of the new
racism is evident in the language of color-blindness. Within this approach, it is
argued that racial conflict and discrimination are things of the past and that race has
no bearing on an individual's or group's location or standing in contemporary
American society. Color-blindness does not deny the existence of race but rather,
claims that race is responsible for alleged injustices that reproduce group inequalities,
privilege whites, and negatively impact on economic mobility, the possession of social
resources, and the acquisition of political power. Put differently, inherent in the logic
of color-blindness is the central assumption that race has no valence as a marker of
identity or power when factored into the social vocabulary of everyday life and the
capacity for exercising individual and social agency. As Charles Gallagher observes,
"Within the color-blind perspective it is not race per se which determines upward
mobility but how much an individual chooses to pay attention to race that
determines one's fate. Within this perspective race is only as important as you allow
it to be."[23] As Jeff, one of Gallagher's interviewees, puts it, race is simply another
choice: "[Y]ou know, there's music, rap music is no longer, it's not a black thing
anymore . . . [W]hen it first came out it was black music, but now it's just music.

It's another choice, just like country music can be considered like white hick music, you know it's just a choice."[24] Hence, in an era "free" of racism, race becomes a matter of taste, lifestyle, or heritage but has nothing to do with politics, legal rights, educational access, or economic opportunities. Veiled by a denial of how racial histories accrue political, economic, and cultural weight to the social power of whiteness, color-blindness deletes the relationship between racial differences and power. In doing so it reinforces whiteness as the arbiter of value for judging difference against a normative notion of homogeneity.[25] For advocates of color-blindness, race as a political signifier is conveniently denied or seen as something to be overcome, allowing whites to ignore racism as a corrosive force for expanding the dynamics of ideological and structural inequality throughout society.[26] Color-blindness, then, is a convenient ideology for enabling whites to disregard the degree to which race is tangled up with asymmetrical relations of power, functioning as a potent force for patterns of exclusion and discrimination including but not limited to housing, mortgage loans, healthcare, schools, and the criminal justice system. If one effect of color-blindness is to deny racial hierarchies, another is that it offers whites the belief not only that America is now a level playing field but also that the success that whites enjoy relative to minorities of color is largely due to individual determination, a strong work ethic, high moral values, and a sound investment in education. In short, color-blindness offers up a highly racialized (though paraded as race-transcendent) notion of agency, while also providing an ideological space free of guilt, self-reflection, and political responsibility, despite the fact that blacks have a disadvantage in almost all areas of social life: housing, jobs, education, income levels, mortgage lending, and basic everyday services.[27] In a society marked by profound racial and class inequalities, it is difficult to believe that character and merit—as color-blindness advocates would have us believe—are the prime determinants for social and economic mobility and a decent standard of living. The relegation of racism and its effects in the larger society to the realm of private beliefs, values, and behavior does little to explain a range of overwhelming realities—such as soaring black unemployment, decaying cities, and segregated schools. Paul Street puts the issue forcibly in a series of questions that register the primacy of and interconnections among politics, social issues, and race.

> Why are African-Americans twice as likely to be unemployed as whites? Why is the poverty rate for blacks more than twice the rate for whites? Why do nearly one out of every two blacks earn less than $25,000 while only one in three whites makes that little? Why is the median black household income ($27,000) less than two thirds of median white household income ($42,000)? Why is the black family's median household net worth less than 10 percent that of whites? Why are blacks much less likely to own their own homes than whites? Why do African-Americans make up roughly half of the United States' massive population of prisoners (2 million) and why are one in three young, black male adults in prison or on parole or otherwise under the supervision of the American criminal justice system? Why do African-Americans continue in severe geographic separation from mainstream society, still largely cordoned off into the nation's most disadvantaged communities thirty years after the passage of the civil rights fair housing legislation? Why do blacks suffer disproportionately from irregularities in the American electoral process, from problems with voter registration to the functioning of voting machinery? Why does black America effectively constitute a Third World enclave of sub-citizens within the world's richest and most powerful state?[28]

Add to this list the stepped-up resegregation of American schools and the growing militarization and lock-down status of public education through the widespread use of zero-tolerance policies.[29] Or the fact that African American males live on average six years less than their white counterparts. It is worth noting that nothing challenges the myth that America has become a color-blind, postracist nation more than the racialization of the criminal justice system since the late 1980s. As the sociologist Loic Wacquant has observed, the expansion of the prison-industrial complex represents a "de facto policy of 'carceral affirmative action' towards African-Americans."[30] This is borne out by the fact that while American prisons house over 2 million inmates, "roughly half of them are black even though African-Americans make up less than 13 percent of the nation's population. . . . According to the Justice Policy Institute there are now more black men behind bars than in college in the United States. One in ten of the world's prisoners is an African-American male."[31]

As one of the most powerful ideological and institutional factors for deciding identities are categorized and power, material privileges, and resources distributed, race represents an essential political category for examining the relationship between justice and a democratic society. But color-blindness is about more than the denial of how power and politics operate to promote racial discrimination and exclusion; it is also an ideological and pedagogical weapon powerfully mobilized by the conservatives and the Right for arguing that because of the success of the civil rights movement, racism has been eliminated as an institutional and ideological force, thus eradicating the need for government-based programs designed to dismantle the historical legacy and effects of racism in all dimensions of the social order.

Within the last twenty years, a more virulent form of the new racism has appeared that also affirms the basic principles of color-blindness; but instead of operating primarily as a discourse of denial regarding how power and politics operate to promote racial discrimination and exclusion, neoliberal racism is about the privatization of racial discourse. It is also proactive, functioning aggressively in the public arena as an ideological and pedagogical weapon powerfully mobilized by various conservatives and right-wing groups. Neoliberal racism asserts the insignificance of race as a social force and aggressively roots out any vestige of race as a category at odds with an individualistic embrace of formal legal rights. Focusing on individuals rather than on groups, neoliberal racism either dismisses the concept of institutional racism or maintains that it has no merit. In this context, racism is primarily defined as a form of individual prejudice while appeals to equality are dismissed outright. For instance, racial ideologues Richard J. Herrnstein and Charles Murray write in *The Bell Curve*: "In everyday life, the ideology of equality censors and straitjackets everything from pedagogy to humor. The ideology of equality has stunted the range of moral dialogue to triviality. . . . It is time for America once again to try living with inequality. . . ."[32] Arguing that individual freedom is tarnished if not poisoned by the discourse of equality, right-wing legal advocacy groups such as the Center for Individual Rights (CIR) and the Foundation for Individual Rights in Education argue that identity politics and pluralism weaken rather than strengthen American democracy because they pose a threat to what it means for the United States "to remain recognizably American"—which translates into preventing marginalized groups of color from shaping dominant values, practices, and public spaces,[33] But the advocacy groups do more than define American culture in racist and retrograde terms; they also aggressively use their resources—generously provided by prominent right-wing conservative organizations such as the Lynde and Harry Bradley Foundation, the John M. Olin Foundation, the Adolph Coors Foundation, and the Scaife Family Foundation—to challenge racial preference policies that are not based on a "principle of state neutrality."[34] Advocates of neoliberal racism have successfully challenged a number of cases before the Supreme Court over the legality of affirmative action programs, campus speech codes, hiring practices, the Violence Against Women Act, and the elimination of men's sports teams in higher education.[35] Hence, neoliberal racism provides the ideological and legal framework for asserting that since American society is now a meritocracy, government should be race neutral, affirmative action programs should be dismantled, civil rights laws discarded, and the welfare state eliminated. As Nikhil Aziz observes, "The Right argues that, because racism has been dealt with as a result of the Civil Rights Movement, race should not be a consideration for hiring in employment or for admission to educational institutions, and group identities other than 'American' are immaterial."[36]

Neoliberal racism is unwilling to accept any concept of the state as a guardian of the public interest. Motivated by a passion for free markets that is matched only by an antigovernment fervor, neoliberal racism calls for a hollowing out of the social welfare functions of the state, except for its role in safeguarding the interests of the privileged and in strengthening its policing functions. Rejecting a notion of the public good for private interest, advocates of neoliberal racism want to limit the state's role in public investments and social programs as a constraint on both individual rights and the expression of individual freedom. In this view, individual interests override any notion of the public good, and individual freedom operates outside of any ethical responsibility for its social consequences. The results of this policy are evident in right-wing attacks on public education, health care, environmental regulations, public housing, race-based scholarships, and other public services that embrace notions of difference. Many of these programs benefit the general public, though they are relied on disproportionately by the poor and people of color. As Zsuza Ferge points out, what becomes clear about neoliberal racism is that "the attack on the big state has indeed become predominantly an attack on the welfare functions of the state . . . The underlying motif is the conviction that the supreme value is economic growth to be attained by unfettered free trade equated with freedom *tout court*. . . . The extremely individualist approach that characterizes this ethic justifies the diagnosis of many that neoliberalism is about the 'individualization of the social.' "[37] By preventing the state from addressing or correcting the effects of racial discrimination, state agencies are silenced, thus displacing "the tensions of contemporary racially charged relations to the relative invisibility of private spheres, seemingly out of reach of public policy intervention."[38]

The relentless spirit of self-interest within neoliberal racism offers an apology for a narrow market-based notion of freedom in which individual rights and choices are removed from any viable notion of social responsibility, critical citizenship, and substantive democracy. By distancing itself from any notion of liberal egalitarianism, civic obligation, or a more positive notion of freedom, neoliberal racism does more than collapse the political into the personal—invoking character against institutional racism and individual rights against social wrongs—indeed, it claims, as Jean and John Comaroff argue that

> [t]he personal is the only politics there is, the only politics with a tangible referent or emotional valence. It is in these privatized terms that action is organized, that the experience of inequity and antagonism takes meaningful shape. . . . [Neoliberalism] is a culture that . . . re-visions persons not as producers from a particular community, but as consumers in a planetary marketplace.[39]

Neoliberalism devitalizes democracy because it has no language for defending a politics in which citizenship becomes an investment in public life rather than an obligation to consume, relegated in this instance to an utterly privatized affair. The discourse of neoliberal racism has no way of talking about collective responsibility, social agency, or a defense of the public good. The absences in its discourse are not innocent. They both ignore and perpetuate the stereotypes, structured violence, and massive inequalities produced by the racial state, the race-based attack on welfare, the destruction of social goods such as schools and healthcare, and the rise of the prison-industrial complex. And its attack on the principles of equality, liberty, economic democracy, and racial justice, in the final analysis, represents "a heartless indifference to the social contract, or any other civic-minded concern for the larger social good."[40] In Fact, Neoliberalism has played a defining role in transforming the social contract to the carceral contract, which substitutes punishment for social investment. Hence, it is not surprising how neoliberal arguments embracing the primacy of individual solutions to public issues such as poverty or the ongoing incarceration of black males are quick to defend public policies that are both punitive and overtly racist such as workfare for welfare recipients or the public shaming rituals of prison chain gangs, with an overabundance of black males always on display. Neoliberal racism's "heartless indifference" to the plight of the poor is often mirrored in an utter disdain for human suffering, as in Shelby Steele's nostalgic longing for a form of social Darwinism in which "failure and suffering are natural and necessary elements of success."[41] Or, more recently in the racist comments of a right-wing talk radio host who stated that a "huge percentages" of hurricane Katrina evacuees from New Orleans "were parasites, like ticks on a dog . . . coming to a community near you.[42]"

It is interesting that whenever white racism is invoked by critics in response to the spectacle of racism, advocates of color-blindnessness and neoliberal racism often step outside of the privatizing language of rights and have little trouble appropriating victim status for whites while blaming people of color for the harsh conditions under which so many have to live in this country. And in some cases, this is done in the name of a civility that is used to hide both the legacy and the reality of racism and a commitment to equality as the cornerstone of racial progress. A classic example of the latter can be found in *The End of Racism* by Dinesh D'Souza. He writes:

> Nothing strengthens racism in this country more than the behavior of the African-American underclass which flagrantly violates and scandalizes basic codes of responsibility and civility. . . . If blacks as a group can show that they are capable of performing competitively in schools and the workforce, and exercising both the rights and responsibilities of American citizenship, then racism will be deprived of its foundation in experience.[43]

Spectacles of Race

Scripted denials of racism coupled with the spectacle of racial discourse and representations have become a common occurrence in American life. Power-evasive strategies wrapped up in the language of individual choice and the virtues of self-reliance provide the dominant modes of framing through which the larger public can witness in our media-saturated culture what Patricia Williams calls "the unsaid, filled by stereotypes and self-identifying illusion, the hierarchies of race and gender circulating unchallenged," enticing audiences who prefer "familiar drama to the risk of serious democratization."[44] In what follows, I want to address the controversy surrounding the racist remarks made by Trent Lott at Strom Thurmond's centennial birthday celebration and how the Lott affair functions as an example of how controversial issues often assume the status of both a national melodrama and a scripted spectacle. I also want to analyze how this event functioned largely to privatize matters of white racism while rendering invisible the endorsement of systemic and state-fashioned racism. The Lott affair functions as a public transcript in providing a context for examining the public pedagogy of racial representations in media and print culture that is often framed within the ideology of the new racism in order to displace any serious discussion of racial exclusion in the United States. Finally, I offer some suggestions about how to respond politically to neoliberal racism and what the implications might be for a critical pedagogical practice aimed at challenging and dismantling it.

While attending Strom Thurmond's 100th birthday party on December 5, 2002, the then Senate majority leader, Trent Lott, offered the following salute to one of the most legendary segregationists alive: "I want to say this about my state: When Strom Thurmond ran for President, we voted for him. We're proud of it. And if the rest of the country had followed our lead, we wouldn't have had all these problems over all these years, either."[45] Of course, for the historically aware, the meaning of the tribute was clear, since Thurmond had run in 1948 on a racist Dixiecrat ticket whose official campaign slogan was "Segregation Forever!"

It took five days before the story got any serious attention in the national media. But once the story broke, Lott offered an endless series of apologies that included everything from saying he was just "winging it" (until it was revealed that he made an almost identical remark as a congressman at a Reagan rally a few decades earlier) to having found "Jesus," to proclaiming he was now "an across the board" advocate of affirmative action.[46] The Lott story evoked a range of opinions in the media extending from a craven defense provided by conservative columnist Bob Novak (who argued that Lott's racist comments were just a slip of the tongue), to vociferous moral condemnation from all sides of the ideological spectrum. Once Lott's voting record on civil rights issues became public, he became an embarrassment and liability to those politicians who denounced open racial bigotry but had little to say about structural, systemic, and institutional racism.[47] Under pressure from his Republican party colleagues, Lott eventually resigned as Senate majority leader, but retained his Senate seat, and the story passed in the national media from revelation to spectacle to irrelevance. The shelf-life of the spectacle in the dominant culture is usually quite long—witness the Gary Conduit affair—except when it offers the possibility for revealing how racist expressions privately license relations of power that reproduce a range of racial exclusions in the wider social order.

Lott's remarks cast him as a supporter of the old racism—bigoted, crude, and overtly racist. And, for the most part, the wrath his remarks engendered from the Republican Party and its media cheerleaders was mainly of the sort that allowed the critics to reposition themselves in keeping with the dictates of the logic of color-blindnessness and neoliberal racism. In doing so, they distanced themselves from Lott's comments as a safe way to attest their disdain for the old racist bigotry and to provide a display of their moral superiority and civility while at the same time distancing themselves from what Robert Kuttner has called some "inconvenient truths" when it came to talking about race. As Kuttner observes, "[His] stated views made it more difficult for the Republican party to put on minstrel shows and offer speeches dripping with compassion, while appointing racist judges, battling affirmative action, resisting hate crimes legislation, and slashing social outlays that help minorities. Lott made it harder to hold down black voting in the name of 'ballot security' while courting black voters, and disguising attacks on public education as expanded 'choice' for black parents and stingy welfare reform as promoting self-sufficiency."[48] Of course, singling out Lott also suggested that he was, as an editorial in the *Wall Street Journal* claimed, a one-of-kind bad apple, an unfortunate holdover from a Jim Crow era that no longer exists in America. David Brooks, the editor of the conservative *National Review*, proclaimed with great indignation that Lott's views were not "normal Republican ideas" and, to prove the point, asserted that after hanging out with Republicans for two decades, he had "never heard an overtly racist comment."[49]

Brooks, like many of his fellow commentators, seems to have allowed his ode to racial cleansing to cloud his sense of recent history. After all, it was only about a decade ago that the late Kirk Fordice, a right-wing Republican, ended his victorious campaign for governor of Mississipi—orchestrated largely as an attack on crime and welfare cheaters—with a "still photograph of a Black woman and her baby."[50] And of course, this was just a few years after George H. W. Bush ran his famous Willie Horton ad and a short time before Dan Quayle in the 1992 presidential campaign used the racially coded category of welfare to attack a sitcom character, Murphy Brown. Maybe David Brooks was just unaware of the interview that John Ashcroft had given in 1999 to the neo-Confederate magazine *Southern Partisan*, "in which he 'vowed to do more' to defend the legacy of Jefferson Davis."[51] Or, as *New York Times* writer Frank Rich puts it in response to the apparent newfound historical amnesia about the overt racism displayed by the Republican Party in more recent times:

> Tell that to George W. Bush, who beat John McCain in the 2000 South Carolina primary after what *Newsweek* called "a smear campaign" of leaflets, e-mails and telephone calls calling attention to the McCains' "black child" (an adopted daughter from Bangladesh). Or to Sonny Perdue, the new Republican governor of Georgia, elected in part by demagoguing the sanctity of the confederate flag.[52]

One telling example of how the Trent Lott affair was removed from the historical record of racialized injustices, the realm of political contestation, and, indeed, any critical understanding of how racializing categories actually take hold in the culture can be found in the December 23, 2002 devoted in entirety issue of *Newsweek*, which was devoted in entirety to the public uproar surrounding Lott's racist remarks.[53] *Newsweek* featured a 1962 picture of Lott on its cover with the caption "The Past That Made Him—and May Undo Him: Race and the Rise of Trent Lott." The stories that appeared in the magazine portrayed Lott either as an odd and totally out-of-touch symbol of the past ("A Man Out of Time," as one story headline read) or as an unrepentant symbol of racism that was no longer acceptable in American public life or in national politics. *Newsweek* ended its series on Lott with a short piece called "Lessons of the Trent Lott Mess."[54] The author of the article, Ellis Cose, condemned Lott's long history of racist affiliations, as did many other writers, but said nothing about why they were ignored by either the major political parties or the dominant media over the last decade, especially given Lott's important standing in national politics. It is interesting to note that Lott's affiliation with the neo-Confederate group—the Council of Conservative Citizens (CCC)—a neo-Confederate group that succeeded the notorious white Citizens Council, once referred to as the "uptown Klan," was revealed in a 1998 story by Stanley Crouch, a writer for the *New York Daily News*. Surprisingly, the article was ignored at the time by both prominent politicians and by the dominant media. At issue here is the recognition that the history of racism of which Trent Lott participated is not merely his personal history but the country's history and, hence, should raise far more serious considerations about how the legacy of racism works through the nation's cultural, economic, and social fabric. While Lott has to be held accountable for his remarks, his actions cannot be understood strictly within the language of American individualism—that is, as a bad reminder that the legacy of racism lives on in some old-fashioned politicians who cannot escape their past. In fact, Lott's remarks as well as the silence that allowed his racist discourse to be viewed in strictly personal and idiosyncratic terms must be addressed as symptomatic of a larger set of racist historical, social, economic, and ideological influences that still hold sway over American society. Collapsing the political into the personal, and serious reporting into talk-show clichés, Cose argues that the reason a person like Lott is serving and will continue to serve in the Senate sharing power with America's ruling elite, is that "Americans are very forgiving folks."[55] This response is more than simply inane; it is symptomatic of a culture of racism that has no language for or interest in understanding systemic racism, its history, or how it is embodied in most ruling political and economic institutions in the United States. Or, for that matter, why it has such a powerful grip on American culture. The Trent Lott affair is important not because it charts an influential senator's fall from grace and power in the wake of an unfortunate racist remark made in public, but because it is symptomatic of a new racism that offers no resources for translating private troubles into public considerations.

The public pedagogy underlying the popular response to Lott's remarks reveals how powerful the educational force of the culture is in shaping dominant conventions about race. Mirroring the logic of neoliberalism, the overall response to Lott both privatized the discourse of racism and attributed a racist expression to an unfortunate slip of the tongue, or a psychological disposition, or the emotive residue of a man who is out of step with both his political party and the spirit of his country. But such expressions are not simply the assertions of a prejudiced individual; but also it is a mode of exclusion, rooted in forms of authority; largely used to name, classify, order, and devalue people of color. As David Theo Goldberg observes:

> As a mode of exclusion, racist expression assumes authority and is vested with power, literally and symbolically, in bodily terms. They are human bodies that are classified, ordered, valorized, and devalued. . . . When this authority assumes state power, racialized discourse and its modes of exclusions become embedded in state institutions and normalized in the common business of everyday institutional life. . . . As expressions of exclusion, racism appeals either to inherent superiority or to differences. These putative differences and gradations may be strictly physical, intellectual, linguistic, or cultural. Each serves in two ways: they purport to furnish the basis for justifying differential distributions or treatment, and they represent the very relations of power that prompted them.[56]

As part of the discourse of denial, the Trent Lott episode reveals how a politics of racial management consigns racism to an outdated past, a narrow psychologism, the private realm of bad judgment or personal indiscretion. But racial discourse is not simply about private speech acts or individualized modes of communication; it is also about contested histories, institutional relations of power, ideologies, and the social gravity of effects. Racist discourses and expressions should alert us to the workings of power and the conditions that make particular forms of language possible and others seemingly impossible, as well as the modes of agency they produce and legitimate— an issue almost completely ignored in the mainstream coverage of the Lott affair. What was missing from such coverage is captured by Teun A. Van Dijk in his analysis of elite discourse and racism:

> Racism, defined as a system of racial and ethnic inequality, can survive only when it is daily reproduced through multiple acts of exclusion, inferiorization, or marginalization. Such acts need to be sustained by an ideological system and by a set of attitudes that legitimate difference and dominance. Discourse is the principal means for the construction and reproduction of this sociocognitive framework.[57]

Conclusion

Any attempt to address the politics of the new racism in the United States must begin by reclaiming the language of the social and affirming the project of an inclusive and just democracy. This suggests addressing how the politics of the new racism is made invisible under the mantle of neoliberal ideology—that is, raising questions about how neoliberalism works to hide the effects of power, politics, and racial injustice. What is both troubling and must increasingly be made problematic is that neoliberalism wraps itself in what appears to be an unassailable appeal to common sense. As Jean and John Comaroff observe:

> there is a strong argument to be made that neoliberal capitalism, in its millennial moment, portends the death of politics by hiding its own ideological underpinnings in the dictates of economic efficiency: in the fetishism of the free market, in the inexorable, expanding 'needs' of business, in the imperatives of science and technology. Or, if it does not conduce to the death of politics, it tends to reduce them to the pursuit of pure interest, individual or collective.[58]

Defined as the paragon of all social relations, neoliberalism attempts to eliminate an engaged critique about its most basic principles and social consequences by embracing the "market as the arbiter of social destiny."[59] More is lost here than neoliberalism's willingness to make its own assumptions problematic. Also lost is the very viability of politics itself. Neoliberalism in this instance empties the public treasury, hollows out public services, and limits the vocabulary and imagery available to recognize anti-democratic forms of power and narrow models of individual agency. It also undermines the socially discursive translating functions of any viable democracy by undercutting the ability of individuals to engage in the continuous translation between public considerations and the private interests.[60] Divested of its political possibilities and social underpinnings, freedom finds few opportunities for rearticulating private worries into public concerns individual discontent into collective struggle.[61] Hence, the first task in engaging neoliberalism is to reveal its claim to a bogus universalism and to make clear how it functions as a historical and social construction. Neoliberalism hides the traces of its own ideology, politics, and history either by rhetorically asserting its triumphalism as part of the "end of history" or by proclaiming that capitalism and democracy are synonymous. What must be challenged is neoliberalism's "future tense narrative of inevitability, [instead] demonstrating that the drama of world history remains wide open."[62]

But the history of the changing economic and ideological conditions that gave rise to neoliberalism must be understood in relation to the corresponding history of race relations in the United States and abroad. Most important, since the history of race is either left out or misrepresented by the official channels of power in the United States, it is crucial that the history of slavery, civil rights, racial politics, and ongoing modes of struggle at the level of everyday life be remembered and used pedagogically to challenge the historical amnesia that feeds neoliberalism's ahistorical claim to power and the continuity of its claims to common sense. The struggle against racial injustice cannot be separated from larger questions about what kind of culture and society is emerging under the imperatives of neoliberalism, what kind of history it ignores, and what alternatives might point to a substantive democratic future.

Second, under neoliberalism all levels of government have been hollowed out and largely reduced either to their policing functions or to maintaining the privileges of the rich and the interests of corporate power holders—both largely white. In this discourse, the state is not only absolved of its traditional social contract of upholding the public good and providing crucial social provisions and minimal guarantees for those who are in need of such services; it also embraces a notion of color-blind racelessness. State racelessness is built on the right-wing logic of "rational racists" such as D'Souza, who argues, "[w]hat we need is a separation of race and state."[63] As David Theo Goldberg points out, this means that the state is now held

> to a standard of justice protective of individual rights and not group results. . . . This in turn makes possible the devaluation of any individuals considered not white, or white-like, the trashing or trampling of their rights and possibilities, for the sake of preserving the right to *private* "rational discrimination" of whites. . . . [Thus] racist discrimination becomes privatized, and in terms of liberal legality state protected in its privacy.[64]

Defined through the ideology of racelessness, the state removes itself from either addressing or correcting the effects of racial discrimination, reducing matters of racism to individual concerns to be largely solved through private negotiations between individuals, and adopting an entirely uncritical role in the way in which the state shapes racial policies and their effects throughout the economic, social, and cultural landscape. Lost here is any critical engagement with state power and how it imposes immigration policies, decides who gets resources and access to a quality education, defines what constitutes a crime, how people are punished, how and whether social problems are criminalized, who is worthy of citizenship, and who is responsible for addressing racial injustices. As the late Pierre Bourdieu argued, there is a political and pedagogical need, not only to protect the social gains, embodied in state policies, that have been the outcome of important collective struggles, but also "to invent another kind of state."[65] This means challenging the political irresponsibility and moral indifference that are the organizing principles at the heart of the neoliberal vision. As Bourdieu suggests, it is necessary to restore the sense of utopian possibility rooted in the struggle for a democratic state. The racial state and its neoliberal ideology need to be challenged as part of a viable antiracist pedagogy and politics.

Antiracist pedagogy also needs to move beyond the conundrums of a limited identity politics and begin to include in its analysis what it would mean to imagine the state as a vehicle for democratic values and a strong proponent for social and racial justice. In part, reclaiming the democratic and public responsibility of the state would mean arguing for a state in which tax cuts for the rich, rather than social spending, are seen as the problem; using the state to protect the public good rather than waging a war on all things public; engaging and resisting the use of state power to define the public sphere as utterly white; redefining the power and role of the state so as to minimize its policing functions and strengthen its accountability to the public interests of all citizens rather than to the wealthy and corporations. Removing the state from its subordination to market values means reclaiming the importance of social needs over commercial interests democratic politics over corporate power; it also means addressing a host of urgent social problems that include but are not limited to the escalating costs of healthcare, housing, the schooling crisis, the growing gap between the rich and poor, the environmental crisis, the rebuilding of the nation's cities and impoverished rural areas, the economic crisis facing most of the states, and the increasing assault on people of color. Rather than abolish the state, its purpose, value, and control must be democratized. The struggle over the state must be linked to a struggle for a racially just, inclusive democracy. Crucial to any viable politics of antiracism is the role the state will play as a guardian of the public interest and as a force in creating a multiracial democracy.

Third, it is crucial for any antiracist pedagogy and politics to recognize that power does not just inhabit the realm of economics or the state, but is also intellectual, residing in the educational force of the culture and its enormous powers of persuasion. This means that any viable antiracist pedagogy must make the political more pedagogical by recognizing how public pedagogy works to determine and secure the ways that racial identity, issues, and relations are produced in a wide variety of sites including schools, cable and television networks, newspapers and magazines, the Internet, advertising, churches, trade unions, and a host of other public spheres in which ideas are produced and distributed. This, in turn, means becoming mindful of how racial meanings and practices are created, mediated, reproduced, and challenged through a wide variety of "discourses, institutions, audiences, markets, and constituencies which help determine the forms and meaning of publicness in American society."[65] The crucial role that pedagogy plays in shaping racial issues reaffirms the centrality of a cultural politics that recognizes the relationship between issues of representation and the operations of power, the important role that intellectuals might play as engaged, public citizens, and the importance of critical knowledge in challenging neoliberalism's illusion of unanimity.

But an antiracist cultural pedagogy also suggests the need to develop both a language of critique and possibility, and to wage individual and collective struggles in a wide variety of dominant public spheres and alternative counterpublics. Public pedagogy as a tool of antiracist struggle understands racial politics, not only as a signifying activity through which subject positions are produced, identities inhabited, and desires mobilized, but also as the mobilization of material relations of power as a way of securing, enforcing, and challenging racial injustices. While cultural politics offers an opportunity to understand how race matters and racist practices take hold in everyday life, such a pedagogical and cultural politics must avoid collapsing into a romanticization of the symbolic, popular, or discursive. Culture matters as a rhetorical tool and mode of persuasion, especially in the realm of visual culture, which has to be taken seriously as a pedagogical force, but changing consciousness is only a precondition to changing society and should not be confused with what it means to actually transform institutional relations of power. In part, this means contesting the control of the media by a handful of transnational corporations.[67] The social gravity of racism as it works through the modalities of everyday language, relations, and cultural expressions has to be taken seriously in any antiracist politics, but such a concern and mode of theorizing must also be accompanied by an equally serious interest in the rise of corporate power and "the role of state institutions and agencies in shaping contemporary forms of racial subjugation and inequality."[68] Racist ideologies, practices, state formations, and institutional relations can be exposed pedagogically and linguistically, but they cannot be resolved merely in the realm of the discursive. Hence, any viable antiracist pedagogy needs to draw attention to the distinction between critique and social transformation, to critical modes of analysis and to the responsibility of acting individually and collectively on one's beliefs.

Another important consideration that has to be included in any notion of antiracist pedagogy and politics is that of connecting matters of racial justice to broader and more comprehensive political, cultural, and social agendas. Neoliberalism exerts a powerful force in American life because its influence and power are spread across a diverse range of political, economic, social, and cultural spheres—from schools to newspapers to the visual media. Its ubiquity is matched by its aggressive pedagogical attempts to reshape the totality of social life in the image of the market, reaching into and connecting a wide range of seemingly disparate factors that bear upon everyday life in the United States. Neoliberalism is persuasive because its language of commercialism, consumerism, privatization, freedom, and self-interest resonates with and saturates so many aspects of public life. Differences, in this discourse, are removed from matters of equity and power and are reduced to market niches. Agency is privatized and social values are reduced to market-based interests. And, of course, a democracy of involved is replaced by a democracy of consumers. Progressives, involved citizens, and other groups who are concerned about matters of race and difference need to maintain their concerns with particular forms of oppression and subordination; yet, at the same time, the limits of various approaches to identity politics must be recognized so as not to allow them to become either fixed or incapable of making alliances with other social movements as part of a broader struggle over not just particular freedoms but also the more generalized freedoms associated with an inclusive and radical democracy.

I have not attempted to be exhaustive in suggesting what it might mean to recognize and challenge the new racism that now reproduces more subtle forms of racial subordination, oppression, and exclusion, though I have tried to point to some pedagogical and political concerns that connect racism and neoliberal politics. The color line in America is neither fixed nor static. Racism as an expression of power and exclusion takes many meanings and forms under different historical conditions. The emphasis on its socially and historically constructed nature offers hope because it suggests that what can be produced by dominant relations of power can also be challenged and transformed by those who imagine a more utopian and just world. The challenge of the color line is still with us today and needs to be recognized not only as a shameful example of racial injustice but also as a reprehensible attack on the very nature of democracy itself.

Notes

1. W.E.B. Du Bois, *The Souls of Black Folk in Three Negro Classics* (New York: Avon Books, 1965), p. 221.
2. It is important to note that while such overt modes of expression may be true of antiblack racism, they certainly do not characterize the racist policies being enacted by the United States against immigrants and nationals from the Middle East. The racial profiling, harassment, and use of outright unconstitutional means to intimidate, deport, and jail members of the Arab and Muslim populations in the United States represent a most shameful period in this country's ongoing history of state-sanctioned racist practices. Thus while the focus of this chapter is on black-white relations, I am not suggesting that racism only encompasses strictly black-white interactions. Obviously, any full account of racism would have to be applied to a wide range of groups who constitute diverse peoples of color and ethnic origin.
3. Howard Winant, "Race in the Twenty-First Century," *Tikkun* 17, no. 1 (2002): 33.
4. Cited in David Shipler, "Reflections on Race," *Tikkun* 13, no. 1 (1998): 59.
5. Dinesh D'Souza, *The End of Racism* (New York: The Free Press, 1995); Jim Sleeper, *Liberal Racism: How Fixating On Race Subverts the American Dream* (Lanham, MD: Rowman and Littlefield, 2002); Stephan and Abigail Thernstrom, *America in Black and White: One Nation, Indivisible* (New York: Simon and Schuster, 1999).
6. Cited in Tim Wise, "See No Evil: Perception and Reality in Black and White," *ZNet Commentary* (August 2, 2002). Available online at http://www.znetcommentary@tao.ca. The Gallup Poll on Black-White Relations in the United States—2001 Update is available online at http://www.gallup.com/poll/specialReports/.
7. As Greg Winter points out, The Center for Equal Opportunity and the American Civil Rights Institute, two groups that oppose affirmative action, have launched a new offensive "against scholarships and summer programs intended to ease minority students into college

life." See Greg Winter, "Colleges See Broader Attack on Their Aid to Minorities," *The New York Times*, March 30, 2003, A15.

8. Following is a representative example of works that point to the pervasive racism at work in American life: Howard Winant, *The World is a Ghetto: Race and Democracy Since World War II* (New York: Basic Books, 2001); Manning Marable, *The Great Wells of Democracy: The Meaning of Race in American Life* (New York: Basic Civitas Books, 2002); David Theo Goldberg, *The Racial State* (Malden, MA: Blackwell Books, 2002); Steve Martinot, *The Rule of Racialization: Class, Identity Governance* (Philadelphia: Temple University Press, 2003).

9. Michael Omi, "Racialization in the Post–Civil Rights Era," in Avery Gordon and Christopher Newfield, eds., *Mapping Multiculturalism* (Minneapolis: University of Minnesota Press, 1996), 183.

10. Jack Geiger, "The Real World of Race," *The Nation*, December 1, 1997, 27.

11. See, for instance, Shelby Steele, "The Age of White Guilt," *Harper's Magazine*, November 2002, 33–42.

12. This position is fully developed in Shelby Steele, *The Content of Our Character* (New York: Harper, 1990).

13. John McWhorter, "Don't Do Me Any Favors," *The American Enterprise Magazine*, April/May 2003, http://www.theamericanenterprise.org/taeam03d.htm.

14. Zygmunt Bauman, *The Individualized Society* (London: Polity Press, 2001), 205.

15. Charles Murray, *Losing Ground: American Social Policy, 1950–1980* (New York: Basic Books, 1985).

16. For an excellent analyses of this shift in race relations, see Eduardo Bonilla-Silva, *White Supremacy and Racism in the Post–Civil Rights Era* (Boulder, CO: Lynne Rienner Publishers, 2001) and Amy Elizabeth Ansell, *New Right, New Racism: Race and Reaction in the United States and Britain* (New York: New York University Press, 1997).

17. Douglas Kellner, "Globalization and New Social Movements: Lessons for Critical Theory and Pedagogy," in Nicholas Burbules and Carlos Torres, eds., *Globalization and Education* (New York: Routledge/Falmer, 2000), 307.

18. Bauman, *Individualized Society*, 159.

19. Lewis H. Lapham, "Res Publica," *Harper's Magazine*, December 2001, 8.

20. Zygmunt Bauman, *Globalization: The Human Consequences* (New York: Columbia University Press, 1998), 47.

21. Ansell, *New Right, New Racism*, 111.

22. Ibid., 20–21.

23. Charles Gallagher, "Color-Blind Privilege: The Social and Political Functions of Erasing the Color Line in Post Race America," unpublished essay, 12.

24. Ibid., 11.

25. This issue is taken up brilliantly in David Theo Goldberg, *Racial State* (Malden, MA: Blackwell Books, 2002), especially 200–238.

26. Manning Marable, "Beyond Color-blindness," *The Nation*, December 14, 1998, 29.

27. For specific figures in all areas of life, see Bonilla-Silva, *White Supremacy*, especially the chapter "White Supremacy in the Post–Civil Rights Era," 89–120.

28. Paul Street, "A Whole Lott Missing: Rituals of Purification and Racism Denial," *Z Magazine*, December 22, 2002, http://www.zmag.org/content/print_article.cfm?itemID=2784&seciton.

29. I address these issues in detail in Henry A. Giroux, *Public Spaces, Private Lives: Democracy Beyond 9/11* (Lanham, MD: Rowman and Littlefield, 2002). See also, Jonathan Kozul, *The Shame of The Nation: The Restoration of Apartheid Schooling in America* (New York: Crown, 2005).

30. Loic Wacquant, "From Slavery to Mass Incarceration: Rethinking the 'Race Question' in the U.S.," in *New Left Review* (January–February 2002): 44.

31. Paul Street, "Mass Incarceration and Racist State Priorities at Home and Abroad," *DissidentVoice*, March 11, 2003, 6–7, http://www.dissidentvoice.org/Articles2/Street_MassIncarceration.htm.

32. Richard J. Herrnstein and Charles Murray, *The Bell Curve: Intelligence and Class Structure in American Life* (New York: The Free Press, 1994), 533–534, 551.

33. Nikhil Aziz, "Moving Right On! Fairness, Family, and Faith," *The Public Eye* 16, no. 2 (Summer 2002): 5.

34. See "Civil rights" within the Mission section of the CIR's website: http://www.cur-usa.org/civil_rights_theme.html.

35. For an excellent summary and analysis of many of these legal cases, see Aziz, "Moving Right On!"

36. Ibid., p. 15.

37. Zsuza Ferge, "What are the State Functions That Neoliberalism Wants to Eliminate?" in *Not For Sale: In Defense of Public Goods*, ed. Antole Anton, Milton Fisk, and Nancy Holmstrom (Boulder, CO: Westview Press, 2000), 183.

38. Goldberg, *Racial State*, 217. The ideas in the sentence prior to this quote are also taken from Goldberg's text.

39. Jean Comaroff and John L. Comaroff, "Millennial Capitalism: First Thoughts on a Second Coming," *Public Culture* 12, no. 2 (2000): 305–306.

40. Aziz, "Moving Right On!" 6.

41. Cited in Philip Klinker, "The 'Racial Realism' Hoax," *The Nation*, December 14, 1998, 37.

42. Bob Normon, "Savage Station." *Miami New Times* (September 22, 2005) available online: www.Miaminewtimes.com /Issues/2005-09-22/News/metroy.html.

43. D'Souza, *End of Racism*, 268.

44. Patricia J. Williams, *Seeing a Color-Blind Future: The Paradox of Race* (New York: The Noonday Press, 1997), 18, 26.

45. John Meacham, "A Man Out of Time," *Newsweek*, December 23, 2003, 27.

46. Ibid.

47. On Trent Lott's voting record on matters of race, see Derrick Z. Jackson, "Brother Lott's Real Record," *Boston Globe*, December 18, 2002, http://www.commondreams.org/views02/1218-09.htm.

48. See Robert Kuttner, "A Candid Conversation About Race in America," *Boston Globe*, December 27, 2002, http://www.commondrems.org/views02/1225-02.htm.

49. David Brooks, "We Don't Talk This Way," *Newsweek*, December 23, 2002, 31.

50. Cited in David Roediger, *Toward the Abolition of Whiteness* (London: Verso, 1994), 8.

51. Frank Rich, "Bonfire of the Vanities," *New York Times*, December 21, 2002, A35.

52. Ibid. There is, of course, the most recent racist remark by former secretary of education William Bennett, who stated on his radio talk show that "you could abort every black baby in this country and your crime rate would go down." Cited in Mark Sorkin, "Bill Bennett's Abortion Fantasies," *The Nation*, October 21, 2005. Available online: www.commondreams.org/views05/1004-30.html.

53. I have taken this ideas from David Theo Goldberg, *Racial Subjects: Writing on Race in America* (New York: Routledge, 1997), 17–26.

54. Ellis Cose, "Lessons of the Trent Lott Mess," *Newsweek*, December 23, 2002, 37.

55. Ibid.

56. David Theo Goldberg, "Racialized Discourse" in *Racist Culture* (Malden, MA: Blackwell, 1993), 54–56.

57. Teun A. Van Dijk, "Denying Racism: Elite Discourse and Racism" in Philomena Essed and David Theo Goldberg, eds., *Race Critical Theories* (Malden, MA: Blackwell, 2002), 323–323.

58. Comaroff and Comaroff, "Millennial Capitalism," 322.

59. James Rule, "Markets, in Their Place," *Dissent*, Winter 1998, 31.

60. Bauman, *Individualized Society*, 107.

61. Ibid.

62. Leerom Medovoi, "Globalization as Narrative and Its Three Critiques," *The Review of Education, Pedagogy & Cultural Studies* 24, no. 1&2 (2002): 66.

63. D'Souza, *End of Racism*, 545.

64. Goldberg, *Racial State*, 229.

65. Pierre Bourdieu and Gunter Grass, "The 'Progressive' Restoration: A Franco-German Dialogue," *New Left Review* 14 (March-April 2002): 71.

66. John Brenkman, "Race Publics: Civic Illiberalism, or Race After Reagan," *Transition* 5, no. 2 (Summer 1995): 8.

67. On this subject, see Robert W. McChesney and John Nichols, *Our Media, Not Theirs* (New York: Seven Stories, 2002).

68. David Goldberg and John Solomos, "Introduction to Part III," in David Goldberg and John Solomos, eds., *A Companion to Ethnic and Racial Studies* (Malden, MA: Blackwell, 2002), 231.

11

Disposable Youth, Racism, and the Politics of Zero Tolerance

In many ways, the United States appears to be a country that is under siege. Faced with increasing threats of terrorism in the aftermath of the horrible events of September 11, Americans are both concerned about their safety and fearful that the Bush administration will sacrifice the country's most basic freedoms in the name of national security. At the same time, the economy is in a recession, with over three million workers having lost their jobs under the Bush administration, and the outlook for those who are working-class and middle-class is far from optimistic. Similarly, economic insecurity and the attack on civil liberties take on an ominous air in light of an endless series of scandals revealing the most blatant and pernicious examples of greed and corruption at the highest levels of corporate America. Moral panic fueled by economic insecurity, a crisis around civil liberties, a war in Iraq that is bankrupting social services, and widespread political corruption make democracy appear even more fragile in the United States in this time of civic and political crisis.

At the same time, there is an ongoing and growing resistance to the passing of antiterrorist laws such as the USA PATRIOT Act—which gives extensive and wide-reaching powers to government agencies, including the rights to monitor what people read in libraries, to engage in wiretaps, to snoop around in places of worship, and to listen in on what clients say to their lawyers—and the now suspended Operation TIPS (Terrorism Information and Prevention System), designed to recruit millions of workers and citizens to act as government snitches while bolstering an expansive internal spying network that would provide "extra eyes and ears for law enforcement" in order to report "suspicious and potentially terrorist related activity." There are also protest movements challenging the Bush administration's unsubstantiated arguments for invading Iraq, and the all-too-cozy entanglements between officials in the highest levels of government and corrupt business executives associated with multinational corporations that have engaged in disreputable business practices in Iraq as well as in reconstruction efforts in the Gulf states following hurricanes Rita and Katrina. Yet, at the same time, there is a thunderous silence on the part of many critics and academics regarding the ongoing insecurity and injustice experienced by young people in this country, which is now being intensified as a result of the state's increasing resort to repression and punitive social policies. The current concerns about terrorism and security almost completely ignore what these terms mean outside of a violent attack against property and persons. There is a sense of moral and political indifference, if not cynicism, about the forms of domestic terrorism suffered by children who are poor, hungry, homeless, neglected, lack medical care, or suffer physical abuse by adults.

Children have fewer rights than almost any other group and fewer institutions protecting these rights. Consequently, their needs and concerns, if not entirely framed within the privatized discourse of the family, are made public most clearly in the moral panics mobilized around children being abducted or preyed upon by pedophiles or other evil assailants. The response to such events, tellingly, is more "get tough on crime policy," never an analysis of the systemic failure to provide safety and security for children through improved social provisions. In public life more generally, discussions of the future and its implications for social responsibility rarely include the responsibilities of adults toward children. Rather, when children are not absent from public discourse altogether, they appear as objects, defined through the debasing discourses of advertising, consumerism, and criminality.

No longer seen as a crucial social investment for the future of a democratic society, youth are now demonized by the popular media and derided by politicians looking for quick-fix solutions to crime. In a society deeply troubled by their presence, youth prompt in the public imagination a rhetoric of fear, control, and surveillance—made all the more visible with the 2002 Supreme Court decision upholding the widespread use of random drug testing of public school students. Such testing of all junior and senior high school students who desire to participate in extracurricular activities registers a deep distrust of students and furthers the notion that youth have become a generation of suspects. Schools increasingly resemble prisons, and students begin to look more like criminal suspects who need to be searched, tested, and observed under the watchful eye of administrators, who, in turn, appear to be less concerned with educating them than with policing their every move. Trust and respect now give way to fear, disdain, and suspicion. Moreover, this hostility of adults toward young people is increasingly being translated into social policies that signal the shrinking of democratic public spheres, the hijacking of civic culture, and the increasing militarization of public space. Police and drug-sniffing dogs now become a common fixture in public schools. In many suburban malls, young people, but especially youth of color, cannot even shop or walk around without either appropriate identification cards or the company of their parents. Excluded from public spaces outside of schools that once offered young people opportunities to learn a sport, play music, hang out in a youth club, attend alternative educational clubs, and develop their own talents and sense of self-worth, young people are now forced to hang out in the streets, while increasingly subject to police surveillance, antigang statues, and curfew laws, especially in poor, urban neighborhoods.

Instead of providing a decent education to poor young people, we serve them more standardized tests and house too many of them in underfunded and underserved schools; instead of guaranteeing young people decent healthcare, jobs, and shelter, we offer them the growing potential of being incarcerated, buttressed by the fact that the United States is the only industrialized country that sentences minors to death and spends "three times more on each incarcerated citizen than on each public school pupil";[1] instead of providing them with vibrant public spheres, we offer them a commercialized culture in which consumerism is the only value through which they can define their individual and collective identities.

The shameful state of many of the children in America can be seen in some of the statistics that suggest a profound failure on the part of one of the richest democracies in the world: over 12.9 million children [21.9%] live in poverty and 9.3 million in 2005 were without health insurance; 5.6 million young people between the ages of sixteen and twenty-four are out of work and the joblessness rate among youth has surged by 16 percent since the year 2000. The *New York Times* reported in 2005 that the "Employment rate for the Nation's Teenagers in the first 11 months of 2004— just 36.3 percent—was the lowest it has ever been since the Federal Government began tracking teenage employment in 1948."[2] When broken down along racial categories, the figures become even more deplorable. For example, in 1998, "36 percent of black and 34 percent of Hispanic children lived in poverty, compared with 14 percent of white children,"[3] and the poverty rates since then have risen even higher. In some states such as the District of Columbia, the child poverty rate is as high as 45 percent and "in Chicago, only one of every 10 black teenagers found employment in 2004."[4] As the Bush administration provides the lion's share of huge tax cuts for the upper 1 percent of the population, it has eliminated tax cuts for over 16 million children in low-income families. Moreover, tax cuts have resulted in the loss of over $75 billion from state budgets, producing cutbacks in many social programs that directly affect children. In states such as Oregon, Massachusetts, and California, teachers have been fired, the school year shortened, and extracurricular programs eliminated. In fact, one telling consequence of the Bush administration's budget for 2006 is that "Nutritional assistance for impoverished mothers and their small children . . . will be cut by 9.6 percent; some 740,000 fewer people would receive assistance."[5] While the United States ranks first among all nations in military technology, military exports, defense expenditures, and the number of millionaires and billionaires, it is ranked eighteenth in the gap between rich and poor children, twelfth in the percent of children in poverty, seventeenth in the efforts to lift children out of poverty, and twenty-third in infant mortality. In short, economically, politically, and culturally, the situation of youth in the United States is intolerable and unforgivable.

At a time when people who are committed to exclusion have been appointed to the highest positions in government, there are mounting ideological, institutional, and political pressures among conservatives, liberals, and others to remove youth from the inventory of ethical and political concerns that legitimize and provide individual rights and social provisions for members of a democratic society. I refer specifically to the growing support among the American people for public policies that increasingly address social problems by relying on the police, courts, and prison system. This is clear not only in the widespread use of zero tolerance policies in the criminal justice system and the public schools—with their mutual emphasis on mandatory intolerance—but also in the emergence of degrading representations, repressive practices, and policies that target young people across a wider variety of public spheres. For example, within the last decade, youth have become public enemy number one—blamed in the press, in Hollywood film, and on an endless array of right-wing talk shows for nearly all of our major social ills extending from violence and drug use to the breakdown of family values. Even the Bush administration could not resist bashing youth by running a series of antidrug ads suggesting that youth who use drugs are responsible for terrorists acts.

But there are more insightful, generous, and ethical understandings of youth that can be drawn upon to challenge the current pejorative representations of youth as dangerous, shiftless, and selfish. Critics from John Dewey to Paulo Freire have always embraced the utopian notion that the model of the good life should not be cut off from the model of the good society, and that the greatest investment in the good life should be made in the children of any given society. One finds, for instance, that Martin Luther King, Jr., dedicated his entire life to the assumption that the public good, collective struggle, equity, racial justice, civil disobedience, and compassion were at the heart of what it meant to provide the conditions for children to inherit a future in which they experienced the benefits of a meaningful and multiracial democracy. In a series of lectures aired by the Canadian Broadcasting Corporation in December 1967, he argued the following:

> When an individual is no longer a true participant, when he no longer feels a sense of responsibility to his society, the content of democracy is emptied. When the culture is degraded and vulgarity enthroned, when the social system does not build security but induces peril, inexorably the individual is impelled to pull away from a soulless society. This process produces alienation—perhaps the most pervasive and insidious development in contemporary society.[6]

I want to build on this insight and its implications for children by arguing that we are a society that faces the problem of losing a generation of young people, especially young people of color, to a system of increasing repression, moral indifference, and racism. Equally important is the recognition that this crisis facing young people is fundamentally about the crisis of democracy itself. In the spirit of revitalizing, expanding, and deepening the possibilities of a strong democracy, educators, parents, students, and critical citizens are currently faced with the challenge of revitalizing the legacy of militant hope and engaged struggle that celebrates a long history in America, indebted to the principles of justice, human rights, freedom, and democratic public life.

In light of these concerns, I want to examine in greater detail the social and political costs of the growing popular perception of youth, but especially youth of color, as a generation of suspects, and how the latter assessment is increasingly being translated into social policies that signal the shrinking of democratic public spheres and the increasing militarization of public space. It is against this growing threat to basic civil liberties, democracy, homeless youth, and youth of color that I want to address the related issues of zero tolerance policies and the increase in domestic militarization. While my focus is on the relationship between education and zero tolerance policies, my analysis points to a broader set of repressive conditions that not only target young people across a wider variety of public sites, but also undermine the guarantee of rights and the institutional structures that are characteristic of a meaningful democracy.

Zero Tolerance and the Politics/Color of Punishment

When the "War on Poverty" ran out of steam with the social and economic crisis that emerged in the 1970s, there was a growing shift at all levels of government from an emphasis on social investments to an emphasis on public control, social containment, and the criminalization of social problems. The criminalization of social issues started with President Lyndon Johnson's Omnibus Crime and Safe Streets Act of 1968 (a bill that was debated in Congress after the assassination of Dr. Martin Luther King), entered a second phase with President Ronald Reagan's war on drugs and the privatization of the prison industry in the 1980s, and moved into a third phase with the passage of a number of anticrime bills by President Bill Clinton's administration, including the Anti-Terrorism and Effective Death Penalty Act, coupled with the escalating war on immigrants in the early 1990s and the rise of the prison-industrial complex by the close of the decade.[7] This view of social issues has now become a part of everyday culture and provides a common reference point that extends from governing prisons and regulating urban culture to running schools. This is most evident in the emergence of zero tolerance laws that have swept the nation since the 1980s, and gained full legislative strength with the passage of the Violent Crime Control and Law Enforcement Act of 1994. Following the mandatory sentencing legislation and get-tough policies associated with the "war on drugs," this bill calls for a "three strikes and you're out" policy, which puts repeat offenders, including nonviolent offenders, in jail for life, regardless of the seriousness of the crime. The general idea behind the bill is "to increase the prison sentence for a second offense and require life in custody without parole for a third offense."[8] It also provides sixty new offenses punishable by death, while at the same time limiting the civil rights and appeal process for those inmates sentenced to die. In addition, the largest single allocation in the bill is for prison construction.[9] The prison market, estimated to be worth $37.8 billion a year, is larger than the major league baseball industry, and it "employs more than 413, 000 people, having more than doubled in the last twenty years."[10] Since the Crime Bill was passed in 1994, the prison industry has become big business, with many states spending "more on prison construction than on university construction."[11] Yet, even as the crime rate plummets dramatically, more people, especially people of color, are being arrested, harassed, punished, and put in jail.[12] As is widely reported, the United States is now the biggest jailer in the world, with 6.5 million people either in jail or under corrections supervision.[13] Between 1985 and 2005 the prison population grew from 744,206 to 2.2 million (approaching the combined populations of Idaho, Wyoming, and Montana), and prison budgets jumped from $7 billion in 1980 to $40 billion in 2000.[14] Put another way, the United States is "spending $35,000 a year to maintain one prisoner in a minimum-security cell . . . [while] it costs nearly $80,000 a year to confine a prisoner in a maximum-security cell. [In addition,] we are building over a hundred new prison cells a day."[15]

The explosion in the prison population has also resulted in a big increase in the move toward privatizing prisons.[16] By the close of 1997, at least 105 for-profit private prisons existed in the United States, "each receiving some form of federal subsidy with limited federal protection of prisoners' rights or prison conditions."[17] Prisoners, especially the widely disproportionate pool of African American inmates, which has tripled since 1980, provide big business with not only "a new source of consumers but a reservoir of cheap labor."[18] Of the two million people behind bars, 70 percent are people of color with 50 percent being African Americans, while 17 percent are Latinos.[19] The racist significance of this figure can be measured by a wide range of statistics. For instance, law professor David Cole, in *No Equal Justice*, points out that while "76 percent of illicit drug users were white, 14 percent black, and 8 percent Hispanic—figures which roughly match each group's share of the general population," African Americans constitute "35 percent of all drug arrests, 55 percent of all drug convictions, and 74 percent of all sentences for drug offences."[20] A Justice Department report points out that on any give day in this country "more than a third of the young African-American men aged 18–34 in some of our major cities are either in prison or under some form of criminal justice supervision."[21] The same department reported in April 2000 that "black youth are forty-eight times more likely than whites to be sentenced to juvenile prison for drug offenses."[22] The Report of the National Criminal Justice Commission noted in 1996 that "spending on crime fighting has risen three times faster than defense spending," and the biggest beneficiary appears to be "private businesses [that] reap enormous profits from the fear of crime and the expansion of the criminal justice system."[23] Moreover, as many critics of the private prison system have pointed out, it "is particularly disturbing that corporations should be making a profit from policies that are not in the public interest— such as excessive prison sentences and the incarceration of nonviolent offenders."[24] At a time when over one million black men and women are interned in jails in the United States, "the concept of private companies profiting from prisoners evokes the convict leasing system of the Old South."[25]

The increased use of zero tolerance policy functions not only to contain "minority populations" and provide new sources of revenue; it also actively promotes and legitimates retrograde social policies. For example, an increasing number of states, including California and New York, are now spending more on prison construction than on higher education, and the impact on minorities of color has been devastating. Paul Street illustrates this point. He claims that in Illinois, for every "African-American enrolled in [its] universities, two-and-a-half Blacks are in prison or on parole . . . [while] in New York . . . more Blacks entered prison just for drug offenses than graduated from the state's massive university system with undergraduate, masters, and doctoral degrees combined in the 1990s."[26] Moreover, many states are also hiring more prison guards than teachers. A study by the Correctional Association of New York and the Washington, D.C.–based Justice Policy Institute claims that millions of dollars are being diverted from the public university budget in New York into prison construction. The reports point out that "between fiscal year 1988 and fiscal year 1998, New York's public universities saw their operating budgets plummet by 29% while funding for prisons rose 76%. In California, the average prison guard now earns $10,000 more than the average public school teacher, and increasingly more than many professors working in the state university system.[27] As the "prison-industrial complex" becomes a dominant force in the economy of states such as California, competing with land developers and service industries, it does more than rake in huge profits for corporations; it also contributes to what Mike Davis calls a "permanent prison class" fed by the rising "market" of black offenders disenfranchised of their political and economic rights.[28] Sustaining this "permanent prison class," in part, is a prison-industrial complex that offers itself as a high-powered growth industry to many rural communities throughout the United States that have been "recently hollowed-out by the de-industrializing and family farm–destroying gales of the 'free-market' system."[29] Attempting to provide jobs and protect their local economies, rural communities in places such as Sayre, Oklahoma, with a population of 4,114 have become part of a prison-industrial lobby that supports tougher crime laws, harsher sentences, and more funding for prison construction, even as crime rates continue to fall throughout the country. And such lobbying efforts seem to be working. Calvin Beale, a senior demographer at the Economic Research Service of the Agriculture Department, claims "an average of 25 new rural prisons opened each year in the 1990's, up from 16 in the 1980's and 4 in the 1970's."[30]

What are we to make of a society that turns to prison construction as a way of reviving its slagging economy, that constructs social policies that increasingly portray youth, especially youth marginalized because of their color and class, as a generation of suspects? What are we to make of a social order whose priorities suggest to poor, urban youth of color that it is easier for them to be sent to jail than to be given a decent education? What is the lesson to be learned when a society invests more in prisons than in those public institutions that educate young people to become critical and productive citizens? In this instance, the culture of domestic militarization, with its policies of containment, brutalization, and punishment, becomes more valued by the dominant social order than any consideration of what it means for a society to expand and strengthen the mechanisms and freedoms of a fully realized democracy.[31]

Zero tolerance policies have been especially cruel in the treatment of juvenile offenders.[32] Rather than attempting to work with youth and make an investment in their psychological, economic, and social well-being, a growing number of cities are passing sweep laws—curfews and bans against loitering and cruising—designed not only to keep youth off the streets, but to make it easier to criminalize their behavior. For example, within the last decade, "45 states . . . have passed or amended legislation making it easier to prosecute juveniles as adults," and in some states "prosecutors can bump a juvenile case into adult court at their own discretion."[33] A particularly harsh example of these draconian measures can be seen in the passing of Proposition 21 in California. The law makes it easier for prosecutors to try in adult court teens fourteen and older who are convicted of felonies. These youth would automatically be put in adult prisons and be given lengthy mandated sentences. As Louise Cooper points out, "It also . . . increases the discretionary powers for routine police surveillance, random searches and arrest of young people."[34] The overall consequence of the law is to largely eliminate intervention programs, increase the number of youth in prisons, especially minority youth, and keep them there for longer periods of time. Moreover, the law is at odds with a number of studies that indicate that putting youth in jail with adults both increases recidivism and poses a grave danger to young offenders who, as a Columbia University study suggested, are "five times as likely to be raped, twice as likely to be beaten and eight times as likely to commit suicide than adults in the adult prison system."[35]

Paradoxically, the moral panic against crime that increasingly feeds the calls for punishment rather than rehabilitation programs for young people exists in conjunction with the disturbing fact that the United States is currently one of only seven countries (Congo, Iran, Nigeria, Pakistan, Saudi Arabia, and Yemen) in the world that permits the death penalty for juveniles and, in the last decade, has executed more juvenile offenders than all six other countries combined.[36] Similarly, the U.S. is only one of a small number of countries in which young people who committed a crime before the age of eighteen are "serving life without parole." Over two thousand American prisoners who were youngsters when they committed their crimes will never get paroled.[37]

The National Criminal Justice Commission report claims that while "get tough" policies are likely to be more severe when dealing with children, they are particularly repressive when applied to youth of color, especially as a result of the war on drugs and the more recent eruption of school shootings. Numerous studies have documented that, unlike middle-class white youth, minority youth are:

> more likely to be arrested, referred to court, and placed outside the home when awaiting disposition of their cases. . . . [A]ll things being equal, minority youths face criminal charges more often than white youths for the same offenses. Also, African-American youths are charged more often than whites with a felony when the offense could be considered a misdemeanor. . . . Minority youth are also more likely to be waived to adult court, where they will face longer sentences and fewer opportunities for rehabilitative programs.[38]

Fed by widespread stereotypical images of black youth as superpredators and black culture as one of criminality, minority youth face not only a criminal justice system that increasingly harasses and humiliates them, but also a larger society that increasingly undercuts their chances for a living wage, quality jobs, essential social services, and decent schools.[39] Within such a context, the possibility for treating young people of color with respect, dignity, and support vanishes, and with it the hope of overcoming a racial abyss that makes a mockery out of justice and a travesty of democracy.

The growing influence of zero tolerance laws in the United States can be seen in the application of such laws in areas as different as airport security, the criminal justice system, immigration policy, and drug testing programs for athletes. The widespread use of these policies has received a substantial amount of critical analyses within the last decade. Unfortunately, these analyses rarely make connections between the criminal justice system and what is going on in public schools.[40] I want to focus on this issue and, in doing so, take up Manning Marable's significant claim: "One of the central battlegrounds for democracy in the U.S. in the twenty-first century will be the effort to halt the dismantling of public education and public institutions in general for the expansion of [the] prison-industrial complex."[41]

Schooling and the Pedagogy of Zero Tolerance

Across the nation, school districts are lining up to embrace zero tolerance policies. Emulating state and federal laws passed in the 1990s, such as the federal Gun-Free Schools Act of 1994, that were based on mandatory sentencing and "three strikes" policies, many educators first invoked zero tolerance rules against those kids who brought guns to schools. But over time the policy was broadened and now includes a range of behavioral infractions, from possessing drugs to harboring a weapon to *threatening* other students—all broadly conceived. For instance, in many districts, school administrators "won't tolerate even one instance of weapon possession, drug use, or harassment."[42]

Unfortunately, any sense of perspective seems lost, as school systems across the country clamor for metal detectors, armed guards, see-through knapsacks, and, in some cases, armed teachers. Some school systems are investing in new software in order to "profile" students who might exhibit criminal behavior.[43] Overzealous laws relieve educators of exercising deliberation and critical judgment as more and more young people are either suspended or expelled from school, often for ludicrous reasons. For example, two Virginia fifth-graders who allegedly put soap in their teacher's drinking water were charged with a felony.[44] Officials at Rangeview High School in Colorado after unsuccessfully trying to expel a student because they found three baseball bats on the floor of his car ended up suspending him.[45] In a similar litany of absurdities, *USA Today* reported that two Illinois seven-year-olds were "suspended for having nail clippers with knifelike attachments."[46] Jesse Jackson offers the example of a student who was suspended on a weapons charge because school officials discovered a little rubber hammer as part of his Halloween costume. Jackson provides another equally revealing example of a student brought up on a drug charge because he gave another youth two lemon cough drops.[47] Images of young children handcuffed, sitting in adult courts before stern judges, are increasingly matched by depictions of schools showing the foreboding presence of hired armed guards in the corridors, patrolled cafeterias, locked doors, video surveillance cameras, electronic badges, police dogs, and routine drug searches. In fact, a five-year old African American girl who was unruly in her Florida Kindergarten class was handcuffed by St. Petersburg Police officers.[48] As compassion and understanding give way to rigidity and intolerance, schools become more militarized and appear as adjuncts, if not conduits, to the penal system.

Zero tolerance does more than offer a simple solution to a complex problem; it has become a code word for a "quick and dirty way of kicking kids out" of school rather than creating safe environments for them.[49] For example, the *Denver Rocky Mountain News* reported in June 1999 that "partly as a result of such rigor in enforcing Colorado's zero tolerance law, the number of kids kicked out of public schools has skyrocketed since 1993—from 437 before the law to nearly 2,000 in the 1996–1997 school year."[50] In Chicago, the widespread adoption of zero tolerance policies in 1994 resulted in a 51 percent increase in student suspensions for the next four years, and a 3,000 percent increase in expulsions, jumping "from 21 in 1994–95 to 668 in 1997–98."[51] Within such a climate of disdain and intolerance, expelling students does more than pose a threat to innocent kids; it also suggests that local school boards are refusing to do the hard work of exercising critical judgment, trying to understand what conditions undermine school safety, and providing reasonable support services for all students as well as viable alternatives for the troubled ones. As the criminalization of young people finds its way into the classroom, it becomes easier for school administrators to punish students rather than listen to them, or, for that matter, to work with parents, community justice programs, religious organizations, and social service agencies.[52] Even though zero tolerance policies clog up the courts and put additional pressure on an already overburdened juvenile justice system, educators appear to have few qualms about implementing them. And the results are far from inconsequential for the students themselves.

Most insidiously, zero tolerance laws, while a threat to all youth and to any viable notion of equal opportunity through education, reinforce in the public imagination the image of students of color as a source of public fear and a threat to public school safety. Zero tolerance policies and laws appear to be well-tailored for mobilizing racialized codes and race-based moral panics that portray black and brown urban youth as a frightening and violent threat to the safety of "decent" Americans. Beyond the high-profile zero tolerance cases, the policies alone reinforce the racial inequities that plague school systems across the country. For example, Tamar Lewin, a writer for the *New York Times*, has reported on a number of studies, illustrating "that black students in public schools across the country are far more likely than whites to be suspended or expelled, and far less likely to be in gifted or advanced placement classes."[53] Even in a city such as San Francisco, considered a bastion of liberalism, African American students pay a far greater price for zero tolerance policies. Libero Della Piana reports, "According to data collected by Justice Matters, a San Francisco agency advocating equity in education, African Americans make up 52 percent of all suspended students in the district—far in excess of the 16 percent of the general population."[54] On a national scale, Marilyn Elias reported in *USA Today*: "In 1998, the first year national expulsion figures were gathered, 31% of kids expelled were black, but blacks made up only 17% of the students in public schools."[55]

Feeding on moral panic and popular fear, zero tolerance policies not only turn schools into an adjunct of the criminal justice system; they also further rationalize misplaced legislative priorities. And that has profound social costs. Instead of investing in early childhood programs, repairing deteriorating school buildings, or hiring more qualified teachers, schools now spend millions of dollars to upgrade security, even when such a fortress mentality defies the simplest test of common sense. For example, school administrators at Fremont High School in Oakland, California, decided to build a new $500,000 security fence "while the heating remained out of commission."[56] Another instance of such irrationality can be found, as I mentioned earlier, in the fact that many states now spend "more on prison than on university construction."[57] Young people are quickly realizing that schools have more in common with military boot camps and prisons than they do with other institutions in American society. In addition, as schools abandon their role as democratic public spheres and are literally "fenced off" from the communities that surround them, they lose their ability to become anything other than spaces of containment and control. In this context, discipline and training replace education for all but the privileged, as schools increasingly take on an uncanny resemblance to oversized police precincts, tragically disconnected both from the students who inhabit them and the communities that give meaning to their historical experiences and daily lives. As schools become militarized, they lose their ability to provide students with the skills to cope with human differences, uncertainty, and the various symbolic and institutional forces that undermine political agency and democratic public life itself.

Schooling and the Crisis of Public Life

I want to conclude by arguing that, as parents, educators, and concerned citizens, we need to rethink what it would mean to interrogate and break away from the destructive representations and racist practices of zero tolerance policies as they work to reinforce modes of control and repression in a number of powerful institutional spheres. We need to recognize, once again, that the crisis of race and youth in the U.S. is symptomatic of the crisis of democracy. In spite of the message we often get from the media, the enemy of democracy is not difference but bigotry. For many youth, the future appears to be a repeat of the present, a period not unlike what the singer and songwriter Gil Scott-Herron once called "winter in America." The time for social change has never been so urgent, since the fate of an entire generation of young people is at stake. Educators, parents, and other concerned citizens need to understand more clearly, as the writer Jack Geiger reminds us, how racism in this country "distorts individual relationships and magnifies such major social policy issues as poverty, crime, drugs, gangs, welfare, joblessness, and the failure of inner-city schools, which are, in American social and political discourse, racially coded."[58] In addition, as parents, critical citizens, and educators we need to reject a growing commercial culture that reduces social values to market relations, limits the obligations of citizenship to the act of consuming, and dismisses racial and economic justice as the product of a bygone era. This is what Dr. King meant when he told a group of young people: "Make a career of humanity. Commit yourself to the noble struggle for equal rights. You will make a greater person of yourself, a greater nation of your country, and a finer world to live in."[59] Under the present circumstances, it is time to remind ourselves that collective problems deserve collective solutions and that what is at risk is not only a generation of young people now considered to be a generation of suspects, but the very promise of democracy itself.

Notes

1. Heather Wokusch, "Leaving Our Children Behind," *Common Dreams News Center*, July 8, 2002, http://www.commondreams.org/views02/0708-08.htm.
2. Bob Herbert, "The Young and the Jobless," *The New York Times*, May 12, 2005, p. A27.
3. These figures are taken from *Childhood Poverty Research Brief 2*, "Child Poverty in the States: Levels and Trends From 1979 to 1998," http://www.nccp.org.
4. Bob Herbert, "The Young and Jobless," *New York Times*, May 12, 2005, A27, http://www.commondreams.org/views03/0602-06.htm.
5. Edmund L. Andrews, "White House Budget Projections Suggest Pain, Much of It Political," *The New York Times*, February 11, 2005, A17.
6. Martin Luther King, Jr., "The Trumpet of Conscience," *A Testament of Hope: The Essential Writings and Speeches of Martin Luther King, Jr.*, ed. James M. Washington (New York: HarperCollins, 1986), 644.
7. For a history of these events, see Christian Parenti, "The 'New' Criminal Justice System: State Repression From 1968–2001," *Monthly Review* 53, no. 3 (2001): 19–28.
8. Steven R. Donziger, ed. *The Real War on Crime: The Report of the National Criminal Justice Commission* (New York: Harper Perennial, 1996), 19.
9. For specifics on this bill, see C. Stone Brown, "Legislating Repression: The Federal Crime Bill and the Anti-Terrorism and Effective Death Penalty Act," in Elihu Rosenblatt, *Criminal Injustice: Confronting the Prison Crisis* (Boston: South End, 1996), 100–107.

10. Cited in Silva J. A. Calvi, "The Craze of Incarceration," *The Progressive*, May 2001, 40–41.

11. Anthony Lewis, "Punishing the Country," *New York Times*, December 2, 1999, A1.

12. For some extensive analyses of the devastating affects the criminal justice system is having on black males, see Michael Tonry, *Malign Neglect: Race, Crime, and Punishment in America* (New York: Oxford University Press, 1995); Jerome Miller, *Search and Destroy: African-American Males in the Criminal Justice System* (Cambridge, UK: Cambridge University Press, 1996); David Cole, *No Equal Justice: Race and Class in the American Criminal Justice System* (New York: The New Press, 1999); David Garland, *The Culture of Control: Crime and Social Order in Contemporary Society* (Chicago: University of Chicago Press, 2001).

13. Parenti, "The 'New' Criminal Justice System," 19.

14. These figures are taken from the following sources: Lewis, "Punishing," A1; Gary Delgado, "Mo' Prisons Equals Mo' Money," *Colorlines*, Winter 1999–2000, 18; Fox Butterfield, "Number in Prison Grows Despite Crime Reduction," *New York Times*, August 10, 2000, A10. See also the special issue of *Monthly Review* 53, no. 3 (July/August 2001) on "Prisons and Executions, The U.S. Model." As of 2001, there are 6.6 million people in the correctional system, with 1.9 million in either prison or jail. Three percent of the U.S. population is under the supervision of the correctional system. See *USA Today*, "Record Numbers Behind Bars," August 26, 2002, 3A.

15. Manning Marable, "Green Party Politics" (speech, Denver, Colorado, June 24, 2000), 3.

16. Prisoners being held in private facilities make up the fastest-growing segment of the jail and prison population in the United States. At the same time, only 7 percent of prisons and jails are privately run. It is worth noting that such prisons have bad track records concerning human rights and providing decent services. They are also actively opposed by correction guards unions. Cited in Lisa Featherstone, "A Common Enemy: Students Fight Private Prisons," *Dissent*, Fall 2000, 78.

17. Robin D. G. Kelley, *Yo' Mama's Disfunktional!* (Boston: Beacon, 1997), 98.

18. Ibid.

19. Cited in David Barsamian, "Interview with Angela Davis," *The Progressive*, February 2001, 35.

20. Cole, *No Equal Justice*, 144.

21. Donziger, ed., *The Real War on Crime*, 101.

22. Cited in Eyal Press, "The Color Test," *Lingua Franca*, October 2000, 55.

23. Donziger, ed., *The Real War on Crime*, xii.

24. Featherstone, "A Common Enemy," 78.

25. Ibid., 81.

26. Paul Street, "Race, Prison, and Poverty: The Race to Incarcerate in the Age of Correctional Keynesianism," *Z Magazine*, May 2001, 25.

27. Cited from Eric Lotke, "The Prison-Industrial Complex," *Multinational Monitor*, November 1996, http://www.igc.org/ncia/pic.html.

28. Mike Davis, "The Politics of Super Incarceration," in Rosenblatt, 73.

29. Street, "Race, Prison, and Poverty," 28.

30. Peter T. Kilborn, "Rural Towns Turn to Prisons to Reignite Their Economies," *New York Times*, August 1, 2001, A1.

31. Even more shameful is that fact that such discrimination against African Americans is often justified from elite institutions such as Harvard University by apologists such as lawyer Randall Kennedy who argue that such laws, criminal policies, and police practices are necessary to protect "good" blacks from "bad" blacks who commit crimes. See Randall Kennedy, *Race, Crime, and the Law* (New York: Pantheon, 1997).

32. For a moving narrative of the devastating effects of the juvenile justice system on teens, see Edward Humes, *No Matter How Loud I Shout: A Year in the Life of Juvenile Court* (New York: Touchstone, 1996).

33. Margaret Talbot, "The Maximum Security Adolescent," *New York Times Magazine*, September 10, 2000, 42.

34. Louise Cooper, "Youth Activists Fight Prop 21," *Against the Current* 86 (May/June 2000): 12.

35. Cited in Evelyn Nieves, "California Proposal Toughens Penalties for Young Criminals," *New York Times*, March 6, 2000, A1, A15.

36. Cited in Sara Rimer and Raymond Bonner, "Whether to Kill Those Who Killed As Youths," *New York Times*, August 22, 2000, A16.

37. Adam Liptak, "Locked Away Forever After Crimes as Teenagers," *The New York Times*, October 3, 2005, A1.

38. Donziger, ed., *The Real War on Crime*, 123.

39. When Tom Smith of the National Opinion Research Center at the University of Chicago asked respondents to compare blacks and other minorities "on a variety of personal traits in 1990, he found that 62% of nonblack respondents thought that blacks were lazier than other groups, 56% felt they were more prone to violence, 53% say they are less intelligent, and 78% thought they were less self-supporting and more likely to live off welfare." Cited in Douglas S. Massey and Nancy A. Denton, *American Apartheid* (Cambridge, MA: Harvard University Press, 1993), 95. I mention this study as simply one example of the widespread racism that permeates American culture. Of course, while blacks are not the only group victimized by stereotypes, unlike many other groups, they often do not have the material resources to fight back and prevent such stereotypes from spreading and influencing individual behavior and social policy. Hence, African Americans, especially black youth, as a group are more likely to suffer the abuse generated by such stereotypes. For a more extensive study of the ongoing presence of racism in American society, see David K. Shipler, *A Country of Strangers: Blacks and Whites in America* (New York: Vintage, 1998); Ronald Walters, "The Criticality of Racism," *Black Scholar* 26, no. 1 (Winter 1996): 2–8. Of course, one could compile an endless list of sources on the latter subject. I only mention three because of limited space.

40. A typical example can be seen in Talbot, 41–47, 58–60, 88, 96. Talbot takes up the "get tough" policies that currently characterize the juvenile justice system but makes no connections to wider social, economic, or political considerations or, for that matter, to the related assaults on teens taking place in a variety of spheres outside of the criminal justice system.

41. Marable, "Green Party Politics," 5.

42. Kate Beem, "Schools Adopting Safety Measures," *Centre Daily Times*, March 3, 2000, 3A.

43. See Brian Moore, "Letting Software Make the Call," *Chicago Reader* 29, no. 49 (September 8, 2000): 18.

44. Ellen Goodman, " 'Zero Tolerance' Means Zero Chance for Troubled Kids," *Centre Daily Times*, January 4, 2000, 8.

45. Editorial, "Zero Tolerance is the Policy," *Denver Rocky Mountain News*, June 22, 1999, 38A.

46. Editorial, "Growing Zeal for Zero Tolerance Ignores Needs of Troubled Youth," *USA Today*, November 22, 1999, 27A.

47. Jesse Jackson, "First-Class Jails, Second-Class Schools" (interview, *Rethinking Schools*, Spring 2000, 16).

48. BBCNews, "US Police Handcuff Five-year Old," *BBCNews.com*, April 23, 2005. Available online: http://news.bbc.co.uk/2/hi/Americas/4475513.stm.

49. Goodman, " 'Zero Tolerance' Mean Zero Chance," 8.

50. Editorial, "Zero Tolerance is the Policy," 38A.

51. Gregory Michie, "One Strike and You're Out: Does Zero Tolerance Work? Or Does Kicking Kids Out of School Just Make Things Worse?" *Chicago Reader* 29, no. 49 (September 8, 2000): 24.

52. It was reported in the *New York Times* that in responding to the spate of school shootings, the FBI has provided educators across the country with a list of behaviors that could

identify "students likely to commit an act of lethal violence." One such behavior is "resentment over real or perceived injustices." The reach of domestic militarization becomes more evident as the FBI not only takes on the role of monitoring potentially disruptive student behavior, but also positions teachers as adjuncts to the criminal justice system. The story and quotations appear in Editorial, "F.B.I. Caution Signs for Violence In Classroom," *New York Times*, September 7, 2000, A18.

53. Tamar Lewin, "Study Finds Racial Bias in Public Schools," *New York Times*, March 11, 2000, A14.

54. Libero Della Piana, "Crime and Punishment in Schools: Students of Color are Facing More Suspensions Because of Racially Biased Policies," *San Francisco Chronicle*, February 9, 2000, A21.

55. Marilyn Elias, "Disparity in Black and White?" *USA Today*, December 11, 2000, 9D.

56. Della Piana, "Crime and Punishment in Schools," A21.

57. Cited in Lewis, "Punishing the Country," A31.

58. Jack Geiger, "The Real World of Race," *The Nation*, December 1, 1997, 28.

59. Martin Luther King, Jr., "Speech Before the Youth March for Integrated Schools," in *A Testament of Hope*, ed. Washington, 22.

PART V
MILITARIZATION, MASCULINITY, AND THE SPECTRE OF FASCISM

WAGING WAR ON DEMOCRACY

THE MILITARIZING OF PUBLIC SPACE

We are in a Hobbesian world, which rests on fear, not on hope. It is in this sense that we can speak of the end of political modernity, since for several centuries politics appeared to be charged with strengthening and making more effective the demands of peoples and individuals for freedom, initiative, and equality of opportunity. It is no surprise to see some dictator place everything at the service of absolute power, even personal enrichment, but the sickness has spread everywhere, to the point that the language used by so many leaders—in the first place by President Bush—now looks like a self-fulfilling prophecy. The political field is declared independent of any social purpose. The spirit of war dictates to politics, even as it takes no account of the demands that should come from below. We can only hope that the events we are experiencing sensitize us to the urgency of reinventing the social basis of all democratic politics.

—Alain Touraine, "Meaningless Politics," 2003[1]

Under the Bush administration, American power is being restructured domestically around a growing culture of fear and a rapidly increasing militarization of public space. As U.S. military action is spreading abroad under the guise of an unlimited war against terrorism, public spaces on the domestic front are increasingly being organized around values supporting a highly militarized, patriarchical, and jingoistic culture that is undermining "centuries of democratic gains."[2] The process of militarization—the increasing centrality of the military in shaping American culture, society, and foreign policy—has a long history in the United States and takes on different forms under different historical conditions.[3] Michael S. Sherry defines militarization as "the process by which war and national security became consuming anxieties and provided memories, models, and metaphors that shaped broad areas of national life."[4] Catherine Lutz adds to that definition:

[Militarization is] an intensification of the labor and resources allocated to military purposes, including the shaping of other institutions in synchrony with military goals. Militarization is simultaneously a discursive process, involving a shift in general societal beliefs and values in ways necessary to legitimate the use of force, the organization of large standing armies and their leaders, and the higher taxes or tribute used to pay for them. Militarization is intimately connected not only to the obvious increase in the size of armies and resurgence of militant nationalisms and militant fundamentalisms but also to the less visible deformation of human potentials into the hierarchies of race, class, gender, and sexuality, and to the shaping of national histories in ways that glorify and legitimate military action.[5]

Unlike the old style of militarization in which all forms of civil authority are subordinate to military authority, the new biopolitics of militarization is organized to engulf the entire social order, legitimating its values as a central rather than peripheral aspect of American public life. Moreover, the values of militarism are no longer limited to a particular group or sphere of society. On the contrary, Jorge Mariscal points out: "In liberal democracies, in particular, the values of militarism do not reside in a single group but are diffused across a wide variety of cultural locations. In twenty-first century America, no one is exempt from militaristic values because the processes of militarization allow those values to permeate the fabric of everyday life."[6] The growing influence of the military presence and ideology in American society is made visible, in part, by the fact that the United States has more police, prisons, spies, weapons, and soldiers than at any other time in its history. This radical shift in the size, scope, and influence of the military can be seen in the redistribution of domestic resources and government funding away from social programs into military-oriented security measures at home and into war abroad. As Richard Falk has pointed out, "The U.S. Government is devoting huge resources to the monopolistic militarization of space, the development of more usable nuclear weapons, and the strengthening of its world-girdling ring of military bases and its global navy, as the most tangible way to discourage any strategic challenges to its preeminence."[7] According to journalist George Monbiot, the federal government "is now spending as much on war as it is on education, public health, housing, employment, pensions, food aid and welfare put together."[8] Moreover, the state itself is being radically transformed into a national security state, increasingly put under the sway of the military-corporate-industrial-educational complex. The military logic of fear, surveillance, and control is gradually permeating our public schools, universities, streets, popular culture, and criminal justice system.

Since the events of 9/11 and the wars in Afghanistan and Iraq, the military has assumed a privileged place in American society. President Bush not only celebrates the military presence in American culture; he cultivates it by going out of his way to give speeches at military facilities, talk to military personnel, and address veterans' groups. He often wears a military uniform when speaking to "captive audiences at military bases, defense plants, and on aircraft carriers."[9] He also takes advantage of the campaign value of military culture by using military symbolism as a political prop in order to attract the widest possible media attention. One glaring example was evident on May 1, 2003, when Bush landed in full aviator flight uniform on the USS *Abraham Lincoln* in the Pacific Ocean, where he officially proclaimed the end of the Iraqi war. There was also the surprise trip to Baghdad to spend Thanksgiving Day (2003) with the troops, an event that attracted worldwide coverage in all the media. Since his reelection in 2004, Bush has showcased defense experts, such as Dick Cheney, Donald Rumsfeld, Condoleezza Rice, and now defeated Paul Wolfowitz, as the most visible and key representatives of a government whose power reflects what

President Eisenhower long ago labeled the "military-industrial complex" and viewed as a dire threat to American democracy.[10] But Bush has done more than take advantage of the military as a campaign prop to sell his domestic and foreign policies. His administration, along with the Republican Party, which now controls all three branches of government, has developed a new, if not dangerous, "and unprecedented confluence of our democratic institutions and the military."[11]

Writing in *Harper's Magazine*, Kevin Baker claims that the military "has become the most revered institution in the country."[12] Andrew J. Bacevich, professor of International Relations at Boston University, argues that "to a degree without precedent in U.S. history, Americans have come to define the nation's strength and well-being in terms of military preparedness, military action, and the fostering of (or nostalgia for) military ideals."[13] Soon after the Iraqi war in 2003, a Gallup Poll reported that over 76 percent of Americans "expressed 'a great deal' or 'quite a lot' of confidence in their nation's military." Among a poll of twelve hundred students conducted by Harvard University, 75 percent believed that the military would most of the time "do the right thing." In addition, the students "characterized themselves as hawks over doves by a ratio of two to one."[14] Popular fears about domestic safety and internal threats, accentuated by endless terror alerts, have created a society that increasingly accepts the notion of a "war without limits" as a normal state of affairs. But fear and insecurity do more than produce a collective anxiety among Americans, exploited largely to get them to believe that they should vote Republican because it is the only political party that can protect them. In addition to producing manufactured political loyalty, such fears can also be manipulated into a kind of "war fever." In such cases, as Robert Lifton points out, "War then becomes heroic, even mythic, a task that must be carried out for the defense of one's nation, to sustain its special historical destiny and immortality of its people."[15]

The mobilization of war fever, intensified through a politics of fear, carries with it a kind of paranoid edge, endlessly stoked by government alerts and repressive laws, and has been used "to create the most extensive national security apparatus in our nation's history."[16] Military support is also reproduced in the Foxified media, which—in addition to constantly marketing the flag and interminably implying that critics of American foreign policy are traitors—offer up seemingly endless images of brave troops on the front line, heroic stories of released American prisoners, and utterly privatized commentaries on those wounded or killed in battle.[17] *Time Magazine* embodied this representational indulgence in military culture by naming "The American Soldier" as the 2003 "Person of the Year." Not only have such ongoing and largely uncritical depictions of war injected a constant military presence in American life; they have also helped to create a civil society that has become aggressive in its warlike enthusiasms. But more is at work here than simply the exploitation of troops for higher ratings or the attempts by right-wing political strategists to keep the American public in a state of permanent fear so as to remove pressing domestic issues from public debate. There is also the attempt by the Bush administration to convince as many Americans as possible that, under the current "state of emergency," the use of the military internally in domestic affairs is perfectly acceptable, and evident in the increasing propensity to use the military establishment "to incarcerate and interrogate suspected terrorists and 'enemy combatants' and keep them beyond the reach of the civilian judicial system, even if they are American citizens."[18] It is also evident in the attempts by the federal government to try terrorists in military courts and to detain prisoners "outside the provisions of the Geneva Convention as prisoners of war . . . at the U.S. Marine Corps base at Guantanamo, Cuba, because that facility is outside of the reach of the American courts."[19]

As the military becomes more popular in American life, its underlying values, social relations, ideology, and hypermasculine aesthetic begin to spread out into other aspects of American culture. Citizens are recruited as foot soldiers in the war on terrorism, urged to spy on their neighbors' behaviors, watch for suspicious-looking people, and supply data to government sources in the war on terrorism. As permanent war becomes a staple of everyday life, flags increasingly appear on storefront windows, lapels, cars, houses, SUVs, and everywhere else, as a show of support for both the expanding interests of empire abroad and the increasing militarization of the culture and social order at home. Major universities now compete for defense contracts and rush to build courses and programs that cater to the interests of the Department of Homeland Security. A number of universities, such as Penn State, not only offer degrees in Homeland Security; they also establish formal ties with government agencies concerned with National Security. Congress recently passed legislation that would "stiffen penalties for colleges that bar military recruiters from their campuses."[20] JROTC programs are increasingly becoming a conventional part of the school day. As a result of President Bush's No Child Left Behind Act, "schools risk losing all federal aid if they fail to provide military recruiters full access to their students; the aid is contingent with complying with federal law."[21] Schools were once viewed as democratic public spheres that would teach students how to resist the militarization of democratic life, or at least to learn the skills to peacefully engage domestic and international problems. Now they serve as recruiting stations for students to fight enemies at home and abroad.

Militarization abroad cannot be separated from the increasing militarization of society at home. War takes on a new meaning in American life as wars are waged on drugs; social policies are criminalized; youth are tried as adults; incarceration rates soar among the poor, especially people of color; and schools are increasingly modeled after prisons. Schools represent one of the most serious public spheres to come under the influence of military culture and values. Tough love now translates into zero tolerance policies that turn public schools into disciplinary institutions that increasingly fail to recognize students' rights. Additionally, as educators turn over their responsibility for school safety to the police, the new security culture in public schools has turned them into "learning prisons," most evident in the ways in which schools are being "reformed" with the addition of armed guards, barbed-wired security fences, and lockdown drills.[22] Recently, in Goose Creek, South Carolina, police conducted an early morning drug-sweep at Stratford High School. When the police arrived they drew guns on students, handcuffed them, and made them kneel facing the wall.[23] No drugs were found in the raid. Though this incident was aired on the national news, there were barely any protests from the public.

And judging from Bush's 2005 State of the Union Address, the Bush administration will continue to allocate funds for "educational reform," intended both to strip young people of the capacity to think critically by teaching them that learning is largely about test-taking and to prepare them for a culture in which punishment has become the central principle of reform. Bush cannot fully fund his own educational reform act, but he pledged in his address an additional $23 million to promote drug testing of students in public schools. Once again, fear, punishment, and containment override the need to provide healthcare for 9.3 million uninsured children, increase the ranks of new teachers by at least 100,000, fully support Head Start programs, repair deteriorating schools, and improve those youth services that will break for many poor students the direct pipeline from school to the local police station, the courts, or prison.

The rampant combination of fear and insecurity that is so much a part of a permanent war culture in the United States seems to bear down particularly hard on children. In many poor school districts, specialists are being laid off and crucial mental health services are being cut back. As Sara Rimer recently pointed out in the *New York Times*, much needed student-based services and traditional, if not compassionate, ways of dealing with student problems are now being replaced by the juvenile justice system, which functions "as a dumping ground for poor minority kids with mental health and special-education problems. . . . The juvenile detention center has become an extension of the principal's office."[24] For example, in some cities, ordinances have been passed that "allow for the filing of misdemeanor charges against students for anything from disrupting a class to assaulting a teacher."[25] Children are no longer given a second chance for minor behavior infractions, nor are they simply sent to the guidance counselor, principal, or to detention. They now come under the jurisdiction of the courts and juvenile justice system.

The militarization of public high schools has become so commonplace that, even in the face of the most flagrant disregard for children's rights, it is justified by both administrators and the public on the grounds that it keeps kids safe. In [pre-Katrina] Biloxi, Mississippi, surveillance cameras were installed in all of its five hundred classrooms. The school's administrators called this "school reform" but none of them asked the question about what they are teaching kids who are put under constant surveillance. At the same time as children encounter a profound distrust on the part of adult society, they are being educated to passively accept military-sanctioned practices organized around maintaining control, surveillance, and unquestioned authority, all conditions central to a police state and to a unique form of protofascism. It gets worse. Some schools are actually using sting operations in which undercover agents who pretend to be students are used to catch young people suspected of selling drugs or committing any one of a number of school infractions. The consequences of such actions are far-reaching. As Randall Beger points out:

> Opponents of school-based sting operations say they not only create a climate of mistrust between students and police, but they also put innocent students at risk of wrongful arrest due to faulty tips and overzealous police work. When asked about his role in a recent undercover probe at a high school near Atlanta, a young-looking police officer who attended classes and went to parties with students replied: "I knew I had to fit in, make kids trust me and then turn around and take them to jail."[26]

Under the auspices of the national security state and the militarization of domestic life, containment policies become the principal means to discipline working-class youth and restrict their ability to think critically and engage in oppositional practices. Marginalized students learn quickly that they are surplus populations and that the journey from home to school no longer means they will next move into a job; on the contrary, school now becomes a training ground for their "graduation" into containment centers such as prisons and jails that keep them out of sight, patrolled, and monitored so as to prevent them from becoming a social canker or political liability to those white and middle-class populations concerned about their own safety. Schools increasingly separate students marginalized by class and color, and as such have become prison-like in their role as social institutions. This follows the argument of David Garland, who points out, "Large-scale incarceration functions as a mode of economic and social placement, a zoning mechanism that segregates those populations rejected by the depleted institutions of family, work, and welfare and places them behind the scenes of social life."[27]

Instances of domestic militarization and the war at home can also be seen in the rise of the prison-industrial-educational complex and the militarization of the criminal justice system. The traditional "distinctions between military, police, and criminal justice are blurring."[28] The police now work in close collaboration with the military. This takes the form of receiving surplus weapons, technology/information transfers, the introduction of SWAT teams modeled after the Navy Seals—which are experiencing a steep growth in police departments throughout the U.S.—and a growing reliance on military models of crime control.[29] This growth of the military model in American life has played a crucial role in the paramilitarizing of the culture, which provides both a narrative and legitimation "for recent trends in corrections, including the normalization of special response teams, the increasingly popular Supermax prisons, and drug war boot camps."[30] In the paramilitaristic perspective, crime is no longer seen as a social problem. Crime is now viewed both as an individual pathology and as a matter of punishing rather than rehabilitating the "enemy." Unsurprisingly, paramilitary culture increasingly embodies a racist and class-specific discourse, and "reflects the discrediting of the social and its related narratives."[31] This is particularly evident as America's inner cities are being singled out as dangerous enclaves of crime and violence. The consequences for those communities have been catastrophic, as can be seen in the cataclysmic rise of the prison-industrial complex. As Sanho Tree points out:

> With more than 2 million people behind bars (there are only 8 million prisoners in the entire world), the United States—with one-twenty-second of the world's population—has one-quarter of the planet's prisoners. We operate the largest penal system in the world, and approximately one quarter of all our prisoners (nearly half a million people) are there for nonviolent drug offenses.[32]

As I mentioned in an earlier chapter, of the two million people behind bars, nearly 70 percent of the inmates are people of color: 50 percent are African American and 17 percent are Latino.[33] When poor youth of color are not being warehoused in dilapidated schools or incarcerated, they are being aggressively recruited by the Army to fight the war in Iraq. For example, Carl Chery recently reported:

> With help from *The Source* magazine, the U.S. military is targeting hip-hop fans with custom made Hummers, throwback jerseys and trucker hats. The yellow Hummer,

spray-painted with two black men in military uniform, is the vehicle of choice for the U.S. Army's "Take It to the Streets campaign"—a sponsored mission aimed at recruiting young African Americans into the military ranks.[34]

It seems that the Army has discovered hip-hop and urban culture, and rather than listening to the searing indictment of poverty, joblessness, and despair that is one of their central messages, the Army recruiters appeal to their most commodified elements by letting the "potential recruits hang out in the Hummer, where they can pep the sound system or watch recruitment videos."[35] Of course, they won't view any videos of Hummers being blown up in the war-torn streets of Baghdad.

Domestic militarization is also widespread in the realm of culture and functions as a mode of public pedagogy, instilling the values and the aesthetic of militarization through a wide variety of pedagogical sites and cultural venues. From video games to Hollywood films to children's toys, popular culture is increasingly bombarded with militarized values, symbols, and images. For instance, Humvee ads offer up the fantasy of military glamour and machismo, marketed to suggest that ownership of these military-designed vehicles first used in Desert Storm guarantees virility for its owners and promotes a mixture of fear and admiration from everyone else. One of the fastest growing sports for middle-class suburban youth is the game of paintball, "in which teenagers stalk and shoot each other on 'battlefields'. (In San Diego, paintball participants pay an additional $50 to hone their skills at the Camp Pendleton Marine Base)."[36] Military recruitment ads flood all modes of entertainment, using sophisticated marketing tools and offering messages that resonate powerfully with young people and particular forms of masculinity that directly serve as an enticement for recruitment. For example, the website for the U.S. Marines, www.marines.com, opens with the sound of gunfire and then provides the following message: "We are the warriors, one and all. Born to defend, built to conquer. The steel we wear is the steel within ourselves, forged by the hot fires of discipline and training. We are fierce in a way no other can be. We are the marines."

The military has found numerous ways to take advantage of the intersection between popular culture and the new electronic technologies. Even as such technologies are being used to recruit and train military personnel, they are also tapping into the realm of popular culture with its celebration of video games, computer technology, the Internet, and other elements of visual culture used by teenagers.[37] Video games such as *Doom* have a long history of using violent graphics and shooting techniques that appeal to the most hyper modes of masculinity. The Marine Corps was so taken in the mid-1990s with *Doom* that they produced their own version of the game, *Marine Doom*, and made it available to download for free. One of the developers of the game, Lieutenant Scott Barnett, claimed at the time that it was a useful game to keep marines entertained. The interface of military and popular culture has not only been valuable in providing video game technology for diverse military uses; it has also resulted in the armed forces developing partnerships "with the video game industry to train and recruit soldiers."[38] The military uses the games to train recruits, and the game makers offer products that have the imprimatur of a first-class fighting machine. Moreover, the popularity of militarized war games is on the rise. Nick Turse argues that the line between entertainment and war is disappearing:

> [A] "military-entertainment complex" [has] sprung up to feed the military's desire to bring out ever-more-realistic computer and video combat games. Through video games, the military and its partners in academia and the entertainment industry are creating an arm of media culture geared toward preparing young Americans for armed conflict.[39]

Combat teaching games offer a perfect fit between the Pentagon, with its accelerating military budget, and the entertainment industry, with annual revenues of $479 billion, which include $40 billion from the video game industry. The entertainment industry offers a stamp of approval for the Pentagon's war games, and the Defense Department provides an aura of authenticity for corporate America's war-based products. While collaboration between the Defense Department and the entertainment industry has been going on since 1997, the permanent war culture that now grips the United States has given this partnership a new life and has greatly expanded its presence in popular culture.

The U.S. Army purchased and now maintains its own video game production studio, developing online software that appeals to computer-literate potential recruits. Capitalizing on its link with industry, a host of new war games are in production. The most attractive feature of the software is the shooting game "that actually simulates battle and strategic-warfare situations."[40] When asked about the violence the games portray, Brian Ball, the lead developer of the game, was crystal clear about the purpose of the video: "We don't downplay the fact that the Army manages violence. We hope that this will help people understand the role of the military in American life."[41] One of the most popular and successful recruiting video games, *America's Army*, teaches young people how "to kill enemy soldiers while wearing your pajamas [and also provides] plenty of suggestions about visiting your local recruiter and joining the real U.S. Army."[42] Clive Thompson argues that "more than 10 million people have downloaded . . . *America's Army* [which] the Army gives away as a recruiting tool."[43] The game, free to use on many gaming websites and also distributed as a free CD-ROM, has become so popular that the Army staged a tournament in New York City and had recruiters waiting at the door.[44] In fact, *America's Army* is one of the most popular video games of all time.

Using the latest versions of satellite technology, military-industry collaboration has also produced *Kuma: War*. This game was developed by the Department of Defense and Kuma Reality Games and is available online. It is a subscription-based product that "prepares gamers for actual missions based on real-world conflicts" and is updated weekly.[45] The game allows players to recreate actual news stories such as the raid American forces conducted in Mosul, Iraq, in which Saddam Hussein's two sons, Uday and Qusay, were killed. The game's "Mission 58" embodies the neoconservative fantasy of empire with its "Assault on Iran" storyline. Gamers can take advantage of real "true to life satellite imagery and authentic military intelligence, to jump from the headlines right into the frontlines of international conflict."[46] Of course, the realities of carrying 80 lb. knapsacks in 120 degree heat, the panic-inducing anxiety and fear of real people shooting real bullets or planting real bombs to kill or maim you and your fellow soldiers, and the months, if not years, away from family, are not among those experiences reproduced for instruction or entertainment. Young people no longer learn military values in training camp or in military-oriented schools. These values are now disseminated through the pedagogical force of popular culture itself, which has become a major tool used by the armed forces to educate young people about the ideology and social relations that inform military life—minus a few of the unpleasantries. The collaboration between the military and entertainment complexes offers up a form of public pedagogy that "may help to produce great battlefield decision makers, but . . . strike from debate the most crucial decisions young people can make in regard to the morality of a war—choosing whether or not to fight and for what cause."[47]

In light of the militaristic transformation of the country, attitudes toward war play have changed dramatically and can be observed in the major increase in the sales, marketing, and consumption of military toys, games, videos, and clothing. Corporations recognize that there are big profits to be made at a time when military symbolism gets a boost from the war in Iraq and from the upsurge in patriotic jingoism. The popularity of militarized culture is apparent not only in the sales of video combat games, but also in the sales of children's toys. Major retailers and major chain stores across the country are selling out of war-related toys. KB Toys retail stores in San Antonio, Texas, sold out in one day an entire shipment of fatigue-clad plush hamsters that dance to military music, and store managers were instructed "to feature military toys in the front of their stores."[48] Moreover, sales of action figures have soared. For example, "between 2001 and 2002, sales of G.I. Joe increased by 46 percent, Hasbro reported. And when toy retailer Small Blue Planet launched a series of figures called 'Special Forces: Showdown With Iraq,' two of the four models sold out immediately."[49] KB Toys took advantage of the infatuation with action toys related to the war in Iraq by marketing a doll that is a pint-sized model of George W. Bush dressed in the U.S. pilot regalia he wore when he landed on the USS *Abraham Lincoln*. Japanese electronic giant SONY attempted to cash in on the war in Iraq by patenting the term "Shock and Awe" for use with video and computer games. The phrase, referring to the massive air bombardment planned for Baghdad in the initial stages of the war, was coined by Pentagon strategists as part of a scare tactic to be used against Iraq. Additionally, the *New York Times* reported that after September 11, 2001, "nearly two-dozen applications were filed for the phrase, 'Let's Roll.' " The term was made famous by one of the passengers on the ill-fated hijacked plane that crashed in a field in Pennsylvania.

Even in the world of fashion, the ever-spreading chic of militarization and patriotism is making its mark. Army-Navy stores are doing a brisk business not only selling American flags, gas masks, aviator sunglasses, night-vision goggles, and other military equipment, but also clothing with the camouflage look.[50] Even chic designers are getting into the act. For instance, at a recent fashion show in Milan, Italy, many designers were "drawn to G.I. uniforms [and were] fascinated by the construction of military uniforms." One designer "had beefy models in commando gear scramble over tabletops and explode balloons."[51]

Fascism in both its old and new forms views life as a form of permanent warfare and, in doing so, subordinates society to the military, rather than viewing the military as subordinate to the needs of a democratic social order. Militarism in this scenario diminishes both the legitimate reasons for a military presence in society and the necessary struggle for the promise of democracy itself. As Umberto Eco points out, under the rubric of its aggressive militarism, protofascist ideology argues that "there is no struggle for life but, rather, life is lived for struggle."[52] The ideology of militarization is central to any understanding of protofascism since it appeals to a form of irrationality that is at odds with any viable notion of democracy. For instance, militarization uses fear to drive human behavior, and the values it promotes are mainly distrust, patriarchy, and intolerance. Within this ideology, masculinity is associated with violence, and action is often substituted for the democratic processes of deliberation and debate. Militarization as an ideology is about the rule of force and the expansion of repressive state power. In fact, democracy appears as an excess in this logic and is often condemned as being a weak system of government.

Echoes of this antidemocratic sentiment can be found in the passages of the Patriot Act with its violation of civil liberties, in the rancorous patriotism that equates dissent with treason, and in the discourse of public commentators who, in the fervor of a militarized culture, fan the flames of hatred and intolerance. One example that has become all too typical emerged after the September 11 attacks. Columnist Ann Coulter, in calling for a holy war on Muslims, wrote, "We should invade their countries, kill their leaders and convert them to Christianity. We weren't punctilious about locating and punishing only Hitler and his top officers. We carpet-bombed German cities; we killed civilians. That's war. And this is war."[53] While this statement does not reflect the mainstream of American opinion, the uncritical and chauvinistic patriotism and intolerance that inform it have become standard fare among many conservative radio hosts in the United States and are increasingly produced and legitimated in a wide number of cultural venues. As militarization spreads through the culture, it produces policies that rely more on force than on dialogue and compassion; it offers up modes of identification that undermine democratic values and tarnish civil liberties; and it makes the production of both symbolic and material violence a central feature of everyday life. As Kevin Baker points out, we are quickly becoming a nation that "substitute[s] military solutions for almost everything, including international alliances, diplomacy, effective intelligence agencies, democratic institutions—even national security."[54] By blurring the lines between military and civilian functions, militarization deforms our language, debases democratic values, celebrates fascist modes of control, defines citizens as soldiers, and diminishes our ability as a nation to uphold international law and support a democratic global public sphere. Unless militarization is systemically exposed and resisted at every place where it appears in the culture, it will undermine the meaning of critical citizenship and do great harm to those institutions that are central to a democratic society.

As militarization spreads its influence both at home and abroad, a culture of fear is mobilized in order to put into place a massive police state intent on controlling and manipulating public speech while making each individual a terrorist suspect subject to surveillance, fingerprinting, and other forms of "electronic tattooing." But the increasing danger of militarization is also evident in the attempt by the corporate-military-media complex to create those ideological and pedagogical conditions in which people either become convinced that the power of the commanding institutions of the state should no longer be held accountable or believe that they are powerless to challenge the new reign of state terrorism. And as militarization spreads its values and power throughout American society and the globe, it works to eliminate those public spaces necessary for imagining an inclusive democratic global society. Militarization and the culture of fear that legitimates it have redefined the very nature of the political and, in doing so, have devalued speech and agency as central categories of democratic public life. And it is precisely as a particular ideology and cultural politics that they have to be opposed.

As the forces of militarization are ratcheted up within multiple spaces in the body politic, they increasingly begin to produce the political currency of fascism in the United States. Both exposing and resisting such an ideology should be one of the primary responsibilities of intellectuals, activists, parents, youth, community members, and others concerned about the fate of democracy on a global scale. Working both within and outside of traditional public spheres such as the media, churches, schools, and universities, individuals and groups can expose the ideology of militarization in all its diversity and how it runs the danger of turning the United States into a military state while at the same time undermining crucial social programs, constitutional liberties, and valuable public spaces. Such intellectual work should take place across nation-states among researchers, academics, intellectuals, and others who produce ideas in the service of social justice, and such work should promote both indignation and collective resistance. This is the pedagogical task that must confront the politics and ideology of militarization. The spreading militarization both at home and abroad demands a new politics of resistance that expands the relationship between politics and everyday life. According to Arundhati Roy, this new politics of resistance requires:

> [F]ighting to win back the minds and hearts of people. . . . It means keeping an eagle eye on public institutions and demanding accountability. It means putting your ear to the ground and listening to the whispering of the truly powerless. It means giving a forum to the myriad voices from the hundreds of resistance movements across the country which are speaking about *real* things—about bonded labor, marital rape, sexual preferences, women's wages, uranium dumping, unsustainable mining, weavers' woes, farmers' suicides. It means fighting displacement and dispossession and the relentless, everyday violence of abject poverty. Fighting it also means not allowing your newspaper columns and prime-time TV spots to be hijacked by their spurious passions and their staged theatrics, which are designed to divert attention from everything else.[55]

At the same time, progressives everywhere have to reinvent the possibility of an engaged politics and real strategies of resistance. This suggests not only working through traditional spheres of political contestation, such as elections or union struggles or various means of education. Collective struggle must combine the tasks of a radical public pedagogy with massive acts of nonviolent collective disobedience. Such acts can serve to educate, to mobilize, and to remind people of the power of alliances, demonstrations, long-term commitments, and of the importance of struggles that change both ideas and relations of power. By making militarization visible through the force of words and peaceful resistance, politics can become both meaningful and possible as a contested site through which people can challenge both locally and within international alliances the obscene accumulation of power symptomatic of the increasing militarization of public space as well as the creeping fascism that is spreading throughout the United States and across the globe. Arundhati Roy is right in her incessant and courageous call to globalize dissent; but, if dissent is to work, it must have a focus that cuts across empires, nation-states, and local space, a focus that cuts to the heart of a clear and present danger to global democracy and social justice. Local strategies are inadequate to challenge the diverse forms of militarization that are both mobile and global challenging militarization in all of its expressions is a direct strike at the heart of a policy that has exceeded its usefulness for democracy and has now formed a dreadful pact with a dangerous authoritarianism. We find ourselves in the midst of a war globally; it is not simply a war against terrorism, but a war against democratic solidarity, a war in which a democratic future both at home and abroad stands in the balance.

Notes

1. Alain Touraine, "Meaningless Politics," *Constellations* 10, no. 3 (September 2003): 311.
2. Susan Buck-Morss, *Thinking Past Terror: Islamism and Critical Theory on the Left* (New York/London: Verso, 2003), 33.
3. John R. Gillis, ed., *The Militarization of the Western World* (New Brunswick, NJ: Rutgers University Press, 1989). On the militarization of urban space, see Mike Davis, *City of Quartz* (New York: Vintage, 1992) and Kenneth Saltman and David Gabbard, eds., *Education as Enforcement: The Militarization and Corporatization of Schools* (New York: Routledge, 2003). For the current neoconservative influence on militarizing American foreign policy, see Donald Kagan and Gary Schmidt, *Rebuilding America's Defenses*, which is one of many reports outlining such an issue and developed under the auspices of The Project for the New American Century (http://www.newamericancentury.org).
4. Michael S. Sherry, *In the Shadow of War: The United States Since the 1930s* (New Haven, CT: Yale University Press, 1995), xi.
5. Catherine Lutz, "Making War at Home in the United States: Militarization and the Current Crisis," *American Anthropologist* 104, no. 3 (September 2003): 723.
6. Jorge Mariscal, " 'Lethal and Compassionate': The Militarization of US Culture," *CounterPunch*, May 5, 2003, http://www.counterpunch.org/mariscal05052003.html.
7. Richard Falk, "Will the Empire be Fascist?" http://www.transnational.org/forum/meet/2003/Falk_FascistEmpire.html.
8. George Monbiot, "States of War," *The Guardian/UK*, October 14, 2003, http://www.commondreams.org/views03/1014-09.htm.
9. Mariscal, " 'Lethal and Compassionate.' "
10. David Harvey, *The New Imperialism* (New York: Oxford University Press, 2005), 192.
11. Kevin Baker, "We're in the Army Now: The G.O.P.'s Plan to Militarize Our Culture," *Harper's Magazine*, October 2003, 38.
12. Ibid., 37.
13. Andrew J. Bacevich, *The New American Militarism* (New York: Oxford University Press, 2004), 2.
14. Ibid.
15. Ruth Rosen, "Politics of Fear," *San Francisco Chronicle*, December 30, 2003, http://www.commondreams.org/views02/1230-02, htm.
16. Ibid.
17. Fox News's and MSNBC's Iraq war coverage was named by *Time Magazine*, no less, in its "The Year in Culture" section as "the worst display of patriotism" for 2003. See *Time Magazine*, January 5, 2004, 151.

18. Richard H. Kohn, "Using the Military at Home: Yesterday, Today, and Tomorrow," *Chicago Journal of International Law* 94, no. 1 (Spring 2003): 174–175.

19. Ibid.

20. Kelly Field, "Colleges That Ban Military Recruiters Would Lose Additional Funds Under New Legislation," *Chronicle of Higher Education*, Daily News Online, October 11, 2004, http://chronicle.com/cgi2-bin/printible.cgi?article=http://chronicle.c . . . See also print article, Kelly Field, "Colleges Risk Losing More Funds for Banning Military Recruiters," *Chronicle of Higher Education*, October 22, 2004, A36.

21. David Goodman, "Covertly Recruiting Kids," *Baltimore Sun*, September 29, 2003, http://www.commondreams.org/views03/1001–11.htm.

22. Gail R. Chaddock, "Safe Schools at a Price," *Christian Science Monitor*, August 25, 1999, 15.

23. Tamar Lewin, "Raid at High School Leads to Racial Divide, Not Drugs," *New York Times*, December 9, 2003, A16.

24. Sandra Rimer, "Unruly Students Facing Arrest, Not Detention," *New York Times*, January 2, 2004, 15.

25. Ibid.

26. Randall Beger, "Expansion of Police Power in the Public Schools and the Vanishing Rights of Students," *Social Justice* 29, no. 1&2 (2002): 124.

27. David Garland cited in Melange, "Men and Jewelry; Prison as Exile: Unifying Laughter and Darkness," *Chronicle of Higher Education*, July 6, 2001, B4.

28. Peter B. Kraska, "The Military-Criminal Justice Blur: An Introduction," in *Militarizing the American Criminal Justice System*, ed. Peter B. Kraska (Boston: Northeastern University Press, 2001), 3.

29. See Christian Parenti, *Lockdown America: Police and Prisons in the Age of Crisis* (London: Verso Press, 1999).

30. Kraska, "Military-Criminal Justice Blur," 10.

31. Jonathan Simon, "Sacrificing Private Ryan: The Military Model and the New Penology," in *Militarizing the American Criminal Justice System*, ed. Kraska, 113.

32. Sanho Tree, "The War at Home," *Sojourner's Magazine*, May–June 2003, 5.

33. Cited in David Barsamian, "Interview with Angela Davis," *The Progressive*, February 2001, 35.

34. Carl Chery, "U.S. Army Targets Black Hip-Hop Fans." *The Wire/Daily Hip-Hop News*, October 21, 2003, http://www.sohh.com/article_print.php?content_ID=5162.

35. Ibid.

36. Mariscal, " 'Lethal and Compassionate.' "

37. For a list of such "toys," see Nicholas Turse, "Have Yourself a Pentagon Xmas," *The Nation*, January 5, 2004, 8. For a more extensive list, see http://www.tomdispatch.com.

38. Matt Slagle, "Military Recruits Video-Game Makers," *Chicago Tribune*, October 8, 2003, 4.

39. Nick Turse, "The Pentagon Invades Your X Box," *Dissident Voice*, December 15, 2003, http://www.dissidentvoice.org/Articles9/Turse_Pentagon-Video-Games.htm.

40. R. Lee Sullivan, "Firefight on Floppy Disk," *Forbes Magazine*, May 20, 1996, 39–40.

41. Gloria Goodale, "Video Game Offers Young Recruits a Peek at Military Life," *The Christian Science Monitor*, May 31, 2003, 18.

42. Wayne Woolley, "From 'An Army of One' to Army of Fun: Online Video Game Helps Build Ranks," *Times-Picayune*, September 7, 2003, 26.

43. Clive Thompson, "The Making of an X Box Warrior," *New York Times Sunday Magazine*, August 22, 2004, 35.

44. See ibid., 34–37.

45. This description comes from *Gaming News*, October 2003, http://www.gamerstemple.com/news/1003/100331.asp.

46. Ibid.

47. Turse, "Pentagon Invades."
48. Maureen Tkacik, "Military Toys Spark Conflict on Home Front," *Wall Street Journal*, March 31, 2003, B1.
49. Amy C. Sims, "Just Child's Play," *Fox News Channel*, August 21, 2003, http://www.wmsa. net/news./Fox News/fn-030822_childs_play.htm.
50. Mike Conklin, "Selling War at Retail," *Chicago Tribune*, May 1, 2003, 1.
51. Both quotes are from Cathy Horyn, "Macho America Storms Europe's Runways," *New York Times*, July 3, 2003, A1.
52. Umberto Eco, "Eternal Fascism: Fourteen Ways of Looking at a Blackshirt," *New York Review of Books*, November-December 1995, 13.
53. This quotation by Coulter has been cited extensively. See: http://www.coulterwatch. com/files/BW_2–003-bin_Coulter.pdf.
54. Baker, "We're in the Army Now," 38.
55. Arundhati Roy, *War Talk* (Cambridge, MA: South End, 2003), 37–38.

13

PRIVATE SATISFACTIONS AND
PUBLIC DISORDER

FIGHT CLUB, PATRIARCHY, AND THE POLITICS OF MASCULINE VIOLENCE

If it has now become easier to imagine the end of the earth and of nature rather than the end of capitalism, as Fredric Jameson argued in *The Seeds of Time*, it is due in large part to the redoubled efforts of a global, neoliberal capitalism.[1] The breathless rhetoric of the global victory of free-market rationality, spewed forth by the mass media, right-wing intellectuals, and governments alike, has found its material expression in an all-out attack on democratic values and on the very notion of the public. Within the discourse of neoliberalism—which construes profit-making as the essence of democracy and provides a rationale for a handful of private interests to control as much of social life as possible in order to maximize their personal profit—issues regarding persistent poverty, inadequate healthcare, racial apartheid in the inner cities, and the growing inequalities between the rich and the poor have been either removed from the inventory of public discourse and social policy or factored into talk-show spectacles. The latter highlight private woes bearing little relationship either to public life or to potential remedies that demand collective action.

As the laws of the market take precedence over the laws of the state as guardians of the public good, the government increasingly offers little help in mediating the interface between the advance of capital and its rapacious commercial interests. Neither does it aid noncommodified interests and nonmarket spheres that create the political, economic, and social conditions vital for critical citizenship and democratic public life. Within the discourse of neoliberalism that has taken hold of the public imagination, there is no vocabulary in which to speak about political or social transformation. There is no collective vision, no social agency to challenge ruthless downsizing, the ongoing liquidation of job security, or the elimination of benefits for people now hired on part-time. In the midst of this concerted attack by big business on the public, market-driven consumerism continues to mobilize desires in the interest of producing market identities and market relationships. These ultimately appear, as Theodor Adorno once put it, as nothing less than "a prohibition on thinking itself."[2]

It is in this context of the ongoing assault on the public by a free-market economy and corporate culture that turns everything it touches into an object of consumption that David Fincher's film, *Fight Club*, needs to be considered. Ostensibly, *Fight Club* offers a critique of late capitalist society and the misfortunes generated by its obsessive concern with profits, consumption, and the commercial values that underline its market-driven ethos. But *Fight Club* is less interested in attacking the broader material relations of power and strategies of domination and exploitation associated with neoliberal capitalism than it is in rebelling against a consumerist culture that dissolves the bonds of male sociality and puts into place an enervating notion of male identity and agency. The onslaught of reviews accompanying the film's premier celebrated it as a daring social critique[3]—the filmic equivalent of magazines like the *Baffler* or *Adbusters*, or even of political protests in Seattle, Washington, D.C., Windsor, Geneva, and Prague against international agents of capitalism like the World Bank, the World Trade Organization, and the International Monetary Fund. But the truth is that *Fight Club* has nothing to say about the structural violence of unemployment, job insecurity, cuts in public spending, and the destruction of institutions capable of defending social provisions and the public good. On the contrary, *Fight Club* defines the violence of capitalism almost exclusively in terms of an attack on traditional (if not to say regressive) notions of masculinity and, in doing so, reinscribes white heterosexuality within a dominant logic of stylized brutality and male bonding that appears predicated on the need to denigrate and wage war against all that is feminine. In this instance, the crisis of capitalism is reduced to the crisis of masculinity, and the nature of the crisis lies less in the economic, political, and social conditions of capitalism itself than in the rise of a culture of consumption in which men are allegedly domesticated, rendered passive, soft, and emasculated.

Fight Club, along with films such as *Pulp Fiction, Rogue Trader, American Psycho, Boiler Room, Pusher,* and *Shadow Boxer,* inaugurates a new subgenre of cult film that combines a fascination with the spectacle of violence, enlivened through tired narratives about the crisis of masculinity, with a superficial gesture toward social critique designed to offer the tease of a serious independent/art film.[4] While appearing to address important social issues, these films end up reproducing the very problems they attempt to address. Rather than turning a critical light on crucial social problems, such films often trivialize them within a stylized aesthetic that revels in irony, cynicism, and excessive violence. Violence in these films is reduced to acts of senseless brutality, pathology, and an indifference to human suffering. Reproducing such hackneyed representations of violence ("senseless," "random"), they conclude where engaged political commentary should begin. Yet I am less interested in moralizing about the politics of David Fincher's film than I am in reading it as a form of public pedagogy that offers an opportunity to engage and understand its politics of representation as part of broader commentary on the intersection of consumerism, masculinity, violence, politics, and gender relations. Moreover, *Fight Club* signifies the role that Hollywood films play as teaching machines. A far cry from simple entertainment, such films function as public pedagogies by articulating knowledge to effects, purposely attempting to influence how and what knowledge and identities can be produced within a limited range of social relations. At the same time, I recognize that such texts "are radically indeterminate with respect to their meaning,

[and] any reading of a text must be determined by factors not prescribed by the text itself."[5]

As public pedagogies, texts such as *Fight Club* attempt to bridge the gap between private and public discourses, while simultaneously putting into play particular ideologies and values that resonate with broader public conversations regarding how a society views itself and the world of power, events, and politics. Reading a film such as *Fight Club* in more specific terms suggests engaging how it offers up particular notions of agency in which white working-class and middle-class men are allowed to see themselves as oppressed and lacking because their masculinity has been compromised by and subordinated to those social and economic spheres and needs that constitute the realm of the feminine.

In taking up these issues, I first analyze the narrative structure of the film, addressing its simultaneous critique of consumerism and its celebration of masculinity. In doing so, I address critically the representational politics that structure *Fight Club*—especially its deeply conventional views of violence, gender relations, and masculinity—and how such representations work in conjunction with a deeply entrenched culture of cynicism. Finally, I argue that such cynicism, far from being innocent, works in tandem with broader public discourses to undermine the faith of individuals and groups to engage in the possibility of a politics designed to struggle against the rising tide of antidemocratic forces and movements that threatens the already weakened fabric of democracy in the U.S. Obviously, I am not arguing that Hollywood films such as *Fight Club* are a cause of these problems, but rather are symptomatic of a wider symbolic and institutional culture of cynicism and senseless violence that exerts a powerful pedagogical influence on shaping the public imagination. In treating *Fight Club* as a pedagogical and political text, my aim is to reveal its socially constructed premises, demystify its contradictions, and challenge its reactionary views. In part, I want to both ask questions about *Fight Club* that have not been generally asked in the popular press and engage how dominant public pedagogies prevent us from asking such questions in the first place. In addition, I take up the role that *Fight Club* and other cultural texts might provide as public pedagogies that can be read against themselves; that is, how such texts can be deconstructed and reworked theoretically within a wider set of associations and meanings that can be both challenged and rearticulated in order to strengthen rather than weaken a public politics, while furthering the promise of democratic transformation.

Fight Club and the Crisis of Everyday Life

In [commercial cinema's] seeming transformation of violence into entertainment, choreography, and macho ebullience, one could say that the reality of violence has been infantilized. One cannot take it too seriously. And yet, one is compelled to ask if any idiom of violence can be regarded as "innocent," distanced from reality through its apparent autonomy of signs.[6]

White, heterosexual men in America have not fared well in the nineties or in the new millennium. Not only have they been attacked by feminists, gays, lesbians, and various subaltern groups for a variety of ideological and material offenses; they have also had to endure a rewriting of the very meaning of masculinity.[7] As Homi Bhabha has stated, the manifest destiny of masculinity with its hard-boiled, tough image of manliness has been disturbed, and its blocked reflexivity has been harshly unsettled.[8] Moreover, the shift from a manufacturing base to an information-based economy, from the production of goods to the production of knowledge has offered men, at least according to Susan Faludi, fewer and fewer meaningful occupations.[9] Consequently, the male body has been transformed from an agent of production to a receptacle for consumption. A rampant culture of consumption, coupled with a loss of manufacturing and middle-management jobs, presents white males with an identity crisis of unparalleled proportions. The male hero of the modern-day workforce is no longer defined in the image of the tightly hewn worker using his body and labor to create the necessities for everyday life. The new workforce hero is now modeled on the image of the young computer whiz yuppie who defines his life and goals around hot start-up e-commerce companies, day trading, and other "get-rich-before-I'm 21" schemes as well as the conspicuous consumption of expensive products. Moreover, as white heterosexual working-class and middle-class men face a life of increasing uncertainty and insecurity, they no longer have easy access to those communities in which they can inhabit and take for granted a form of masculinity that defines itself in opposition to femininity. In simple terms, the new millennium offers white heterosexual men nothing less than a life in which ennui and domestication define their everyday existence.

David Fincher's 1999 film *Fight Club*, based on a novel by Chuck Palahniuk, attempts to critically engage the boredom, shallowness, and emptiness of a stifling consumer culture, redefine what it might mean for men to resist compromising their masculinity for the sofa or cappuccino maker that "speaks them," and explore the possibilities for creating a sense of community in which men can reclaim their virility and power. The film opens with an inside shot of Jack's (played by Edward Norton) brain, tracking a surge of adrenalin that quickly finds an opening in Jack's mouth and then exits up the barrel of a gun. Jack then proceeds to lead the audience into the nature of his predicament and, in doing so, narrates his journey out of corporate America and his evolving relationship with Tyler Durden (Brad Pitt), who functions as Jack's alter-ego and significant other. The first section of the film functions primarily as a critique of contemporary consumerism and how corporate culture positions men in jobs and lifestyles that are an affront to both their manhood and male sociality, leaving them to seek refuge in communities of self-help/support— portrayed as the dreaded cult of victimhood—that only accentuate the contemporary crisis of masculinity. As the film unfolds, Jack is portrayed as a neoliberal Everyman— an emasculated, repressed corporate drone whose life is simply an extension of a reified and commodified culture.

As a recall coordinator, Jack travels around the country investigating accidents for a major auto company in order to decide whether it's cheaper for the corporation to process recalls or payment to a likely number of lawsuits. Alienated from his job, utterly lacking any sense of drive or future, Jack's principal relief comes from an unsatiable urge for flipping through and shopping from consumer catalogues. A slave to the "IKEA nesting instinct," Jack self-consciously offers up rhetorical questions, such as, "What kind of dining set defines me as a person?" But Jack's IKEA-designed apartment appears to offer him no respite from the emptiness in his life, and his consumerist urges only seem to reinforce his lack of enthusiasm for packaging himself as a corporate puppet and presenting himself as a Tom Peters up-and-coming "brand name."[10] Tormented by the emptiness of his daily life and suffering from near terminal insomnia, Jack visits his doctor claiming he is in real pain. His thirty-something doctor refuses to give him drugs and tells him that if he really wants to see pain to visit a local testicular cancer survivor group. Jack not only attends the self-help meeting, but discovers that the group offers him a sense of comfort and community, and in an ironic twist, he becomes a support group junkie. At his first meeting of the Remaining Men Together survival group, Jack encounters Bob (Meat Loaf Aday), a former weightlifter who has enormous breasts (described as "bitch tits") as a result of hormonal treatments. The group allows Jack to partici-pate in a form of male bonding that offers him an opportunity to release his pent-up emotions and provides a cure for his insomnia. Bob becomes a not-too-subtle symbol in the film, personifying how masculinity is both degraded (he has breasts like a woman) and used in a culture that relies upon the "feminine" qualities of support and empathy rather than the "masculine" attributes of strength and virility to bring men together. When Bob hugs Jack and tells him, "You can cry now," *Fight Club* does more than mock new age therapy for men; it is also satirizing and condemning the "weepy" process of femininization that such therapies sanction and put into place.

Jack eventually meets Marla (Helena Bonham Carter), a disheveled, chain-smoking, slinky street urchin who is also slumming in the same group therapy ses-sions as Jack. Jack views Marla as a tourist—addicted only to the spectacle of the meetings. Marla reminds him of his own phoniness and so upsets him that his insom-nia returns, and his asylum is shattered. Jack can't find emotional release with another phony in the same session. In the voice-over, Jack claims that "if I had a tumor I would name it Marla." Once again, repressed white masculinity is thrown into a cri-sis by the eruption of a trivialized version of post-60s femininity that signifies as the antithesis of domestic security, comfort, and sexual passivity—offering only neu-rosis and blame in their place. We now begin to understand Jack's comment in the beginning of the film, after the gun is pulled from his mouth, that "Marla is at the root of it."

On the heels of this loss, Jack meets Tyler Durden (Brad Pitt) on an airplane. Tyler is the opposite of Jack—a bruising, cocky, brash soap salesman, part-time waiter, and movie projectionist with a whiff of anarchism shoring up his speech, dress, and body language. If Jack is a model of packaged conformity and yuppie depthlessness, Tyler is a no-holds-barred charismatic rebel, who as a part-time movie projectionist offers his own attack on family values by splicing frames of pornography into kiddie films, or when working as a banquet waiter in a luxurious hotel urinates into the soup to be served to high-paying yuppie customers. Tyler also creatively affirms his disgust for women by making high-priced soaps from liposuctioned human fat and proudly telling Jack that he is "selling rich ladies their own fat asses back to them at twenty dollars a bar." Jack is immediately taken with Tyler, who taunts him with the appel-lation "IKEA boy" and offers himself as Jack's personal guide to the pitfalls of con-sumer culture. Mesmerized by Tyler's high-octane talk and sense of subversion, Jack exchanges phone numbers with him.

When Jack returns home, he finds that his apartment has been mysteriously blown to bits. He calls Tyler, who meets him at a local bar and tells him that things could be worse: "a woman could cut of your penis while you are sleeping and toss it out the window of a moving car." Tyler then launches into a five-minute, cliché-ridden tirade against the pitfalls of bourgeois life, mixing critique with elements of his own philosophical ramblings about the fall of masculinity. He tells Jack that issues such as crime and poverty don't trouble him. According to Tyler, the real problems men like him confront are "celebrity magazines, television with five hundred channels, some guy's name on my underwear, Rogaine, Viagra, Olestra." And as for the IKEA consumer hype of an idyllic domesticated existence, Tyler indignantly tells Jack, "Things you own end up owning you. . . . Fuck Martha Stewart. . . . Fuck off with your sofa units. . . . [S]top being perfect. Let's evolve." And evolve they do. As they leave the bar, Tyler offers Jack the opportunity to move in with him in what turns out to be a dilapidated, abandoned house near a toxic dump.

Then the magic happens. Before they go back to Tyler's place, Tyler asks Jack to hit him, which Jack does, and then Tyler returns the favor. Pain leads to exhilaration, and they sit exhausted, bloodied, and blissful after their brute encounter. Soon Tyler and Jack start fighting repeatedly in a bar parking lot, eventually drawing a crowd of men who want to participate in brutally pummeling each other. Hence, Fight Club, a new religion and secret society open only to males, is born. Groups of men soon afterwards start meeting in the cellar of a local nightclub in order to beat each other's heads into a bloody mess so as to reclaim their instincts as hunters within a society that has turned them into repressed losers and empty consumers. While Tyler enumerates several rules for the members of Fight Club ("The first rule of Fight Club is that you don't talk about Fight Club"), the one that actually captures the driving sentiment of his philosophy is the exhortation that "Self-improvement is masturbation . . . self-destruction is the answer." For Tyler, physical violence becomes the necessary foundation for masculinity, and collective terrorism the basis for politics itself. In other words, the only way Tyler's followers can become agents in a society that has deadened them is to get in touch with their primal instincts for competition and violence, and the only way their masculine identity can be reclaimed is through the literal destruction of their present selves—beating each other senseless—and their only recourse to community is to collectively engage in acts of militia-inspired terrorism aimed at corporate strongholds.

Eventually Jack has second thoughts about his homoerotic attraction to Tyler as a self-styled antihero when Tyler's narcissism and bravado mutate into an unbridled megalomania that appears more psychotic than anarchistic. Before long, Tyler is spending more and more time with Marla, who appears, to Jack's chagrin, to be screwing Tyler on an almost hourly basis. And Tyler ups the stakes of Fight Club by turning it into Operation Mayhem, a nationwide organization of terrorist thugs whose aim is to wage war against the rich and powerful. The acts of "resistance" carried out by Operation Mayhem, composed of Fight Club graduates, range from what has been described as "culture jamming" (transforming advertising billboards into political slogans; replacing airline safety cards with ones whose images depict the real outcome of a plane crash) to various forms of petty vandalism (demagnetizing an entire store worth of video rentals; encouraging pigeons to shit all over a BMW dealership) to outright anarchic violence against what Tyler sees as the central symbols of domesticated masculinity: computers, the chief agents behind the end of industrialization; yuppie coffee bars, taken as symptomatic of the fetishization and feminization of a drink once associated with labor; and credit-card companies, whose products lie at the very center of contemporary consumer culture.[11] Eventually, the line between taking painful risks as part of the redeeming power of "masculine recovery" and the performance of barbaric fantasies worthy of the most ruthless right-wing militia movements becomes blurred. Before long, one of Operation Mayhem's terrorist forays is botched, and one of their members is killed by the police. The victim is Bob, the oversized testicular cancer survivor who has recently reaffirmed his own manliness by joining Fight Club. Jack is shocked by the killing, which in turn enables him to recognize that Tyler has become a demagogue and that Fight Club has evolved into a fascist paramilitary group more dangerous than the social order it had set out to destroy.

In a psychic meltdown that is long overdue, Jack realizes that he and Tyler are the same person, signaling a shift in the drama from the realm of the sociological to the psychological. Jack discovers that Tyler has planned a series of bombings around the unmentioned city and goes to the police to turn himself in. But the cops are members of Operation Mayhem and attempt to cut off his testicles because of his betrayal. Once more Jack rescues his manhood by escaping and eventually confronting Tyler in a building that has been targeted for demolition by Operation Mayhem. Jack fares badly in his fight with Tyler and ends up at the top of the building with a gun in his mouth. Jack finally realizes that he has the power to take control of the gun and must shoot himself in order to kill Tyler. He puts the gun in his mouth and pulls the trigger. Tyler dies on the spot, and Jack mysteriously survives. Marla is brought to the scene by some Operation Mayhem members. Jack orders them to leave, and he and Marla hold hands and watch as office buildings explode all around them. In an apparent repudiation of all that he/Tyler has been about, Jack turns to Marla and tells her not to worry, "You met me at a weird time in my life," suggesting that life will get better for the both of them in the future.

Consumerism, Cynicism, and Hollywood Resistance

Consumerism . . . is less of an ideological falsification of well-being than a mark that no benefit exterior to the system can be imagined.[12]

As I have attempted to demonstrate, central to *Fight Club* is the interrelated critique of late capitalism and the politics of masculinity. The protagonists, Jack and Tyler, represent two opposing registers that link consumerism and masculinity. Jack is representative of a generation of men condemned to corporate peonage whose emotional lives and investments are mediated through the allure of commodities and goods. No longer a producer of goods, Jack exemplifies a form of domesticated masculinity— passive, alienated, and without ambition. On the other hand, Tyler exemplifies an embodied masculinity that refuses the seductions of consumerism, while fetishizing forms of production—from soaps to explosives—the ultimate negative expression of which is chaos and destruction. Tyler represents the magnetism of the isolated, dauntless antihero whose public appeal is based on the attractions of the cult-personality rather than on the strengths of an articulated, democratic notion of political reform. Politics for Tyler is about doing, not thinking. As the embodiment of aggressive masculinity and hyperindividualism, Tyler cannot imagine a politics that connects to democratic movements, and is less a symbol of vision and leadership for the new millennium than a holdover of early-twentieth-century fascist ideologies that envisioned themselves as alternatives to the decadence and decay of the established order of things. Tyler, played by the Hollywood superstar Brad Pitt (a contradiction that cannot be overlooked), seems appropriate as the founding father of Operation Mayhem—a vanguardist political movement, hierarchically organized through rigid social relations and led by a charismatic cult leader, that is represented as the only enabling force to contest the very capitalism of which it is an outgrowth. If Jack represents the crisis of capitalism repackaged as the crisis of a domesticated masculinity, Tyler represents the redemption of masculinity repackaged as the promise of violence in the interests of social and political anarchy.

While *Fight Club* registers a form of resistance to the rampant commodification and alienation of contemporary neoliberal society, it ultimately has little to say about those diverse and related aspects of consumer culture and contemporary capitalism structured in iniquitous power relations, material wealth, and hierarchical social formations. *Fight Club* largely ignores issues surrounding the breakup of labor unions, the slashing of the U.S. workforce, extensive plant closings, downsizing, outsourcing, the elimination of the welfare state, the attack on people of color, and the growing disparities between the rich and the poor. All of these issues get factored out of *Fight Club's* analysis of consumerism and corporate alienation. Hence, it comes as no surprise that class as a critical category is nonexistent in this film. When working-class people do appear, they are represented primarily as brown shirts, part of the nonthinking herd looking for an opportunity to release their tensions and repressed masculine rage through forms of terrorist violence and self-abuse. Or they appear as people who willingly take up jobs that are dehumanizing, unskilled, and alienating. There is one particularly revealing scene in *Fight Club* that brings this message home while simultaneously signaling a crucial element of the film's politics. At one point in the story, Tyler takes Jack into a convenience store. He pulls out a gun and forces the young Korean clerk to get on his knees. Putting the gun to the clerk's head, Tyler tells him he is going to die. As a kind of parting gesture, he then asks Raymond, the clerk, what he really wanted to be in life. A veterinarian, Raymond replies, but he had to drop out of school because of a lack of money. Tyler tells him that if he isn't on his way to becoming a veterinarian in six weeks, he is going to come back and kill him. He then lets Raymond go and tells Jack that tomorrow morning will be the most important day in Raymond's life because he will have to address what it means to do something about his future. Choice for Tyler appears to be an exclusively individual act, a simple matter of personal will that functions outside of existing relations of power, resources, and social formations. As Homi Bhabha points out, this notion of agency "suggests that 'free choice' is inherent in the individual [and] . . . is based on an unquestioned 'egalitarianism' and a utopian notion of individualism that bears no relation to the history of the marginalized, the minoritized, the oppressed."[13]

This privatized version of agency and politics is central to understanding Tyler's character as emblematic of the very market forces he denounces. For Tyler, success is simply a matter of getting off one's back and forging ahead; individual initiative and the sheer force of will magically cancel out institutional constraints, and critiques of the gravity of dominant relations of oppression are dismissed as either an act of bad faith or the unacceptable whine of victimization. Tyler hates consumerism, but he values a "Just Do It" ideology appropriated from the marketing strategists of the Nike corporation and the ideology of the Reagan and Bush eras. It is not surprising that in linking freedom to the dynamics of individual choice, *Fight Club* offers up a notion of politics in which oppression breeds contempt rather than compassion, and social change is fueled by totalitarian visions rather than democratic struggles. By defining agency through such a limited (and curiously Republican Party) notion of choice, *Fight Club* reinscribes freedom as an individual desire rather than the "testing of boundaries and limits as part of a communal, collective process."[14] In the end, *Fight Club* removes choice as a "public demand and duty" and, in doing so, restricts the public spaces people are allowed to inhabit as well as the range of subject positions they are allowed to take up.[15] Those spaces of debate, dialogue, and resistance such as union halls, democratic social movements, clubs, churches, and other educational/political sites simply disappear in this film. Hence, it is no wonder that *Fight Club* is marked by an absence of working men and women who embody a sense of agency and empowerment, focusing instead on largely middle-class heterosexual white men who are suffering from a blocked hypermasculinity.

Consumerism in *Fight Club* is criticized primarily as an ideological force and existential experience that weakens and domesticates men, robbing them of their primary role as producers whose bodies affirm and legitimate their sense of agency and control. The importance of agency is not lost on director David Fincher; but it is restricted to a narrowly defined notion of masculinity that is as self-absorbed as it is patriarchal.[16] Fincher is less interested in fighting oppressive forms of power than he is in exploring how men yield to it. Freedom in *Fight Club* is not simply preoccupied with the depoliticized self; it also lacks a language for translating private troubles into public rage, and as such succumbs to the cult of immediate sensations in which freedom degenerates into collective impotence. Given Fincher's suggestion that men have no enduring qualities outside of their physicality, resistance and affirmation are primarily taken up as part of a politics of embodiment that has little concern for critical consciousness, social critique, or democratic social relations of resistance. In *Fight Club*, the body is no longer the privileged space of social citizenship or political agency, but becomes "the location of violence, crime, and [aggression]."[17] What changes in *Fight Club* is the context enabling men to assault each other; but the outside world remains the same, unaffected by the celebration of a hypermasculinity and violence that provides the only basis for solidarity.[18]

Fight Club's critique of consumerism suffers from a number of absences that need to be addressed. First, the film depicts capitalism and the ideology of consumerism as sutured, impenetrable, and totalizing, offering few if any possibilities for resistance or struggle, except by the heroic few. There is no sense of how people critically mediate the power of capitalism and the logic of consumerism, turn it against itself, and, in doing so, offer up daily possibilities for resistance, survival, and democratic struggles.[19]

No space exists within *Fight Club* for critical engagements, political understanding, and enlightened forms of social change. Moreover, consumerism, for David Fincher, can only function within the libidinal economy of repression, particularly as it rearticulates the male body away from the visceral experiences of pain, coercion, and violence toward the more "feminized" notions of empathy, compassion, and trust. Hence, masculinity is defined in opposition to both femininity and consumerism, while simultaneously refusing to take up either in a dialectical and critical way.

Second, *Fight Club* functions less as a critique of capitalism than as a defense of a highly stereotypical and limited sense of masculinity that is seen as wedded to the immediacy of pleasure sustained through violence and abuse. Once again, *Fight Club* becomes complicitous with the very system of commodification it denounces since both rely upon a notion of agency largely constructed within the immediacy of pleasure, the cult of hypercompetitiveness, and the market-driven desire of winning and exercising power over others. Third, *Fight Club* resurrects a notion of freedom tied to a Hobbesian world in which cynicism replaces hope, and the ideology of the "survival of the fittest" becomes literalized in the form of a clarion call for the legitimation of dehumanizing forms of violence as a source of pleasure and sociality. Pleasure in this context has less to do with justice, equality, and freedom than with hyper modes of competition mediated through the fantasy of violence. More specifically, this particular rendering of pleasure is predicated on legitimating the relationship between oppression and misogyny, and masculinity gains its force through a celebration of both brutality and the denigration of the feminine. Hence, *Fight Club* appears to have no understanding of its own articulation with the very forces of capitalism it appears to be attacking, and this is most evident in its linking of violence, masculinity, and gender. In other words, *Fight Club*'s vision of liberation and politics relies on gendered and sexist hierarchies that flow directly from the consumer culture it claims to be criticizing.

Violence and the Politics of Masculinity

Unlike a number of Hollywood films in which violence is largely formulaic and superficially visceral, designed primarily to shock, titillate, and celebrate the sensational, *Fight Club* uses violence as both a form of voyeuristic identification and a pedagogical tool. Although *Fight Club* offers up a gruesome and relentless spectacle of bare-knuckled brutality, blood-curdling and stylistic gore, violence becomes more than ritualistic kitsch: it also provides audiences with an ideologically loaded context and mode of articulation for legitimating a particular understanding of masculinity and its relationship to important issues regarding moral and civic agency, gender, and politics. Violence in *Fight Club* is treated as a sport, a crucial component that lets men connect with each other through the overcoming of fear, pain, and fatigue, while reveling in the illusions of a paramilitary culture. For example, in one vivid scene, Tyler initiates Jack into the higher reaches of homoerotically charged sadism by pouring corrosive lye on his hand, watching as the skin bubbles and curls. Violence in this instance signals its crucial function in both affirming the natural "fierceness" of men and in providing them with a concrete experience that allows them to connect at some primal level. As grotesque as this act appears, Fincher does not engage it—or similar representations in the film—as expressions of pathology.[20] On the contrary, such senseless brutality becomes crucial to a form of male bonding, glorified for its cathartic and cleansing properties.[21] By maximizing the pleasures of bodies, pain, and violence, *Fight Club* comes dangerously close to giving violence a glamorous and fascist edge.[22] In many respects, *Fight Club* mimics fascism's militarization and masculinization of the public sphere with its exultation of violence "as a space in which men can know themselves better and love one another legitimately in the absence of the feminine."[23] As a packaged representation of masculine crisis, *Fight Club* reduces the body to a receptacle for pain parading as pleasure, and, in doing so, fails to understand how the very society it attempts to critique uses an affirmative notion of the body and its pleasures to create consuming subjects. Terry Eagleton captures this sentiment:

> Sensation in such conditions becomes a matter of commodified shock-value regardless of content: everything can now become pleasure, just as the desensitized morphine addict will grab indiscriminately at any drug. To posit the body and its pleasures as an unquestionably affirmative category is a dangerous illusion in a social order which reifies and regulates corporeal pleasure for its own ends just as relentlessly as it colonizes the mind.[24]

But the violence portrayed in *Fight Club* is not only reductionistic in its affirmation of physical aggression as a crucial element of male bonding; it also fails to make problematic those forms of violence that individuals, dissidents, and various marginalized groups experience as daily acts of oppression deployed by the state, racist and homophobic individuals, and a multitude of other oppressive social forces. What are the limits of romanticizing violence in the face of those ongoing instances of abuse and violence that people involuntarily experience everyday because of their sexual orientation, the color of their skin, their gender, or their class status?[25] There is no sense in *Fight Club* of the complex connections among the operations of power, agency, and violence, or of how some forms of violence function to oppress, infantilize, and demean human life.[26] Nor is there any incentive—given the way violence is sutured to primal masculinity—to consider how violence can be resisted, alleviated, and challenged through alternative institutional forms and social practices. It is this lack of discrimination among diverse forms of violence and the conditions for their emergence, use, and consequences, coupled with a moral indifference to how violence produces human suffering, that positions *Fight Club* as a morally bankrupt and politically reactionary film.[27] Representations of violence, masculinity, and gender in *Fight Club* seem all too willing to mirror the pathology of individual and institutional violence that informs the American landscape, extending from all manner of hate crimes to the far Right's celebration of paramilitary and protofascist subcultures.

Fight Club does not rupture conventional ways of thinking about violence in a world in which casual violence and hip nihilism increasingly pose a threat to human life and democracy itself. Violence in this film functions largely through a politics of denial, insulation, and disinterest, and the film is unable to criticize with any self-consciousness the very violence that it gleefully represents and celebrates. *Fight Club* portrays a society in which public space collapses and is filled by middle-class white men—disoriented in the pandemonium of conflicting social forces—who end up with a lot of opportunities for violence and few, perhaps none at all, for argument and social engagement.[28] Macho ebullience in *Fight Club* is directly linked to the foreclosure of dialogue and critical analysis, and moves all too quickly into an absolutist rhetoric that easily lends itself to a geography of violence in which there are no ethical discriminations that matter, no collective forces to engage or stop the numbing brutality and rising tide of aggression. While Jack renounces Tyler's militia-like terrorism at the end of *Fight Club*, it appears as a meaningless gesture of resistance, as all he can do is stand by and watch as various buildings explode all around him. The message here is entirely consistent with the cynical politics that inform the film— violence is the ultimate language, referent, and state of affairs through which to understand all human events, and there is no way of stopping it. This ideology becomes even more disheartening given the film's attempt to homogenize violence under the mutually determining forces of pleasure and masculine identity formation, as it strategically restricts not only our understanding of the complexity of violence, but also, as Susan Sontag has suggested in another context, "dissolves politics into pathology."[29]

The pathology at issue—one that is central to *Fight Club*—is the film's intensely misogynist representation of women, and its intimation that violence is the only means through which men can be cleansed of the dire effect women have on the shaping of their identities. From the first scene of *Fight Club* to the last, femininity is cast as the binary opposite of masculinity. Women are both the other and a form of pathology. Jack begins his narrative by claiming that Marla is the cause of all of his problems. Tyler consistently tells Jack that men have lost their manhood because they have been feminized; they are a generation raised by women. And the critical commentary on consumerism presented throughout the film is really not a serious critique of capitalism as much as it is a criticism of the feminization and domestication of men in a society driven by relations of buying and selling. Consumerism is criticized because it is womanish stuff. Moreover, the only primary female character, Marla, appears to exist simultaneously to make men unhappy and to service their sexual needs. Marla has no identity outside of the needs of the warrior mentality and the chest-beating impulses of men who revel in patriarchy and enact all of the violence associated with such traditional, hypermasculine stereotypes.[30]

But representations of masculinity in *Fight Club* do more than reinscribe forms of male identity within a warrior mentality and space of patriarchical relations. They also work to legitimate unequal relations of power and oppression, while condoning a view of masculinity predicated on the need to wage violence against all that is feminine both within and outside of their lives.[31] Masculinity in this film is directly linked to male violence against women by virtue of the way in which it ignores and thus sanctions hierarchical, gendered divisions and a masculinist psychic economy. By constructing masculinity on an imaginary terrain in which women are foregrounded as the other, the flight from the feminine becomes synonymous with sanctioning violence against women as it works simultaneously to eliminate different and opposing definitions of masculinity. Male violence offers men a performative basis on which to construct masculine identity, and it provides the basis for abusing and battering an increasing number of women. According to the National Center for

Victims of Crime, an estimated 6 million women are assaulted by a male partner each year in the United States and, of these, 1.8 million are severely assaulted.[32] Affirming stereotypical notions of male violence, while remaining silent about how such violence works to serve male power in subordinating and abusing women, both legitimates and creates the pedagogical conditions for such violence to occur. *Fight Club* provides no understanding of how gendered hierarchies mediated by a misogynist psychic economy encourage male violence against women. In short, male violence in this film appears directly linked to fostering those ideological conditions that justify abuse toward women by linking masculinity exclusively to expressions of violence and defining male identity against everything that is feminine.

Fight Club as Public Pedagogy

There is a link between epistemology and morality: between how we get to know what we know (through various, including electronic media) and the moral life we aspire to lead. . . . Terrible things, by continuing to be shown, begin to appear matter-of-fact, a natural rather than man-made catastrophe. Zygmunt Bauman has labeled this the "production of moral indifference."[33]

While *Fight Club* generated a number of critical commentaries, few reviewers addressed the misogynistic nature of the film or the warrior mythology of the 1980s that it so closely resembled ideologically and politically.[34] In some cases, high-profile critics such as Janet Maslin, writing in the *New York Times*, not only defended the film as a serious attempt to examine the "lure of violence" in a "dangerously regimented, dehumanized culture," she also condemned as mindless those critics who might view the film as a nihilistic "all-out assault on society."[35] Oddly enough, Twentieth Century Fox, the studio that produced *Fight Club*, viewed such criticism as dangerous rather than simply mindless, and proceeded to withdraw all of its movie advertising in the trade paper *The Hollywood Reporter*, because it had published two critical reviews of the film. But while such politics were not new to Hollywood, the overt attempts by a major studio to censor the voices of dissent—because some critical reviews spoke to the willing use of political power by corporate institutions in the cultural sphere to close down democratic relationships, denigrate women, and celebrate mindless violence—should have nevertheless elicited public outrage. Certainly, Twentieth Century Fox had little to fear from the "progressive" critics who largely praised the film. For example, Amy Taubin, writing for *Sight and Sound*, extolled the film for "screwing around with your bio-rhythms" and for expressing some "right-on-the—*zeitgeist* ideas about masculinity."[36] Taubin, it seems, was also bowled over with Brad Pitt's newfound masculinity, and claimed that "Pitt has never been as exquisite as he is with a broken nose and blood streaming down his cut body."[37] Susan Faludi made the remarkable statement in *Newsweek* that *Fight Club* is a *"feminist film"* (my emphasis).[38] It seemed that the connection between *Fight Club*'s underlying misogynist premises and its similarity to a number of recent Hollywood films that offered denigrating images of women had been lost on critics such as Maslin, Taubin, as well as the feminist-backlash expert, Faludi. Even worse, the online journal *Slate* argued that veteran rock video director Fincher had transformed cinema with his hip digital editing style and that the most "thrilling thing about *Fight Club* isn't *what it says* but how . . . Fincher pulls you into its narrator's head and simulates his adrenalin rushes" (my emphasis).[39] Gary Crowdus reviewing the video release of *Fight Club* praised it as a "pitch-black comedy, an over-the-top, consciously outrageous social satire, characterized by excess and satire."[40] The violence in this film for Crowdus was merely an expression of comic fun, and for those critics who missed it, each scene of violence "simply provided a comic or dramatic context for every fight, with each bout functioning in terms of character development or to signal a key turning point in the plot."[41] Largely formalist in nature, Crowdus's praise of the film completely ignored how it might be taken up as a form of public pedagogy or public transcript. There is no sense of how *Fight Club* resonated and functioned through its refusal to rupture dominant codes within a much larger discursive arena in which violence, masculinity, and sexism are being presented by the right-wing and dominant media. Crowdus made the mistake of treating this text as if it were merely hermetic, and, in doing so, he appeared unable to engage it through a language of articulation that addresses *Fight Club* in the context of contemporary representations and politics, particularly with respect to the interrelationships of gender, violence, and masculinity.

Fight Club's overall success with a large number of critics was also buoyed by an ongoing series of interviews with its stars, Edward Norton, Brad Pitt, and Helena Bonham Carter, as well as a number of well-placed interviews with the film's director, David Fincher.[42] Norton, for example, argued that the film is about young men having a problem defining their manhood and that it has little to do with fighting: "The fight club is not about fighting; it is a manifestation of a desire to strip away everything and rediscover yourself."[43] Norton went so far as to claim that *Fight Club* is really a comedy similar to the classic coming-of-age film *The Graduate*. One of the more incredible comments came from Helena Bonham Carter, who defended the film by claiming that Fincher is a feminist. In describing why she took on the role of Marla, she stated, "The script was awfully dark, and in bad hands it could have been immature or possibly even irresponsible. But after meeting him, I could tell that it wasn't going to be a concern. He's not just an all-out testosterone package. He's got a healthy feminist streak."[44] Fincher appeared at times to be caught on the defensive in having to provide some theoretical explanation and ethical justification for the film. Claiming that *Fight Club* was a film "that's downloaded in front of you. It doesn't wait for you," he seemed to suggest that many critics were tripping over themselves trying to understand the film. He has also argued that while the film is a coming-of-age narrative, he doesn't "purport for a second to know what a film should be, what entertainment should be, how much it should teach, how much it should titillate. I am just trying to make a good, funny movie."[45] And, of course, the implication is that neither should his audience know these things. Fincher's comments were more than disingenuous; they represented, at the very least, an apologetic discourse for the increasing merger of over-the-top violence, hypermasculinity, and sexist inscriptions of women in Hollywood films.[46]

All of these comments exhibit a cavalier indifference to the ways in which films operate as public pedagogies within a broader set of articulations. That is, they ignore how such films function as public discourses that address or at least resonate with broader issues in the historical and sociopolitical context in which they are situated.

There is no sense of how *Fight Club*—or films in general—bridge the gap between public and private discourses, playing an important role in placing particular ideologies and values into public conversation while offering a pedagogical space for addressing specific views of how everyday lives are intertwined with politics, social relations, and existing institutional formations. For instance, Fincher seems completely unaware of how his portrayal of violence and hypermasculinity resonates with the reactionary mythology of warrior culture that reached its heyday during Ronald Reagan's presidency and found its cultural embodiment in figures such as John Wayne, Oliver North, and a host of Hollywood movies celebrating rogue warriors such as *Lethal Weapon, Missing in Action, Robocop*, and *Rambo*.[47]

Given the enormous violence, misogyny, aggression, and political indifference that permeate contemporary daily life, it is crucial to understand how representations of male violence, scorn for everything that is feminine, and a protofascist politics in a film such as *Fight Club* resonate with a broader assemblage of historical and contemporary forces to reproduce, rather than challenge, some of the more oppressive forces in American society. Clearly, many supporters of *Fight Club* as well as Fincher and the film's stars appear completely indifferent to the kind of ideological work *Fight Club* performs in linking masculinity, violence, and politics at a historical moment when public politics is collapsing into privatized discourses and pleasures, and the crisis of masculinity is widely perceived as the most important manifestation of changing economic conditions. While it would be easy to dismiss the comments by Fincher, Norton, and Bonham Carter as nothing more than self-serving publicity—or simply idiotic in light of the representational politics of the film—such comments exemplify a period in which, as Hannah Arendt has pointed out in another context, violence might best be understood by connecting it less to people who are "cold-blooded enough to 'think the unthinkable,' [than to the fact] that they do not think."[48] Against the emergence of films such as *Fight Club* and the refusal on the part of critics and others to link the violence in the film to the violence directed against women, public life, and democracy itself, progressives and others need to question not only the conditions for the production of such films, but also how they work to construct particular definitions of agency. Such questions are crucial if progressives are going to rightfully explore what tools are needed to resist such romanticized notions of violence and masculinity.

Equally important is the need to understand *Fight Club* within both the heritage and the growing reemergence of fascist cultural formations.[49] Paul Gilroy argues convincingly that contemporary formations are organized around "the special investment that fascist movements have made in the ideal of fraternity" as well as the "comprehensive masculinization of the public sphere and the militaristic style with which this has been accomplished in many different settings . . . [and] the strongly masculinist character derived principally from the exultation of war."[50] *Fight Club* emulates elements of what Gilroy calls a generic fascism, partially rehabilitating certain fascist ideas and principles that debase civic culture, and it does so by allowing an "armed and militarized political subject . . . to know itself" through the aestheticization of politics in which libidinal pleasure, paramilitary rituals, and authoritarian rule intersect to authenticate "proto-fascistic, fascistic, and pseudo-fascistic forms of political culture."[51] Home-grown fascism may be easy to spot in the growing presence and violence of neo-Nazi organizations and other hate groups such as the National Association for the Advancement of White People, but it is less obvious in those popular modes of representation and image-making, including films such as *Fight Club*, that feature excessive doses of paramilitary spectacle, appeal to the logic-defying patterns of conspiracy theory, and mobilize forms of identification around the temptations of fascist investments in militarized forms of male bonding and solidarity. Gilroy rightly argues that militarization was and remains the center of fascist style and aesthetic values that increasingly find their most persuasive expressions in the pedagogical space that links entertainment with politics. Fincher's film reminds us: "The heritage of fascist rule survives inside democracy as well as outside it."[52]

In opposition to films such as *Fight Club*, progressives need to consider developing pedagogies of disruption that unsettle the commonsensical assumptions and ways of thinking that inform films and other cultural texts, particularly those that construct and legitimate certain subject positions, identities, values, and social relations that both celebrate pathological violence and render hypermasculine culture as a space in which to reinscribe the hierarchies of gender, race, sexuality, and politics. James Snead is right when he argues:

> Mass culture in America today consists of an entirely new set of artifacts—mass visual productions. These new artifacts require new ways of seeing and new ways of thinking about what we are seeing. . . . We have to be ready, as film-goers, not only to see films, but also to see through them; we have to be willing to figure out what the film is claiming to portray, and also to scrutinize what the film is actually showing. Finally, we need to ask from whose social vantage point any film becomes credible or comforting, and ask why?[53]

But this should not suggest that educators, progressives, and others simply need to teach students and others the skills of critical literacy in order, for instance, to demythologize specific representations of violence or to engage gendered representations in radically new ways. This is an important but inadequate strategy. We need to go beyond questions of literacy and critique to issues of politics, power, and social transformation.

At the very least, the emergence of films such as *Fight Club* suggests that progressives need a new civic language and vocabulary to address the relevance of culture, politics, and pedagogy in order not just to understand how to read texts critically, but also to comprehend how knowledge circulates through various circuits of power in order to put into place images, experiences, representations, and discourses that objectify others and create the ideological conditions for individuals to become indifferent to how violence in its diverse expressions promotes human suffering. This suggests developing forms of public pedagogy not only that critically engage how language, images, sounds, codes, and representations work to structure basic assumptions about freedom, citizenship, public memory, and history, but that are also attentive to how the material relations of power that produce and circulate forms of common sense can be challenged and transformed on both a national and transnational level. In this instance, public pedagogy links knowledge to power in an effort to understand how to effect social change. At stake here is both recognizing and developing a new vision of what we want the future to be, and struggling to acknowledge not only that the fundamental nature of cultural politics and knowledge production has changed dramatically in the last fifty years, but that culture industries and visual culture have become the primary pedagogical/political forces/spaces in shaping consciousness and legitimating dominant social practices. This is not meant to suggest that culture exists in opposition to what some have called a material politics, as much as it points to the necessity of recognizing the pedagogical nature of any attempt to both unlearn and relearn what it might mean to challenge those commonsense assumptions and institutional forms that shape oppressive relations, regardless of how and where they manifest themselves.

Films such as *Fight Club* become important as public pedagogies because they play a powerful role in mobilizing meaning, pleasures, and identifications. They produce and reflect important considerations of how human beings should live, engage with others, and define themselves, and they address how a society should take up questions fundamental to its survival. At the same time, if we are to read films such as *Fight Club* as social and political allegories articulating deeply rooted fears, desires, and visions, they have to be understood within a broader network of cultural spheres and institutional formations such as schools, the media, talk radio, and films rather than as isolated texts. The pedagogical and political character of such films resides in the ways in which they align with broader social, sexual, economic, class, and institutional configurations that reproduce what it means to be a man, woman, gay, worker, child, and citizen in a democratic society.

Needless to say, *Fight Club*, as well as any other cultural text, can be read differently by different audiences, and this suggests the necessity to take up such texts in the specificity of the contexts in which they are received. But at the same time, educators, social critics, and others can shed critical light on how such texts work pedagogically to legitimate some meanings, invite particular desires, and exclude others. Acknowledging the educational role of such films requires that educators and others find ways to make the political more pedagogical. One approach would be to develop a pedagogy of disruption that would attempt to make students and others more attentive to visual and popular culture as an important site of political and pedagogical struggle. Such a pedagogy would raise questions regarding how certain meanings under particular historical conditions become more legitimate as representations of the real than others, or how certain meanings take on the force of commonsense assumptions and proceed relatively unchallenged in shaping a broader set of discourses and social configurations. Such a pedagogy would raise questions about how *Fight Club*, for instance, resonates with the ongoing social locations and conditions of fear, uncertainty, sexism, and political despair through which many people now live their lives. More specifically, a pedagogy of disruption would engage a film's attempts to shift the discourse of politics away from issues of justice and equality and toward a focus on violence and individual freedom as part of a broader neoliberal backlash against equity, social citizenship, and human rights. Such an approach would not only critically engage the dominant ideologies of masculinity, violence, and sexism that give *Fight Club* so much power in the public imagination, but also work to expose the ideological contradictions and political absences that characterize the film by challenging it as symptomatic of the growing reaction against feminism, the right-wing assault on the welfare state, and the increasing use of violence to keep in check marginalized groups such as young black males who are now viewed as a threat to order and stability.

Any attempt to critically address *Fight Club* and the implications it suggests for the changing nature of representational politics must also acknowledge that power is never totalizing and that, even within an increasingly corporatized social landscape, there are always cracks, openings, and spaces for resistance. *Fight Club* reminds us of the need to reclaim ethics, politics, and critical agency as important to the struggle against the rising tide of violence, human suffering, and the spectre of fascism that threatens all vestiges of democratic public life. Precisely because of its ideological implications, *Fight Club* posits an important challenge to anyone concerned about the promise of democracy, and what it might mean for critical intellectuals and others to take a stand against the dominant media, while providing opportunities to develop what Paul Gilroy calls in another context, "minimal ethical principles."[54] At the heart of such an engagement is the need to accentuate the tension between the growing threat to public life and the promise of a democracy that would both remember the history of human suffering and work to prevent its reoccurrence. The political limits of *Fight Club*'s attack on capitalism and consumerism should point to the need for a more sustained and systematic critique of the dire conditions of contemporary social life, especially as such conditions encourage a critique of neoliberalism that does not confuse it with fascism, but rather points to those elements within global capitalism that remind us of what makes fascism possible.

Notes

1. Fredric Jameson, *The Seeds of Time* (New York: Columbia University Press, 1994), xii.
2. Theodor W. Adorno, *Critical Models* (New York: Columbia University Press, 1993), 290.
3. See, for example, Janet Maslin, "Such a Very Long Way from Duvets to Danger," *New York Times*, Friday, October 15, 1999, B14; Amy Taubin, "So Good It Hurts," *Sight and Sound*, November 1999, 16; and Gary Crowdus, "Getting Exercised Over *Fight Club*," *Cineaste* 25, no. 4 (2000): 46–48.
4. This genre was an outgrowth of a number of films, beginning with Quentin Tarantino's *Reservoir Dogs*. James Wolcott has labeled this genre as "scuzz cinema . . . which earns its name from the pervasive, in-your-face, foulmouthed scuzzines of its low-life characters, situations, and atmosphere, all of which convey the bottom falling out of civilization" (148). The infatuation with violence, cynicism, glitz, and shoot-outs in diners got a remake by adding a more updated gesture toward social relevance, i.e., a critique of suburban life, consumerism, etc.
5. Eleanor Byrne and Martin McQuillan, *Deconstructing Disney* (London: Pluto, 1999), 3–4.
6. Rustom Bharacuha, "Around Aydohya: Aberrations, Enigmas, and Moments of Violence," *Third Text* 24 (Autumn 1993): 56.
7. Needless to say, feminist and gay theorists have been analyzing the politics of masculinity for quite some time. For an important series of theoretical analyses on the changing nature of masculinity in Hollywood cinema that draws on many of these traditions, see Stevan Cohan and Ina Rae Hark, eds., *Screening the Male: Exploring Masculinities in Hollywood Cinema* (New York: Routledge, 1993).
8. Homi Bhabha, "Are You a Man or a Mouse," in *Constructing Masculinity*, ed. Maurice Berger, Brian Wallis, and Simon Watson (New York: Routledge, 1995), 57–65.
9. Susan Faludi, *Stiffed* (New York: W. Morrow, 1999).

10. Tom Peters adds a new twist in applying the logic of the market to everyday life by arguing that everyone should define themselves as a saleable item, a commodity. Specifically, Mr. Peters argues that everyone should come to see and treat themselves as brands. According to Peters, the one sure way of being successful in life is to market yourself as a brand name. Or, as Mr. Peters puts it: "It's this simple. You are a brand. You are in charge of your brand. There is no single path to success. And there is no one right way to create a brand called You. Except this: Start today. Or Else." See Tom Peters, "This Brand Called You," *Fast Company*, August–September 1997, 94.

11. This paragraph on Operation Mayhem is taken from Henry A. Giroux and Imre Szeman, "IKEA Boy and the Politics of Male Bonding: *Fight Club*, Consumerism, and Violence," *New Art Examiner*, December/January 2000/2001, 60.

12. Bill Readings, *The University in Ruins* (Cambridge, MA: Harvard University Press, 1996), 48.

13. Homi K. Bhabha, "The Enchantment of Art," in *The Artist in Society*, ed. Carol Becker and Ann Wiens (Chicago: New Art Examiner, 1994), 33.

14. Ibid.

15. Ibid.

16. For some excellent commentaries on the politics of masculinity, see R.W. Connell, *Masculinities* (Berkeley: University of California Press, 1995); Maurice Berger, Brian Wallis, and Simon Watson, eds., *Constructing Masculinities* (New York: Routledge, 1995); Paul Smith, ed., *Boys: Masculinities in Contemporary Culture* (Boulder, CO: Westview, 1996).

17. Paul Gilroy, " 'After the Love Has Gone': Bio-Politics and Etho-Politics in the Black Public Sphere," *Public Culture* 7, no. 1 (1994): 58.

18. For an interesting commentary on the way in which dominant forms of masculinity work to reproduce particular notions of racism, see Robin D. G. Kelley, "Confessions of a Nice Negro, or Why I Shaved My Head," in *(Speak My Name): Black Men On Masculinity and the American Dream*, ed. Don Belton (Boston: Beacon, 1997), 15–28.

19. For an interesting analysis of what might be called the dialectic of consumerism, see Robert Miklitsch, *From Hegel to Madonna: Towards a General Economy of 'Commodity Fetishism'* (Albany: SUNY Press, 1998).

20. Susan Bordo offers a number of critical insights around the relationship between art and its growing tendency to celebrate and "become more sympathetic of the pathologies of our culture than of exposing them." See Bordo, *Twilight Zones: The Hidden Life of Cultural Images* (Berkeley: University of California Press, 1999), 27.

21. Dr. Nadine Hoover is on target when she argues, "There is something terribly wrong with our society when abuse becomes a means of bonding." Hoover cited in Andrew Jacobs, "Violent Cast of High School Hazing Mirrors Society, Experts Say," *New York Times*, March 5, 2000, NE 27–28.

22. The classic work on the relationship between fascism, male violence, and hatred of women is Klaus Theweleit, *Male Fantasies, Vol. 1 and 2* (Minneapolis: University of Minnesota Press, 1987, 1989).

23. Paul Gilroy, *Against Race* (Cambridge, MA: Harvard University Press, 2000), 146.

24. Terry Eagleton, *The Ideology of the Aesthetic* (Cambridge: Basil Blackwell, 1990), 344.

25. One wonders how Fincher would retheorize the relationship between misogyny and the celebration of violence in *Fight Club* in light of the attack by mobs of young men against a number of women in Central Park after the Puerto Rican Day parade in New York City during the summer of 2000. Of course, it would be fatuous to claim that utterly misogynist films such as *Fight Club* are directly responsible for the recent incident in which fifty-six women were attacked by roving bands of young men who doused them with water, groped them, and ripped off their clothes. But I don't think it would be unreasonable to argue that misogynist films such as *Fight Club* help to legitimate such acts, because they

exercise a pedagogical force shaped largely by a dominant politics of sexist representations that contributes to an increasing climate of hatred and objectification of women.

26. Commenting on the kind of violence that is often ignored in films such as *Fight Club*, Holly Sklar writes, "Imagine [films such as *Fight Club* giving] sustained national attention to the violence waged on the mind, body, and spirit of crumbling schools, [or to] low teacher expectations, employment and housing discrimination, racist dragnets, and every-day looks of hate by people finding you guilty by suspicion." See Sklar, "Young and Guilty by Stereotype," *Z Magazine*, July/August 1993, 53.

27. For a masterful analysis of the complexities of theorizing violence as well as a critique of its romanticization, see John Keane, *Reflections on Violence* (New York: Verso, 1996).

28. This theme is take up in a number of recent books, such as Jeffrey C. Goldfarb, *The Cynical Society: The Culture of Politics and the Politics of Culture in American Life* (Chicago: University of Chicago Press, 1991); Joseph N. Capella and Kathleen Hall Jamieson, *Spiral of Cynicism: The Press and the Public Good* (New York: Oxford University Press, 1997); Russell Jacoby, *The End of Utopia* (New York: Basic Books, 1999); William Chaloupka, *Everybody Knows: Cynicism in America* (Minneapolis: University of Minnesota Press, 1999); Zygmunt Bauman, *In Search of Politics* (Stanford, CA: Stanford University Press, 1999); Carl Boggs, *The End of Politics: Corporate Power and the Decline of the Public Sphere* (New York: Guilford Press, 2000).

29. Cited in Carol Becker, "The Art of Testimony," *Sculpture* 16, no. 3 (March 1997): 28.

30. For one of the most popular celebrations of this warrior mentality, see Robert Bly, *Iron John: A Book About Men* (Reading, MA: Addison-Wesley, 1990). For a sustained critique of this position, see James William Gibson, *Warrior Dreams: Paramilitary Culture in Post-Vietnam America* (New York: Hill and Wang, 1994).

31. This theme is explored in Tania Modleski, *Feminism Without Women* (New York: Routledge, 1991).

32. Cited from the National Center of Victims of Crime website: http://207.222.132.10/index%7E1.htm.

33. Geoffrey Hartman, "Public Memory and Its Discontents," *Raritan* 8, no. 4 (Spring 1994): 28, 26.

34. On the cult of warrior mythology and its relationship to male violence, see the exceptionally important work done on this subject by Gibson, *Warrior Dreams*.

35. Janet Maslin, "Such a Very Long Way from Duvets to Danger," *New York Times*, Friday, October 15, 1999, B14.

36. Taubin, "So Good It Hurts," 16.

37. Ibid., 17.

38. Susan Faludi, "It's 'Thelma and Louise' for Guys," *Newsweek*, October 25, 1999, 89.

39. David Edelstein, "Boys Do Bleed," *Slate*, October 15, 1999, 4, http://www.slate.com/.

40. Crowdus, "Getting Exercised Over *Fight Club*," 46.

41. Ibid., 47.

42. See, for example, Bob Strauss, "Actors Defend Ultra Violent Film," *Arizona Republic*, October 15, 1999, D1; Gavin Smith, "Inside-Out-on-One With David Fincher," *Film Comment*, Sept/October 1999, 58–67.

43. Edward Norton cited in Barry Koltnow, "Club's Call to Arms is Not Call to Violence," *Center Daily Times*, October 19, 1999, 11C.

44. Cited in Benjamin Svetkey, "Blood, Sweat and Fears," *Entertainment Weekly*, October 15, 1999, 28.

45. Both quotations from ibid., 26, 31.

46. I take up this issue in Henry A. Giroux, *Fugitive Cultures* (New York: Routledge, 1996), and *Channel Surfing: Racism, the Media and the Destruction of Today's Youth* (New York: St. Martin's, 1998).

47. This issue is taken up brilliantly in Susan Jeffords, *Hard Bodies: Hollywood Masculinity in the Reagan Era* (New York: Rutgers University Press, 1994). Of course, this type of representation is ongoing and can be found in recent films such as *Saving Private Ryan, The Thin Red Line,* and *Three Kings.*

48. Hannah Arendt, "On Violence," in *Crisis of the Republic* (New York: Harvest, 1969), 108.

49. See, for example, Martin A. Lee, *The Beast Reawakens: Fascism's Resurgence From Hitler's Spymasters to Today's Neo-Nazi Groups and Right-Wing Extremists* (New York: Routledge, 2000).

50. Gilroy, *Against Race*, 146.

51. Ibid., 150; 158.

52. Ibid., 152.

53. James Snead, *White Screens/Black Images* (New York: Routledge, 1994), 131, 142.

54. Gilroy, *Against Race*, 5.

Part VI

Youth, Pedagogy, and the Politics of Hope

THE ABANDONED GENERATION

THE URBAN DEBATE LEAGUE
AND THE POLITICS OF POSSIBILITY

One of the most serious, yet unspoken and unrecognized, tragedies in the United States is the condition of its children. We live in a society in which too many young people are poor, lack decent housing and healthcare, attend decrepit schools filled with overworked and underpaid teachers, and, by all standards, deserve more in a country that prides itself on its level of democracy, liberty, and alleged equality for all citizens. For many young people, the future looks bleak, filled with the promise of low-paying, low-skilled jobs, the collapse of the welfare state, and, if you are a person of color and poor, the threat of either unemployment or incarceration. Dietrich Bonhoeffer, the Protestant theologian, believed that the ultimate test of morality resided in what a society does for its children. If we take this standard seriously, American society has deeply failed its children and its commitment to democracy.

The argument presented here suggests that it is time for educators, community leaders, parents, young people, and others to take a stand and remind themselves that collective problems deserve collective solutions and that what is at risk is not only a generation of young people, but the very promise of democracy itself. The National Association of Urban Debate Leagues (UDLs) represents a promising, innovative effort to reinforce substantive democratic education and tradition by fostering rigorous and passionate discussions about social change and how it is to be achieved. The Urban Debate League approaches matters of school equity, reform, and agency through the use of academic debate as a way to help urban public school students learn the skills, disciplines, knowledge, and values that enable them to become critically literate and effectively engaged citizens. It organizes debate teams in urban public schools, holds competitions among schools all over the country, and supports the ongoing education of urban school teachers helping them to recognize the political, pedagogical, and civic value of debate leagues while actively learning how to organize and engage students in such debates. What is so important about the UDL program is that it is not merely interested in teaching debating skills to students—though learning how to do library research, electronic retrieval, critical analysis, and policy evaluation is not inconsequential, it is simply not enough. Instead, debating is viewed as a form of critical literacy that empowers students, especially underrepresented races, ethnicities, and females, not only with high-powered academic skills but also with the essential critical knowledge and beliefs necessary to convince them that they can become both effective advocates for democracy *and* leaders in a world that they must learn how to influence and govern. Operating with the assumption that to be voiceless is to be powerless, the UDL organizes high school debates around the understanding that to have a voice students must learn from and construct pedagogical practices that make knowledge meaningful in order to be critical and critical in order to be transformative. And the space of the debate provides exactly the public sphere where students learn how to invest in ideas, engage in dialogue with others, respect the positions of those different from their own, and do so in the spirit of contributing to both a wider public discourse and a more vibrant public life. The UDL believes that excellence cannot be abstracted from equity, and that historically academic debate was largely the province of white, privileged youth from affluent suburban and private schools. The interscholastic debate experience provided these students with important communicative skills, modes of literacy, research opportunities, and the ability to travel and meet students from similar privileged backgrounds. Needless to say, such students enjoyed all the privileges debate leagues afforded them, but the benefits were exclusively class-based, and the very notion of the debate as a performative event was viewed as limited to the ranks of the elite. The UDL has attempted to change the class dynamics of the sphere of high school debating by purposely enlisting working-class youth, minorities of color, and young women into debating leagues in order not only to raise their possibilities for going on to higher education, but also to connect them to those discourses that are crucial to engaged forms of citizenship, public policy, democratic values, and what it might mean to imagine a future that does not merely imitate the present. The UDL believes that matters of literacy, critical understanding, and intervention in the world are linked to matters of advocacy, which presupposes that notions of critical consciousness and learning are inextricably connected to social change. I believe in Urban Debate Leagues because their organizers and participants believe it is not only possible to think against the grain, but crucial to act in ways that demonstrate political conviction, civic courage, and collective responsibility.

Youth and the Crisis of the Future

Any discourse about the future has to begin with the issue of youth because young people embody the projected dreams, desires, and commitment of a society's obligations to the future. In many respects, youth not only register symbolically the importance of modernity's claim to progress; they also affirm the importance of the liberal democratic tradition of the social contract in which adult responsibility is mediated through a willingness to fight for the rights of children, enact reforms that invest in their future, and provide the educational conditions necessary for them to make use of the freedoms they have while learning how to be critical citizens. Within such a modernist project, democracy is linked to the well-being of youth, while the status of how a society imagines democracy and its future is contingent on how it views its responsibility toward future generations. But the category of youth does more than affirm modernity's social contract, rooted in a conception of the future in which adult commitment and intergenerational solidarity are articulated as a vital public service; it also affirms those vocabularies, values, and social relations central to a politics capable of both defending vital institutions as a public good and contributing to the quality of public life. Such a vocabulary is particularly important for both public and higher education, institutions that often define and address their highest ideals through the recognition that how they educate youth is connected to both the democratic future they hope for and their claim as important public spheres.

Yet as the twenty-first century unfolds, it is not at all clear that we believe any longer in youth, the future, or the social contract, even in its minimalist version. Since the 1980s, we have been told that there is no such thing as society and, indeed, following that nefarious pronouncement, institutions committed to public welfare have been disappearing ever since. Those of us who, against the prevailing common sense, insist on the relationship between public and higher education and the future of democracy have to face the disturbing reversal in priorities with regard to youth and education that now defines the United States, especially with the reelection of George W. Bush in 2004. Increasingly, children seem to have no standing in the public sphere as citizens, and thus are denied any sense of entitlement and agency. Their voices and needs are almost completely absent from the debates, policies, and legislative practices that are constructed in terms of their needs. This is not to suggest that adults do not care about youth, but most of the concerns are framed within the realm of the private sphere of the family. Children seem absent from any public discourse about the future and the responsibilities such a discourse implies for adult society.

Worth repeating is the fact that the hard currency of human suffering as it impacts on children can be seen in some of the astounding statistics that suggest a profound moral and political contradiction at the heart of the United States, one of the richest democracies in the world: 21.9 percent of children live in poverty and one in three will be poor at some point in their childhood; 1.35 million children are homeless; one in eight children or 9.3 million lack healthcare insurance; millions lack affordable childcare and decent early childhood education; one in ten teens between the ages of sixteen to nineteen is a school dropout, and one in seven never graduates from high school. Yet in many states, more money is being spent on prison construction than on education; nationally, more money is spent on beauty products than on public education; and the infant mortality rate in the United States is the highest of any industrialized nation.[1]

Urban Debate Leagues have started in major cities, from New York to Los Angeles, which are on the front lines in this country's war against youth. Urban Debate Leagues prove that, rather than being occasions for despair, the problems we face offer opportunities for organizing our passions and energies in order to reaffirm democratic commitments to equality, liberty, justice, and critical citizenship. Edward Lee, a graduate from an Atlanta public school's debate program, describes debate as "a pedagogical tool desperately needed to prevent an ever-increasing number of academically underprivileged children from wasting away in misery and hopelessness."[2] Indeed the foundations for new Urban Debate Leagues are currently being set up around the country, demonstrating the broader truth that the time has come for adults and young people to organize together, to create the conditions necessary to reject cynicism, and to struggle collectively for a more just world and the possibility of a realizable democracy. Lee offers a compelling vision for advancing the struggle for human dignity and democracy by building more UDLs. He asks us to "imagine graduating from high school each year millions of underprivileged teenagers with the ability to articulate their needs, the needs of others, and the ability to offer solutions."[3]

Education and the Challenge of Revitalizing Democratic Public Life

As those public spaces disappear that once offered forums for debating norms, critically engaging ideas, making private issues public, and evaluating judgments, it becomes critical for educators to raise fundamental questions about what it means to revitalize public life, politics, and ethics in ways that take seriously such values as patriotism, "citizen participation . . . political obligation, social governance, and community."[4] Educators are confronted with the problem as well as the challenge of analyzing, engaging, and developing those public spheres that help create citizens who are equipped to exercise their freedoms, competent to question the basic assumptions that govern political life, and skilled enough to participate in shaping the social, political, and economic orders that govern their lives. Two factors, however, work against such developments. First, there are very few public spheres left that provide the space for such conversations to take place. For instance, high school gyms are increasingly used by companies, while many privately owned coffee shops don't allow UDLs to meet. Second, it is increasingly difficult for young people and adults to translate private problems into public concerns or to relate public issues to private considerations. For many young people and adults today, the private sphere has become the only space in which to imagine any sense of hope, pleasure, or possibility. Reduced to the act of consuming, citizenship is "mostly about forgetting, not learning."[5]

The decline of democratic values and informed citizenship can be seen in research studies done by The Justice Project in 2001 in which a substantial number of teenagers and young people were asked what they thought democracy meant. The answers testified to a growing depoliticization of American life and largely consisted of statements along the following lines: "Nothing," "I don't know," or "My rights, just like, pride, I guess, to some extent, and paying taxes," or "I just think, like, what does it really mean? I know it's our, like, our government, but I don't know what it technically is."[6] The transition from being ignorant about democracy to actually supporting antidemocratic tendencies can be seen in a number of youth surveys that have been taken since 2000. For instance, a survey released by the University of California, Berkeley, revealed that 69 percent of students support school prayer and 44 percent of young people aged fifteen to twenty-two support government restrictions on abortions. A 2004 survey of 112,003 high school students on First Amendment rights showed that one third of students surveyed believed that the First Amendment went too far in the rights it guarantees and 36 percent believed that the press enjoyed too much freedom.[7] This suggests not just a failing of education, but a crisis of citizenship and democracy.

One consequence of the decline in democratic values and citizenship literacy is that all levels of government are being hollowed out, their role reduced to dismantling the gains of the welfare state as they increasingly construct policies that criminalize social problems and prioritize penal methods over social investments. When citizenship is reduced to consumerism, it should come as no surprise that people develop an indifference to civic engagement and participation in democratic public life. Unlike some theorists who suggest that politics as critical exchange and social engagement is either dead or in a state of terminal arrest, I believe that the current depressing state of politics points to an urgent challenge: reformulating the crisis of democracy as a fundamental crisis of vision, meaning, education, and political agency. Central to my argument is the assumption that politics is not simply about power, but also, as Cornelius Castoriadis points out, "has to do with political judgments and value choices," meaning that questions of civic education—learning how to become a skilled citizen—are central to democracy itself.[8]

Educators at all levels need to challenge the assumption that politics is dead, or the nature of politics will be determined exclusively by government leaders and experts in the heat of moral frenzy. Educators need to take a more critical position, arguing that knowledge, debate, and dialogue about pressing social problems offer individuals and groups some hope in shaping the conditions that bear down on their lives. Public civic engagement is essential if the concepts of social life and the public sphere are to be used to revitalize the language of civic education and democratization as part of a broader discourse of political agency and critical citizenship in a global world. Linking the social to democratic public values represents an attempt, however incomplete, to link democracy to public action, as part of a comprehensive attempt to revitalize civic activism and citizen access to decision-making while simultaneously addressing basic problems of social justice and global democracy.

Educators within public schools need to find ways to engage political issues by making social problems visible and by debating them in the political sphere. They also need to be at the forefront of the defense of the most progressive historical advances and gains of the state. French sociologist Pierre Bourdieu is right when he calls for collective work by educators to prevent those who are mobilized against the welfare state from destroying the most precious democratic conquests in labor legislation, health, social protection, and education.[9] At the very least, this would suggest that educators should defend schools as democratic public spheres, struggle against the de-skilling of teachers and students that has accompanied the emphasis on teaching for test-taking, and argue for pedagogy grounded in democratic values rather than testing schemes that severely limit the creative, ethical, and liberatory potential of education.

Urban Debate Leagues represent one reason for hope. Hope is more than romantic idealism; it is the condition that highlights images of an alternative politics and pedagogy. Hope is not simply wishful thinking; it is written into those various struggles waged by brave men and women for civil rights, racial justice, decent working conditions, and a society cleansed of war. Hope is the refusal to stand still in the face of human suffering, and it is learned by example, inflamed by the passion for a better life, and undertaken as an act of civic courage. The work of Urban Debate Leagues provides a tangible reason to be hopeful. Urban debaters, as they devour newspapers and periodicals, confront information detailing certain realities about our world including the use of war, the severity of environmental degradation, and the increasing gap between the rich and working poor. In the face of these realities, the mere optimistic tendency to expect the best possible outcome cannot and does not suffice. The students and teachers who participate in UDLs hold on to hope because they have seen loved ones get kicked and stand back up. Those attracted to UDLs understand that when a person gets kicked and stands back up, she asserts her basic human dignity. Urban debaters bring hope with them to the activity, and then, through their participation in debate, they gather the tools necessary to be the architects of a new, more equitable future.

Administrators at all levels feel pressured by the imposition of high-stakes testing regiments to improve standardized test performance in their districts. The message they receive is clear: turn schools into testing factories and punish them if they do not succeed in raising test scores. The hidden curriculum is that testing be used to ensure that teachers are de-skilled as they are reduced to mere technicians, and that students be treated as customers in the marketplace rather than as engaged, critical learners. The high stakes mean that schools either can receive extra money or be shut down, and such tests put enormous pressure on teachers to teach to the test, abandon their sense of creativity and autonomy in the classroom, ignore the specificities of children's lives and problems, and, in general, be less attentive to the vast differences that often exist among students. As conception is divorced from implementation, teachers are often stripped of their authority, skills, and creative possibilities, and are reduced to technicians—drill sergeants working under the imperatives of a handful of corporate test makers.

Under such conditions, teachers are prevented from taking risks and designing their own lessons as the pressure to achieve passing test scores produces highly scripted and regimented forms of teaching. In this context, worksheets become a substitute for critical teaching, and rote memorization takes the place of in-depth thinking. Learning discrete facts and skills in reading and math becomes more important than genuine understanding and the ability to engage knowledge with thoughtfulness and critical analytical skills. The type of pedagogy fostered by high-stakes testing is at odds with learning that stresses creativity, critical thinking, leadership skills, autonomy, and self- and social development. Pedagogy as a critical practice in which students learn to be attentive and responsible to the memories and narratives of others disappears within test-driven learning. Unfortunately, the reductive transmission, or banking approach to pedagogy underscored in current federal reforms cancels out some of the most important aspects of critical teaching: making knowledge relevant to students' lives; providing supportive environments in which students can learn; and developing a range of teaching approaches and forms of assessment based on the recognition that not every student learns the same way.

In a world where high-stakes testing is a given, it is crucial to invest in substantive efforts that help schools reach accountability measures by improving the quality of teaching and learning. Urban Debate Leagues represent one crucial and exciting way to improve an urban public school system's curriculum and its academic ethos and norms. I am enormously impressed with the way that UDLs support teachers who seek to build classrooms and schools that represent student voice, formulate rigorous and critical investigations into pressing issues of social concern, and prepare students to be active and engaged learners. The UDL movement understands that we cannot afford to stifle the critical and creative impulses and passions of our teachers and students. In UDLs, teachers and students who might otherwise fall through the cracks instead find an outlet. In the words of Anthony Grobe, an English teacher at Cleveland Naval Academy in St. Louis, "Coaching energizes me after a long school day. The passion and commitment of my debaters validate my work as a teacher. The after school practices are invigorating, the students are excited about ideas. They work with each other in order to research and write about issues concerning their lives."[10] The work of Urban Debate Leagues is also aligned with forms of assessment that enhance the possibility for self- and social empowerment among children, forms of assessment that promote critical modes of inquiry and creativity as opposed to those that shut down self-respect and motivation by instilling a sense of failure or humiliation. UDLs embody an effort to improve education by embracing assessments that get students to reflect on their work and the work of others—as a measure of deliberation, critical analysis, and dialogue. The way that UDLs approach the question of assessment makes it clear that accountability needs to be part of a broader agenda for equity and must be understood within a notion of schooling that rejects learning simply as the mastery of discrete skills and bodies of information.

Despite the war against youth and efforts to dismantle the notion and reality of quality public education, many young people and educators around the country are choosing to embrace a politics of hope. Urban Debate Leagues and other local efforts to ignite student passion for substantive democracy as well as racial and economic justice demonstrate that power as a form of domination is never absolute and that oppression always produces some form of resistance. Fortunately, UDLs are adding their voices to a larger chorus as more and more young people nationally and internationally are mobilizing and struggling to construct an alternative future in which their voices can be heard as part of a broader movement to realize genuine democracy and social justice. The message that appears to unite this generation of youth—and it is a message that resonates deeply with the UDL movement—is that a more democratic and just world is possible. Such a world, however, can only be realized through the collective struggles of many people willing to unite in their efforts to make real the possibilities and promises of a truly democratic world order.

Notes

1. These figures are taken from The Children's Defense Fund, "The State of America's Children 2004," July 13, 2004, http://www.childrensdefense.org/pressreleases/040713.aspx.
2. Edward Lee, "Memoir of a Former Urban Debate League Participant," *Contemporary Argumentation and Debate* 19 (1998): 93–96.
3. Open Society Institute, "High School Debate: Changing Lives with the Power of Words," *U.S. Program Notes: A Newsletter of the Open Society Institute*, July 1999, 5.
4 Carl Boggs, *The End of Politics* (New York: Guilford Press, 2000), ix.
5. Zygmunt Bauman, *Globalization: The Human Consequences* (New York: Columbia University Press, 1998), 82.
6. Cited in Ann Greenberg, "What Young Voters Want," *The Nation*, February 11, 2001, 15.
7. The first survey was conducted by the Pew Charitable Trusts and is available on the web at www.pewtrusts.com/pdf/pp_paces.pdf. The second survey was conducted by The John S. and James L. Knight Foundation, "High School: Leaving the First Amendment Behind," http://www.jideas.org/Knight%20fdtn%20report%20final.pdf. See also, BBC News,

"US Teens 'Reject' Key Freedoms," *BBC News.com*, February 1, 2005. Available online: http://News.bbc.co.uk/2/hi/Americas/4225013.stm

8. Cornelius Castoriadis, "Institution and Autonomy," in Peter Osborne, *A Critical Sense: Interviews with Intellectuals* (New York: Routledge, 1996), 8.

9. Pierre Bourdieu, *Acts of Resistance* (New York: Free Press, 1998).

10. This quote is taken from an interview with Anthony Grobe. The excerpt is available online at http://www.urbandebate.org/endorsements.

15
Putting Youth Back into Politics

Reclaiming Education and
Hope in Dark Times

Introduction from Canada

As someone who has recently relocated from the United States to Canada, I am deeply concerned that Canada not emulate the domestic and foreign policies that have been unleashed by the reactionary presidency of George W. Bush. Many Canadians are distrustful, if not appalled, by "the public religiosity" of a right-wing regime in Washington, which not only appears "under the control of Christian *jihadists* confronting Islamist *jihadists*," but is also waging a war on any vestige of the public good, especially the social contract and the welfare state, two elements of Canadian society that are central to its commitment to social justice and democracy.[1]

Similarly, most Canadians refuse to endorse Bush's failed war in Iraq, his ruinous economic policies, his fraudulent case for a missile defense system, and his outsourcing of torture. But as skeptical and critically thoughtful as Canadians are of Bush's foreign and domestic policies, I think Canadian academics, politicians, journalists, and other intellectuals should give more attention to the degree to which the Bush administration increasingly wages an assault against young people in the United States and, in doing so, loses all semblance of moral and political credibility. Of course, many people are aware of how U.S. policies have drastically affected the lives of children in other countries—such as Iraq, before and after the recent invasion—but there appears to be less known about the war being waged at home against youth. In this chapter, I focus on what it might mean in a democracy to take children seriously as a moral referent, in order not only to gauge the health of children in a democratic society, but also to define our obligations to future generations of young people. Children constitute a powerful referent for addressing war, poverty, education, and a host of other important social issues. As a symbol of the future, children provide adults with an important moral compass to assess what Jacques Derrida calls the promises of a "democracy to come."[2] While the context from which I explore these matters is rooted in the U.S. society I recently left, I believe that the issues I speak to regarding the connection between the crisis of youth and the crisis of democracy have important implications for how Canadians address their own concerns about the interface among politics, ethics, and youth. This is particularly the case because of the power the United States exercises throughout the world and the threat that it poses to both the very idea of social justice and the possibilities of expanding and deepening global democracy in the twenty-first century.

We live at a time in which the loss of American standing in the world is related directly to the United States's ill-fated war in Iraq, its reckless free-market triumphalism deciding the fate of most nations of the world, and its increasing support at the highest levels of government for domestic Christian right-wing groups. What is often ignored by many critics with their singular fixation on the war abroad is the war that is also being waged on the home front.[3] This war can be seen not only in the crushing assault on unions and civil liberties, but also in the restructuring of the tax system to benefit the rich and drain resources from the poor and the middle class. The war at home has been exacerbated by the ascendancy of neoliberal corporate culture into every aspect of American life. As I have mentioned repeatedly throughout this book, neoliberalism consolidates economic power in the hands of the few, aggressively attempts to destroy the welfare state, subordinates the needs of society to the dictates of corporate power, views misfortune as a weakness, and deems public services and goods an unconscionable luxury.[4] With few exceptions, the project of democratizing public goods, redistributing resources, and addressing important social problems has fallen into disrepute in the popular imagination as the logic of the market undermines the most basic social solidarities. The consequences include not only a weakened social state, but a growing sense of insecurity, cynicism, and political retreat on the part of the general public. The incessant calls for self-reliance that now dominate public discourse betray an eviscerated and refigured state that neither provides adequate safety nets for its populace, especially those who are young, poor, or racially marginalized, nor gives any indication that it will serve the interests of its citizens in spite of constitutional guarantees. In fact, as the state is being reconfigured, it is increasingly becoming more concerned with punishing and policing than with nurturing and investing in the public good. In short, private interests trump social needs; economic growth becomes more important than social justice; and the militarization and commercialization of public space now define what counts as the public sphere.

This dystopian recognition points to dire political, social, and economic consequences for young people and for the very nature of democracy itself. Democracy increasingly appears damaged, if not fatally wounded, as those who are young, poor, immigrants, or people of color are excluded from the operations of power, the realm of politics, and crucial social provisions. For over a century, most Americans have embraced as a defining feature of politics the idea that all levels of government would assume a large measure of responsibility for providing the resources, social provisions, security, and modes of education that enable young people to be prepared for the present while offering them a better future as the meaning and depth of an inclusive democracy are simultaneously expanded. But just as education has been separated from any viable notion of politics, youth have been separated from the discourse of either the social contract or any ethical notion of what it might mean for society to provide young people with the prospects of a decent and democratic future. Youth increasingly have come to be seen as a problem rather than as a resource for investing in the future. Framed largely as a generation of suspects, they are now treated as either a disposable population, fodder for a barbaric war in Iraq, or the source of most of society's problems. Youth now constitute a crisis that has less to do with improving the future than with denying it. Punishment and fear have replaced compassion and social investment as the most important modalities mediating the relationship of youth to the larger social order.

No longer "viewed as a privileged sign and embodiment of the future," youth are now demonized by the popular media and derided by politicians looking for quick-fix solutions to crime.[5] Bestselling authors Lt. Col. Dave Grossman and Gloria DeGaentano argue in their *Stop Teaching Our Kids to Kill* that young people are more violent than ever before because of what they learn in popular culture and, by default, the authors suggest that young people need to be subjected to more extended disciplinary measures.[6] Hollywood movies consistently represent youth as either dangerous, utterly brainless, or simply without merit. The marketplace only imagines students either as consumers or as branded billboards as it offers for sale sexuality, beauty, and athleticism embodied in music, clothes, accessories, and a host of other consumer products. Market relations executives are now gloating over their discovery that eight- to fourteen-year-olds constitute a new market for "sexy" fashions such as the La Senza Girl bra, heavy makeup, and magazines like *Twist, J-14, Teen Vogue*, and *M* that read like adult fashion magazines. At the same time, in a society deeply troubled by their presence, youth prompt in the public imagination a rhetoric of fear, control, and surveillance as well as laws and policies that threaten to fine youth for wearing baggy pants, subject youth to antigang laws that punish kids for violating certain dress codes, and offer them schools that are modeled after prisons. In the case of the latter, federal laws now provide financial incentives to schools that implement zero tolerance policies, in spite of their proven racial and class biases; drug-sniffing dogs and cameras have become a common feature in schools; and administrators willingly comply with federal laws that give military recruiters the right to access the names, addresses, and telephone numbers of students in both public schools and higher education. Trust and respect now give way to fear, disdain, and suspicion. Children have fewer rights than almost any other group and fewer institutions protecting these rights. For instance, while young children need a parent's permission to get a tattoo or abortion in many states, they can be convicted of a serious crime and put to death long before their eighteenth birthday. The United States is one of the few countries in the world that sentences minors to death, while spending "three times more on each incarcerated citizen than on each public school pupil."[7] As Marian Wright Edelman, founder and president of the Children's Defense Fund, points out,

Fifty years after *Brown v. Board of Education* and 40 years after President Johnson declared a War on Poverty, many minority and lower income children still lack a fair chance to live, learn, thrive and contribute in America. The great unfinished business of our nation in this first decade of the 21st century is to open wide the doors of equal education and economic opportunity to every child in America. It's time to build a powerful 21st century movement to emancipate our children from racial injustice and poverty. We must summon the moral, political, and financial courage to make sure that we truly leave no child behind.[8]

Yet the Bush administration seems intent on pursuing a "war [in Iraq] whose central feature is the government's consistent, disastrous denial of reality," just as it drains the public treasury of billions of dollars through tax cuts for the rich and appropriations for a bloated military budget.[9] The idea, not to mention the reality, of justice seems dead on arrival, as the Bush regime consistently and aggressively attempts to generate retrograde policies intent on increasing corporate power, expanding the reach of its influence, and wasting billions of dollars on a rapacious empire-building agenda. Justice seems to take a backseat in Bush's 2006 budget proposal. For instance, the Bush administration proposes to cut back funding for Upward Bound and Talent Search, two programs that benefit disadvantaged students, while at the same time it has allocated $127 billion to the Pentagon to build a robot army.[10] According to a representative from the U.S. Joint Forces Research Center, the virtue of the robot army is that there "are no prohibitions against robots making life-or-death decisions."[11] All of this may be good news for those die-hard members of the Christian Right, free-market fundamentalists, and power-hungry neoconservatives who are doing everything they can, not only to render democracy irrelevant, but also to disempower an entire generation of children, whose future is being mortgaged off to the vagaries of corporate power and religious fanaticism. Instead of providing a decent critical education to poor young people, President Bush and his cohorts serve them more standardized tests, enforce abstinence programs instead of sex education, hand out Bibles, inculcate right-wing Christian values, and advocate creationism at the expense of reason.[12] Youth who are poor fare even worse and often find themselves in classes that are overcrowded, lack basic resources, and are subject to policies largely designed to warehouse young people rather than educate them with even minimal basic literacy skills. Instead of providing young people with vibrant public spheres, the Bush government offers them a commercialized culture in which consumerism is the only condition of citizenship.

Rather then being viewed as at-risk, children in George Bush's America are now seen as the risk itself and are treated as either disposable or a drain on the national treasury. Equal education, economic opportunity, decent healthcare, and the most basic social provisions are now out of reach for millions of children who are poor, deprived of health insurance, abused, and sadly undereducated. The Bush administration's answer to the plight of children in America can be seen in his proposed $2.5 trillion budget for 2006. Laura Flanders defines Bush's budget as a hit list targeting teens and kids because it "calls for cuts in emergency medical services for children, cuts in K-12 education funding, cuts in vocational education and cuts in programs like Head Start. There are food-stamp cuts and a five-year freeze on child care. A $41 million college loan program is eliminated. The whole National Youth Sports Program which has provided athletics for low income kids is cut, as in cut out."[13]

The hypocrisy underlying these cuts becomes more obvious when cuts in education are examined, especially since Bush's "compassionate conservativism" defines itself largely through educational reforms. In fact, of the 150 programs designed to be radically cut back, "one out of every three of the targeted programs concerns education . . . [with cuts of] $2.2 billion for high school programs . . . $440 million in Safe and Drug-Free School grants, $500 million in education technology state grants,

$225 million for the Even Start literacy program, [and] $280 million for Upward Bound programs for inner-city youths."[14] Paul Krugman calls Bush's latest budget projections a form of class warfare, since he "takes food from the mouths of babes and gives the proceeds to his millionaire friends."[15] In his 2006 budget proposals, Bush calls for terminating aid for over 300,000 people receiving food stamps and denies childcare assistance to over 300,000 children from working-class families, while at the same time phasing out a limit on tax exemptions for high-income families that would give taxpayers with incomes over $1 million an average tax cut of more than $19,000.[16] In this case, savage cuts in education, nutritional assistance for impoverished mothers, veterans' medical care, and basic scientific research help fund tax cuts for the inordinately rich.

How might youth fare in the midst of such a crisis, particularly concerning their need for decent schools, qualified teachers, and a critically informed education? Rather than invest in young people, the Bush administration either punishes them through retrograde policies or simply ignores their needs. One example of how the Bush administration views the education of young people is shown by an incident in which the newly appointed secretary of education, Margaret Spellings, on the second day of her job, launched a public attack against the children's television show *Postcards from Buster*.[17] The show is about a rabbit who travels all over America visiting families of various and diverse backgrounds. Unfortunately, according to Spellings, the show was no longer fit to be aired because in one of the episodes a family consisted of a lesbian couple with children. This does not simply suggest an inept public official who would like to teach children that tolerance rather than bigotry is the enemy of democracy. It also reveals a powerful representative of the Bush administration whose disregard for children is evident in her undemocratic embrace of censorship and her politically inspired tirades and threats to decrease funding for PBS, another apparently left-wing public service that poses a threat to free-market fundamentalism. Ms. Spellings' actions inspired Frank Rich, a writer for the *New York Times*, to claim that "Ms. Spellings' threats against PBS are only the latest chapter in a continuing saga at an education department that increasingly resembles an authoritarian government's ministry of information" and that clearly has little regard for young people.[18]

Youth has become one of the most visible symbols onto which class and racial anxieties are projected. The very troubled state of young people confronts us with the broken promises of capitalism in the age of outsourcing, contract work, deindustrialization, and deregulation. It also represents a collective fear of the consequences wrought by systemic class inequalities, racism, and a culture of downsizing and deficits that have created a generation of unskilled and displaced youth that has been expelled from shrinking markets, blue-collar jobs, and any viable hope in the future. Indeed, as Bob Herbert has pointed out, more than five million youth between the ages of eighteen and twenty-four are out of school, work, and hope. In the inner cities, youth hopelessness is increasingly matched with a mix of violence, drug trafficking, and an exaggerated "tough guy" masculinity. But as Earl Ofari Hutchinson makes clear,

It's not just drugs and hopelessness that drive young men, especially young Black men, to kill and dodge bullets. The huge state and federal cutbacks in job training and skills programs, the brutal competition for low and semi skilled service and retail jobs from immigrants [along with] the high number of miserably failing inner-city public schools . . . have turned thousands of Blacks into education cripples. These students are desperately unequipped to handle the rapidly evolving and demanding technical and professional skills in the public sector and the business world of the 21st century.[19]

In the degraded economic, political, and cultural geography of neoliberal capitalism, youth occupy a "dead zone" in which the spectacle of commodification exists side by side with the imposing threat of the prison-industrial complex and the elimination of basic civil liberties. As market fundamentalism frees itself from political power, it has disassociated economics from its social costs, and "the political state has become the corporate state."[20] Under such circumstances, the state does not disappear, but as Pierre Bourdieu has brilliantly reminded us is refigured, as its role in providing social provisions, intervening on behalf of public welfare, and regulating corporate plunder is weakened.[21] The neoliberal state no longer invests in solving social problems; it now punishes those who are caught in the downward spiral of its economic policies. Punishment, incarceration, control, and surveillance represent the face of the new, expanded National Security state. One consequence is that the implied contract between the state and its citizens is broken, and social guarantees for youth as well as civic obligations to the future vanish from the agenda of public concern. Similarly, as market values supplant civic values, it becomes increasingly difficult "to translate private worries into public issues and, conversely, to discern public issues in private troubles."[22] Alcoholism, homelessness, poverty, and illiteracy, among other issues, are seen not as social but as individual problems—matters of character, individual fortitude, and personal responsibility. Ardent consumers and disengaged citizens provide fodder for a growing cynicism and depoliticization of public life at a time when there is an increasing awareness not just of corporate corruption, financial mismanagement, and systemic greed, but also of the recognition that a democracy of critical citizens is being replaced quickly by a democracy of consumers. The desire to protect market freedoms and wage a war against terrorism has, ironically, not only ushered in a culture of fear, but also dealt a lethal blow to civil freedoms. At the heart of this contradiction is both the fate of democracy and the civic health and future of a generation of children and young people.

For many young people and adults today, the private sphere has become the only space in which to imagine any sense of hope, pleasure, or possibility. Culture, as an activity in which young people actually produce the conditions of their own agency through dialogue, community participation, public stories, and political struggle, is being eroded. In its place we are increasingly surrounded by a "climate of cultural and linguistic privatization" in which culture becomes something that is consumed, and the only kind of acceptable speech is that of the fast-paced shopper.[23] The war against youth can be understood, in part, through those central values and practices that characterize a market fundamentalism that emphasizes commercial forces and profit margins while narrowing the legitimacy of the public sphere. In spite of neoconservative and neoliberal claims that economic growth will cure social ills, the market has no way of dealing with poverty, social inequality, or civil rights issues. It has no vocabulary for addressing respect, compassion, decency, and ethics, or, for that matter, what it means to recognize antidemocratic forms of power. These are political issues, not merely economic concerns. In contrast, a political system based on democratic principles of inclusiveness and nonrepression can and does provide citizens with the critical tools necessary for them to participate in investing public life with vibrancy while expanding the foundations of freedom and justice.

The current state of youth bears heavily on both public and higher education. Childhood as a core referent for a vibrant democracy and for an embrace of social justice appears to be disappearing in a society that not only rejects the promise of youth, but the future itself "as an affective investment."[24] The crisis of youth signals a dangerous state of affairs for the future; it also portends a crisis in the very idea of the political and ethical constitution of the social and in the possibility of articulating the relevance of democracy itself. In what follows, I want to argue that youth as a referent refers not only to young children, but also to those youth who inhabit the institutions of higher learning and who are poised to become adults by virtue of the knowledge, capacities, and skills they learn as critical citizens, workers, and intellectuals.

Higher Education and the Crisis of the Social

Within the last two decades a widespread pessimism about public life and politics has developed in the United States. Individual rights now outweigh collective concerns as market ideals have taken precedence over democratic values. In the vocabulary of neoliberalism, the public collapses into the personal, the personal becomes "the only politics there is, the only politics with a tangible referent or emotional valence," and it is within such an utterly personal discourse that human actions are shaped and agency is privatized.[25] Under neoliberalism, hope becomes dystopian as the public sphere disappears and, as Peter Beilharz argues, "politics becomes banal, for there is not only an absence of citizenship but a striking absence of agency."[26]

As economic and financial power is increasingly separated from the specificity of traditional politics and public obligations, corporations are less subject to the control of the state, and "there is a strong impulse to displace political sovereignty with the sovereignty of the market, as if the latter has a mind and morality of its own."[27] Under the auspices of neoliberalism, the language of the social is either devalued or ignored, as public life is reduced to a form of pathology, and all dreams of the future are now modeled around the narcissistic, privatized, and self-indulgent needs of consumer culture and the dictates of the alleged "free" market. Samuel Weber has suggested that what seems to be involved in such a transformation is "a fundamental and political redefinition of the social value of public services in general, and of universities and education in particular."[28]

Within this impoverished sense of politics and public life, the university is increasingly being transformed into a training ground for the corporate workforce, with the loss of any notion of higher education as a crucial public sphere in which critical citizens and democratic agents are formed. In the age of money and profit, academic subjects gain stature almost exclusively through their exchange value on the market. This is all the more so as the Bush administration attempts to privatize higher education, cut student aid, plunder public services, and push states to the brink of financial disaster. As higher education increasingly becomes a privilege rather than a right, many working-class students either find it financially impossible to enter college or, because of increased costs, have to drop out. Those students who have the resources to stay in school are feeling the tight pressures of the job market and rush to take courses and receive professional credentials in business and the bio-sciences as the humanities lose majors and downsize. Not surprisingly, students are now referred to as "customers," while faculty are rewarded less for their scholarship than their ability to secure funds and generate grants from foundations, corporations, and other external sources. Rather than being rewarded for critically inventive teaching and rigorous research, faculty are now valued as multinational operatives, even as the majority of their colleagues are increasingly reduced to contract employees.

Under the reign of neoliberalism and corporate culture, the boundaries between commercial culture and public culture become blurred as universities rush to embrace the logic of industrial management while simultaneously forfeiting those broader values central to a democracy and capable of limiting the excesses of corporate power. As higher education is corporatized, young people find themselves on campuses that look more like malls, and they are increasingly taught by professors who are hired on a contractual basis, have obscene workloads, and can barely make enough money to pay the loans for their cars. Tenured faculty are now called upon to generate grants, establish close partnerships with corporations, and teach courses that have practical value in the marketplace. There is little in this vision of the university that imagines young people as anything other than fodder for the corporation.

Educated Hope in Dark Times

In opposition to the corporatization of higher education and the devaluing of the capacities of young people, there is a prominent educational tradition in the United States extending from Thomas Jefferson to John Dewey in which the future of the university is premised on the recognition that in order for freedom to flourish in the worldly space of the public realm, citizens have to be formed, educated, and socialized. Dewey, for example, argued that higher education should provide the conditions for people to involve themselves in the deepest problems of society, to acquire the knowledge, skills, and ethical responsibility necessary for "reasoned participation in democratically organized publics."[29] C. Wright Mills challenged schooling as a form of corporate training and called for fashioning higher education within a public philosophy committed to a radical conception of citizenship, civic engagement, and public wisdom.[30] Education in these contexts was linked to public life through democratic values such as equality, liberty, and freedom, rather than as an adjunct of the corporation whose knowledge and values were defined largely through the prism of commercial interests. Education was crucial to a notion of individual agency and public citizenship, integral to defending the relationship between an autonomous society—rooted in an ever-expanding process of self-examination, critique, and reform—and autonomous individuals, for whom critical inquiry is propelled by the need to engage in an ongoing pursuit of ethics and justice as a matter of public good. In many ways, higher education has been faithful, at least in theory, to a project of modern politics, in which its purpose was to create citizens capable of defining and implementing universal goals such as freedom, equality, and justice as part of a broader attempt to deepen the relationship between an expanded notion of the social and the enabling ground of a vibrant democracy.

If the rise of the corporate university is to be challenged and education is to become a meaningful site for educating youth for a democratic future, educators and others need to reclaim the meaning and purpose of higher education as an ethical and political response to the demise of democratic public life. At stake here is the need to insist on the role of the university as a public sphere committed to deepening and expanding the possibilities of democratic identities, values, and relations. This approach suggests new models of leadership based on the understanding that the real purpose of higher education means encouraging people to think beyond the task of simply getting a lucrative job. Beyond this ever-narrowing instrumental justification, there are the more relevant goals of opening up higher education to all groups, creating a critical citizenry, providing specialized work skills for jobs that really require them, democratizing relations of governance among administrators, faculty, and students, and taking seriously the imperative to disseminate an intellectual and artistic culture. Higher education may be one of the few sites left in which students can learn how to mediate critically between democratic values and the demands of corporate power, between identities founded on democratic principles and identities engulfed by forms of unbridled individualism that promote competitiveness, self-interest, profit-making, and greed. This view suggests, once again, that higher education needs to be defended through intellectual work that self-consciously recalls the tension between the democratic imperatives and possibilities of public institutions and their everyday realization within a society dominated by a market fundamentalism. Higher education should be defended as a space of critical education where teachers and students have the chance to resist those modes of pedagogy, time, and rationality that refuse to include questions of judgment and issues of responsibility. Understood as such, higher education should be viewed as neither an exclusively consumer-driven product nor as a form of training and career preparation, but as a mode of learning that renders all individuals fit "to participate in power . . . to the greatest extent possible, to participate in a common government," and to be capable, as Aristotle reminds us, of both governing and being governed.[31] Addressing education as a democratic endeavor begins with the recognition that higher education is more than an investment opportunity; citizenship is about more than consuming; learning is about more than preparing for a job; and democracy is about more than making choices at the local mall.

Reclaiming higher education as a public sphere begins with the crucial project of challenging corporate ideology and its preference of market time over public time. Market time fosters a narrow sense of leadership, agency, and public values and is largely indifferent to those noncommercial concerns that are critical to a just society. The values of hierarchy, materialism, competition, and excessive individualism are enshrined under market time and play a defining role in how it allocates space, manages the production of particular forms of knowledge, guides research, and regulates pedagogical relations. Market time accentuates privatized and competitive modes of intellectual activity, largely removed from public obligations and social responsibilities. Public time, on the other hand, rejects the fever-pitch appeals of "just in time" or "speed time," demands often made within the context of "ever faster technological transformation and exchange" and buttressed by corporate capital's golden rule: "time is money."[32] Public time slows time down, neither as a simple refusal of technological change nor as a rejection of all calls for efficiency, but as an attempt to create the institutional and ideological conditions that promote long-term analyses, historical reflection, and deliberations over what our collective actions might mean for shaping the future. Rejecting an instrumentality that evacuates questions of history, ethics, and justice, public time fosters dialogue, thoughtfulness, and critical exchange. Public time offers room for knowledge that contributes to society's self-understanding, enables it to question itself, and seeks to legitimate intellectual practices that not only are collective and noninstrumental, but that also deepen democratic values while encouraging pedagogical relations that question the future in terms that are political, ethical, and social. At stake here is the important task of redefining higher education as a democratic public sphere not only to assert the importance of public time, but also to reconfigure it so that "economic interests cease to be the dominant factor in shaping attitudes" about the social as a realm devoid of politics and democratic possibilities.[33] Higher education is a hard-won democratic achievement, and it is time that parents, faculty, students, college alumni, and concerned citizens reclaim it as a fundamental public good rather than a mere training ground for corporate interests, values, and profits. Education is not only about issues of work and economics, but also about questions of justice, social freedom, and the capacity for democratic agency, action, and change as well as the related issues of power, exclusion, and citizenship. These are educational and political issues and should be addressed as part of a broader concern for renewing the struggle for social justice and democracy.

Academics and Public Life

Institutions of higher education must be seen as deeply moral and political spaces in which intellectuals assert themselves not merely as professional academics, but as citizens whose knowledge and actions presuppose specific visions of public life, community, and moral accountability. This view suggests that higher education be defended, not as an adjunct of the corporation, but as a vital public sphere in its own right, one that has deeply moral and educative dimensions that directly impact on civic life. This defense must be maintained by academics redefining their roles as public intellectuals who can move between academic institutions and other public spheres in which knowledge, values, and social identities are produced.

If the university is to remain a site of critical thinking, collective work, and public service, educators will have to redefine the knowledge, skills, research, and intellectual practices currently being favored in the university. Central to such a challenge is the necessity to define intellectual practice "as part of an intricate web of morality, rigor and responsibility" that enables academics to speak with conviction, enter the public sphere in order to address important social problems, and demonstrate alternative models for what it means to bridge the gap between higher education and the broader society.[34] Under such conditions, it is crucial to construct intellectual practices that are collegial rather than competitive, that refuse the instrumentality and privileged isolation of the academy, that link critical thought to a profound impatience with the status quo, and that connect human agency to the idea of social responsibility.

Increasingly as universities are shaped by a culture of fear in which dissent is equated with treason, the call to be objective and impartial can easily echo what George Orwell referred to as the official truth or the establishment point of view, however unconscious or unintentional. Lacking a self-conscious democratic political project, the role of the university intellectual is often reduced to that of a technician or functionary engaged in formalistic rituals and unconcerned with the disturbing and urgent problems that confront the larger society. In opposition to this view, I argue that public intellectuals—and perhaps especially those concerned with research into aspects of childhood and youth—should combine the mutually interdependent roles of critical educator and active citizen. This suggests finding ways to connect the practice of class-room teaching to the operation of power in the larger society. I think Edward Said is on target when he argues that the public intellectual must function within institutions, in part, as an exile, as someone whose "place it is publicly to raise embarrassing questions, to confront orthodoxy and dogma, to be someone who cannot easily be co-opted by governments or corporations."[35] In this perspective, the educator as public intellectual becomes responsible for linking the diverse experiences that produce knowledge, iden-tities, and social values in the university to the quality of moral and political life in the wider society. Vaclav Havel captures this sentiment in arguing that intellectuals have a responsibility to engage in practical politics, to see "things in more global terms . . . build people-to-people solidarity . . . foster tolerance, struggle against evil and violence, promote human rights, and argue for their indivisibility."[36]

I think that these concerns about the responsibility of academics as public intel-lectuals are especially important with respect to how young people in education programs are taught to educate and nurture people younger than themselves. One of the ways in which university teachers in education programs can reach out to influence the future is to make it clear to their own students that they bear a responsibility to educate critically the students they will be interacting with once they graduate from college. The importance of such an educational challenge and project can be seen in a recent survey conducted by the John S. and James L. Knight Foundation, which found that 36 percent of U.S. high school students believed that "newspapers should get government approval of stories before publishing."[37] Clearly, it is precisely the lack of education about student rights, First Amendment freedoms, and the meaning of a substantive democracy that provides the conditions for such views, which are much closer to fascism than to what it means to be a critical citizen in a democracy. Moreover, this type of political illiteracy and historical amnesia poses as much of a threat to Canadian children as it does to American youth.[38] Critical education cannot be decoupled from political democracy and should take place at all levels of school-ing; but it must gain its momentum in those colleges and universities among students who will go back to the schools, churches, synagogues, and business world in order to produce new ideas, concepts, and democratic ways of understanding the world in which young people live.

Intellectuals who feel an increased sense of responsibility for humanity may not be able to, and do not necessarily have to, explain the problems of the world in terms that purport to be absolute or all-encompassing. Nor should they limit their responsibility to the sphere of the university or the media. On the contrary, public intellectuals need to approach social issues with humility, mindful of the multiple connections and issues that tie humanity together; but they need to do so as border intellectuals moving within and across diverse sites of learning as part of an engaged and practical politics that recognizes the importance of "asking questions, making distinctions, restoring to memory all those things that tend to be overlooked or walked past in the rush to collective judgment and action."[39] Within this discourse, the experiences that constitute the production of knowledge, identities, and social values in the university are inextricably linked to the quality of moral and political life in the wider society.

If educators are to function as public intellectuals, then they need to provide the opportunities for students to learn that the relationship between knowledge and power can be emancipatory, that their histories and experiences matter, and that what they say and do count in their struggle to unlearn dominating privileges, productively reconstruct their relations with others, and transform, when necessary, the world around them. More specifically, such educators need to argue for forms of pedagogy that close the gap between the university and everyday life. Their curriculum needs to be organized around knowledge of communities, cultures, and traditions that give students a sense of history, identity, and place. Edward Said is again helpful. Said urges academics and students to accept the demands of "worldliness," which implies "lifting complex ideas into the public space," recognizing human injury outside of the academy, and using theory as a form of criticism to change things.[40] Worldliness requires not being afraid of controversy, making connections that are otherwise hidden, deflating the claims of triumphalism, and bridging intellectual work and the operation of politics. It means combining rigor and clarity, on the one hand, and civic courage and political commitment, on the other. Following Said, I am calling for the transgressing of the often rigid division between academic culture and popular culture as well as between disciplines, and for expanding pedagogical practice as a form of cultural politics by making all knowledge subject to serious analysis and interrogation, and, in so doing, making visible the operations of power that connect such knowledge to specific views of authority, cultural practice, and the larger world.

Educators need to construct pedagogical approaches that do more than make learning context-specific; in effect, they need to challenge the content of established canons and, similarly, to expand the range of cultural texts that count as "really useful knowledge." As public intellectuals, university teachers must begin to use those electronically mediated knowledge forms that constitute the terrain of mass and popular culture. I am referring here to the world of media texts—videos, films, music, and other mechanisms of popular culture that operate through a combination of visual and print culture. What I am suggesting here is that educators challenge the traditional definition and site of pedagogy by widening the application of pedagogy to a variety of cultural locations and, in doing so, alert students to how public pedagogy operates through the educational force of the culture at large.

The content of the curriculum should affirm and critically enrich the meaning, language, and knowledge forms that students actually use to negotiate and inform their lives. Academics can in part exercise their role as public intellectuals via such curricula by giving students the opportunity to understand how power is organized through the enormous number of "popular" cultural spheres that range from libraries, movie theaters, and schools, to high-tech media conglomerates that circulate signs and meanings through newspapers, magazines, advertisements, new information technologies, machines, films, and television programs. University intellectuals must draw a lesson from cultural studies in extending the historical and relational definition of cultural texts while redefining, how in Toni Morrison's terms, "knowledge, however mundane and utilitarian, plays about in linguistic images and forms cultural practices."[41] Needless to say, this position challenges Roger Kimball's claim that "Popular culture is a tradition essential to uneducated Americans."[42] Of course, what is at stake is not only important questions about how knowledge is produced and taken up, but what it means to provide the conditions for students to become competent and critically versed in a variety of literacies while at the same time expanding the conditions and options for the roles they might play as cultural producers (as opposed to simply teaching students to be critical readers).

Although it is central for university teachers to enlarge the curriculum to reflect the richness and diversity of the students they actually teach, they also need to decenter the curriculum. That is, as Stanley Aronowitz points out, students should be actively involved in governance, "including setting learning goals, selecting courses, and having their own, autonomous organizations, including a free press."[43] Not only does the distribution of power among teachers, students, and administrators provide the conditions for students to become agents in their learning process; it also provides the basis for collective learning, civic action, and ethical responsibility. Moreover, student agency emerges from a pedagogy of lived experience and struggle, not from mere formalistic mastery of an academic subject.

I have suggested that educators need to become provocateurs. They need to take a stand while refusing to be involved in either a cynical relativism or doctrinaire politics. This suggests that central to intellectual life is the pedagogical and political imperative that academics engage in rigorous social criticism while becoming a stubborn force that can challenge false prophets, fight against the imposed silence of normalized power, "refuse to allow conscience to look away or fall asleep," and critically engage all those social relations that promote material and symbolic violence.[44] At the same time, such intellectuals must be deeply critical of their own authority and how it structures classroom relations and cultural practices. In this way, the authority they legitimate in the classroom (as well as in other public spheres) would become both an object of self-critique and a critical referent for expressing a more "fundamental dispute with authority itself."[45]

Central to my argument is the need for educators to define themselves less as narrow specialists, classroom managers, or mouthpieces for corporate culture than as engaged public intellectuals willing to address those economic, political, and social problems that must be overcome if both young people and adults are going to take seriously a future that opens up rather than closes down the promises of a viable and substantive democracy. There is a lot of talk among social theorists about the death of politics and the inability of human beings to imagine a more equitable and just world in order to make it better. I would hope that, of all groups, educators would be the most vocal and militant in challenging this assumption by making it clear that at the heart of any form of critical education is the assumption that learning should be used to expand the public good and promote democratic social change, especially for young people. Public and higher education may be one of the few spheres left where the promise of youth can be linked to the promise of democracy. Education in this instance becomes both an ethical and political referent in that it not only furnishes an opportunity for adults to provide the conditions for young people to become critically engaged social agents, but also offers the symbols of a future in which democracy creates the conditions for each generation of youth to struggle anew to sustain the promise of a democracy that has no endpoint and must be continuously expanded into a world of new possibilities and opportunities for keeping justice and hope alive.

In conclusion, I want to suggest that struggles over how we view, represent, and treat young people must be understood as part of a larger public dialogue about how to imagine a future linked to the creation of a strong inclusive democracy while simultaneously articulating a new vocabulary, a set of theoretical tools, and social possibilities for envisioning civic engagement and political transformation. We have entered a period in which the war against youth, especially poor youth of color, offers no apologies because it is too arrogant and ruthless to imagine any resistance. But the collective need and potential struggle for justice should never be underestimated even in the darkest of times. I realize this sounds a bit utopian, but we have few choices if we are going to fight for a future that enables teachers, parents, students, and others to work diligently and tirelessly in order to make hope practical for all members of society and especially for young people, who deserve a future that does a great deal more than endlessly repeat the present.

Notes

1. Reg Whitaker, "Living with Bush's America—Remaining True to Ourselves Will See Canadians Through the Next Four Years," *Literary Review of Canada*, January/February 2005, 5.
2. Jacques Derrida, "The Future of the Profession or the Unconditional University," in *Derrida Down Under*, ed. Laurence Simmons and Heather Worth (Auckland, NZ: Dunmarra Press, 2001), 253.
3. Francis Fox Ivan, *The War at Home: The Domestic Costs of Bush's Militarism* (New York: The New Press, 2004).
4. I analyze neoliberalism in great detail in Henry Giroux, *The Terror of Neoliberalism* (Boulder, CO: Paradigm, 2004).
5. Lawrence Grossberg, "Why Does Neo-Liberalism Hate Kids? The War on Youth and the Culture of Politics," *The Review of Education, Pedagogy & Cultural Studies* 23, no. 2 (2001): 133.
6. Lt. Col. Dave Grossman and Gloria DeGaentano, *Teaching Our Kids to Kill* (New York: Crown, 1999).
7. Heather Wokusch, "Leaving Our Children Behind," *Common Dreams News Center*, July 8, 2002, 1, http://www.commondreams.org/views02/0708-08.htm.
8. Press Release, "The State of America's Children 2004," *Children's Defense Fund*, July 13, 2004, http://www.childrensdefense.org/pressreleases/040713.aspx.
9. Ellen Willis, "Historical Analysis," *Dissent*, Winter 2005, 113.
10. Jeffrey Selingo, "Bush Budget Takes Aim at Student Aid and Research," *Chronicle of Higher Education*, February 18, 2005, A5, A21–A24.

11. Paul Ford, "Weekly Review," *Harper's Online*, February 22, 2005, http://www.harpers.org/WeeklyReview.html.
12. Anne E. Kornblut, "Bush Urges Rigorous High School Testing," *New York Times*, January 13, 2005, 26; I have taken up this critique in great detail in Henry A. Giroux, *The Abandoned Generation* (New York: Palgrave, 2004).
13. Laura Flanders, "Bush's Hit List: Teens and Kids," *Common Dreams News Center*, February 13, 2005, http://www.commondreams.org/views05/0213-11.htm.
14. Mike Allen and Peter Baker, "$2.5 Trillion Budget Plan Cuts Many Programs," *Washington Post*, February 7, 2005, A01.
15. Paul Krugman, "Bush's Class-War Budget," *New York Times*, February 11, 2005, A23.
16. Ibid.
17. Ginger McCall, "Secretary of Ed.'s Attack on Cartoon Spells Trouble," *Pitt News*, February 2, 2005, 1.
18. Frank Rich, "The Year of Living Indecently," *New York Times*, February 6, 2005, AR1.
19. Earl Ofari Hutchinson, "Crips, Bloods and Laura Bush," *Black America Today*, February 7, 2005, http://www.blackamericatoday.com/article.cfm?ArticleID=745.
20. Noreena Hertz, *The Silent Takeover: Global Capitalism and the Death of Democracy* (New York: The Free Press, 2001), 11.
21. Pierre Bourdieu, *Acts of Resistance: Against the Tyranny of the Market* (New York: The New Press, 1998); Pierre Bourdieu et al., *The Weight of the World: Social Suffering in Contemporary Society* (Stanford, CA: Stanford University Press, 1999).
22. Zygmunt Bauman, *In Search of Politics* (Stanford, CA: Stanford University Press, 1999), 2.
23. Naomi Klein, *No Logo* (New York: Picador, 1999), 177.
24. Grossberg, "Why Does Neo-Liberalism Hate Kids?" 133.
25. Jean Comaroff and John L. Comaroff, "Millennial Capitalism: First Thoughts on a Second Coming," *Public Culture* 12, no. 2 (2000): 305–306.
26. Peter Beilharz, *Zygmunt Bauman: Dialectic of Modernity* (London: Sage, 2000), 160.
27. Comaroff and Comaroff, "Millennial Capitalism," 332.
28. Cited in Roger Simon, "The University: A Place to Think?" in *Beyond the Corporate University*, ed. Henry A. Giroux and Kostas Myrsiades (Lanham, MD: Rowman and Littlefield, 2001), 47–48.
29. Cited in Frank Hearn, *Reason and Freedom in Sociological Thought* (Boston: Unwin Hyman, 1985), 175. The classic statements by Dewey on this subject can be found in John Dewey, *Democracy and Education* (1916; repr., New York: The Free Press, 1997); see also, John Dewey, *The Public and Its Problems* (Columbus: Ohio University Press, 1954).
30. C. Wright Mills, *Power, Politics, and People*, ed. Irving Louis Horowitz (New York: Oxford University Press, 1963).
31. Cornelius Castoriadis, "The Nature and Value of Equity," in *Philosophy, Politics, Autonomy: Essays in Political Philosophy* (New York: Oxford University Press, 1991), 140.
32. Jerome Bind, "Toward an Ethic of the Future," *Public Culture* 12, no. 1 (2000): 52.
33. Cornelius Castoriadis, "The Greek Polis and the Creation of Democracy," in *Philosophy, Politics, Autonomy*, 112.
34. Arundhati Roy, *Power Politics* (Cambridge, MA: South End, 2001), 6.
35. Edward Said, *Representations of the Intellectual* (New York: Pantheon, 1994), 11.
36. Vaclav Havel, "The Responsibility of Intellectuals," *New York Review of Books*, June 22, 1995, 37.
37. Greg Toppo, "U.S. Students Say Press Freedoms Go too Far," *USA Today*, January 30, 2005, http://www.usatoday.com/news/education/2005-01-30-students-press_x.htm.
38. I am indebted to Perry Nodelman for this insight about the wider pedagogical influences our students can have on younger students.
39. Said, *Representations*, 52–53.
40. Edward Said, "Scholarship and Commitment: An Introduction," *Profession* (2000): 7.

41. Toni Morrison, *Playing in the Dark: Whiteness and the Literary Imagination* (Cambridge, MA: Harvard University Press, 1992), 49–50.

42. Kimball cited in Lawrence W. Levine, *The Opening of the American Mind* (Boston: Beacon, 1996), 19.

43. Stanley Aronowitz, "A Different Perspective on Educational Equality," *The Review of Education, Pedagogy and Cultural Studies* 16, no. 2 (1994): 24.

44. All of these ideas and the quotation itself are taken from Edward Said, *Humanism and Democratic Criticism* (New York: Columbia, 2004), 142.

45. R. Radhakrishnan, "Canonicity and Theory: Toward a Poststructuralist Pedagogy," in *Theory/Pedagogy/Politics*, ed. Donald Morton and Mas'ud Zavarzadeh (Urbana: University of Illinois Press, 1991), 112–135.

16

TRANSLATING THE FUTURE

SPEAKING TO GRADUATING YOUTH

I am honored to accept this honorary degree on this important occasion today, and to be with all of you in sharing this wonderful achievement of graduating from Memorial University. As a father of three teenage boys, I also want to congratulate those family members, friends, and others whose support throughout the years helped to make it possible for you to achieve this tremendous milestone in your life. It is a humbling task to stand before you and say something worthy of this memorable event. Needless to say, I am mindful of a comment made by the late United States Supreme Court Justice, Harry Blackman, who stated that "a commencement speaker was like the corpse at an old-fashion Irish wake: he was necessary to justify the occasion but no one expected him to say anything."[1]

Of course, Blackman highlighted that position only to resist it. The great philosopher, Hannah Arendt, certainly took Blackman's caveat seriously by insisting that speeches made by award recipients should be less about individual merit than about accepting the award and speaking our gratitude for it by "ignoring ourselves and acting entirely within the framework of our attitude toward the world, toward a world and public to which we owe the space to which we speak and in which we are heard."[2] And it is precisely in this spirit of affirming public discourse, civic morality, and what it might mean to conduct your lives as engaged citizens attentive to the suffering of others and the fragility of democracy itself that I want to frame my brief remarks.

I have been writing about education, social justice, and democracy in the United States for over thirty years. I have done so not because I am motivated by some lofty notion of the perfect society, but because I believe that it is impossible to talk about the future without highlighting the crucial importance of youth, who, more than any other group, embody the projected desires, dreams, and commitment of society's obligations to the future. This recognition echoes a classical principle of modernity in which youth both symbolized society's responsibility to the future and offered a measure of its progress. Youth, in this instance, provides a moral and political referent for how we translate the future and how we meet our responsibility to supply the resources, social provisions, and modes of education that enable young people to work toward the promise of an inclusive, sustainable, and peaceful global democracy.

Within such a project, democracy is measured by the well-being of youth, while the status of how a society imagines the promise of democracy is contingent on how it views its planetary responsibility toward future generations. As you move from the university to the larger world, how you become responsible to your own sense of responsibility will be inextricably linked to what kind of world you make for your own children.

As you well know, the futures we inherit are not of our own making, but the futures we create for the generations of young people who follow us arise out of our ability to imagine a better world, to recognize our responsibility to others, and to define the success of a society to the degree that it can address the needs of coming generations to live in a world in which the obligations of a global democracy and individual responsibility mutually inform each other. Translating the future in such terms poses a serious and important challenge for your generation because the language of democracy and social justice has come under serious attack within the last few decades. Not only has a widespread pessimism about public life and politics developed in countries such as the United States, as politics is devalued and public space is commercialized or privatized, but the very idea of justice is under attack as the language of the social contract and democracy is either devalued or ignored. Dreams of the future are now manufactured in the Pentagon, corporate board rooms, or in Hollywood. In a post-9/11 world, the space of shared responsibility has given way to a space of shared fears; the obligations of citizenship are reduced to the imperatives of consumerism; and the public sphere, emptied of all substantive content, becomes a playground for endlessly enacting and reinforcing the banal privatized fantasies of shopping malls and celebrity culture, which means putting up with the likes of Paris Hilton.

Hopefully, this will not be the model through which you will imagine the future after you leave here today. But dreaming a more just and democratic future means you will have to build upon and continue your education, which should begin with the recognition that justice is the merging of hope, imagination, reason, and moral responsibility, tempered by the recognition that the pursuit of happiness and the good life is a collective affair. Where does education fit into all of this? Education suggests developing a language and set of strategies for translating private troubles into public considerations and public issues into individual and collective rights. Rather than widen the gap between the public and private, you will need a vocabulary for understanding how private problems and public issues constitute the very lifeblood of politics. I stress this point because you are living in a world that is increasingly collapsing the public into the private, creating conditions in which public discourse and politics disappear only to be replaced by a litany of individual flaws to be borne in isolation. You see the signs of this everywhere. Poverty is now a problem of individual character. Racism is merely individual discrimination or prejudice. Homelessness is reduced to a choice made by lazy people. Misfortune is viewed as a private disgrace or deserving of only a sneer. At the level of social policy, public officials make lyrical pronouncements suggesting that a crisis such as water pollution can be solved by buying bottled water. Politics takes many forms but central to it is the need for citizens to be able to translate individual problems into public concerns. And that is going to be your job. You leave here today with degrees in engineering, computer science, history, social work, and so many other fields. Today, I ask you to think of yourselves as competent professionals who also have a special obligation as civic leaders. Leadership, as the great sociologist, Zygmunt Bauman, reminds us, is the ability to be an expert in translation, to be able to question the basic assumptions central to a democracy, to learn how to govern and not simply be governed, to be capable of promoting a vision of the better society, and to raise important questions about what education should accomplish in a democracy.[3]

I believe that one of the many great challenges facing your generation is how to resist the manufactured cynicism, moral despair, and social Darwinism—with its cult of competitiveness and war against all ethic—served up in all the spheres of public life and mirrored daily in reality TV shows such as *Survivor, Temptation Island, The Biggest Loser,* and *The Bachelor.* Democratic politics needs leaders, while manufactured cynicism needs celebrity idols. The other great challenge facing your generation is the need to develop a language of not only critique—one that refuses to equate democracy with market relations and consumerism—but also a language of hope.

Vibrant democratic cultures and societies refuse to live in an era of foreclosed hope. Such societies embrace hope, not as some utopian dream or privatized fantasy, but as a way of anticipating a better world in the future, by combining reason with a gritty sense of reality and its limits, and by realizing your potential as full human beings. The French philosopher, Alan Badiou, argues that hope as an educational project means "showing how the space of the possible is larger than the one assigned— that something else is possible, but not everything is possible."[4] Any viable notion of hope has to foreground issues of both understanding and social responsibility and address the implications the latter has for a democratic society. As the artist and politician, Vaclav Havel, has noted, "Democracy requires a certain type of citizen who feels responsible for something other than his [or her] own well-feathered little corner; citizens who want to participate in society's affairs, who insist on it; citizens with backbones; citizens who hold their ideas about democracy at the deepest level, at the level that religion is held, where beliefs and identity are the same."[5]

Responsibility breathes hope into politics and suggests both a different future and the possibility of politics itself. At the same time, hope not only offers long-term visions and possibilities; it also makes moral responsibility the condition for politics and agency because it recognizes the importance of young people becoming accountable for others through their ideas, language, and actions. At the center of politics is not a battle between the Left and Right, liberals and conservatives, but between hope and despair. In opposition to a world in which the public sphere has been annexed by the private, and happiness has been deregulated and commodified, hope offers neither an image of a scientifically engineered future nor a blueprint for a future without imperfections or contradictions, but a belief that different futures are possible, holding open matters of dialogue, contingency, context, and indeterminacy. The challenge of hope for your generation poses the important question of how to reclaim social agency within a broader struggle to deepen the possibilities for social justice and global democracy. This position is echoed by the feminist scholar, Judith Butler, who argues, "For me, there is more hope in the world when we can question what is taken for granted, especially about what it is to be human."[6] Zygmunt Bauman elaborates this idea further, arguing that any viable notion of democracy is dependent upon a culture of questioning, whose purpose is to "keep the forever unexhausted and unfulfilled human potential open, fighting back all attempts to foreclose and pre-empt the further unravelling of human possibilities, prodding human society to go on questioning itself and preventing that questioning from ever stalling or being declared finished."[7]

To reclaim hope in the service of planetary democracy is an act of daring that I hope your generation readily confronts and succeeds in establishing. You live in a world in which democracy, if it is to survive, needs to be sustained by new global public spaces and spheres. The lesson here is that democracy is very fragile, takes many forms, and it is never guaranteed. It is up to your generation to confront the dark forces afoot globally trying to eclipse the promise of democracy. Hints of such forces can be seen in alarming tendency toward barbarism reflected in the torture chambers of Abu Ghraib, the widening economic inequalities between the rich and poor, the increasing religious fundamentalism around the globe, the ongoing militarization of public space and surveillance in public schools, the ravaging of the planet for profit, and the attack on critical dissent in the universities and elsewhere. The future is now in your hands, and it is a future that needs your skills, critical judgment, sense of responsibility, compassion, imagination, and humility. Rather than trade in your dreams of a better world for a home security system or gated community, I urge you to "connect your utopian passions with a practical politics" in order to define what is still possible in a democracy.[8] Everything is possible for you, but it can only happen if you can imagine the unimaginable, think differently in order to act differently, and "give imaginative shape to humanity's hope for a better and more inclusive future."[9] To quote Bono, a rock star with a political sensibility: "This is a time for bold measures. This is the country, and you are the generation."[10]

Notes

1. I came across this citation in James Freedman, "What a Liberal Education Makes of Us," *Whitman College Magazine Online*, Summer 1999, http://www.whitman.edu/magazine/summer1999/jfreedmanspeech.html (accessed April 14, 2005).
2. Hannah Arendt, "On Humanity in Dark Times: Thoughts About Lessing," in *Men in Dark Times* (New York: Harcourt, 1968), 3.
3. Zygmunt Bauman, "Introduction," *Society under Siege* (Malden, MA: Blackwell, 2002), 170.
4. Alain Badiou, *Ethics: An Essay on the Understanding of Evil* (London: Verso, 1998), 115–116.
5. Cited in Paul Berman, "The Philosopher-King is Mortal," *The New York Times Magazine*, May 11, 1997, 36.
6. Cited in Gary A. Olson and Lynn Worsham, "Changing the Subject: Judith Butler's Politics of Radical Resignification," *JAC: Journal of Advanced Composition* 20, no. 4 (2000): 765.
7. Zygmunt Bauman and Keith Tester, *Conversations with Zygmunt Bauman* (Malden, MA: Polity, 2001), 4.
8. Russell Jacoby, *Picture Imperfect: Utopian Thought for an Anti-Utopian Age* (New York: Columbia University Press, 2005), 148.
9. Bram Dijkstra, "The Dialectics of Hope versus the Politics of Stasis in Art," *Tikkun* 19, no. 6 (November/December 2004): 62.
10. Bono, "Because We Can, We Must," *Almanac Between Issues* (commencement address, University of Pennsylvania, May 19, 2004, http://www.upenn.edu/almanac/between/2004/commence-b.html).

INDEX

1984 (Orwell), 32, 103
60 Minutes, 46, 53, 139

Abu Ghraib, 26, 59–61, 63, 65, 82, 104,
    106–107, 256
    public perception of, 46–47
    torture at, 53–57
    see also torture
abuse
    child, 129–135, 137, 139–140, 142–143
    of prisoners, 104, 106–112
academia
    and dissent, 19–20
    and public life, 246–250
    viewed as elitists, 19
ACLU, 75, 106
Adorno, Theodor, 143, 205
    critique of nationalism, 63
    and importance of critical education,
        58–60, 64–65
    and role of education after Auschwitz,
        61–62
affirmative action, 44, 152, 154, 160–161,
    163–164
Afghanistan, 32, 46, 81, 104, 107–108, 192
African Americans, 25, 80, 133, 152, 154,
    160, 179–180, 184, 196–197
Al Qaeda, 45, 105
Alterman, Eric, 105, 108
America in Black and White (Thernstrom),
    152
America's Army (video game), 32, 61, 198
American Association of University
    Professors, 92
Amnesty International, 105, 107–108
Ansell, Elizabeth, 157–158

anti-intellectualism, 16, 29, 80
antiracist ideologies, 156, 168–169
Arar, Maher, 106
Arendt, Hannah, 117, 219, 253
Aronowitz, Stanley, 8, 113, 249
Ashcroft, John, 62, 71, 73–74, 81, 164
Atta, Mohammad, 78, 105
Auletta, Ken, 105
Auschwitz, 53, 55, 57–61, 63, 65
authoritarianism
    Bush and, 26–27, 33–35, 56, 62–64,
        101, 104
    religious fundamentalism and, 72–73,
        80–81, 84–85
    U.S. government's trend toward, 11–12,
        23, 38
Aziz, Nikhil, 161

Bacevich, Andrew J., 31, 193
Badiou, Alain, 13, 255
Baker, Kevin, 193, 200
Barnett, Scott, 197
Baudrillard, Jean, 111
Bauman, Zygmunt, 17, 61, 83, 155, 157,
    217, 255
BBC, 46
Beale, Calvin, 181
beauty pageants, child, 129, 133–143
    genealogy of, 136–140
    and shock of the real, 133–136
Bechtel, 89
Beger, Randall, 195
Beilharz, Peter, 243
Bell Curve, The (Herrnstein and
    Murray), 160
Bhabha, Homi K., 207, 212

bigotry, 43, 65, 76, 80–81, 154, 163–164, 185, 241
Billington, Hardy, 77
bin Laden, Osama, 81, 105
Blackman, Harry, 253
Bloch, Ernst, 82
Bob Jones University, 28, 71
Bollinger, Lee C., 93–94
Bonhoeffer, Deitrich, 50, 229
Bourdieu, Pierre, 97, 168, 233, 242
Boykin, William, 81
Brooks, David, 164
Brooks, Renana, 102
Brown, Janice Rogers, 103
Bush, George H.W., 164
Bush, George W., 237, 240–241, 243
    aboard USS *Abraham Lincoln,* 53, 192, 199
    and Abu Ghraib, 55–56, 60
    abuse of power, 10, 34–35, 37
    corporatization and, 89, 91, 95
    and domestic policy, 25–26, 44–47, 62–63, 175, 177–178
    and education, 15–18
    election of, 24–25
    and foreign policy, 26–27
    fundamentalism and, 27–33
    and militarization of public space, 191–195, 199
    and newspeak, 101–111, 113
    reelection of, 12–14, 16, 23, 27–28, 31–33, 37, 71, 75–77, 192, 231–232
    religious Right and, 71–81, 84
Butler, Judith, 255
Byrd, Robert, 46

Calvin Klein, 141
Canada, 12, 92, 237
capitalism
    authoritarianism and, 64
    effects on education, 90, 96–97, 241–242
    global, 35, 155, 222
    neoliberal, 11, 25, 62, 82, 166, 205–206
career training versus critical education, 18, 25, 36, 45, 47, 91–92, 162, 208, 212, 241, 243, 245
Carroll, James, 63

Carter, Helena Bonham, 209, 218–219
Castoriadis, Cornelius, 233
Center for Individual Rights (CIR), 160
Cheney, Dick, 46, 63, 77, 104–105, 108, 111, 192
Chery, Carl, 196
child abuse, 106, 129–135, 137, 139–140
    politics of, 140–143
child care, 130, 240
childhood, 3, 129–131, 133–135, 184, 231, 247
Children's Defense Fund, 239
Chomsky, Noam, 95
citizenship, effects of consumerism on, 24–25, 27, 93–94, 97
civic responsibility, 15, 24, 76, 157
civil liberties, 10, 14, 26, 31, 62, 64, 104, 175, 178, 200, 238, 242
Civil Rights Movement, 43–44, 153, 161
class, 44–45, 180–181
    struggle, 10–11
    warfare, 103, 241
Clear Channel, 30
'Clear Skies' initiative, 104
Clinton, Bill, 23–24, 31, 130, 179
Coburn, Tom, 74
Cold War, 45, 63, 119
Cole, David, 180
Colorado, 76, 132, 183
color-blindness, 154, 158–160, 162
Comaroff, John, 57, 162, 166
consumerism, 7, 15, 24, 34, 62, 142, 156–157, 169, 176–177, 205–208, 211–214, 216, 222, 233, 240, 254–255
Cooper, Louise, 181
corporatization, 16–18, 50, 89, 91–92, 94, 96, 155, 222, 244
    opposition to, 244–246
Council of Conservative Citizens (CCC), 165
Crash (film), 125
creationism, 9, 28, 73, 77, 240
crime, 164, 168, 176, 179–182, 185, 196, 210, 213, 215, 217, 239
critical pedagogy, 7–9, 11, 13, 15, 17, 19, 119
    educational implications of, 4–6
    status in United States, 7–8, 11–12

Crouch, Stanley, 165

cultural politics, 3, 7, 23, 81, 84, 109, 114, 117, 120–121, 125–126, 141, 143, 169, 201, 221, 248

cynicism, 5, 7, 13, 15, 27, 36, 38, 43, 49, 58, 83, 103, 105, 110–112, 153, 176, 206–207, 211, 214, 232, 238, 242, 255

    culture of, 34, 207

Daily Show, 105

Davis, Mike, 180

debate, 229–231, 232–235

Defense Department, 32, 81, 198

Defense of Marriage Act, 75

DeLay, Tom, 73, 105

DeMint, Jim, 74

democratic idealism, 62–63

depoliticization, 15, 35, 232, 242

deregulation, 24–25, 30, 82, 156, 241

Derrida, Jacques, 20, 237

Dewey, John, 34, 47, 178, 244

Disney, 3, 135

dissent, 13–14, 16, 24, 26, 33, 37, 50, 53, 55–56, 60, 72, 84, 96, 101, 125, 200, 202, 217, 247, 256

    education and, 19–20

Dobbs, James, 72

Dobson, James, 72, 76

documentary film, 119, 125

dogmatism, 13

Dominionism, 77

Dowd, Maureen, 76

downsizing, 24, 61, 92–94, 139, 157, 212, 241, 244

drugs, war on, 179, 182

D'Souza, Dinesh, 152, 162, 167

Du Bois, W.E.B., 34, 47, 151–152

Dubroff, Jessica, 134

Dyson, Michael, 152

Eco, Umberto, 101

Edelman, Marian Wright, 239

education

    and challenge of revitalizing democratic public life, 232–235

    corporatization of, 17–18

    and crisis of the social, 243–244

    critical, 8–9, 15, 17–18, 27, 29, 32–35, 37–38, 49, 59, 61, 65, 95, 110, 112, 114, 121, 143, 240, 245–247, 250

    cultural role of, 6

    positivist view of, 8–10

    public skepticism regarding, 44–45

    reform, 10, 194, 240

efficiency, cult of, 17, 62, 92, 166, 246

Ehrenreich, Barbara, 83

Eisenhower, Dwight, 192–193

Elkind, David, 139

End of Racism (D'Souza), 152, 162

England, Lynndie, 54

evangelicals, 25, 28–29, 34, 71–79, 103

Even Start, 241

faith-based initiatives, 77, 79–80

Falk, Richard, 192

Falwell, Jerry, 72, 75–76

family values, 71–72, 130, 135, 142, 178, 209

fear

    culture of, 13–15, 25–27, 56, 62, 81, 83, 111, 191, 200–201, 242, 247

    politics of, 31–34, 191–193, 195, 197–198

feminism, 72, 74–75, 93, 120, 123, 137, 207, 217–218, 221, 255

    backlash against, 139–140

Ferge, Zsuza, 161

Ferguson, Niall, 63

Fight Club (film)

    consumerism and masculinity in, 211–214

    and crisis of everyday life, 207–211

    as public pedagogy, 217–222

    violence in, 214–217

films

    cultural politics of, 117–126, 214

    militarized values and, 197

    as public pedagogy, 206–207, 209, 217–221, 248–249

    see also Hollywood

Fincher, David, 206, 208, 213–214, 217–220

Fish, Stanley, 94

Flanders, Laura, 240

Fletcher, Adam, 109

Fordice, Kirk, 164
Fox News, 26, 46, 55, 193, 217
Freechild Project, 109
freedom
    academic, 15–16, 96
    social, 25, 246
Freire, Paulo, 83, 178
Fremont High School, 184
Frist, Bill, 75
fundamentalism
    militaristic, 80–82
    religious, 9–11, 15–16, 62–65, 73–78,
        80–84, 94, 110, 256
    and threats to democracy, 27–38

Gallagher, Charles, 158
Garland, David, 196
GATT, 155
Geiger, Jack, 185
Geneva Conventions, 46, 60, 194, 206
Gerad, Nona, 93
Geras, Norman, 110
Gilroy, Paul, 219–220, 222
Girl X, 133
Giroux, Susan Searls, 15–16, 43
Goldberg, David Theo, 34, 166–167
Graner, Charles E., 54
Gray, Herman, 120
Greider, William, 26
Griffin, Pam, 137
Gross, Terry, 103
Grossberg, Lawrence, 8, 120
Guantanamo, prison camp at, 64,
    106–108, 194
Gun-Free Schools Act (1994), 182

Hager, David, 79
Halliburton, 89
Hanley, Larry, 91
hardness, ideology of, 60–61
Harris, Marly, 139
Havel, Vaclav, 247, 255
Head Start, 104–105, 195, 240
healthcare, 25, 27–28, 60, 62, 82–83, 90,
    102, 132, 159, 162, 176, 195, 205,
    229, 231, 240
Hedges, Chris, 72, 76
Herbert, Bob, 23, 102, 104, 106

Hersh, Seymour, 46
Hertzberg, Hendrik, 78
Higher Education Act (1998), 14–15
Hitchins, Christopher, 110
Hollywood, 11, 117–120, 126, 132, 177,
    197, 206–207, 214, 217–219
    see also films
Holocaust, 57–58, 101, 103
Homeland Security, 89, 194
homosexuality, 29, 72–75, 93, 135, 207, 241
hooks, bell, 8, 122
hope, educated, 37, 83, 121, 244
Horton, Willie, 164
Hostettler, John, 75
Hough, Joseph, 73
Human Rights Watch, 105
humanism, secular, 72, 74, 82, 85
Hurricane Katrina, 27, 44, 80, 102, 162,
    175, 195
Hussein, Saddam, 45–46, 53–54, 81,
    105, 198
Hutchinson, Earl Ofari, 241

Ignatieff, Michael, 63–64, 110
images, power of, 53–56, 60
inclusive democracy, 4–5, 9, 37, 48, 84,
    168, 250
indifference, 13, 27, 46, 53, 57, 60–62,
    111–112, 153, 157, 162, 168, 176,
    178, 206, 215, 217–219, 233
individualism, 7, 24–25, 27, 62, 81–82, 95,
    151, 153–155, 157, 159, 161, 163,
    165, 167, 169, 212, 245
innocence
    child abuse and, 140–142
    child beauty pageants and, 132–140
    politics of, 129–132
International Monetary Fund (IMF),
    97, 206
Internet, 6, 15, 48, 55, 84, 109–110, 168,
    197
Iraq, 10, 12, 14, 16, 26, 29, 31–32, 44–46,
    60, 63, 78, 80–81, 89, 104–105,
    107–108, 175, 192–193, 196,
    198–199, 237–240
    visual representations of war in, 53–57
Israel, 16, 78
It Takes a Family (Santorum), 71

Jackson, Jesse, 183
Jacoby, Susan, 78
Jameson, Fredric, 205
Jesus Day, 77
Jim Crow laws, 152, 164
jingoism, 12, 24, 60, 125, 199
Johnson, Hans, 27
Johnson, Lyndon, 179, 239
Jong-Il, Kim, 81
JROTC programs, 194
justice, 6–15, 19–20, 153–160, 164,
        166–170, 175, 177–178, 180,
        182–185, 231–233, 235, 237–240,
        243–246, 250, 253–255
    distributive, 10
    racial, 12–13, 17, 154–157, 162, 169,
        178, 233
Justice Matters, 184
Justice Project, 232
Justice Sunday, 75

Kaiser, Jo Ellen Green, 36
Kellner, Doug, 124
Kennedy, Edward, 130
Kerry, John, 77
Kimball, Roger, 249
King, Larry, 108
King, Martin Luther, 158, 178–179, 185
Klaas, Polly, 133
Koran, defilement of, 107
Kozol, Jonathan, 47
Krugman, Paul, 27, 33, 105, 241
Ku Klux Klan, 71
Kuma: War (video game), 198
Kuttner, Robert 164
Kyoto protocol, 106

LaCour, V.J., 138
language, as authoritarian tool, 101–106,
        109–112, 114
    see also newspeak
Lapham, Lewis, 72, 76
Lee, Edward, 231–232
Lee, Spike, 122
Lefkow, John, 73
Left Behind series, 137, 194
Lewin, Tamar, 184
Lieberman, Joseph, 111

Lifton, Robert, 193
Lippman, Walter, 47, 50
literacy, 6, 20, 47, 99, 119, 121–122, 130,
        220, 230, 232, 240–242, 247
    and school reform, 4
Lott, Trent, 102, 163–166
Lutz, Catherine, 191

Macdonald, Dwight, 101, 112
manipulation, 73, 102–103, 193
Mansfield, Stephen, 78
Marable, Manning, 182
Marine Doom (video game), 197
Mariscal, Jorge, 12, 192
Mark, Ellen, 137
masculinity, 32, 58, 60–61, 119,
        122–123, 189, 197, 200,
        206–219, 221, 241
Maslin, Janet, 217
Mbembe, Achille, 12
McDonald's, 9, 90
McKinley, William, 34
McWhorter, John, 153–154
media
    age, 6
    culture, 47, 49, 141, 198
    cultural influence of, 6, 18
Media Education Foundation, 109
Medicaid, 25
Meet the Press, 75, 105
Miles, Margaret, 122
militarization, 10–12, 18, 26–27,
        31–34, 55–56, 60–63, 126, 160,
        176, 178, 181, 183–184, 191–192,
        194–197, 199–202, 219–220,
        238–240
Miller, Lois, 138
Miller, Matt, 111
Mills, C. Wright, 244
Monbiot, George, 192
Moon, Sun Myung, 72
moralism, 10, 28–29, 63, 71–72, 74
Morrison, Toni, 249
Moss, Kate, 138, 141
Mouse That Roared, The (Giroux), 3
MoveOn.org, 109
Moyers, Bill, 28, 30, 38, 72
Murray, Charles, 154, 160

NAFTA, 155

Nation, The, 95, 182, 229

National Association of Evangelicals, 71, 76

National Criminal Justice, 180, 182

nationalism, 61–63, 192

neoliberalism, 4, 10–11, 14–15, 18, 23–25, 27, 35–36, 38, 44, 49, 61–62, 81–82, 97, 112–113, 121, 160–170, 205–206, 208, 212, 221–222, 238, 242–244
  and privatization, 154–156
  and racism, 156–163

New Deal, 25, 62

New Right, 157–158

newspeak, 101–103, 105, 108–110, 112
  see also language, as authoritarian tool

Newsweek (magazine), 107–108, 164–165, 217

Nike, 90, 113, 213

No Child Left Behind Act, 194

Norquist, Grover, 103

Norton, Edward, 208, 218–219

O'Connor, Sandra Day, 75

Olivieri, Nancy, 92

Omi, Michael, 153

Orwell, George, 27, 32, 101, 103–105, 107–113, 247

outsourcing, 24, 65, 82, 94, 212, 237, 241

Pageant Life (magazine), 136–138

Paige, Rod, 30, 74

Palahniuk, Chuck, 208

Patriot Act, 34, 175, 200

patriotism, 11, 24, 33, 47, 55–56, 102, 111, 119, 125, 199–200, 232
  and social policy, 62–63
  and treason, 16, 26, 44, 60, 200, 247

PBS, 74, 241

Pell Grants, 91

Penn State University, 3, 15–17, 32, 93

Pepsi, 9, 90

Perkins, Tony, 75

Perlstein, Rick, 31

Piana, Libero Della, 184

Pitt, Brad, 208–209, 212, 217–218

Pollitt, Katha, 80

popular culture, 4, 6, 18, 29, 60, 123, 130, 143, 192, 197–199, 221, 239, 248–249

Poster, Mark, 113

Postman, Neil, 129–130

poverty, 23, 25, 28, 30–31, 62, 79, 82–83, 89, 119, 123, 130, 132–133, 157, 159, 162, 177, 179, 185, 197, 201, 205, 210, 231, 237, 239–242, 254

Powell, Colin, 46, 78

power, abuse of, 13, 95, 109–110, 112

powerlessness, 101, 105, 121, 138, 141, 153, 201, 230

prison-industrial complex, 32–33, 90, 153, 159–160, 162, 179–182, 196, 242

privatization, 9–10, 28–29, 34, 43–44, 81–82, 111–112, 114, 151, 153–154, 156–157, 160, 162–170, 242–243, 245, 254–255

professionalism, cult of, 93–94

propaganda, 11, 30, 45, 50, 93

public perception
  of Iraq invasion, 45–46
  of torture at Abu Ghraib, 46–47

public policy, 15, 27, 89, 91, 152, 161, 230
  and corporate education, 91–92

Putin, Vladimir, 78, 104, 106

Quitting America (Robinson), 12

racelessness, 167–168

racism, 3, 12, 18, 23, 28, 44, 55–56, 61, 64, 76, 110, 123, 125, 132, 142, 151–170, 175, 177–181, 183, 185, 196, 215, 241, 254
  neoliberal, 154, 156, 158, 160–164
  spectacles of, 163–166

Ramsey, JonBenet, 132–137, 139

Rapture, 71–73, 75–77, 79, 81, 83

Rather, Dan, 107, 135

Reagan, Ronald, 23, 44, 163, 179, 213, 219

reality television, 60–61, 255

recruitment, military, 32–33, 61, 74, 175, 194, 196–198, 239

Red Cross, 107

Reed, Ralph, 71

Rehnquist, William, 75

Republicans, 16, 28, 72, 75, 77, 130, 163–164, 193, 213

Rice, Condoleezza, 46, 192

Rich, Frank, 30, 84, 135

Ricoeur, Paul, 37
Rimer, Sara, 195
robber baron, 34, 62, 71
Roberts, John, 75–76
Robertson, Pat, 72–73
Robinson, James, 78
Robinson, Randall, 12
Roe v. Wade, 28, 76
Rosen, Ruth, 103
Rothschild, Matthew, 77
Rove, Karl, 34
Roy, Arundhati, 201–202
Rumsfeld, Donald, 46, 63, 108, 192
Russell, Bertrand, 47

Safer, Morley, 139
Said, Edward, 20, 94–95, 109, 247–248
Santorum, Rick, 16, 71, 74
Scalia, Antonin, 71
Schiavo, Terry, 73
Schwarzenegger, Arnold, 32
Scott-Herron, Gil, 185
separation of church and state, 33, 71,
    74–75, 79, 81–82, 104
September 11, 2001, 16, 26, 45, 95, 102,
    106, 175, 199–200
    effects on American culture, 10
sex education, 73, 79, 240
sexism, 3, 123, 132, 140, 142, 214, 218, 221
Sherry, Michael S., 191
Shesol, Jeff, 31
Silber, John, 92
Sklar, Holly, 26
Sleeper, Jim, 152
Smith, Roger, 57
Snead, James, 122, 220
social Darwinism, 27, 34, 155, 255
Social Security, 33, 102
Sontag, Susan, 47, 54, 61, 216
Souls of Black Folks (Du Bois), 151
Southern Partisan (magazine), 164
Soyinka, Wole, 84
Spanier, Graham, 32
Spellings, Margaret, 241
standardized testing, 176, 234, 240
Steele, Shelby, 153, 162
Stop Teaching Our Kids to Kill (Grossman
    and DeGaentano), 239

Street, Paul, 159, 180
Streisand, Barbara, 72
Suarez, J.P., 104
Sucker-Free City (film), 122
Sullivan, Andrew, 79–80
Supreme Court, 71, 75–76, 131, 152, 161,
    176, 253
surveillance, 24, 26, 33, 149, 176, 183, 192,
    195, 200, 239, 242, 256
Suskind, Ron, 79

Take Back Higher Education (Giroux), 16
Talent Search, 240
taxes, 9, 24, 103
terrorism, 11, 26, 33, 56, 64, 81, 106,
    175–176, 179, 191, 194, 201–202,
    210, 216, 242
Thompson, Clive, 198
Timmendequas, Jesse, 134
TIPS (Terrorism Information and
    Prevention System), 175
torture, 46, 53–57, 60, 63–64, 103–104,
    106–108, 237, 256
    see also Abu Ghraib
totalitarianism, 33, 213
Traditional Values Coalition, 28
Turse, Nick, 197

unions, 23, 121, 155–156, 168
United Nations, 79
United States
    antidemocratic threats within, 20,
        27–34, 72, 80–82, 89, 94, 200,
        207, 232, 243
    foreign policy, 14, 16, 31–32, 53, 78,
        104, 108, 111, 125, 191, 193
    state of politics in, 15–16, 43
    and unilateralism, 10, 44, 62–63, 104
United Students Against Sweatshops, 97
universities
    adjunct professors and, 90–93, 96,
        183–184, 244, 246
    corporatization of, 17–18, 90–91,
        92–94
    strategy to retake, 94–97
    and tenure, 89, 92–94
Upward Bound, 240
Urban Debate Leagues (UDLs), 229–235

Van Dijk, Teun A., 166
Vidal, Gore, 120
video games, 32, 48, 61, 121, 197–198
Village Voice (newspaper), 31, 129, 135

Wacquant, Loic, 160
Walkerdine, Valerie, 140
Wall Street Journal (newspaper), 164
Wallis, Jim, 25, 78–79
Weber, Samuel, 243
welfare, 82–83, 132, 143, 161–162, 212,
    221, 229, 231–233, 237–238
  cuts to, 23–25, 130, 164
West, Cornel, 32, 77, 129, 140, 152
White, Curtis, 111
Whitman, Walt, 23
Why We Fight (film), 125

Williams, Patricia, 152, 163
Wills, Garry, 73
Wilson, William Julius, 153
Wolf, Naomi, 138
Wolfowitz, Paul, 63, 192
Woodward, Bob, 78
work
  full-time, 90, 92–96, 156
  part-time, negative effects of, 18, 24,
    92–94, 96, 156, 205, 209
World Bank, 9, 155, 206
World Trade Organization, 97,
    155, 206

zero tolerance, 33, 47, 175, 177–178, 239
  and racism, 179–182
  schooling and, 182–184, 185